ETHICS

ETHICS

Twelve Lectures on the
Philosophy of Morality

David Wiggins

HARVARD UNIVERSITY PRESS

Cambridge, Massachusetts
2006

Library of Congress Cataloging-in-Publication Data

Wiggins, David.
  Ethics : twelve lectures on the philosophy of morality / David Wiggins.
    p. cm.
  Includes bibliographical references and index.
  ISBN 0-674-02214-9 (alk. paper)
    1. Ethics. I. Title.
BJ21.W49 2006
170—dc22   2005056707

Contents

Preface

The lectures that make up this book will not introduce their ground level subject matter from scratch. They cannot introduce to someone who has never heard of these things or asked a question about them such subjects as good and evil and the nature of our concern with them; or things required, permissible, or forbidden; or things that make life significant; or acts one is responsible for . . . Rather, they introduce the *philosophy* of these subjects, the inquiry that is variously called moral philosophy or ethics. The book will serve best and most usefully perhaps as a second introduction to this subject, a reintroduction, so to say, designed for those who want to start again without presupposing anything from their previous acquaintance with philosophy. Nevertheless, in demanding hardly anything except the reader's willingness to confront the philosophical prose of authors such as Hume or Kant or John Stuart Mill—in requiring little more of a reader than the constant readiness to consult a good medium-sized dictionary, even for the case of words that seem familiar—I hope the book may meet the needs of some mature persons with no previous knowledge of philosophy.

The aim is to approach each topic from a standing start. No more is taken for granted than a readiness to resolve to read some day in the not too distant future a few wonderful works written at various times between the fourth century B.C. and the twentieth century A.D. Some of these rank among the finer works of Western literature. We shall not start from zero, but the immediate prerequisite is that the reader should have some grasp of moral notions—an operational but not necessarily articulate grasp, preferably undisturbed by theory yet tending already in the direction of a speculative interest in the ethical.

There is another way in which there is no prospect of a start from zero. No author treating these questions can *himself* start from scratch. In moral philosophy, whatever may hold of other branches of philosophy, the theoretical understanding of that which is in all other ways familiar to us accumulates very slowly. For that reason, the perceptions of our predecessors are integral to any alert or thoughtful consideration of the central questions. Among these predecessors, three philosophers stand out: Aristotle, in his *Nicomachean Ethics,* on which we shall draw occasionally; David Hume, in his *Treatise of Human Nature,* book III, and his *Enquiry Concerning the Principles of Morals;* and Immanuel Kant, represented for present purposes by his *Foundations of the Metaphysics of Morals.* It would be silly to deny that someone can take a serious interest in moral philosophy without reading any of these writers—just as silly as to deny that they can address the questions treated later without special reference to the various other texts to be adduced there. But anyone who intends to go by that road will know already how to draw on some alternative tradition of ethical speculation. There are many to choose from.

We begin with the first and most fundamental question, the content of morality and the nature of the moral motive (Lectures 1 to 9); then we move outward towards justice and the link between the moral and the political (Part II = Lecture 10); finally, in Part III (Lectures 11 and 12), we touch upon the 'metaethical'—the questions of the reality and objectivity of the ethical as such—in the hope of controlling a copious source of misconception and confusion. In 9.18 following, and several times in the lectures that lead up to that point, we venture closer to the place where angels might reasonably fear to tread, namely the ethical and other conditions for human felicity—a question that needs to be pursued more single-mindedly than is possible here, but in some other place on some other day.

In assembling, revising, and extending these lectures I was assisted at the initial stage by spending the month of September 1997 in

Bellagio under the hospitable auspices of the Rockefeller Foundation. For the years 2001–2, 2002–3, and 2003–4 the Leverhulme Trust helped me immeasurably by a generous grant in aid of secretarial assistance. I record here my gratitude to both these foundations. I owe further gratitude to the referees for Harvard University Press for numerous friendly comments and more suggestions than there was space to accommodate. I am further indebted to the Press for engaging Angela Blackburn, a peerlessly wise copyeditor and counsellor. Among colleagues, I want to thank warmly Roger Crisp, Anthony Price, Jeffrey Seidman, John Tasioulas, Stephen Mulhall, Véronique Munoz-Dardé, Sophie Botros, G. A. Cohen, R. V. Scruton, and James Griffin, who were kind enough to read some long, long stretches of text and point out various misconceptions or missed opportunities. In 1981–2 John McDowell and I gave a class together about moral philosophy. In ways hard now to detail, Lecture 11 is indebted to the discussions to which that gave rise and to the comments that J. L. Mackie and H. L. Hart made to us at that time. Further, more specific, and no less important acknowledgments are made in footnotes. I owe a different but no lesser debt of gratitude to Mrs Sally Nabavian and Mrs Jo Cartmell for their indispensable and skilful work in transposing handwritten copy onto disk and entering endless corrections to the same. I am very grateful too for the kindly assistance of Colin Cook, Andy Davies, Thomas Moore, and Hilla Wait in the Faculty of Philosophy, 10 Merton Street, Oxford. A debt of a different kind is owed to New College, Oxford—a veritable oasis in the man-made (manager-made) desert fast encroaching upon the ground where once learning was cultivated, shared, and perpetuated for its own sake—and to its librarian, Mrs Naomi van Loo.

Grateful acknowledgment is made for permission to reprint material first published elsewhere: the epigraph to Lecture 7, from R. M. Hare, 'What Makes Choices Rational', *Review of Metaphysics* 32 (1979), reprinted by permission of Professor John Hare; quoted passage on pp. 179–80 from R. M. Hare, 'A Philosophical Autobiography', *Utilitas* 14.3 (2002); quoted passage on pp. 197–9 from

John Rawls, 'The Basic Structure as Subject,' *American Philosophical Quarterly* 14 (1977); Lecture 10, a version of which was pub-
lished in *Mind* 109 (2004), by permission of Oxford University Press;
Lecture 11, a version of which was published in *Ratio* 18 (2005),
copyright © Blackwell Publishing Ltd., 2005; lines from the poem
'Sonnet' by William Empson used as an epigraph to Lecture 11, from
The Complete Poems of William Empson (University Press of Florida,
2001); and Lecture 12, one part of which was published in Brad
Hooker, ed., *Truth in Ethics* (Oxford: Blackwell, 1996), © Blackwell
Publishing Ltd., 1996.

Most of the lectures that make up this book were first written in
response to the needs, which were acute, and the reactions, which
were instructive and generous, of six generations (1988–94) of mature
part-time students in the philosophy department of Birkbeck College, a University of London night school in the centre of London.
In this time-hallowed place, drawing now towards its bicentenary,
the established interests of colleagues and the exigencies of timetable
and curriculum (requirements as if carved in stone) enforced upon
me a six-year half-respite from questions more habitual to me of
metaphysics, ancient philosophy, and philosophical grammar and
logic. That respite strengthened my resolve to convert a preoccupation with Aristotle and certain themes arising from Aristotle's and
Hume's ethics into the wherewithal to give a more general course
on ethics. The lectures that resulted (which, despite the textual approach, are purely philosophical in their aspiration) I now dedicate,
blots and all, to those generations and their successors at Birkbeck.

New College, Oxford
May, 2005

I

Morality: Its motive and content

Overview

0.1. Lectures 1–5 of our study are dedicated to Hume and Kant and the rival answers we shall construct on behalf of each of them to a question about moral motivation which Plato was among the first to raise. This is a question we shall divide into two questions linked together in a way that is designed to relieve the heavy burden placed upon these subjects by the moral sceptic. Then we look in the direction of the answers to the same questions that are to be found in utilitarians such as Jeremy Bentham and J. S. Mill. After that we consider new arguments for similar conclusions offered by their twentieth-century inheritors. Conspicuous among these inheritors is the moral philosopher R. M. Hare, who is sharply contrasted with another exponent of a constructional method, John Rawls. In Lecture 8, we cross-examine more recent, self-styled consequentialist accounts of the content and nature of morality and the moral motive. Wherever an obligation or duty lies upon an agent to do some act, the consequentialist will seek to derive this duty or obligation, not through distinctively ethical-cum-agential considerations, but more simply and directly (as if distrusting the shape imposed on matters by ethical notions) from the pre-ethical net balance of advantages over disadvantages of the act's being realized. For further and necessary refinements of this characterization, see 8.3. Consequentialism represents itself as a canonical form of rationality, with would-be *a priori* claims to that status. But we shall say that this claim rests on an assumption which there is simply no need to make and a pressing reason *not* to make.

The true reasonableness of ordinary morality and the rationale for the concepts and conceptions that it deploys, including our non-consequentialist ideas of agency and responsibility, will better appear when it becomes plainer, as it will in Lecture 9, how ordinary morality can give expression to an ethic of solidarity and reciprocity such as Philippa Foot has defended. Such an ethic accords to agents who live by it their own share in the full variety of good reasons that there are for each of an entire range of morally admirable acts and attitudes. This is to say that a true answer to Plato's question will begin as a set of reminders. No doubt the rest of that answer will need to engage somehow with the question of happiness, the matter briefly resumed in the concluding pages of Lecture 9 and the last pages of the whole book. That is the grain of truth in sceptical and cynical challenges to morality from which we begin in Lecture 1. But let us not confuse this grain of truth or the inscrutabilities of happiness itself with the absurd claim that self-love is the motive that underlies all the other motives of ordinary human agents.

Lecture 9 not only refers back to Plato's question in Lecture 1. It develops the hidden affinity between Hume's and Aristotle's ideas of ethical formation. In this way it points forward to a question in political philosophy that will be taken up in Part II.

0.2. There is nothing inevitable in our choice, here or in subsequent parts, of authors, texts, and subjects, but there is nothing capricious either. For our starting in the place where we start, and our heading in the direction along which we seek to advance, will familiarize the reader with a significant part of the intellectual, cultural, and historical background for a large quantity of work in moral philosophy. The last thing the reader needs at this point is an author who strains constantly to contribute to disputations that are all the rage but ephemeral, who begins far from the real centre, or who closes out half of the subject in order to focus on that which is in fashion.

In what spirit do I urge that we treat with texts and authors singled out here for special attention? In the spirit of looking first for the things each author points to and asking how much truth we find in the author's perceptions; and in the spirit of doing the best we can with the notions by which the author makes sense of those perceptions. There is more to be got from a good author's text than we shall recover from received stereotypes of his or her doctrines. So far as we have strength, we must read our writers' words themselves and try to construe them against the larger background of their whole philosophy. But then at the next stage—if our interest is philosophical rather than historiographical and we want the books we read to contribute to a cumulative advance in a shared understanding—we must dare to inquire how readily Hume's ethical perceptions and notions can be cut loose from his philosophy of impressions and ideas, or Kant's from his transcendental idealism, or Aristotle's from his metaphysics of entelechy, actuality, potentiality, and form.

The very idea of our attempting such acts of expropriation may cause consternation in some quarters. But given that our chief need is to arrive at a true conception of the ethical subject matter, how can we help but seek to make our own that which our authors show us? If we seek in this cause to make the most of the plurality of observations and insights we inherit and carry forward, then we shall have to take courage from the thought that true perceptions can scarcely conflict. Nor can sound notions be at cross-purposes or spoil for a fight. Momentarily (or every now and then), if or when we strain to attend to a text in order to make the most of an author's insights, the scholar may approve of what we are attempting. But our real task is not historical. The task is for reader and author to decide how we ourselves are to answer the various questions proposed at 1.1.

In this book, ancient moralists such as Plato and Aristotle play a subsidiary role. If the verdicts we reach upon modern accounts of morality, or the answers we propose for the various questions we pursue, appear to leave everything open to the renewal of ancient initiatives in the field, this may excite a reader to hasten back to Aristotle himself (as the lectures themselves sometimes do). Aristotle's *Nicomachean Ethics*, the principal text, may best be studied

in the translations by W. D. Ross and Roger Crisp.[1] The interest of
Aristotle's treatise has persisted through countless shifts in virtue
and manners. It will surely survive many more. In the earlier lectures,
where Hume and Kant play the central roles, it would have confused
the matters treated to admit a tritagonist. For that reason, Aristotle
is shifted into a supernumerary role, as a perennial source of distinctive insights and perceptions and a formative influence upon the
present author.

0.3. With so much said, I exhort the reader, in considering that
which is laid out in all three parts of this book, to draw constantly
upon his or her lived experience in the world, enlarging that experience by imaginative reference to some larger stretch of human
history and human discourse. As part of the very same effort, let
the reader try constantly to understand the *literal meaning* (as well
as any further meanings) of the forms of words with which we respond to lived experience. Let the reader never forget the things he
or she already knows about our subject matter. For in the matters
we are concerned with, philosophy itself will lack all authority unless, from the outset, it pays eager attention to that which is always
present, on the surface or some way below the surface, in the ordinary thoughts and ideas of ordinary, passably good, passably sensible people—and present there entirely independently of the min-
istrations of philosophy. For the first aim of philosophical ethics is
not to supersede or to streamline the moral ideas that the reader
brings to the subject, or to lord it over ordinary notions, not yet to
put them to the test by instantly transposing everything into the
language of planning, execution, and command. Better counsel,
counsel too rarely heeded but familiar from the writings of Bernard
Williams, will be to study our moral ideas for themselves and for all
they are worth, avoiding every preconception of what they 'must'
be like.

1. See the 'Note on five texts' at the end of the book.

0.4. In that spirit, moral philosophy and the theory of the practical are treated here as a branch of speculative philosophy. When the subject is treated on these terms, moral philosophy ought to bear the same sort of relation to morals as philosophy of mathematics bears to mathematics or philosophy of science bears to science or philosophy of mind (the descriptively or phenomenologically based variety, I mean) bears to mind. Even more than questions about numbers, nature or mind, these questions about good and bad, ought and ought not, must and must not . . . , are apt to stir our eager curiosity. By all means, let us expect moral philosophy to be in some sense *applicable* or *practicable*. If only it will, let the subject expand our thoughts. But nothing at all can be depended upon to come out right in this inquiry unless in the presence of a lively, open-ended, first-level curiosity, a curiosity that is equally keenly directed at the actual content and working of our ethical ideas and at the objects, properties, and situations themselves with which those ideas engage. Even though our interest in the practical is speculative in this way, let us leave the expression 'moral theory' in the hands of those who relish its present connotation of reconstruction or believe that it is the business of moral philosophy to trespass on the preserve of the moralist by remaking first-order morality. Until we attain some speculative understanding, it is too soon for us to commit ourselves to any of that. At the outset, let us bracket all preconceptions and allow the notions we already have to speak to us for themselves.

1

Glaucon's and Adeimantus' interrogation of Socrates

The theoretical examination of the foundation of morals is open to the quite peculiar disadvantage that it is easily regarded as an undermining thereof, which might entail the collapse of the structure itself. For here the practical interest is so close to the theoretical that its well meant zeal cannot easily be restrained from ill-timed interference. Not everyone is capable of clearly distinguishing between the purely theoretical search for objective truth, a search dissociated from all interest, even from that of morality as practised, and a sacrilegious attack on the heart's hallowed conviction.

Schopenhauer, *On the Basis of Morality*, §1

1.1. Ethics is the philosophical study of morals or morality.

(A) It concerns the question of the substance or content of morality, its nature, and its extent.

(B) It concerns the question of the reasons there may be—and the reasons agents may make their own—to participate, persevere, and persist in morality.

(C) Consequentially upon the kind of content and authority that is attributed to it under the heads (A) and (B), the philosophy of morality seeks to determine the logical and metaphysical character of the findings of morality. It studies the questions of the truth, objectivity, relativity, etc., of its judgments and the logical status of the approbation that it extends to some acts and responses but denies to a host of others.

Among further questions there is a question (D) about the relations of morality, meaning, and happiness. But that is a question we shall treat here only obliquely. It will be resumed in a sequel to this book.

Lectures 1–9 of this book are chiefly concerned with different approaches to topic (A) and topic (B): the Humean approach, then the Kantian, then the utilitarian/consequentialist approaches. In advance of extended inquiry under (A) and (B), it would be strange (though I know not everyone thinks it strange) to think that anything at all could be decided about the topic (C). For that reason, this topic (C) is constantly postponed, until Lectures 11 and 12 in fact.

1.2. If we are to study either the content of morality or the motivation to pay heed to it, then what shall we say that morality itself is? What is it about morality that determines or generates this content? What is it about a morality (morality as we think we know it or as others elsewhere know it) possessing this or that content that commands loyalty or respect?—or else provokes disloyalty and disrespect? Surely, in so far as we have reason to care about it or pay attention to what it makes of our acts, characters, and attitudes, indeed in so far as we can inquire at all under the headings (A) and (B) whether committedly or sceptically, we *must already* have some understanding of what morality is. What is that understanding? In order that we may progress with question (B), someone may say, let us hear what it is.

An innocent and reasonable question! Yet, as posed in this way at this early stage, a demand such as this will strike anyone who tries to satisfy it as unfair and much too hard. Struggling to escape from it, we may be tempted to declare that in moral philosophy questions such as this should come last, not first. For at the beginning, we may say, we cannot know whether to give a cynical and/or purely spectatorial answer to the question of what morality is or to look for an answer that leaves in place the momentous claim that we have reasons internal to morality and integral to its content for caring about it. In any case, our respect or our disrespect for it can far outreach our understanding. At this early point (we may try to insist), it is neither fair nor sensible to expect us to be able to *articulate anything* about what morality is.

There is something right about the protest. Yet we cannot simply leave the matter there. We cannot really postpone the whole question if we think that we mean anything by the questions that give us our topics (A) and (B) or we intend to measure up to either of them. By all means, let the question of the nature of morality come at the end, but it must *also* come here, at the outset. Even if we shall scarcely achieve anything very ambitious, how can we refuse to try, in the spirit of making a beginning, to *list or enumerate* some of the familiar concerns (understood in the light of their objects) which seem to us, here and now, to be characteristic of a person who is already inside morality?

Maybe the first thing one should be struck by is not what we do do or want to do, but what we mostly *don't* do and are much exercised not to see done. Is there not something altogether re-markable in the strength and variety of our primitively prohibitive aversions—our aversion to wounding, injury, murder, plunder, or pillage, the abhorrence that we experience against the neglect or abuse of children or other defenceless persons, the horror we feel at the slaughter of the innocent or the repaying of good with gra-tuitous evil? Here are acts whose awfulness we take for granted, acts that shock and surprise us when we see them done and appal us when we consider them as acts we might find ourselves engaged in. Drawing on our intuitive and imaginative shared grasp of moral mat-ters, a moral phenomenologist needs to register the strength and persistence of these responses and the inhibitions associated with them. However provisionally, let us put these first, and resolutely postpone all anxieties about the self-selection that precedes this ref-erence to the *us* who participate in these *aversions of ours* and share in the responses to which *we are provoked* by the outrageous events that are constantly reported—mostly, we always hope, from elsewhen or elsewhere. (The response to such anxieties is at 1.12.)

What comes next? The obvious candidate for the second place in this preliminary enumeration are the simple and positive concerns that arise in us from primitive fellow feeling and find their expression (independently of self-love and sometimes even in opposition to it, or that is how it appears) in our willingness to interest ourselves in the plight of known or identifiable persons, and our readiness, face to face, to enter into cooperative relations with others. (The cynicism so often provoked by the claim that such concerns and feelings are genuine will be countered in 2.6.)

What comes after this? Almost imperceptibly, the concerns placed second seem to merge into a third group of divers much more abstract preoccupations, those proper to public spirit, to devotion to the general interest, or to humanitarian causes. Concerns of these varieties combine very naturally with those of the less abstract second kind, which they have seemed to some philosophers to generalize. Taken together, concerns of the second and third kinds are readily subsumed, one may think, under the general head of the benevolence, beneficence, or humanity that we observe in however varying degrees among persons whom we both like and admire. (The third kind of concern attracts cynicism too. See below, 2.6.)

Finally, fourth by my count, last but not least, come certain intuitive and special preoccupations to which we are party, less clamant than the primitive aversions we began with but perceptibly *more* clamant than benevolence in the abstract or the concerns for the general good of which some philosophers have made so much: preoccupations with justice (in a relatively narrow and specific sense of 'just') or veracity or allegiance or fidelity to promises. Preoccupations of this fourth kind keep company with kindred preoccupations and solicitudes which condemn the omission of particular duties or obligations and the commission of particular acts such as stealing, betrayal of trust, lying, treason, the breaking of promises. . . . Here the rights and expectations of particular people and groups of people will loom large. In the ordinary moral consciousness as we know it, such preoccupations and solicitudes limit or narrowly constrain the working of the second and third kinds of moral concern. One of the things we most dread in ordinary life is collision between the exclusions that flow from our first or most primitive aversions and the apparently no less strict requirements that arise from among this fourth class of concerns.

1.3. Motives and concerns of the four kinds thus provisionally enumerated, once they are translated into settled dispositions and habits of mind, permeate and condition the whole mentality of a human being. We shall refer to them again in Lectures 3 and 9. For short, let us label them (1) prohibitive aversion, (2) cooperative benevolence, (3) generalized beneficence, and (4) observance. Together, one might say, they help to make up an ordinary morality or a first-order moral sensibility—a state of being that is beyond finite description in words and affords an endless fund of responses, verbal and non-verbal responses, to whatever we encounter. However inaccurate and incomplete our fourfold attempt may appear, it is scarcely to be questioned that *some* such system of ideas and practices is ours to deploy. For the appearance is this: that we deploy this system constantly in act and feeling without recourse to calculation; that it oversees and regulates the business of everyday life; that it forms a whole framework within which we deliberate; that it excludes all sorts of act from the space within which we want to rehearse or refine the practical possibilities that are open to us; that it frequently narrows those possibilities to unity. It is equally familiar, though, that this sensibility can make things more difficult for us— most notoriously and obviously, for instance, when it proposes courses of conduct that we want not to follow. It does this more interestingly and problematically when it directs us simultaneously (as sometimes it will) towards *opposite* courses of conduct.[1]

---

1. Formal logic will not criticize the supposition that that is how things are with our duties and obligations. 'I ought to abandon my aged mother and enlist with the Free French' and 'I ought not to abandon my mother and enlist with the Free French' (as potentially uttered, let us suppose, at some time and place in occupied France) are not, strictly speaking, contraries. We have *contraries* only where one or other judgment must be false. Look carefully at the placing of the 'not'. (Contrast the situation with the pair 'I ought to abandon my aged mother and enlist with the Free French' and 'It is not the case I ought to abandon my aged mother and enlist with the Free French', which are indeed contraries.) Here syntax and grammar promote reflection, not least by slowing

That is one source of puzzlement we have from first-order morality. Here is another. Not only does first-order morality harbour demands that cannot together be satisfied. It also provokes passionate disagreements between its adherents, even between adherents of what is recognizably the same specific morality, about all sorts of first-order questions—not least over how to decide which of two practically incompatible moral demands is to be fulfilled, or what can legitimately require an agent to override simple prohibitions against killing or lying or the breaking of promises. Why is it, and what does it show about the status of morality, that so many of these deliverances seem to be *essentially contestable?* (See, in due course, Lectures 11 and 12.)

These are all good questions. Several of them we shall inevitably come back to. (Some of them fall under the heading (C) at 1.1 above.) But they are not the first source of philosophical puzzlement. Intuitively and traditionally, it is not so much the question of what morality comprises (topic A) as the question of what reason there is for us to pay heed to moral demands (topic B) that has been seen as raising the very first question of morality. So let us turn now to that.

1.4. Perfectly ordinary people, when they attempt the things demanded of them under requirements that correspond to the various sorts of concern we have recently identified, may act neither from inclination towards this act (for they may have no inclination to it that antedates the considered choice of that act), nor from personal

---

it down for a moment. But much more needs to be said, if it can really be our duty to do one thing *and* be our duty to do another thing, even where it is impossible for us to do both of these things. For the long term, the reader is referred in these matters to E. J. Lemmon, 'Moral Dilemmas', *Philosophical Review* 77 (1968). One of the beauties of formal logic is how it precisely keeps silent at this point and leaves us free to find our own salvation—the thing we do by thinking further about what matters most and how to make our peace with the claim we decide not to satisfy. In the short term, though, let the reader look yet once more at the placing of the 'not'. The example we have made use of here will be found in J.-P. Sartre's essay, *L'existentialisme est un humanisme* (Paris: Nagel, 1946), trans. B. Frechtman as *Existentialism* (New York: Philosophical Library, 1947, and New York: Citadel, 1957).

interest, nor yet from duress, nor even for the sake of a good reputation. Or so it appears. The appearance is that *sometimes* human
agents act as they do from principled aversion to all visible alternatives, from benevolence or beneficence, or else from an anxious
concern to give proper heed to the demands of gratitude or loyalty
or promise-keeping. In many cases, moreover, the appearance seems
very well entrenched. Yet the finding that people act frequently in
this way will also provoke opposition. It stirs up confusion and
perplexity. How, it is asked, are disinterested motives of the kind we
are attributing to these people possible? And supposing that they be
possible, how can they ever be strong enough to give us any reason
to act in a way that runs contrary to inclination and interest? And
how is it *rational* for us to act so? Surely morality is not a special
form of irrationality.

Philosophers have tried over and over again to attend to these
matters. Among the most striking formulations they have ever received is that given by Plato in book II of the *Republic*. Since that
formulation has become the usual starting point, there is every
reason for us too to begin there.

1.5. In book I of the *Republic,* the sophist Thrasymachus advances the cynical view that that which human beings call justice is
simply the advantage of those who are stronger or more powerful;
that true human excellence consists in injustice. By well-tried means
of interrogation and cross-examination Socrates reduces him to silence. In book II, the brothers Glaucon and Adeimantus declare that
they are unconvinced. They ask Socrates to prove to them that
justice (in a wide sense of the Greek word which more or less coincides with 'morality' as we used the term when we were attempting
our phenomenological fixation of what to mean by that word) is
something quite unlike such irksome necessities as diet or exercise.
What the brothers want to have proved for them is that justice/
morality is something to embrace *for itself and in itself* (without
regard for worldly consequences), as well as for the sake of its consequences. Socrates' declared position is that justice, like health or

sanity or sight, is something to embrace for both these reasons. The brothers challenge him to vindicate this claim. 'By nature,' Glaucon declares, 'to do injustice/wrong is good, to suffer it evil, but there is more evil in suffering injustice/wrong than there is good in inflicting it' (358). In order to provoke Socrates to show that he and his brother are mistaken, Glaucon then declares that justice (= morality) is a compromise between the best, which is doing injustice/ wrong with impunity, and the worst, which is suffering injustice/ wrong without requital. Justice/morality is not something to love for itself and is desirable only for its consequences: 'No one who had the power to inflict injustice/wrong and was anything of a man would ever make a contract of mutual abstention. He would be mad if he did.' 'Those who practise justice/morality do so unwillingly and from their inability to inflict injustice/wrong.'

In order to support these claims, but intending as always to provoke Socrates to explain what is so lovable about justice/morality, Glaucon then proposes a thought experiment by which to contrast the lives of the perfectly unjust/wicked and perfectly just/righteous man. The perfectly unjust/wicked man will be ruthless but so clever and discerning in his acts of ruthlessness that he is never caught or checked. He does the fullest injustice/wrong possible but is reputed to be perfectly just/righteous (361A). Beside him Glaucon sets the truly just/righteous man,

> a simple and noble character, one who desires not to seem but to be good. The semblance [of being just] we must take from him [in our thought experiment]. For if he is reputed just, he will enjoy the honours and rewards that such a reputation earns, and thus it will not be fully apparent . . . whether he is just for justice's sake or for the sake of honours and rewards. He must be stripped of everything except justice and made the very counterpart of the other man. He shall do no injustice *and be reputed altogether unjust, in order that [in our thought experiment] his justice may be tested as being [impermeable to considerations] of ill-repute or its consequences, and he shall go on his way un-*

changed [in his justice] till death, all his life seeming unjust but being just. Thus these two, the just man and the unjust man, will have come to the extremes of justice and injustice and we may judge which of them is the happier. (362D)[2]

Such a challenge seems more than enough; but Glaucon's brother Adeimantus then adds that, because the unjust/wicked man can suborn the gods, the unjust/wicked man has it in his power to bring it about that he himself will flourish for ever and always. The just/ righteous man, on the other hand, will be scourged, racked, fettered, have his eyes burnt out, and at last, after all manner of suffering, be crucified. Nor is that all. Given the fallibility of the gods and the machinations of the unjust/wicked, his justice/righteousness will go unrecognized for all time. No human being or god will ever know about it.

If this is what justice and injustice respectively do for a person 'each of itself, by the power of its own nature, when dwelling in the heart of him who possesses it, hidden from gods and man alike', then the challenge to Socrates is for him to explain what is so lovable for itself about justice and why we should choose it over injustice. What could there be about justice/morality that would prompt any-one to make it welcome and choose it over injustice/moral cynicism? And how could anyone suppose that being just has anything to do with attaining happiness?

1.6. In the *Republic*, Socrates' reaction to Glaucon and Adei-mantus was to prepare to answer what they said exactly as it stood. The answer he gave depended upon a comparison between what health is for the body and what justice/morality is for the soul. (See *Republic* book IV, especially 445. See also book X.) The answer makes it clear that the brothers were wrong if *they thought they knew already what happiness was.* This Socratic answer is a wonderful ethical work. But it has rarely been seen as a satisfactory response

2. Trans. A. D. Lindsay (3rd ed., London: Dent, 1920), my italics.

to the challenge—not least because of the doubtful status of the
Platonic analogy between soul and state on which Plato's own development of the comparison depended, and the doubtful status, in
a situation so extreme as that envisaged for the just man (a situation
where one might think that nobody however wise or just could retain
their sanity or their reason), of considerations relating to the conditions for the health of the soul. Is it not obvious (one thinks), in
recognition of the utterly peculiar and special terms under which
this Platonically just man is doomed to live, that a sane philosophy
of morality must reconcile itself to the near certainty that, in the
thought experiment, the health of the soul itself, along with all happiness and sanity, will long since have flown out of the window?
For the truth is that, once it is taken up by Glaucon and Adeimantus,
who press Socrates so relentlessly, the question that was meant to
be central to moral motivation as such (and is still widely taken to
be central to it) seems to have carried us to a point beyond the
margin of human morality. If that is so, then something has gone
seriously astray in Plato's construction. Would it not be better to try
to understand why this has happened than to attempt the thing
Socrates attempts?

If we take this latter view, then three observations will immediately
suggest themselves about the challenge that the brothers make to
Socrates. I shall set them out in order of ascending importance.

1.7. First, Glaucon and Adeimantus declare that the life that men
want to lead is one of doing injustice/wickedness with impunity. But
it ought to be worth saying somewhere that this rings false. In real
life, it is much truer to say that what most people really want is for
justice to be *dead easy*. It isn't dead easy. But that isn't a point in
favour of Glaucon's description. Of course, if we were the sort of
creatures he seems to describe, then the problem of explaining moral
motivation might be different from the given or actual problem. Nevertheless, the given or actual question under (B) may be far more
interesting.

1.8. Secondly, the two brothers seem to suppose that, if ever we have acted well or justly in Plato's broad sense of 'just', and wherever we have acted otherwise than for the sake of honour or reputation or . . . , then the friend of justice/morality must hope to claim that we have acted *for the sake of justice or morality itself.* Nothing different from that would count, it seems we are being told, as acting fully justly. (Nothing less will suffice for the state of being just that Socrates is to connect with the state of being happy.) The claim is an important one. It is integral to the challenge to Socrates. Moreover, as regards justice *in the narrower or more restricted sense* of securing to each person what is due to them, the Platonic equivalence is plausible. It is borne out by the class of moral concerns placed fourth in our recent phenomenology. (Where one owes money, for instance, one must pay the money simply because it is owed. Where one feels a temptation to take object z from person x, one must leave x in possession of z simply because z belongs to x.) Yes. But, when Glaucon and Adeimantus require that *all* acts of a just/good person should be chosen 'for their own sake', they are generalizing this special finding, generalizing it recklessly. Can that which applies to paying a debt suggest a sense for the phrase 'acting for the sake of morality itself' in which *we already suppose* that every act of a just/good person is done for the sake of justice/morality itself? Consider benevolence and the virtues cognate with it. Benevolence is a virtue which, in real life, we do not insist needs to be practised for the virtue's own sake. On the contrary, we insist that benevolence should be practised for the sake of its beneficiaries. Why should we suppose that *that* means the same as exercising the virtue for its own sake? There is a mass of unfinished business here. If morality or justice in the broad sense is what Glaucon and Adeimantus want Socrates to justify, they should attend far more carefully than they do to the question of what ordinary morality really is and how it coheres with itself.

Even at this early point in the inquiry, a new possibility comes into sight. It may be that genuine morality, without being more self-seeking or less pure than the brothers suppose that it ought to be, is in some respects less relentless, in other respects less simple, and, in further respects, far more interesting than they conceive of its being. May it not denature morality to see every good act as done for the sake of duty itself? It is equally evident that there is far more to morality than the workaday benevolence (or 'altruism') that the brothers pretend, in solidarity with the sophist Thrasymachus, to hold in such contempt. Here too they are guilty of a serious misportrayal of the phenomena of the ordinary life. The time has come to find a picture of morality that represents it neither as a patsy nor as a puritanical despot.

1.9.   Third, and most important, the terms of the thought experiment that the brothers propose are hopelessly skewed. What they want Socrates to study is the motive to do acts of justice/morality and to do them otherwise than out of a concern with avoiding punishment or securing the sort of goods that we endure diet or exercise for. But it quickly appears that the only case that could ever satisfy them under this head is a case where someone sticks so steadfastly to justice, despite the most terrible punishments and discouragements, that all cynical hypotheses wither away and the only possible explanation of their conduct is revealed as a simple, indivisible love of justice/morality itself, perfectly heedless of discouragement or punishment and equally heedless of the promptings of all distinct motives. (See 361a–362d, already quoted in part.) Such a case would indeed be impressive. On these terms, the vindication they seek of justice/morality, so conceived, would be a philosophical tour de force. But to insist that the only cases that can count for anything at all under the heading of justice/morality are cases like this, or to insist that the only thing of any interest is a magnificent and general vindication of justice/morality as Glaucon and Adeimantus misdescribe it, is to confuse cases where there is a pure or unselfish motive to morality with cases where even an utter sceptic could be convinced that there was a pure motive. These will be cases so extraordinary that no other motive *could be conceived* for what is done. But why is certainty of this sort so important for the question that the two brothers began by raising about the foundations of justice? The question they began by raising was a general question. Moreover, scepticism and brute behaviourism in matters of the interpretation of human behaviour really have nothing to do with it.

1.10. At this point, those who prefer to see broad brush-strokes will ask how much the confusions and uncertainties I have imputed to Glaucon and Adeimantus really matter. They will urge that the simplest and best thing for philosophical understanding would still be a straightforward answer to the perplexity that the brothers have expressed. I reply that, in principle, the brothers' confusions might not matter at all—except that the slant they have put upon their thought experiment completely obscures, as if almost deliberately, an all-important possibility: namely that there are many, many moral motives that are both *disinterested and pure*—manifestations neither of self-interest nor of the desire for useful consequences such as good reputation—*yet are not invincibly strong*. The heroism of the Platonically just man is indeed a very special case of purity and strength of motive. But why assume that the relative weakness of the moral motive in the non-heroic cases taints the purity of this motive? We have no reason to think this. Why should one suppose that motives are tainted because, when the acts that they prompt one to do are followed by horrible punishment, the motives themselves grow weaker and weaker or more and more inert? Before they were driven out, were these not motives to kind or considerate action for the sake of the recipient or motives to honest dealing simply for honesty's own sake? If someone stops acting benevolently or scrupulously (or apparently benevolently or scrupulously) because you frighten them out of their wits or torture them close to death, how can that show that, *before* you did this, the person wasn't really behaving benevolently or scrupulously, but acting for some other reason *in order to gain something or avoid something that is out of sight?* All that is shown is that, if you kill off every other motive, self-love will be the only thing that remains.

Do Glaucon and Adeimantus think that morality is inconsistent with the *persistence of self-love?* If so, that seems inconsistent with their interest in the virtuous agent's concern not to destroy his own prospect of ultimate happiness. What is more, if this were their view, then they would need to give good grounds for us to concur with them—just as they need to give reason for their other characterizations of justice/morality. On an ordinary view, the thing morality requires is only the thing the egoist fails in, namely a proper subordination of self-love to other considerations. (What would it be, one might ask, for a person to retain their practical reason and their sanity yet abdicate entirely from self-love?)

It has become perfectly standard in works of social science and economics (see for instance Samuelson's famous textbook of economics) to call 'selfish' all acts that people do in order to further their own self-preservation or at the prompting of self-love. But to speak in this way and refer to agents as doing these things 'selfishly' is an abuse of words which begins by nurturing lazy cynicism and then brings ruinous confusion. First there is a demand, which is confused with morality's demand, whose satisfaction cannot even be conceived; then, when it appears that *that* demand is not satisfiable, little or no attention is paid to the distinctions that morality does make. If we allow it to do so, the language itself will correct these confusions. Listen for one moment, if you will, to the word 'selfish'. This word connotes not self-love as such, but a vice or fault of character, the vice of the egoist who fails to *temper his self-love* by sufficient benevolence towards others or a proper regard for the interests of others.[3]

The idea that, if someone's moral motive is not proof against all fear or weakness, then his motive must really be corrupt or self-interested—and corrupt or self-interested in itself—is one of the most

3. So, in its application to the choice of an act, 'selfish' connotes origination in the self-love of a person who is *not* properly subordinating that motive to benevolence and other considerations. Acting selfishly then is a matter of choosing the act that that sort of person would choose or doing something in the way in which such a person would do it.

insidious of the distortions to which morality is liable. To accept a challenge such as Glaucon's and Adeimantus' just as it stands, a challenge that precisely depends on this distortion—is this not to introduce confusion from the start into the most elementary part of the subject?

1.11.   It is sometimes suggested that, through its own nature, morality invites such distortion. Critics and enthusiasts of morality often seem to be in alliance to suggest that morality is altogether uncircumscribed in where it places its demands, endlessly detailed in the shaping of its demands, and limitless in the extent of these demands.[4] But this way lies confusion and ultimate ruin. Even if morality were the single and most important of all things in life, that would lend it no authority to subjugate or swallow up every distinct concern. To say that something is the most important thing of all does not commit one to denying that anything else has any importance of its own. Where morality does swallow up everything else, moreover, a counter-reaction is inevitable, and will itself be exaggerated. It is to be expected that in the present case, the response to insidious moralism will be an equally frightening immoralism or cynicism. But here, right at the outset, let us insist that philosophy does no one a favour if it acquiesces, even for a moment, in the distortions we are told morality is apt to visit upon itself. If morality seems to need this self-image, maybe philosophers and theologians are more to blame for this than people of ordinary workaday virtue.

1.12.   At the beginning there were two basic topics (A) and (B) in the philosophy of morality. Glaucon's and Adeimantus' concern appeared to relate only to (B). But now let us briefly revisit the disquiet we were caused by the evident interdependence between the question (B) of the motive to morality, which is the question in

---

4. In our first fix on the content of morality, not devised to counter enthusiasm or its obverse, the demand that is most clamant is the *negative* (as with the first kind of moral concern) and the *prescriptively specific* (a 'perfect duty' inviting 'perfect compliance', as with the fourth sort of moral concern).

Republic book II, and the question (A) of what morality is and what its content is. (See 1.2). The perplexity arose from the thought that the reasonableness of the claim of morality—compare topic (B)—must depend on what exactly it is that morality demands or requires or advises. If only we knew for certain what that was, we might make real progress with question (B). But in fact this content of morality—compare topic (A)—can only be determined from such ordinary moral sensibilities as have a strong enough hold on the feelings and thoughts of human beings for us to hear them as reminding us of real concerns and intimating to us real requirements. And that takes us back to questions we have treated as falling under the topic (B). Do these ordinary sensibilities and motivations define an ideal which we, who ask questions such as question (B), have any reason to make our own?

Here was the circle. So far our thought has been to break into the circle by gathering from outside the area of dispute some partial answer to the question (A) and bringing to bear things we think we know already. (See 1.3.) In so far as we proceed in that way, however, we need to acknowledge openly and freely that our procedure is burdened with assumptions and presuppositions that fail to be completely neutral with respect to the question of moral motivation. Total neutrality is impossible. This will neither dismay nor surprise those who see it as the role of philosophy, not to make something out of nothing, but to assist in the process of the emendation and diversification of our convictions.[5] But can nothing more be said?

Close by, moreover, there is another not very different source of unease. Proceeding as we have by the phenomenological method, we have constantly appealed to 'our' feelings, 'our' relations, and 'our' attitudes—as if those who ask the philosophical questions (A) and (B) are a representative sample of humanity, rather than a self-selected group. How could we show that we *are* representative?

---

5. Similar assumptions and presuppositions were already at work in the comments we made at 1.8, 1.9, and 1.10 on Glaucon's and Adeimantus' challenge to Socrates. Glaucon and Adeimantus can say that they too have a right to assumptions. But I think I have shown *their* assumptions really are arbitrary.

The proper response to these several doubts is to begin by refusing to see them as gratuitously brought on by the approach we have pursued. (It is not as if some rival approach could understand the moral motive in abstraction from the content of morality or the content of morality in abstraction from the motive to have regard for morality.) And the next thing we may want to do is to transpose the inquiries (A) and (B) that we began with, as follows:

(A') What is the substance or content (and what is the nature and extent) of that morality, *if there is one*, which there is reason for us (as under (B') and any positive answer there may be to that question) to adhere to?

(B') What reasons are there (if any) for us to adhere to and to persist in a morality that has the content alluded to under (A')?

Alternatively, in a spirit that would have us begin from a position slightly closer to *Republic* book II, we may ask:

(B") What sort of motive can there be for us to care about justice/morality?

(A") How do we need to think of justice/morality, and what content must we think that it has, if we are prepared to see it as furnishing us with any motive at all to persist in any of its distinctive works or aims?

Putting matters in either of these new ways, we can escape from the charge of pursuing a method that makes a blatant assumption in favour of morality or justice. For it is left entirely open under this dispensation whether *satisfactory and satisfactorily matching* answers will ever be found for the questions of content and motivation. It becomes equally evident that the topics (A) and (B) need to be shackled together and attempted within some larger framework of inquiry, namely one containing the whole life that is proper to the creatures whose morality and reasonableness have come into question. In this context, it will be silly to despise a moral philosophy that goes back and forth constantly between (A) and (B), proceeding first by *tâtonnement* or groping about, and then by gradual approximation. It will be silly to complain that there are so few self-sufficient knock-down arguments, and no less silly to look askance at our recourse in 1.2 to the method of moral phenomenology.

If you like, you may see the problem (A)/(B) and its variants as analogous to the problem of solving by trial and error a pair of simultaneous equations. On these terms, any preliminary and provisional fixation of morality's content and motivation can be tested and refined against the joint determinations proposed by *rival* approaches to (A) and (B), taken jointly. What is more, *all* such answers become open to be tested and constructively interrogated within a constituency made progressively larger and larger than that of 'people like us'. The only persons to exclude are those who take a perverse or playful delight in confusion, are cynically determined to belittle any appearance of gathering agreement in thought and feeling, or wilfully despise the dialogical rules severally commended by philosophers as diverse as Socrates, Plato, and C. S. Peirce—: never to answer questions in a manner at variance with what one believes,[6] but always to pay proper heed to any difficulties that appear for it; not to despise that which is good enough for the dialectical context;[7] to make any interim result achieved in that context the basis for the next stage of determining the emended opinion;[8] to seek always to conclude, yet never to cut off inquiry[9] or ring-fence

6. Cp. Plato, *Crito,* 49d1–e2; *Gorgias,* 500b6–7; *Protagoras,* 331c4–d1; *Meno,* 83d1–2; *Republic,* 346a3–4, 539b, which offers a comparison between puppy-dogs who delight in rending and tearing whatever they come across and human beings who celebrate every invitation to disputation by dispensing with the *sincerity* that the dialogical rules must demand.

7. Cp. Plato, *Phaedo* 101d; Aristotle, *Nicomachean Ethics,* 1095b2.

8. Cp. C. S. Peirce's essay, 'On the Fixation of Belief'. On the view of truth that is implicit in that essay see my 'Reflections on Inquiry and Truth Arising from Peirce's Method for the Fixation of Belief', in *Cambridge Companion to C. S. Peirce,* ed. C. Misak (New York: Cambridge University Press, 2004).

9. Cp. C. S. Peirce, *Collected Papers,* ed. C. Hartshorne, P. Weiss, and A. W. Burks (Cambridge, Mass.: Harvard University Press, 1931–58), vol. I, 139.

one's convictions against that which one might learn by one's own experience or by the experience (reported or imaginatively reconstructed) of another.

1.13. For Plato the purpose of such precepts was to guide a search for truth made by the best way, which he took to be shared converse among friends. In choosing perforce a second or third best way, I shall try at each point to imagine a reader as if actually present and enforcing my observance of these rules when I make the case for any particular conclusion or try to gain command over the fixation of philosophical belief. In order to increase the clout of our subject matter itself at the expense of would-be theoretical assumptions and received opinions I shall try to follow certain further precepts. These are: to cleave scrupulously, wherever that is possible, to terminology whose sense is fixed in its context by the language itself (independently of current philosophy and other theoretical subjects, and independently also of the rhetoric or the politics of the present moment); to adhere always to that which can command stable understanding among those who want philosophy to achieve a certain cumulativity of understanding;[10] and to avoid technical terms that are not forced upon us by the insights and perceptions of our predecessors or not absolutely forced upon us by the exigencies of our subject matter itself.

These restrictions may appear draconian. But they do not arise only from the concern to diminish the hold of preconceptions, reader's and author's alike. They are also intended to ensure that

10. Such a philosophy needs a lingua franca or *koine* that will pass muster and command common understanding in the British Isles, in Northern Europe, Australasia, the Indian subcontinent, North America . . . a recognizable continuation, I should hope, of such English as is common to J. S. Mill, William James, Mahatma Gandhi, John Anderson, or John Passmore, a language at once *restricted* by the subtraction of that which now provokes misunderstanding *yet extended* by the free use of the vast linguistic resources that such authors have seen as available to them and that even now the larger and better dictionaries so beautifully explicate. I have to hope that the reader, no less the native speaker than the reader for whom English is a second language, will have the same access to such dictionaries as the author.

what we are saying in philosophy really *means* something. Having superseded the criteria of meaningfulness that Wittgenstein himself put behind him after *Tractatus Logico-Philosophicus* (1921), let us not abandon Wittgenstein's ambition for philosophy, namely for it to insist that something be *meant,* be proposed to cognition, by every sign that figures in any declaration that is put forward. (Compare *Tractatus* 6.53.) Let us never suppose that serious thought can dispense with a constant care for the words which will be as fortresses for it.[11]

The choice of a terminology is never neutral. It imports things and it excludes things. All too often, the technical notions that have been allowed into philosophy are *creative,* not in an intuitive or good sense of 'creative' but in one variant of a specialized or technical sense.[12] This is to say that they may commit the users of the terminology to assumptions—assumptions that may be gratuitous, unclear, or unjustified, or ought, as assumptions in which ordinary thought or practice does not entangle us, to have no place in a philosophy that seeks to begin near the beginning. Another way in which technical terms may be 'creative' appears where the use of

11. 'Words are the fortresses of thought': William Hamilton, *Lectures on Metaphysics and Logic,* vol. III (Edinburgh: William Blackwood, 1874), p. 178, a reference I owe to Roland Hall. Such fortresses will never be built, I believe, among the airless abstractions preferred by those who propose in the place of philosophical ethics a rational choice theory or a microeconomics of human motivation. For a short but exemplary critique of such theories, richly deserving of discussion, refinement, and elaboration, see Simon Blackburn, 'Practical Tortoise Raising', *Mind* 104 (1995), especially pp. 698–711. In the abstract treatments of our subject I complain of and the loose and semi-technical uses of such expressions as 'altruism', 'egoism', 'selfish', 'self-interest', 'preference', 'satisfaction', the difference between accurate and inaccurate description is not something that can be simply or directly heard or felt. The inwardness and outlandishness of the studies just referred to is not the only objection to them. Among the speculative or theoretical rewards of the dogged pursuit of a more ordinary non-philosophical plainness might be the assurance that no substantive claim made by the moral philosopher should rest upon commitments entered into unconsciously or simply by virtue of his or her adopting a certain technical terminology. On 'selfish' etc., see 1.10 (also 1.7, 1.8, 1.9) and below, 2.4–8 (see also 2.12 *ad fin.*).

12. For the technical sense, see Patrick Suppes, *Introduction to Logic* (Princeton: Van Nostrand, 1957), ch. 8. In case this does not spring to mind, I would point out that there is a cognate sense for the very same word in accountancy.

terms of this kind commits their users to questions that warp the intelligence of those who try to answer them—questions that are unnecessary precisely because they are tainted (I mean) by unwarranted assumptions. These dangers already abound, if only because we have to come to terms with problems of this kind that are left to us by our predecessors, along with a legacy of controversy that is kept alive by our failure to hunt down assumptions. Let us try our hardest and best then, even if we cannot make those problems disappear, not to add to them. In listening to what we hear ourselves utter, as in trying to listen to the utterances of others, let us remember that to make sense by what we say in philosophy, to mean *this* rather than *that* by our words, is not something to take for granted, however defeasibly. It is a real and difficult achievement, where failure is something short of final disgrace. It is something to strive for.

2

Hume's genealogy of morals

Self-love, benevolence, reason, and imagination; evil in Hume and in Schopenhauer

I cannot forbear having a curiosity to be acquainted with the principles of moral good and evil, the nature and foundation of government and the cause of those several passions and inclinations which actuate and govern me. I am uneasy to think I approve of one object and disapprove of another; call one thing beautiful and another deformed; decide concerning truth and falsehood, reason and folly, without knowing upon what principles I proceed. I am concerned for the condition of the learned world which lies under such a deplorable ignorance in all these particulars. I feel an ambition to arise in me of contributing to the instruction of mankind, and of acquiring a name by my inventions and discoveries. These sentiments spring up naturally in my present disposition and, should I endeavour to banish them by attaching myself to any other business or diversion, I feel I should be a loser in point of pleasure; and this is the origin of my philosophy.

Hume, *Treatise of Human Nature*, I.iv.7

The social virtues must, therefore, be allowed to have *a natural beauty and amiableness,* which, at first, antecedent to all precept or education, recommends them to the esteem of uninstructed mankind, and engages their affections.

Hume, *Enquiry Concerning the Principles of Morals*, V.1

2.1. Plato's successors in moral philosophy, Aristotle and countless others, have offered all sorts of variants, Judaeo-Christian, secular, and other, upon Socrates' answer to Glaucon and Adeimantus. Siding with morality but wanting philosophy, albeit from a distance, somehow to second morality's best-considered pretensions, they have recruited to the task of lending them some authority either *metaphysics* (in religious and secular variants) or *pure practical reason* (see Lectures 4 and 5), or else *desire*. (How desire? The thought is that desires of persons other than *x*, along with *x*'s own desires, can sometimes make an act binding upon or 'normative for' *x*. This is Utilitarian territory, onto which we advance in Lecture 6.)

A response of an altogether different kind, one addressing the questions of content and of motivation more or less simultaneously (as we have counselled at 1.12) but attempting this in speculative mode without blatant *parti pris* in the cause of morality, may be extracted from the account of morals that is presented by David Hume. This is to be discovered in book III of Hume's *Treatise* and his *Enquiry Concerning the Principles of Morals*. There is little chance of this approach to such questions being properly understood, however, or read as offering even an indirect answer to the problem with which the brothers beset Socrates in the *Republic*, unless we attend to Hume's aims, which are distinctive.

2.2. At least at the outset, Hume's chief aim in moral philosophy is not to find a validation in philosophy for any particular discrimination of good from evil or vice from virtue. It is rather to describe and explain the actual capacities of human beings to make the particular distinctions that they do make. In his plan of investigation, these capacities are to be traced to the presumed, discovered, or hypothetically reconstructed workings and propensities of the human mind. In the *Treatise of Human Nature* Hume says he searched for principles in the moral sphere that would be like the principles which, in the preceding century, Newton had found in the sphere of physics. In this new inquiry, which Hume called moral science but might nowadays have called the anthropology of morals, his explanatory hope was that, wherever some 'principle [had] been found to have a great force and energy in one instance', it would be possible, just as it was in natural science, to 'ascribe to it a like energy in all similar instances'. 'Principles' here are not so much principles in the sense of instructions or precepts or maxims for the conduct of moral agents as principles for judging of character or acts or whatever. They are followed (whether consciously or not) by ordinary thinkers, but studied (and maybe vindicated or refined or even discredited) by the moral scientist. Hume expected that, by proceeding in this way and along a different route from his predecessors, he would be able to improve on all the previous accounts of morality that were known to him, dispensing altogether with the implausibilities of notions on which they had relied, such as 'conformity to reason' and 'eternal fitnesses'.

Further specifying Hume's plan in the light of his mode of executing it, one might describe it as follows: he will explain, as nobody has previously explained, how it is possible for a conscious being to fasten on an object (a person, a custom, a disposition or would-be virtue, a particular character, an act expressive in its context of that character, or the outcome of that act and the state of affairs resulting . . . , or a putative act or putative outcome . . .), to bring the object in question under a standard of virtue or morality (or where applicable, of taste) and then to pass judgment on the object. By examining the indispensable role here of the natural passions and the given faculties, by studying human subjects' received ways of ratifying or correcting the judgments that they arrive at, Hume will achieve an understanding of morals which could never be achieved by trying to understand these subjects as attempting *moral inferences* from one sort of proposition, from something already given as an *is,* to another proposition, a practical conclusion given as an *ought:*

> In every system of morality, which I have hitherto met with, I have always remark'd, that the author proceeds for some time in the ordinary way of reasoning, and establishes the being of a God, or makes observations concerning human affairs; when of a sudden I am surpriz'd to find, that instead of the usual copulations of propositions, *is,* and *is not,* I meet with no proposition that is not connected with an *ought,* or an *ought not.* This change is imperceptible; but is, however, of the last conse-

quence. For as this *ought,* or *ought not,* expresses some new relation or affirmation, 'tis necessary that it shou'd be observ'd and explain'd; and at the same time that a reason should be given, for what seems altogether inconceivable, how this new relation can be a deduction from others, which are entirely different from it. But as authors do not commonly use this precaution, I shall presume to recommend it to the readers; and am persuaded, that this small attention would subvert all the vulgar systems of morality and let us see that the distinction of vice and virtue is not founded merely on the relations of objects nor is perceiv'd by reason. (*Treatise,* III.i.1, end)

Upstaging all systems that he has 'hitherto met with', Hume's own approach to these questions is to discredit any ambition to find that his subjects are engaged (or even *as if* engaged) in deduction. According to his own efforts to 'observe and explain', neither deduction nor yet some easier way of passing from one judgment to another is at issue. The starting point is an object (in the sense of 'object' that we introduced before we quoted *Treatise,* III.i.1). A human subject's arriving at his response to an object and his attainment of a conviction about *ought* (or *good* or *beautiful . . .*) is the culmination of a collusion of feeling and thinking that runs in parallel with the subject's exploration of the world of sense experience, a culmination that involves the subject's grasping of a standard by which to judge in matters of taste and morals. This catching onto the standard is the end product of an apprenticeship in which the joint workings of passion, reason, and imagination are socialized and yet further socialized. In the central or paradigmatic case, a subject moves smoothly and unimpededly (or else defeasibly and reflectively) from an object all the way to a well-considered attitude of approbation or disapprobation.[1]

1. On these terms, Hume is not open to criticism for failing to clarify the nature and the bounds of what *is* or the relations of the province of *is* and the province of *ought.* If we don't start with an *is* at all, but with an object, all that lapses.

I would add that, because that is not his interest here, Hume says nothing in this

In a moment we must rehearse that which Hume sees as leading
a human being through the formative stages to a fully fledged capacity to do all this. But first it will be useful to say a word or two
more about Hume's methodology and his general approach to that
which we now call moral philosophy.

2.3. Human beings appear to themselves very special and peculiar. The morality of human beings is certainly a singular creation.
It does not follow that human animals or human morality have themselves to lie beyond the reach of 'moral science' as Hume came to
conceive this. As his project advances, it is made more and more
evident that to look upon human beings and their morality as natural
things in the way in which Hume interprets his Newtonian aspiration
is not in itself to transform or denature these things.[2] Not only does

---

passage itself about whether or not the conviction reached by the process he himself
intends to describe does represent or does not represent something that *is* (as well as
representing an *ought*). I mean that he does not say whether the conviction itself represents as vicious (or virtuous) what *really is* vicious (or virtuous), represents as beautiful
(or deformed) what *really is* beautiful (or deformed), represents as obligatory what *really
is* obligatory. . . . The logical or ontological or metaphysical standing of the conviction
attained is not Hume's topic in the passage cited. His concern is only to make room
for his own theory (soon to be revealed) of how the conviction is arrived at and to point
to the disadvantages of the theories which his own theory is to supersede. I repeat this.
Neither Hume's theory itself as properly understood, nor the advertisement for it, needs
to rest on an exhaustive or general account of *is* and *ought,* or on a dichotomy between
them. (If that had been the aim, much more care would have been needed to characterize
each.) The only thing that is certain about the proposition that expresses the new
conviction the subject reaches is that the content of the conviction is not exhausted by
the theological or the sociological or the historical. In so far as the proposition in
question relates to something that 'is', this something will have to be a 'new creation',
arising from the 'eternal frame and constitution of animals' (including human animals).
See the last paragraph of Appendix I of the *Enquiry Concerning the Principles of Morals.*
See also Lecture 12, n. 7.

2. Nor need such naturalism generate a naturalistic account of 'good' etc. of the kind
that G. E. Moore anathematized as committing 'the naturalistic fallacy', the fallacy
(roughly speaking) of assimilating other subject matters to the subject matter of experi-
mental science. In the Humean story, the extensions of 'good' and other value predicates
are not determined in the fashion proper to a natural science. For 'nature' and 'natural',
see Moore's *Principia Ethica* (Cambridge: Cambridge University Press, 1903), pp. 40–
1. (For further remarks about Moore, see 7.4, 8.1, 11.1, and 11.5 with n. 14.)

his method make careful accommodation to the peculiarities of its subject matter. It makes room for the possibility that a well-observed description and explanation of morals may prove to vindicate morals—not least by showing the multiplicity and stringency of the constraints that lie upon any first-order ethic that will answer to the strictly unforsakeable needs, aspirations, or expectations of its participants.[3] Linking our actual benevolence with the natural reasons and norms of reasonableness that we observe in human creatures, and seeing that benevolence diverted into further motives that we do in fact have (cp. Lecture 3), the moral scientist must also hope that, towards the end of his work, even the human artifice of justice (in the narrow or specific sense of justice, contrast Platonic justice/righteousness) will eventually be revealed as founded in an interest that is the greatest imaginable, extends to all times and places, and could not possibly be served by any other invention. (Cp. the penultimate paragraph of the *Treatise.*) As part of the same project, the theorist will explore the possibility that it is the same with most of the other dispositions that moralists have singled out as particular moral virtues. Why should they not be vindicated, and vindicated not in an empty or vacuous way but by showing just how hard it would be to dispense with most of the dispositions that are advertised as virtues—even as accolades of this sort are specifically and carefully withheld from dispositions that are wrongly advertised as virtues but are really corrosive of the foundations (as Hume reads them) of morality? Among the corrosive dispositions will be penance, mortification, self-denial, celibacy and other monkish dispositions that stupefy the understanding, harden the heart and sour the temper (cp. *Enquiry*, IX.1, Selby-Bigge, p. 270). In the end, to anyone who feels and thinks through everything that it involves, moral virtue must appear as the finest possible flowering of the original and acquired natures of man—the perfecting adornment or embellishment of man considered as a natural-cum-reasonable being. (Cp. *Enquiry*, IX.1, Selby-Bigge, p. 276.)

3. We shall come back to explanations of this kind in Lectures 11 and 12.

It will be a matter of the greatest consequence to see how it happens, when it happens, that explanation passes into vindication. Meanwhile, one may note how Hume's understanding of explanatory method differs from that of most of his present successors in the social sciences. Hume's approach to the task of explanation is never distorted by excessive admiration for that which is admirable in natural science but inapplicable outside that field. It begins without *parti pris,* but it always leaves room for the theorist to recruit the moral engagement of author, reader, and critic. There is something else that is even rarer in social science. One who recognizes the force of the Humean account of why he, the subject himself, feels or thinks as he does need not find that, if he accepts the explanation, this subverts his finding of moral beauty in this or that act or character. The acceptance of the explanation will not undermine the reasons he would give himself to follow this or that line of action. For the explanation, the conviction, and the reasons will coexist happily enough in the agent's consciousness. Indeed,

> a sense of morals is a principle inherent in the soul, and one of
> the most powerful that enters into the composition. But this
> sense must certainly acquire new force when, reflecting on itself,
> it approves of those principles, from whence it is derived, and
> finds nothing but what is great and good in its rise and origin.
> (*Treatise,* II.iii.6, Selby-Bigge, p. 619)

2.4. So much for the original aim and plan, and so much for further things that might in the end accrue to success in its pursuit. Back now to the beginning. What should the moral scientist postulate as the original propensities and normal workings of the human mind?

According to the *Treatise* and the *Enquiry,* human beings come into the world endowed with the sentiment of self-love, which is the strongest original spring of action that there is, endowed *also* with the weak sentiment of benevolence, and further endowed with the faculties (inter alia) of reason (the capacity to discover truth about the empirical world by perception, to understand relations of ideas, and to find means to given ends),[4] imagination (this subsuming the capacity to produce in response to what prompts a given idea another associated idea), and sympathy, by which Hume means the capacity, available alike to the virtuous and the wicked, to resonate or reverberate to the feelings of others.[5]

In Hume's picture, these primitive endowments work in concert. He does not aim to describe their normal workings as strictly independent of one another. He does, however, assert the irreducibility of benevolence to self-love.[6] What he says is this: 'It is needless to push our researches so far as to ask why we have humanity or fellow-feeling with others. It is sufficient that this is experienced to be a

---

4. To these various offices of reason it is necessary to add something else that does not fall under these offices and is strictly distinct, namely this: to perceive situations previously unencountered as falling under the same preoccupations or concerns (e.g. of benevolence) as more familiar situations fall under, and to see various ends already adopted or acted upon as committing one to yet others that are analogous or apparently on the same footing. See below at 2.11 for Hume's repeated failure to give proper consideration or care to the ordinary idea of the practically reasonable.

5. 'The minds of all men are similar in their feelings and operations, nor can any one be actuated by any affection of which all others are not in some degree susceptible. As in strings equally wound up, the motion of one communicates itself to the rest; so all the affections pass from one person to another and beget correspondent movements in every human creature. When I see the effects of passion in the voice and gesture of any person, my mind immediately passes from these effects to their causes and forms such a lively idea of the passion as is presently converted into the passion itself. In like manner, when I perceive the *causes* of any emotion my mind is convey'd to the effects, and is actuated with a like emotion.' Hume, *Treatise,* III.iii.1, Selby-Bigge, pp. 575–6.

6. Benevolence generates 'non-I desires' in Bernard Williams's sense, desires on x's part that someone other than x should receive some benefit. See his 'Egoism and Altruism', an article I strongly recommend, still there to be found in *Problems of the Self* (Cambridge: Cambridge University Press, 1973). In the absence of good reason to believe that we are massively deluded, it can also generate 'basic non-I desires', as Williams calls them, namely non-I desires that are *not* sustained or held in place by a desire or concern that the desirer himself should receive some benefit or avoid some harm.

In giving such pride of place to benevolence in Hume's theory and in treating sympathy minimally as a psychological principle which can operate (strictly speaking) with or without benevolence, I am following more closely the emphases of the *Enquiry* than of the *Treatise,* which I see as clarifying and as simplifying the *Treatise* in certain ways. There is no reason to believe that the special satisfaction Hume felt in the second *Enquiry* was exclusively bellettristic.

principle in human nature' (*Enquiry*, V.2, second paragraph, foot-note), and this: 'passions . . . composed under the denomination of *self-love* are here excluded from our theory concerning the origin of morals, not because they are too weak, but because they have not a proper direction for that purpose' (*Enquiry*, IX.9, fifth paragraph).

2.5. This last claim is of critical importance to Hume's account of morality and everything else that is supposed to flow from it. But it might be questioned. It seems impossible to make benevolence out of self-love; but someone might attempt to explain benevolence as arising out of self-love plus the resonations of sympathy. The thought might be that sympathy can prompt one to treat another's sufferings as if they were one's own or in the fashion of a benevolent person. Variants on this approach still have their champions. The difficulty Hume would have with their view is that, if sympathy is simply a reverberation (if sympathy is not understood as already directed by benevolence), then the process that the explanation de-scribes cannot be expected to produce anything that will amount to real benevolence. The egoist who was distressed by the sufferings that resonated upon him from someone else for whom he felt no concern would have a better reason to distance himself from the sufferer or drive the sufferer away than to help him. Even in the presence of simple sympathy (of sympathy and only sympathy), self-love *as such* will not have 'a proper direction' for Hume's purpose. It can neither ground benevolence nor deputize for it.

2.6. At this point, more needs to be said positively of benevo-lence, which is the primitive sentiment on which, in Hume's theory of morality, almost everything else is founded. Benevolence is vari-ously described by Hume as fellow feeling or as the spark of friend-ship for human kind. The propensity to feel this sentiment is the same propensity by which we seek, however provisionally or tenta-tively, to respond to the plight of others or to benefit others. It is the propensity by which we conceive disinterested desires that others (especially, in the first instance, those close by, but then, by the workings of sympathy, imagination, and reason, more distant persons too) should be relieved of this or that evil or receive this or that benefit.[7] From this original benevolence, as particularly directed, there springs, Hume says, a more general concern with human interests as such, our own or others', including the interests of those who are further away in space or time or are excluded from the ambit of the solicitudes with which we first embark on a life somewhere inside the ambit of morality:

> There seems a necessity for confessing that the happiness and misery of others are not spectacles entirely indifferent to us; but that the view of the former [i.e. the spectacle of happiness], whether in its causes or effects, like sunshine or the prospect of well-cultivated plains (to carry our pretensions no higher), communicates a secret joy and satisfaction. (*Enquiry*, VI.1, Selby-Bigge, pp. 243–4)

> Any recent event or piece of news, by which the fate of states, provinces or many individuals is affected, is extremely interesting even to those whose welfare is not immediately engaged. Such intelligence is propagated with celerity, heard with avidity, and enquired into with attention and concern. The interest of society appears, on this occasion, to be in some degree the interest of each individual. The imagination is sure to be affected; though the passions excited may not always be so strong and steady as to have great influence on the conduct and behaviour. (*Enquiry*, V.2, Selby-Bigge, p. 223)

> There is some benevolence, however small, infused into our bosom; some spark of friendship for human kind; some particle of the dove kneaded into our frame, along with the sentiments of the wolf and serpent. Let these generous sentiments be supposed ever so weak; let them be insufficient to move even a

7. See again Williams, cited at n. 6.

hand or finger of our body, they must still direct the determinations of our mind, and where everything else is equal, produce
a cool preference of what is useful and serviceable to mankind
above what is pernicious and dangerous. A moral distinction,
therefore, immediately arises; a general sentiment of approbation; a tendency, however faint to the objects of the one, and a
proportionable aversion to those of the other. (*Enquiry*, IX.1,
Selby-Bigge, p. 271)

2.7. Before we seek to know in more detail how this concern for
the general interest can arise from whatever slow process produces
it out of simple benevolence and before we inquire (as we must)
what else can ensue from it, it will be well to protect and extend
this foundation of Hume's system. We must first demystify and sim-
plify benevolence a little; and then (2.8) we must confront the outright scepticism that Hume's conception of benevolence has always
prompted to the adherents of what Hume calls the 'selfish theory'
of human motivation.

It would have been advantageous, and well in line with his conspicuous insistence that gratitude is a natural virtue, for Hume to
have emphasized how, *in action,* the sentiment that he calls benevolence need not begin in thoughts of any great or noble refinement.
It would have been helpful for him to have explored its affinity with
our human propensity to come together with others in enterprises
of shared or shareable benefit and take pleasure in such success as
they achieve without exact regard for our own particular contribution
or for our own particular reward.[8] This propensity deserves much
more study than Humean philosophy has so far accorded to it, as
does the propensity to return good for good—which is only the
expression of a natural virtue Hume is careful to recognize—and to
give evil only in return for evil. Another part of the same scene is
the ordinary readiness of most human beings under ordinary cir-

---

8. In his regard, see J. L. Mackie, 'Norms and Dilemmas', in *Persons and Values*
(Oxford: Oxford University Press, 1985), to which the present paragraph is indebted.

cumstances to presume (albeit slightly riskily) that they will neither be penalized for the benefit they bring to another person nor punished for their preliminary, however tentative, goodwill towards them. (For a further elaboration of this, see below, 2.17.) It is not as if every animal partakes in all these predispositions. Not even every human being does. The claim is only that there is a remarkable *tendency* for most human beings to share in them.[9] From this contingency and others, all sorts of special consequences have followed, most conspicuously, under divers further conditions yet to be described, human morality itself.

2.8. In contrast with the Humean theory of benevolence, some theories make their sole starting point its rival, namely self-love. This 'selfish theory', still discoverable in countless works of social, economic, and biological science and imputed by Hume (with varying degrees of fairness and unfairness) to Epicurus, to Hobbes, and to Locke among others, says that 'all of us, at bottom, pursue only our private interest' (see *Enquiry*, Appendix II); or else it says that 'unknown to ourselves, we seek only our own gratification, even while we appear the most deeply engaged in schemes for the liberty and happiness of mankind' (*Enquiry*, Appendix II).

It may appear that the first point to make about these ideas is that, even if the selfish theorists' denial of the appearances were not so wilful as it is ('to the most careless observer there appear to be such dispositions as benevolence and generosity; such affections as love, friendship, gratitude', Hume says, *Enquiry*, Appendix II), it would *still* be worth marking and celebrating the difference between the virtuous and the vicious form of 'self-love'. Indeed. But, in

---

9. Compare *Treatise*, III.ii.2 (Selby-Bigge, p. 487): 'So far from thinking that men have no affection for any thing beyond themselves, I am of opinion that, though it be rare to meet with one who loves any single person better than himself; yet it is as rare to meet with one in whom all the kind affections taken together do not overbalance all the selfish. Consult common experience.' So much is contingency, no doubt. Think twice, however, before you infer that moral judgments must *themselves* be either contingent or *a posteriori*.

practice, anyone who sets too great a store by this point has almost certainly conceded much more than Hume would think necessary or wise to the selfish theorists. For almost every attack from their quarter upon benevolence (upon altruism, as our contemporaries mostly prefer to say) arises out of rank confusions that call for more direct criticism. The confusions are variations upon a simple theme that may as well be anatomized here and now, once and for all.

If someone wants (however weakly) to do a service (however easy) to someone else, then the thing he or she normally wants is to bring it about that, *in that particular way* (whatever it is), *things should be better for the other person.* The phrase just italicized signals the thing that the benevolent person wants. That is the distinctive content of the original aim. If the person's efforts succeed and the beneficiary is indeed helped by these efforts, then the benevolent agent may, of course, come to feel pleasure. But, *pace* the selfish theory, this pleasure cannot be the thing that this agent was aiming at within the original want. It is not part of the agent's motivation. If you refer back to the specification, there need be no mention there of the agent, let alone of his pleasure. What is more, concerning any pleasure the agent will have, *this* pleasure could never have been the *original aim.* For if the agent had not wanted *something else* (e.g. that the beneficiary should benefit), if he had not wanted it independently of his own future or present experience of pleasure, there would be no accounting for the agent's eventual pleasure or satisfaction. The pleasure, if it is itself to be intelligible, must presuppose some *prior* concern.[10]

Such an exposé of confusion is misunderstood if it is read as a plea for the genuineness of *all* apparent or supposed cases of benevolence. Countless motives other than benevolence may be misrepresented as benevolence. Many, many intentions that benefit another will arise from intentions further back that relate only to

10. See Williams, 'Egoism and Altruism', especially pp. 260-1. More generally, see Bishop Butler's *Fifteen Sermons Preached at the Rolls Chapel* (1726).

self-love. It does not follow that all do or most do. It is true that, in the difficult matter of finding out whether, in this or that particular case, the motives of agents really were benevolent, the mere exposé of confusion does not assist us. The exposé does however vindicate some sort of presumption of innocence in a benevolent motive. For it protects the motive against the muddle in which so many selfish theorists take their peculiar pleasure when they exult in the claim that 'all benevolence is mere hypocrisy, friendship a cheat, public spirit a farce, fidelity a snare to procure trust and confidence' (*Enquiry*, Appendix II). It must never be forgotten that the selfish theory always rested the greater part of its argument on a supposed difficulty in the *very idea* of genuine benevolence. The selfish theory is begotten in fallacy and confusion.

Other selfish theorists are not confused but cynical. They find simple benevolence not so much impossible as absurd or else absurdly improbable. Wherever they furnish reasons for their opinion (something surprisingly rare in practice), they will deserve a separate reply. For the moment, however, we may follow Hume (see *Enquiry*, Appendix II, *ad fin.*) and simply remind them of anger. Suppose that, being angry with someone, I hurt him. Suppose that I punish him and I exult in his suffering. Will the cynic deny that the best explanation of my joy is the fulfilment of my *prior* desire that this person should suffer? Will he say that that is not how my want is properly to be specified? Probably he will not. But then, if we can want one person to suffer, can we not want another person to thrive? If we can be vindictive, why can we not be benevolent? (For more on vindictiveness, see below, 2.14–18.)

So far we have only addressed Hume's first formulation of the selfish theory. (See 2.7.) What then about the second formulation— that, unknown to ourselves, we seek only our own gratification? Pleasure plays an important role within the aetiology of morality and taste, by attaching us to certain characters and qualities that we shall approve. But it cannot follow that, whatever we may approve, we pursue or promote it for the sake of pleasure rather than for the sake of what it is. On this matter, let us give the last word to the great

American philosopher and methodologist of science, C. S. Peirce, where he writes:

> No argument can possibly be a correct one which pretends to disclose to us a fact wholly new without being based on evidence which is new. . . . When Hobbes, for example, would persuade us that no man can act otherwise than for the sake of pleasure, it is clear that this belief would deeply modify our conceptions of men, and our plans of life; but when on asking what supports this momentous conclusion we learn that it is but the simple fact—if it can by dignified by that name—that every man desires to do what he does do, we are led at once to suspect that there is some sophistry in the process by which so novel a conclusion can be drawn from so familiar a premise. (*Collected Papers*, vol. VII, p. 329)

2.9. Supposing that it may be provisionally allowed that it is possible for benevolence to be what it seems, let us at last revert to Humean exposition, which we left in suspense at the end of 2.5. There are now two further questions: what can have made a sentiment as weak as benevolence any rival to a sentiment that is as strong as self-love? And, supposing that benevolence could be such a rival, what extends the workings of humanity or benevolence beyond simple participative impulse, first into warm-hearted goodwill and then, beyond that, into care for the standard of virtue and vice or a dependable concern for anything as abstract as the general good or the public interest?

Hume's answer is as follows. From the beginning of their physical existence, individual human beings, endowed as they are with their benevolence and self-love, are drawn into constant converse with other human beings. They have acute and urgent needs of their own but it soon becomes evident to them that others too have such needs.[11] Precisely for that reason they need to learn to think and speak without any reference to self about whatever it may be that ministers to such needs. In the process of learning the sense of the public language in which there is provision to talk of useful and useless, good and bad, fair and foul, beautiful and ugly, a human being enters into the commitment to learn to depart from his private and particular situation, and see things not only from thence but from the point of view that shall be common between one person and another. (See *Treatise,* III.iii.1 *ad fin.* and *Enquiry,* cited below.) Simply by virtue of their intersubjective significance, these terms, 'good', 'bad', 'fair', 'foul', 'beautiful', 'ugly', force anyone who will seize their proper meaning to transcend that which is good, bad, fair, foul, beautiful, ugly *for him.* In learning to speak the public language of approbation and disapprobation, praise and blame (and arrive at the possibility of agreement with others in judgments), a human being needs to learn to see his responses as answerable to a point of view that lies beyond his own, a point of view that he shares first with others to whose fate he is not entirely indifferent or whose fate he cannot ignore—cannot ignore if he coexists with them or he engages in any cooperative venture with them.

Let it be clear that, at this point, Hume postulates no special diminution of self-love nor any waning in the readiness to make the speaker-relative judgments that arise in the private and particular viewpoint of self-love. All he postulates are *countervailing* tendencies, tendencies arising from benevolence or arising from the same source as benevolence. But as soon as we are drawn onwards and outwards by our need and our benevolence (even as we are drawn by the mind's wont to spread itself constantly on objects that it encounters in the world), and as soon as we come to see things from the common viewpoint that is presupposed to the senses of predi-

11. See Augustine, *Confessions,* I.vi.8: "It is the physical weakness of a baby that makes it seem innocent, not the quality of its inner life. I myself have seen a baby jealous: it was too young to speak, but it was livid with anger as it watched another baby at the breast.'

cates that presuppose it, we are well set to learn a new set of responses and treat our own judgments as answerable to responses
beyond our own responses. Suppose that, in seeking that common
viewpoint and exploring it, we are struck in one way or another by
some object of attention. Then we have to ask ourselves whether
others, especially those who are motivated in the same way to take
up that viewpoint, are similarly struck—rather as, when we seek to
establish the objective contours of a landscape, we need to interest
ourselves in perspectives other than the one we ourselves happen to
enjoy at a given point. From a plurality of perspectives we have to
work backwards to that which they are all perspectives of, allowing
one perspective to supplement or explain or correct the apparent
error in another.[12] Thus Hume writes:

> When [one] bestows on any man the epithets of vicious or
> odious or depraved, he then speaks another language [than that
> of self-love], and expresses sentiments in which he expects all
> his audience are to concur with him. He must here, therefore,
> depart from his private and particular situation, and must choose
> a point of view common to him with others; he must move some
> universal principle of the human frame, and touch a string to
> which all mankind have an accord and symphony. If he mean,
> therefore, to express that this man possesses qualities whose
> tendency is pernicious to society, he has chosen this common
> point of view, and has touched the principle of humanity in
> which every man in some degree concurs. (*Enquiry*, IX.1, Selby-
> Bigge, p. 272)

Marrying this claim with one that Hume makes in the *Treatise*, we
may paraphrase Hume as saying further that, if others do concur,
then the judgment of odiousness is to that extent reinforced. If others

---

12. Cp. *Treatise*, III.iii.1, Selby-Bigge, pp. 582, 583; III.iii.3, Selby-Bigge, p. 603; *Enquiry*, V.2, last footnote: 'We know to correct these inequalities by reflection and retain a general standard of vice and virtue, founded chiefly in general usefulness.'

do not concur, the judgment is a candidate to be corrected or discarded. (There is of course one other possibility, and it is one Hume should have said something about. Sometimes we will stick to our own judgment as sound and incur the responsibility of explaining the discrepancy between our own response and that of others.) In general, one will be right in one's valuations and appraisals, and others will tend to concur in them, just to the extent that one succeeds in homing upon the common standard that is erected upon the interest that people have in common with one another. And now, as the passage just quoted from the *Enquiry* continues:

> While the human heart is compounded of the same elements as at present, it will never be wholly indifferent to public good nor entirely unaffected with the tendency of characters and manners. And though this affection of humanity may not generally be esteemed so strong as vanity or ambition, yet being common to all men, it can alone be the foundation of morals, or of any system of blame or praise. One man's ambition is not another's ambition, nor will the same event or object satisfy both; but the humanity of one man is the humanity of every one, and the same object touches this passion in all human creatures. But the sentiments which arise from humanity are not only the same in all human creatures and produce the same approbation or censure; but they also comprehend all human creatures; nor is there any one whose conduct or character is not, by their means, an object to everyone or censure or approbation. (*Enquiry*, IX.1, Selby-Bigge, p. 222)

The system of blame or praise, the shared standard or the 'abstract rule' that emerge in this way for the evaluation of characters—and (derivatively from that) the evaluation of the acts that issue from characters—rests on an interest that is in each case weak. But it is the only standard that is reliably reinforced. Or, as Hume says earlier in the *Enquiry*:

Every man's interest is peculiar to himself and the aversions and desires which result from it cannot be supposed to affect others in like degree. General language, therefore, being formed for general use must be moulded on some more general views and must affix the epithets of praise or blame in conformity to sentiments which arise from the general interests of the community. (*Enquiry*, V.1, Selby-Bigge, p. 186)

The shared standard, the 'abstract rule' (by which Hume means not so much a command or prescription to be imposed on human behaviour as the way according to which subjects are to evaluate things that they encounter and the norm to which they may be seen to hold their conduct answerable), embodies or condenses views and interests that are general and established in common. But the standard or rule itself is the creation of sentiments and modes of thinking and feeling in which each of us participates. Hence the hope we entertain that Hume can answer our questions (A) and (B) or (A') and (B') by some method of joint determination.

2.10. At the moment of human beings' arriving at the stage where (as in the last citation) they assume full mastery of 'general language' and are begun upon moral thought itself, their imagination, their reason, their powers of analogy and of looking for similar treatment for similar cases and dissimilar treatment for dissimilar cases, will long since have entered into collaboration with their capacity to resonate to the feelings of all others, with their benevolence and with the other traits and tendencies fostered by benevolence.[13] And this will have happened in such a way that the shared standard of morals becomes for each of us a standard of assessment to be applied first to traits and characters, and then (derivatively from these) to actions seen as expressive of traits and characters, and then to the conse-

---

13. Gratitude, for instance, the virtue that Hume rightly treats as natural and might usefully have stressed in its linkage with the equally primitive but more general idea of reciprocity. On that see 2.16–18 below. See also Lecture 9.

quences of actions (cp. *Treatise,* III.iii.1, Selby-Bigge, p. 590). It becomes our own standard, not necessarily uncritically—for we are contributors to it as well as its subjects—nor yet for every case, but presumptively. Moreover, as we become better schooled in that public standard, better equipped to participate in its application, and progressively more engaged with the general concerns that it embodies, we shall come to feel a pleasurable sentiment of a particular kind (or an uneasy sentiment of a particular kind) in the spectacle (or, as Hume calls it, 'the view') of virtuous (vicious) characters and the actions that express them. The time then arrives when we can be relied upon to feel this pleasurable sentiment in the view or spectacle of any mental quality (or the expression of any mental quality) that is useful or agreeable to its possessor or useful or agreeable to others. We are now a member of that collective, that *us,* whom Hume has in mind when he writes:

> When any action or quality of mind pleases us after a certain manner, we say it is virtuous; and when the neglect or non-performance [of an act] displeases us after a like manner, we say that we lie under an obligation to perform it. (*Treatise,* III.ii.5, Selby-Bigge, p. 517)

In Lecture 5 (and then again, for a moment, in Lecture 9), we shall generalize this Humean finding (for the natural and the artificial virtues combined) in the claim that we recognize the duty to do the act A where the neglect or non-performance of the act A displeases us in a certain manner, the manner that goes with the thought that it is reprehensible not to do the act A; and we shall measure the strength and adequacy to the thing that is to be explained of the moral compulsion that Hume sees this sentiment as imposing upon us.

2.11. At this point, let us take stock. Genealogically or aetiologically speaking, the public standard that informs our evaluation of characters, sustains our understanding of the distinction of vice and virtue, and gives us new reasons to act non-egoistically is always an elaboration of natural benevolence. But it is crucially important that that to which it has given rise reaches far beyond that original sentiment. It reaches beyond in at least three ways.

First, the standard of morals is established in the ascent from the level of primitive sentiment to the level of plenary moral thought. In that ascent, we graduate from the merely expressive employment of language to the command of a proper subject matter and content which requires us to deploy the indicative mood and the declarative mode. This is surely the same moment at which the passions Hume calls *the calm passions*—passions easily confounded, Hume says, with the operation of reason—enter fully into their own:

> there are certain calm desires and tendencies which, though they be real passions, produce little emotion, and are more known by their effects than by the immediate feeling or sensation. These desires are of two kinds; either certain instincts originally implanted in our natures, such as benevolence and resentment, the love of life, and kindness to children, or the general appetite to good, and aversion to evil, considered merely as such. (*Treatise,* II.iii.3, Selby-Bigge, p. 417)

Here Aristotelians and others will want to salute Hume's near-readiness to acknowledge the possibilities which Aristotle marked with the notions of *deliberative desire, desiderative reason,* and *ratiocinative desire.* (See *Nicomachean Ethics,* book VI, especially chapter 2, which is devoted to *prohairesis* or choice.) From the calm passions Hume could surely have advanced to something very like the practical reason of Aristotle. Rather than think of the calm passions as desires as such, would it not be more accurate to think of them as representing *potentialities* for desire or as sources or *origins* of desire—sources or origins for desire subtly transformed by the mental operations and processes Hume himself describes? For desires that spring from the calm passions will be newly refined and differentiated and newly subject to criticism. They will know how to give account of themselves, moreover, on the level of reasons (in the plural).

Hume does not avail himself of such possibilities. Or rather he does not put these things down to the credit of reason. He says of the calm passions, which 'determine the will', that, because they 'cause no disorder', they are often 'taken for the determinations of reason, and are supposed to proceed from the same faculty with that which judges of truth and falsehood' (*Treatise,* II.iii.3)—but that it is *wrong* to take them so. Continuing his polemic against philosophers such as Samuel Clarke and Ralph Cudworth and notions such as *eternal fitnesses,* Hume cleaves here to his habitual opposition of reason and passion. He always persists in the idea that the operations of reason and passion can be isolated from one another, considered separately, and then composed. Compare the later passage at *Treatise,* III.ii.2:

> Human nature being composed of two principal parts which are requisite in all its actions, the affections and understanding; it is certain, that the blind motions of the former, without the direction of the latter, incapacitate men for society: and it may be allowed us to consider separately the effects that result from the separate operations of these two component parts of the mind. The same liberty may be permitted to moral, which is allowed to natural philosophers; and it is very usual with the latter to consider any motion as compounded and consisting of two parts separate from each other, though at the same time they acknowledge it to be in itself uncompounded and inseparable. (Selby-Bigge, p. 493)

In his dispute with Clarke and Cudworth, Hume is surely right. But one of the effects of his promoting a campaign against them over every other philosophical concern is for him to make his opponents a present (in effect) of the notion of reason. In this way he creates the impression that anyone who wanted to find some substantive role for reason in connection with the ends of morality or practice would have to side with Clarke and Cudworth. The sad thing is that, once Hume denies, however fairly, that reason *as these philosophers conceive it* can play the role they want it to play or can have anything to do with ordinary reasons for choosing this or that course of action, and once he interpolates his own proposal and circumscribes the role of reason in the way he does, a workaday notion of practical reason becomes, for others who are not seeking to reinstate any view like Clarke's or Cudworth's, very hard to recover. (See 2.4 above, at n. 4.)

Perhaps the best way of bringing it home to Hume that this is a pity is to take seriously the analogy we have found him contemplating between an *action*, which he sees as the joint product of the affections and the understanding taken together, and a *motion*, which natural philosophy will understand as the resultant of two vectors. The analogy is as fruitful for criticism as Hume takes it to be for exposition. For, once we try to work out the analogy and put it into harness with Hume's own theory of morals, we happen on a crucial difference.

In a calculation concerning two vectors, the input each makes can be described once and for all. In an account of the contribution of the affections and the understanding, things are not like this. Suppose that the input of the affections lies at the level of nature or instinct and consists in blind motions or desire-driven strivings that would, unchecked, 'incapacitate men for society'. Suppose that it is by virtue of a simultaneous contribution of the understanding that desire-driven strivings submit to . . . well, submit to what exactly? According to Hume's genealogy of morals, they submit, under the auspices of reason, to sympathy and imagination, and the eventual outcome is the emergence of a standard of morals. Once that standard is established, however, it can *speak back* to the affections in which it is founded. Modified so, the affections can then make *another* contribution to the determination of action. Only at risk of sacrificing the attractive plausibility of his own genealogy of morals can Hume cast doubt on these claims. Their plausibility is only increased if the standard of morals is seen as the product of repeated back and forth between reason and modified affections or modified modified affections or . . . affections.

What happens, once we retell this story, to Hume's analogy with the composition of motions? The analogy seems faint and misleading. It would be one thing for Hume to sum up his own moral genealogy as spelling out the stages of back and forth between the affections and the understanding. It would be another thing altogether—nothing better than bluff, I think—for him to represent that nothing is subtracted and nothing is added if his genealogy is recapitulated as akin to the simple composition of two vectors. Does the genealogy really predict such striking determinacy of outcome as we find in the composition of forces? Can some vector story really condense the whole of Hume's aetiological account? Rather than place reliance on thoughts that encourage a comparison between motion understood in terms of the composition of forces and an interaction of bare passion and bare reason, would it not have been wiser for Hume to exert his right to *interrogate* more carefully and patiently the (mis)conceptions of reason that he was opposing?

2.12. So much for the first of three ways in which the establishment of a public standard reaches beyond the sentiments that made it possible.

Here is the second way: there is no clear limit upon whose happiness or misery can impinge upon the judgments that issue from the public standard. A virtue is any mental quality in anyone (however remote they may be from the one who undertakes to apply the public standard) that occasions the agreeable sentiment of approbation. The standard transcends that which is local to the person who applies it. The standard does not replace the finding of particular duties by a derivation of such duties from some general duty to promote utility or whatever. That is not what Hume is aiming for. (It would duplicate and then confuse his detailed account of how each duty arises.) The standard transcends the local in the sense that it applies itself to cases far outside the time or place of those who arrive at it. It aspires to be a standard that is universal.

And here is a third way: the energy that is mustered from fellow feeling and its allies (mustered from these and self-love, rather) can be *redirected* and put at the disposal of concerns that are essentially alien (Hume will insist) to benevolence. These divergent concerns will be the topic of our next chapter. But a glance back towards 1.2 will suggest the reason why Hume needs to engage with these other concerns. In the construction as we have it so far, Hume has touched on at most three of the four kinds of concern enumerated there. The fourth, namely observance, has yet to make an appearance.

Excursus

2.13. The way is now open to the topic of Lecture 3. Before we enter upon the next layer of Hume's theory, however, let us give some consideration to the *status* of these speculations of Hume's, and try to plot Hume's relation to evolutionary and psychogenetic accounts of the origin of morality. After that, a question will arise concerning evil and the completeness or incompleteness of Hume's theory.

There is the remarkable and extraordinary phenomenon of human morality. It invites wonder and curiosity. Anyone who asks, as Hume did, how it came into being, how it sustains itself, and how exactly it enables its participants to move from an object to a judgment upon this object, must try to see in one single focus (1) the phenomenon itself, however tentatively articulated, and (2) the original constitution of human beings, however boldly and speculatively delineated and however tentatively demarcated from the acquired nature that human beings come to possess under the influence of the circumstances in which they live. On some such basis Hume's moral scientist has to try to construct a historical or psychogenetical narrative.

The disadvantage the moral scientist labours under is that all he knows is the present reality of the phenomenon. He can extend his knowledge backwards only so far as literature, geography, geology, or history permit. His advantage is that, in this task, he can draw on the understanding that he gets from his own participation in the practices whose origin and persistence he has undertaken to explain. He can redeploy his however inarticulate mastery of the notions that animate these practices and mine his participative conception of these notions for their plenary content. His reconstruction cannot, however, make the emergence of the phenomenon appear as inevitable. Nor can his story be checked against a historical record. The thing that counts for most is whether, on the basis of the explanation he offers, it is intelligible how morality *might have* developed and come to mean what it means now.

How is Hume's account to be ranked against rival accounts that have appeared since? The peculiar distinction of his story is that it arises from a vivid and detailed sense of the cohesion of divers moral ideas, a close interest in the inner workings of morality itself, and a sure grasp of what it will take to account for all the moral data on the basis of benevolence, sympathy, imagination, reason, and self-love. That and the inventiveness with which Hume traces the refinements of morality back to these starting points is its lasting beauty. On the other hand, in so far as it simply presupposes the weak sentiment of benevolence, Hume's account will appear incomplete, faint and unsatisfying. 'It is needless to push our researches so far as to ask why we have humanity or fellow-feeling with others. It is sufficient that this is experienced to be a principle in human nature', Hume says in a footnote to *Enquiry,* V.2 (Selby-Bigge, pp. 219–20). We have already quoted these words. In our own times, nobody would be *allowed* to regard it as 'needless to push our researches so far as to ask' where benevolence and humanity themselves come from. That is a difference between Hume's times and ours. But what ought he to have said?

If Hume had been pressed to answer this question and he had been permitted to read advance copies of Darwin's *Origin of Species* and Darwin's subsequent writings, he would surely have emphasized—or so one speculates—how close the founding sentiments of human morality are to the maternal and paternal instincts of most mammals that manifest awareness of family or larger groups. It also

seems plain, as regards the further reaches of the ethical above and
beyond the natural virtues of a parent, that he would have found
almost everything he needed in a passage of Darwin's *Descent of
Man* to which Elliott Sober and David Sloan Wilson have recently
drawn attention:[14]

> It must not be forgotten that although a high standard of mo-
> rality gives but a slight or no advantage to each individual man
> and his children over the other men of the same tribe, yet that
> an increase in the number of well-endowed men and advance-
> ment in the standard of morality will certainly give an immense
> advantage to one tribe over another. There can be no doubt that
> a tribe including many members who, from possessing in a high
> degree the spirit of patriotism, fidelity, obedience, courage, and
> sympathy, were always ready to aid one another, and to sacrifice
> themselves for the common good, would be victorious over most
> other tribes; and this would be natural selection. At all times
> throughout the world tribes have supplanted other tribes; and
> as morality is one important element in their success, the stan-
> dard of morality and the number of well-endowed men will
> everywhere tend to rise and increase. (*Descent of Man* (1871),
> pt. I, p. 166; cp. also pp. 82 and 238)

This sort of explanation is indifferent in itself between the cultural,
the customary, the historical, the genetic, and any mixture of any of
these; but it actively encourages speculation about possible ways[15]

---

14. See their book *Unto Others: the Evolution and Psychology of Unselfish Behavior*
(Cambridge, Mass.: Harvard University Press, 2000).

15. Not least under conditions of cultural differentiation beween groups and cultural
homogenization within them. See K. Sterelny, *Thought in a Hostile World* (Oxford:
Blackwell, 2003). There has been a tendency for those who have wanted to insist (despite
discouragement) upon the possibility of group selection to allow nevertheless that the
conditions favourable to it will be unusual. (Cp. Mackie, 'The Law of the Jungle: Moral
Alternatives and Principles of Evolution', *Philosophy* 53 (1978), repr. in *Persons and
Values*, p. 128: 'There can be genuine cases of group selection. But I admit they are
exceptional.') But however usual or unusual the said conditions may be *in general*, the
peculiar proclivity of *Homo sapiens* towards artifice forbids the assumption that, in the
history of this particular animal, such conditions will be other than normal.

in which certain human attributes that confer advantage on a group at the level of ethos, culture, and custom can simultaneously (i) put the group at an advantage over other groups and (ii) confer advantage even upon members of the group who both have and actualize within the group an above average potentiality to develop these attributes.[16] Why cannot such individual members both enlarge by procreation the class of individuals with potentialities for this form of ethical development and enlarge by their conduct and example the chances (on the level of culture and custom) for the further, better, and more general actualization of such potentialities?

The Darwinian kind of explanation has long been unfashionable. Against such explanations, it has been objected repeatedly that the 'altruism' visible in the fidelity, obedience, etc. of which Darwin speaks confers no advantage for survival on individual altruists, but only handicap; that only under the most unusual conditions could altruists survive to the point of attaining a commanding majority, etc. Those who make such objections will deprecate the recruitment of Hume among the followers on this point of Darwin.

Hume's ideas are wide open to either side of this controversy, but it is never certain—even when it is clear that objectors mean to

16. Harking back to Darwin's own words, consider the 'slight [but appreciable] advantage' conferred on its possessor by the potentiality for courage and one of its lively associates, namely the concern for the good of the group ≏ patriotism. Possessors of attributes such as these may indeed incur 'costs' but certain advantages will also accrue to them within the group. It will be useful at this point for anyone drawn to the rhetoric of 'costs' and the supposedly limitless advantages of 'free riding' to confront a full list of Humean virtues. For a peerless summation of these see Annette Baier, *A Progress of Sentiments* (Cambridge, Mass.: Harvard University Press, 1991, ch. 9; see especially pp. 199–200).

At this point there looms (yet again) the threat of muddle. There is no need for the idea that self-love and primitive benevolence *both* figure within the history of morality to revive or renew the confusions already exposed at 2.8. (In related connections, see also Sober and Wilson, *Unto Others*, pp. 142–9.) In this place as everywhere, let us also remember one of the saner things said by Nietzsche: 'the actual causes of a thing and its eventual uses, the manner of its incorporation into a system of purposes, are worlds apart. . . . all processes in the organic world are processes of outstripping and overcoming: and, in turn, all outstripping and overcoming means reinterpretation, rearrangement, in the course of which the earlier meaning and purpose was necessarily either obscured or lost' (*Genealogy of Morals*, II.xii).

concern themselves with morality proper—what the objectors really mean by 'altruism'. It is hard not to suspect that the objectors' ideas of what morality itself is are just as inaccurate and ill considered as those that Glaucon and Adeimantus propose to Socrates. It is harder still to believe that, taken in the way in which objectors so roughly and readily conceive it, *altruism as such* is either necessary or sufficient for the morality that human beings know. We have studiously avoided the idea that there is some self-sufficient whole dispositional state of human beings called altruism which they must attain either at some point on their road to morality or else at the moment of their attaining to it. Hence our own preference for the now familiar idea of 'benevolence' as it is conceived within Hume's usage and Hume's theory, a pure disposition at once *coexisting* with self-love and *curbing* or *restraining* it. Hence too the care we have tried to exercise at 2.7 (see also 2.18 below) in refining and simplifying the Humean conception of benevolence and the rest, in order to adjust it, still in the spirit of Hume's theory, to the ordinary reality of human conduct and custom that prevails under the ordinary conditions of the social life of human beings and their ordinary expectations of ordinary morality. Ordinary morality, so understood, is no more the weakling it is often modelled or represented as being than it is the bullying, scheming, autocrat/oligarch pictured by the many and various old and new inheritors of Thrasymachus.

It is a fortunate thing for the prospect of an alliance in this matter between Hume and Darwin that controversy in evolutionary theory has recently returned to a point where Darwin's own proposal concerning the evolution of human morality can again receive serious consideration.[17] So much the better if any fresh endeavour to understand the genesis of morality can inherit some of Hume's insights—and so much the better if the new framework for serious consideration of these matters is innocent of the egregious confusions (see 2.7) that we have seen Hume show us ways to avoid.

---

17. See Sober and Wilson, *Unto Others*. See also J. L. Mackie, 'The Law of the Jungle.'

There is one more point (see below, 2.17) that needs to be made about Hume's genealogy of morals. But in advance of our attempting that, there is one more incompleteness that still needs to be signalled in Hume's theory.

2.14. Hume's theory partakes copiously of the benevolence and good humour of its author, whom many of his readers might confidently choose (despite the disadvantage of his reported bulk) for a cheerful and trustworthy companion in shipwreck or other dire straits and hardships. But how will a theory such as Hume's engage with the dark realities of positive evil—with the realities of deliberate brutality, of power-lust, of the eager obedience that those steeped in power-lust know how to exact and require from those weaker than themselves? How can it engage with pitiless indifference, with careless insensibility to the effects of collective actions in which one is indirectly implicated, or (most distinctively) with energetic and unremitting malevolence? A conspicuous example of this last, unfamiliar only in its purity and selflessness, is the motiveless malignity, as Coleridge called it, of Shakespeare's Iago. What is there for Hume to say on this score?[18] Does it not appear that, on pain of his theory's being condemned under the charges of systematic and inevitable incompleteness, its foundation must be extended?

Schopenhauer, who knew Hume's writings well and attempted in his own ethical writings things comparable to Hume's *Enquiry* (see, for instance, *On the Basis of Morality*),[19] would appear to have noticed the same deficit that we are concerned with. In Schopenhauer's moral genealogy, the foundational human impulses are (i) *Egoismus*, 'egoism' (better, perhaps, 'self-love'), (ii) *Mitleid* (roughly speaking) 'compassion' (in which Humean benevolence and fellow feeling may be tinged with pity), and (iii) *Bosheit*, or malice itself. The insights that Schopenhauer himself achieved in this way prompt one to ask

18. 'Absolute, unprovok'd, disinterested malice has never perhaps place in any human breast' is one thing he says. See *Enquiry*, V.2, Selby-Bigge, p. 227.

19. Trans. E. F. J. Payne (Providence, R.I.: Berghahn, 1995); originally published as *Über das Fundament der Moral*, 1841.

whether it would have been open to Hume to have done the same thing.

Objection might be made against a positive answer to this question, on the grounds that it involves a simultaneous postulation (as in Schopenhauer) of benevolence *and* (in effect) of malevolence. But such a would-be logical objection would rest on a confusion. Perhaps the quickest way of exposing the confusion is to think of the supposedly hardest case, where one and the same person is given both to benevolence and to malevolence towards one and the same second person.[20] Suppose that, at some point in their relations, the first of these persons wishes simultaneously that good befall the second person *and* that good *not* befall that second person. Well, even in this case (where the subject may have in due course to force himself to decide something about where he is proposing to go next in the matter), we encounter nothing remotely similar to the blank impossibility of someone's wishing that good befall the person and *not* wishing that good befall the person.[21]

2.15.   Once it becomes clear that there is no logical objection to postulating primitive benevolence *and* primitive malevolence, other questions must arise about the malice that Schopenhauer posits. One

20. Similarly the Roman poet, Catullus, asked how it was possible that he should feel love and loathing at one and the same time for one and the same person. (*Odi et amo. Quare id faciam fortasse requiris. Nescio sed fieri sentio et excrucior:* 'I love and I hate: wherefore I do so you may ask. I do not know, but I feel it happen and I am in torment', Poem LXXXV.)

21. To attempt to describe a case of this last kind would indeed bring one into conflict with the law of non-contradiction. But in the case we began with, which might be observed and which we began by describing, logic may observe a benign silence. Emotions can be contrary to one another. Where this is so, one need not destroy the other. And logic is not in abeyance. As was pointed out in Lecture 1, n. 1, the placing of the sign of negation is always crucial in these matters. In the first description of the case given in the text, the 'not' only qualifies the clause that is embedded (to the effect that good not befall the person). It does not negate 'wish'. The law of non-contradiction is secure; the mindset of the subject of the two states can be safely described; and logic is silent about how the subject should hold in balance the different prospects of doing the different acts that these states of his urge upon him. In so far as he refrains from all relevant action, the subject need not even decide.

might ask how so familiar, so normally circumscribed, so specifically directed a motive as this one (Peter has insulted Paul, so Paul wants to have his own back, etc.), can grow and grow to the point where it will give rise to the colossal and awe-inspiring phenomena of evil which the twentieth century recently supplied to us in such plenty. Another question relates to the original germ of malevolence itself.

In one of the first and fullest books about the political philosophy of the Nazis, and the psychogenesis of Nazism, a work entitled *The War against the West* (London: Gollancz, 1938), Aurel Kolnai, a Hungarian Christianized Jew living in the 1930s in Vienna, gave a part of the answer to the first of these questions. He showed how Nazi ideals and the prodigious evils into which they led represented not so much the inexplicable efflorescence of other-worldly Evil as an unmysterious product of the exaggerated emphasis on certain positive human values—values of patriotism, of national and cultural unity, of military valour, of national glory. . . . These were real values, Kolnai insisted, even when they were relentlessly pursued and promoted at the expense of ordinary pedestrian values such as justice, humanity, charity. . . . They were real values even when they were promoted under the conditions of post-Great War disaffection and humiliation and in despite of ordinary prohibitive aversions of the most fundamental kind. (For prohibitive aversions, see 1.2.)[22]

In the light of the descriptions that Kolnai provided of how the demands of so many other values and concerns were crowded out by those that the Nazis did emphasize, it certainly becomes easier to understand what ordinary malice and the free-floating passion to retaliate against someone or something can make of themselves under the hot-house conditions of patriotism perverted into militarism, and obedience enforced by intimidation. Comprehension can even increase when one adduces a further fact: that one of the most re-

---

22. Similarly, Kolnai later attributed to other ideologies, as to the cast of mind that he called the utopian mentality, a similar power to prompt human beings who are in hot pursuit of some glorious-seeming (however internally incoherent) objective to abdicate (either in enthusiasm and zeal or else in terror) from ordinary inhibitions against murder, intimidation, false witness, false accusation, etc.

markable things about human beings from the evolutionary point of view is the huge variety of environments and geographical, social, or physical conditions to which they can adapt themselves. Instead of relying upon instinct, with which they are relatively poorly provided (too many instincts would make Homo sapiens another, less adaptable, kind of creature), human beings rely over and over again upon their capacity to accommodate their conduct in ways not determined by instinct to whatever they find in the place where find themselves. More particularly, they rely upon their capacity *to imitate the more successful responses of the other human or animate beings they encounter there.*[23] We have all heard endlessly inconclusive discussions about the essential goodness (or not) of human nature. But one of the most deep seated of the constituents of that nature is this capacity for imitation, a capacity which is neutral in itself between good and evil. The most urgent question about possessors of that nature is what they will find in this or that place, context, or culture. What will they have to imitate there? What if anything will prompt them to reflect on what they are doing? To what extent is the responsibility there for good or bad something whole and entire or something divided, subdivided, subsubdivided . . . ?

2.16.   Given some starting point in *Bosheit,* evil is not incomprehensible. But we still need to understand that starting point. How can ordinary malice become the motiveless malignity that Coleridge puzzled over in Shakespeare's Iago? How can there be the pure malignity we hear Mephistopheles condense in the declaration he makes to Faust: 'Ich bin der Geist der stets verneint'—I am the spirit that constantly denies.

None of the accounts of morality we treat in these lectures has a ready-made or purely philosophical answer to such questions. In the case of Hume, I think he would question Schopenhauer's postulation

---

23. See Susan Hurley, 'Imitation, Media Violence and Freedom of Speech', *Philosophical Studies* 117 (2004): 165–218. See also Susan Hurley and N. Chater (eds.), *Perspectives on Imitation: From Neuroscience to Social Science,* 2 vols. (Cambridge, Mass.: MIT Press, 2005).

of *Bosheit,* and prefer to draw attention to the powerful forces already apparent in incidents such as that described by Augustine at *Confessions,* I.vi.8, (which we have already cited at n. 11): 'I myself have seen a baby jealous: it was too young to speak, but it was livid with anger as it watched another baby at the breast.' In this incident (compare the last two paragraphs of Appendix II of the *Enquiry*), as in infant behaviour now studied to such good effect by psychotherapists, psychoanalysts, and other observers,[24] or in ordinary adult retaliation which we see teeter on the edge of implacable spite, Hume might say that a wealth of explanatory possibilities is revealed for the diversification of an explanatory schema that he has found to be adequate for the normal or non-pathological cases that he has preferred to begin by studying.

In reply, Schopenhauer could object that Hume has never really said how, as they stand, Hume's founding principles will ever provide the *first germ* of what is needed. Whence will Hume derive the child's primitive impulse to strike out at those who obstruct its will, to make them suffer or to punish them? *Why is it* that 'every privation is infinitely aggravated by the pleasure of others'? What is to be said about the way in which anger itself can outstrip grief or disappointment? Here is the strength of the case for *Bosheit* as a foundational impulse, the impulse already visible in Augustine's account of infant behaviour. Once we speculate how such jealousy can arise from a baby's hunger or its anxious recollection of hunger, there are two other things we see there: the starting point for a more general insecurity which can grow under adverse conditions into a lust for the unlimited power that a *complete* or *absolute* security would require; and, second, the starting point for something different and much commoner, namely a *muted* or *modified hostility* which is eager and willing, given its cue, to work against primitive benevolence and stands at the ready to thwart putative or possible rivals for the good things of this world.[25]

24. Here see Margot Waddell, *Inside Lives: Psychoanalysis and the Growth of the Personality* (London: Duckworth, 1998; 2nd ed. London: Karnac, 2002), chs. 3 and 4.

25. Max Scheler, in his work *Ressentiment* (see the translation by Lewis B. Coser and William W. Holdheim, Milwaukee, Wis.: Marquette University Press, 1998), adds

2.17.　Finally, let us return to that which prompted us at 2.7 to redescribe primitive benevolence in terms of the cooperative propensity to return good for good and not to give bad except in return for bad. The thought that now suggests itself is that the characterization we gave of the underlying primitive impulse of human constitution was seriously incomplete. It needs to be fuller and more general: *to be ready to cooperate; to be ready always to initiate good; not, other things being equal, to expect bad in return for good; not to give bad unless in return for bad; to give good in return for good, but to be ready to give bad in return for bad.* The first four-fifths of this characterization give a possible schematization of Humean benevolence. In the last nine words, we see the *in itself* blameless enough embryo of Schopenhauer's *Bosheit* or malice. We see the instinct ready and waiting to emerge in motives of narrowly constrained self-defence or retaliation—but ready and waiting *also* for the cue which can precipitate the moral subject, beyond all measured retaliation, into divers pathologies of real evil: 'the real wickedness that seeks quite disinterestedly the pain and injury of others without any advantage to itself'.[26] Thus: 'The thirst for revenge is closely related to wickedness. It repays evil with evil, not from regard for the future, which is the character of punishment, but merely on account of what has happened and is past as such, and thus disinterestedly, not as means but as end, in order to gloat over the offender's affliction caused by the avenger himself.'[27]

---

not only a wealth of further reflections that converge upon these themes, but the words that Milton puts in Satan's mouth: ' . . . the more I see/Pleasures about me, so much more I feel hateful/Torment within me, as from the hateful siege/Of contraries; all good to me becomes/Bane, and in Heaven much worse would be my state' (p. 148).

26. Schopenhauer, *The World as Will and Representation*, trans. E. F. J. Payne (New York: Dover, 1969, vol. I, p. 333, sect. 61.

27. Ibid., sect. 65. In these formulations, is there even an echo of Hume (*Enquiry*, Appendix II): 'Vengeance, from the force alone of passion, may be so eagerly pursued as to make us knowingly neglect every consideration of ease, interest, or safety; and, like some vindictive animals, infuse our very souls into the wounds we give an enemy'? The claim we have made is that in his theory (when that is read just as it stands) Hume

2.18. Back now for a moment to 2.13. A new proposal now suggests itself concerning the division of theoretical labour within the inquiry into origins. Let evolutionary theory and its associates begin with the things human beings have in common with other mammals in order to tell the story of the emergence of primitive reciprocity in the forms in which we have now formulated it. (See 2.17.) Meanwhile, let it be the task of moral philosophy to help tell the long, twisting tale of the founding propensity's transformation into the benevolence/humanity from which flow certain natural virtues and then the extension of these virtues into fully fledged human morality. Let moral philosophy collaborate in this with moral psychology and let it recruit any assistance it can from psychoanalysis or other therapies of the soul in order to describe the several pathologies of evil.

---

reports more convincingly than he *accounts* for retaliation or vengeance, either for the germ or for its development.

For an invaluable supplement to Hume at this point, entirely consistent with Schopenhauer, see Mackie, *Persons and Values,* p. 154.

3

Hume's theory extended

The theory extended to embrace the artificial virtues by the diversion of benevolence and self-love into a new role; the reasonable as a sum of good reasons which agents can appropriate as reasons of their own

All *moral* duties may be divided into two kinds. The *first* are those to which men are impelled by a natural instinct or immediate propensity which operates on them independent of all ideas of obligation and of all views either to public or private utility. Of this nature are love of children, gratitude to benefactors, pity to the unfortunate. When we reflect on the advantage which results to society from such humane instincts, we pay them the just tribute of moral approbation and esteem. But the person actuated by them feels their power and influence antecedent to any such reflection.

The *second* kind of moral duties are such as are not supported by any original instinct of nature, but are performed entirely from a sense of obligation when we consider the necessities of human society and the impossibility of supporting it if these duties were neglected. It is thus that *justice* or a regard to the property of others, *fidelity* or the observance of promises, become obligatory, and acquire an authority over mankind. For as it is evident that every man loves himself better than any other person, he is naturally impelled to extend his acquisitions as much as possible; and nothing can restrain him in this propensity but reflection and experience, by which he learns the pernicious effects of that licence, and the total dissolution of society which must ensue from it. His original inclination, therefore, or instinct is here checked and restrained by a subsequent judgement or observation.

Hume, 'Of the Original Contract'

3.1. There is more for Hume to explain than we have seen him explain so far. But first let us look back. According to Hume's account, the weak but fortifiable sentiment of benevolence and the ever-present sentiment of self-love, under the influence of imagination, reason, and sympathy (the capacity to resonate to the mental states of others), issue in a standard of morals which informs the evaluation of characters, sustains the first understanding of the distinction of vice and virtue, and extends, reinforces, and refines the motivation to act non-egoistically. If someone is party to the standard of morals that Hume describes—and it will be hard in ordinary life for the preponderance of human beings not to be carried along by the processes Hume describes, and hard to struggle against the social forces that make us party to that standard—then it is to be expected that he or she will often be motivated, weakly perhaps but less and less weakly, to act otherwise than upon simple self-love. Indeed, in the important class of cases from which the Humean construction starts out, the emerging standard of morals has only to recognize as a norm what is already latent within our human nature.

> The social virtues of humanity and benevolence exert their influence immediately by a direct tendency or instinct, which chiefly keeps in view the simple object moving the affections and comprehends not any scheme or system nor the consequences resulting from the concurrence, imitation, or example of others. A parent flies to the relief of his child, transported by that natural sympathy which actuates him and which affords no leisure to reflect on the sentiments or conduct of the rest of mankind in like circumstances. A generous man cheerfully embraces an opportunity of serving his friend, because he then feels himself under the dominion of the beneficent affections, nor is he concerned whether any other person in the universe were ever before actuated by such noble motives, or will ever afterwards prove their influence. In all these cases the social passions have in view a single individual object, and pursue the safety or

happiness alone of the person loved and esteemed. With this they are satisfied: in this they acquiesce. And as the good resulting from their benign influence is in itself complete and entire, it also excites the moral sentiment of approbation without any reflection on farther consequences and without any more enlarged views of the concurrence or imitation of the other members of society. (*Enquiry,* Appendix III, Selby-Bigge, pp. 303–4)

This is a description of the ordinary workings of the social virtues— of the virtues that are rooted directly in the weak sentiment of benevolence and need no more than ordinary circumstances for their development. It springs from our first nature to approve them and approve their being approved. But there is much more to morality than non-egoism or the capacity to second the claims of benevolence against those of self-love; and there are other virtues beside those that can exert their influence on an agent both directly and without the assistance of a scheme or system requiring 'concurrence' and 'imitation' on the part of persons distinct from the agent himself. Within a benevolence-based scheme, Hume's theoretical problem (as it plainly appears from the perspective of the *Enquiry*) is to account for loyalty, honesty, allegiance, fidelity to promises, justice (respecting property and so on).[1]

3.2.   Among the further signs that there are virtues that fit imperfectly into Hume's original aetiology of morality is this. There are considerations of justice (in the strict and specific sense of the word) that we frequently allow to defeat or trump the requirements of beneficence. Sometimes justice and private benevolence will call for

1. See 1.1 (last paragraph) and 1.2 (the first paragraph and the concerns subsumed there under (4). And see Hume in the third paragraph of the same appendix: 'the benefit resulting from [the virtues of justice and fidelity] is not the consequence of every individual single act, but arises from the whole scheme or system concurred in' (Selby-Bigge, p. 304).

the same act; but equally often they will not, e.g. where a poor man has wronged a less poor one. Sometimes justice will call for the same act as the concern for the general interest as considered in advance of justice; but no less often it will not, as when a dangerous and seditious bigot is deprived of his lawful inheritance, for instance, or is subjected to criminal violence, or is found guilty of an offence he has not committed. In any such case, Hume wants us to be free to insist that we should side with justice, not with benevolence (whether private or public). Once we appreciate the force of Hume's insistence on this point, we shall see that there are a significant number of virtues whose recognition as virtues will seriously disrupt the pattern of explanation so far expounded. If the weak sentiment of benevolence is to be the whole theoretical origin of morality,[2] then the aetiology of morals must find some way to explain how the force and energy of benevolence can be redirected so as to propel our line of conduct along altogether new channels. Sometimes the redirected force of benevolence will have to work against benevolence itself. It is at this point—it is in order to come to terms with the virtues that do not arise directly or straightforwardly from our benevolence— that Hume invokes the idea of a convention or a compact.

There is a theoretically cognate problem that Hume sees in the ideas of justice and kindred virtues. Hume's exposition of this problem has given his readers much difficulty.[3] We shall expound the problem in his words but interpose brief comments and explanations in square brackets. These interpolations are designed to suggest one particular interpretation. The problem is set out at *Treatise*, III.ii.1:

2. Or if benevolence is to play the foundational role for morality that it inherits from the principles mooted at 2.7 and 2.17.

3. The problem disappears without trace from the account given of the artificial virtues in the *Enquiry*, the work which determines our preferred vantage point. (See Lecture 2, n. 6, second paragraph. For the appellation 'artificial' in the *Enquiry*, see the penultimate footnote of Appendix Three.) Nevertheless, as on some previous occasions, it will further our own philosophical purposes to restore one part of that which Hume painted out from the later account of the principles of morals.

I suppose a person to have lent me a sum of money on condition
that it be restored in a few days; and also suppose that, after
the expiration of the term agreed on, he demands the sum. I
ask, *What reason or motive have I to restore the money?* It will
perhaps be said, that my regard to justice and abhorrence of
villainy and knavery are sufficient reasons for me, if I have the
least grain of honesty, or sense of duty and obligation. And this
answer, no doubt, is just and satisfactory to man in his civilized
state and when trained up according to a certain discipline and
education. But in his rude and more *natural* condition [which
is the place where Hume's aetiology of morals must set out from,
for it is seeking to explain the emergence of the *civilized* state],
if you are pleased to call such a condition natural [it is natural
in this sense: it does not presuppose the emergence so far, of
convention, compact, or any such artifice], this answer would
be rejected as perfectly unintelligible and sophistical. For one in
that situation would immediately ask you wherein consists this
honesty and justice, which you find in restoring a loan and
abstaining from the property of others? It does not surely lie in
the external action. (Selby-Bigge, pp. 479–80)

Here we must break off the citation to ask why we are expected to
agree that the honesty cannot consist in the external action. The
answer is that, according to Hume, 'all virtuous actions derive their
merit only from virtuous motives, and are considered merely as signs
of those motives' (Selby-Bigge, p. 478). For Hume the claim has the
status of a would-be axiom, based in his conception of morality,
which is announced as founded not in the quality of acts per se but
in matters of 'personal merit' and the virtuous motives of individual
moral agents. The passage continues,

[That wherein this honesty and justice consists] does not surely
lie in the external action. It must therefore be placed in the
motive from which the external action is derived. [That is the
effect of the would-be axiom.] This motive [however] can never

be a regard to the honesty of the action. For it is a plain fallacy to say that a virtuous motive is requisite to render an action honest, and at the same time that a regard to the honesty is the motive of the action. (Selby-Bigge, p. 480)

Hume's point is that, if the merit of the action of restoring the money is referred to the merit of the motive and the virtuous disposition associated with that motive, then the merit of that motive itself cannot, on pain of circularity in the explanation, be referred back to the merit of the action. Or, as Hume says,

> We can never have a regard to the virtue of an action, unless the action be antecedently virtuous. No action can be virtuous, but so far as it proceeds from a virtuous motive. A virtuous motive, therefore, must precede the regard to the virtue; and it is impossible that the virtuous motive and the regard to the virtue can be the same.
>
> It is requisite, then, to find some motive to acts of justice and honesty distinct from our regard to the honesty; and in this lies the great difficulty. (Selby-Bigge, p. 480)

Hume finds the further motive that he needs for acts of justice, honesty, fidelity to promises, and so on in the approbation that we feel for acts that conform to a useful convention. This might be a convention or compact that enjoins one to keep one's hands off what others have made, or have had assigned to them by those who have made it, or have had assigned to them by those who had it assigned to them . . . by those who have made it. Or it might be the convention that designates some promissory formula and enjoins one to take all care to do that which, using that formula, one has said one will do. And so on.

How can conventions solve the problem Hume has proposed? Well, the conventions in question may be imagined to be conventions such that, if most people observe them, then things may be expected to be better for almost everyone:

[T]he benefit resulting from [justice and fidelity and so on] is
not the consequence of every individual single act; but arises
from the whole scheme or system concurred in by the whole,
or the greater part of the society. (*Enquiry*, Appendix III, Selby-
Bigge, p. 304)

Conventions or compacts single out practices that will bring a general benefit that appeals to self-love and to the sense of the general
interest; but then, as the practices come into their own and are
sustained in living, we may suppose that *further* merit is conferred,
in all the processes of ethical formation, upon acts or observances
that exemplify these practices, over and above the expected benefit
of the observance itself.[4] If a sense of general interest (as in Appendix
III of the *Enquiry*) or self-love (as in the *Treatise*) or both will *second*
some convention and *approve* it, then the convention can redirect
the activity of virtuous agents into justice or fidelity.

3.3.   In further explanation of how this is meant to work, I shall
set out a suggestion that I owe to Geoffrey Sayre-McCord (personal
communication): 'Once *artifice* is on the scene, so too is the relevant
motivation: a recognition that some given act conforms with a convention that is beneficial. With the appropriate conventions in place,
a person can be motivated by the recognition that the act conforms
to the convention. A person raised in civilized society who has internalized its advantageous conventions will normally be moved by
a recognition that an act conforms to the convention.'
   This suggestion has an attractive concinnity with the passage from
'Of the Original Contract' given at the head of this chapter, a text
that is succinct and has the advantage of showing Hume persevering
in the account of the natural and artificial virtues which he gave in
the *Treatise*. (However inexplicit Hume is about this theory in the

4. For 'act' as I seek to use the term, see n. 8 to Lecture 4, where it becomes even
more important to distinguish acts from actions. Strictly speaking, there is in the present
context a similar need to distinguish two senses of 'observance', in parallel with the
Lecture 4 distinction of 'action' from 'act'.

Enquiry, it is still there. See the penultimate footnote of Appendix Three.) But in the text displayed in the epigraph there are points where the reader may wonder whether Hume is doing the very best for Hume's idea.

Contrary to what Hume seems to suggest at one point, the practices that he says arise from compact or convention and command our approbation surely do not need to depend, either in their origination or for their perpetuation (in moral education and the life that this education looks out towards), upon explicit reference to compact or convention as such. (Compare Sayre-McCord's stipulation 'internalized'.) At the level of discovery, some practices may result from sheer accident or from our falling experimentally into ways of behaving that we then find ourselves encouraged to persist in. Some might even be by-products of natural inclinations to gratitude or reciprocity. Developing further an example Hume provides, let us think of two men who find themselves rowing a boat for the first time in their lives. Imagine that they discover after a while that they row best if they concert their efforts and pull on the oars at the same moment with a similar force. Imagine them settling down to row in that way. It does not matter how it came about that they started to row together in that way, provided that they can continue to do so. And surely they can also continue to do so and further their shared purpose without thought of their coordination's depending on compact or convention. (They need not even have these notions.)

This might make one think that the moral scientist does not need a general theory about how we *arrive at* compacts or conventions. A fortiori, he does not need to invoke the explicit ratiocinations that are spelled out in our epigraph. It ought to be enough to have an account of what sustains a practice, however the practice was first arrived at. And that need not be any one thing. All will be well, in fact, if whatever it is that encourages us to persist in a practice— and prompts us to behave *as if* we adhered to a compact enjoining that persistence—is some habit or disposition that is *already* amenable to Hume's general theory.

On these terms, if this were right so far, what would Hume have to mean by a convention? One might credit him with this answer: either a compact or what *would have been* a compact if it had been entered into *as* a compact; or else a way of behaving in which we come together or have already come together—*convenimus* ('we have come together') and so *conventum est a nobis* ('there has been a coming together by us')—*as if* by a compact. (Let etymology help philosophy here.) In that case, the explicit, conscious, or articulated convention is no more than one special case, a central one perhaps or an essential one for some instances, but by no means the only possible case. The most that we need is a sense of some common interest that is liable to diminution from the non-concurrence of others.

There is more than one reason to take a stand on these points. The first is the wild improbability of the story we find Hume telling in our epigraph. The second is Hume's own description of the honesty and justice that one who has *already* attained 'the civilized state' will find in the act of restoring a loan or in abstention from the property of others. 'Just' and 'honest', so predicated, have a sense that is already downwind (so to speak) of coordination. It is too little too late to try to *make the case for* the acts they denominate by appeal to convention and utility. (That is one part of the oddity of the passage in our epigraph.) The senses of 'just' and 'honest' *presuppose coordination and convention already internalized.*

A third reason for us to be leery of insisting on placing the explicit recognition of convention and its utility within the motivation of persons who are just or honest is that it would expose those who supposedly depended on thinking such thoughts to the idea that, *in this or that special case,* greater public utility would result from ignoring the convention. ('After all, we only have the convention in order to promote utility. But here we can promote utility *better* in another way.') That sort of thought, the direct (short-circuiting) appeal to general benevolence, has had a long history. But it is not the thought that Hume is promoting and that we need to have from him. Hume's aim is to use the idea of a convention in order to *redirect* the sense of common interest (more visible at *Enquiry*, Appendix III) and/or self-love and love of gain (more prominent in the *Treatise,* but tempered there by sympathy). I conclude that, if we are to protect Hume's account of the virtues that are not natural, then we must allow the practices themselves of honesty and justice that he is concerned with to impart to those who live by them a grateful familiarity, a familiarity that comes to shape or reshape their *constitutive* ideas of (their own and others') ongoing happiness and security. That is a point we shall return to below (3.6).

3.4. One more point about our epigraph from 'Of the Original Contract', while we look so closely at it. It would have been helpful if Hume had allowed himself, here and elsewhere, to single out for special attention conventions with a particular further property, over and above their original usefulness or indispensability to us collectively. These are conventions that *each and every* putative participant would be happy to agree to (at least if they know that *some* convention must be agreed) and be happy to prefer over all visible alternatives.[5] Such conventions deserve to be singled out for special attention because this property is bound to have a new and magnified importance when the aetiological examination of moral ideas leads into the question of their vindication. That is not their only importance; a much more general use will be made of such ideas in Lecture 9. In the meanwhile, however, we should note how Hume himself insists at one point (*Treatise,* III.ii.2, Selby-Bigge, p. 498) that 'the

5. See T. M. Scanlon, 'Contractualism and Utilitarianism', in A. Sen and B. Williams (eds.), *Utilitarianism and Beyond* (Cambridge: Cambridge University Press, 1982), pp. 103–28. I mention Scanlon's article not in order to force contractualism onto the Humean scene (that would be an absurdity; see 'Of the Original Contract' (1752), in *Essays Moral, Political, and Literary,* ed. E. F. Miller, rev. ed. (Indianapolis: Liberty Classics, 1987) and see *Enquiry,* Appendix III, Selby-Bigge, p. 306), but in order to make the point that the requirements of an artificial virtue need not to threaten but even to extend the primitive *solidarity* or *reciprocity* on which morality itself depends. See Lecture 9, n. 3, and 9.7.

whole system of [just] actions, concurr'd in by the whole society, is
infinitely advantageous to the whole *and to every part*'. See also 3.5,
below.

3.5. So much for complaints about the ways in which Hume fails
to keep apart questions of aetiology, of phenomenology, and of motivation or fails to do the best for his leading idea. Yet the general
shape of the explanation is clear. He can see virtues such as fidelity,
loyalty, allegiance, honesty and justice as redirections of elements
already accounted for in his theory, and he can explain how the
energy to be mustered from fellow feeling may be put at the disposal
of moral preoccupations and concerns that are not only different
from the concerns of humanity and self-love but seriously at variance
with them. Hume obtains from these redirections the virtues which
he designates *artificial*. He calls them artificial because they are *not*
virtues that arise directly from human nature without the mediation
of some coordinative convention or compact that helps to constitute
the practice defining this or that virtue. He is at liberty, moreover,
without any detriment to the scheme, to insist at the same time how
natural it is (how non-miraculous that is) for us to find our way
into artifices, conventions, and compacts of this kind.[6]

3.6. So far so good,[7] but now we must return once more to the
question of individual motivation. What explains an individual

6. 'Natural may be opposed either to what is *unusual, miraculous* or *artificial*':
Enquiry, Appendix III. These three contrasts generate three Humean senses for the
word. He is entitled to demand that his own uses of 'natural' be interpreted accordingly.
'In so sagacious an animal, what necessarily arises from the exertion of his intellectual
faculties may justly be esteemed natural [non-miraculous]': Appendix III, Selby-Bigge,
p. 307.

7. Except that there is of course a mass of unfinished business, concerning what is
special in the case of each of justice, fidelity, allegiance. . . . On these matters, see Annette
Baier, *A Progress of Sentiments* (Cambridge, Mass.: Harvard University Press, 1991),
especially her chs. 10 and 11.

With respect to justice, any Humean philosophy will surely need in the end to enlarge
the ambit of the virtue, to come to terms with the complexities it imports of grammar
and sense (see 10.7), to account for the peculiar impartiality and sacredness of its re-

person's persistence in ways of acting conformable with useful or agreeable conventions even when such persistence runs contrary to his own interest or contrary to the general interest? How easily can Hume's theory (interpreted as here advocated) manage either of these cases? Well, the person in question may not adhere to them. So the question had better be this: where he does adhere to them, why does he do so? And is it reasonable for him to adhere to them? Hume's explanation would appear to be this:

> [Men] are induced to inculcate on their children, from their earliest infancy, the principles of probity, and teach them to regard the observance of those rules by which society is maintained as worthy and honourable, and their violation as base and infamous. (*Treatise,* III.ii.2, Selby-Bigge, pp. 500–1)

In this connection there is further evidence of Hume's intentions at the beginning of the same section of *Treatise,* where Hume speaks of 'the reasons, which determine us to attribute to the observance or neglect of [the rules of justice] a moral beauty and deformity'. That is what explains our adherence—where we do adhere. We have come to see doing *this* as honest, as fair, as honourable . . . , doing *that* as dishonest, as ugly, as . . . , where the *this* or the *that* are acts, that is *kinds of action,* with which ethical formation has to concern itself.

The attractive feature of this thought, already prefigured at the end of 3.3 above, is that it makes it apparent to theory how, on the inside of a practice, moral subjects can engage in it in exactly the manner in which we suppose that we can, without aetiological reflection about conventions and without consideration of that which has lent *honest, dishonest, mine, thine, faithful, faithless,* etc. the senses that ethical formation gives to them. It makes apparent how we can follow

------

quirements (but see below, nn. 9 and 11, and see 9.10) and (well beyond the Humean point that the virtue is made for a world of scarcity, etc.) to relate justice as protective, reparative, remedial, enabling . . . to the most vital needs and most considerable vulnerabilities of human beings. On that point see Lecture 10, and see 7.20.

in a practice in the manner that Hume himself was describing when he wrote, 'It will perhaps be said that my regard to justice and abhorrence of villainy and knavery are sufficient reasons for me, if I have the least grain of honesty, or sense of duty and obligation.' In the civilized state that Hume took such pains to describe and explain, a person can annex the idea of moral beauty to acts that conform to certain practices, and can annex the idea of moral deformity to their non-performance. Such practices and the acts they call for take on a life of their own in the hearts and minds of ordinary agents who are happy to live under the auspices of the civilization that Hume sees as offering to them the final fulfilment of their natures as reasonable beings.

Such practices and the expectations that they generate are not, of course, proof against violation or abuse. But there are real safeguards of a sort in these ideas that we have of them—the idea of the 'beauty of an observance', the 'deformity of an infraction', and so on. Nor is there any mistake, according to Hume, in these ideas that we have internalized—unless it is a mistake that can be eliminated by piecemeal refinement and internal criticism. 'At our best, this is what we do,' we might say. 'Any alternative to what we do can be considered, or any improvement. But already the thing that we do is the result of indefinitely many reconsiderations and refinements.' It should be added that the requirements of honesty, fair dealing, and so on will not require us to act in this manner when we are dealing with blackguards or fanatics without conscience. The requirements simply set standards that we need strong reasons to depart from. For Hume—as for anyone else with a sense of what is possible here—that is answer enough. It is an illusion, one might say on Hume's behalf (and despite his self-imposed abstinence from the language of practical reason), to suppose that there is any well-founded conception of the reasonable that is so independent of human nature, and so independent of the substance of human life as we know it, that it would enable a judgment to be reached on some *further* question of the reasonableness (or not) of observances which agents can perceive as having the kind of beauty we are here concerned with or as belonging to a system that is 'advantageous to the whole and to every part'. Hume sees no trumping reasonableness, let it be remembered, in the promptings of self-interest. Let the critics who say they want more try to get for themselves a notion of the reasonable that presupposes nothing at all about human nature and its redirections. If they want more, let them say what more they want in those terms. Their difficulty will be this, that

> Where passion is neither founded on false suppositions, nor chooses means insufficient for the end, the [theoretical] understanding can neither justify nor condemn it. It is not contrary to [theoretical] reason to prefer the destruction of the whole world to the scratching of my finger. It is not contrary to [theoretical] reason for me to choose my total ruin, to prevent the least uneasiness of an Indian or person wholly unknown to me.[8]

It is the workaday, non-theoretical reasonableness of the practice, *given* the standing concerns and natural propensities that bring the convention into being, that helps to constitute the moral beauty of the observance. This moral beauty, as revealed to those who simply learn to participate in the practices subject to the convention, affords the major part of what gives any individual agent a good reason to conform and 'observe'.

In this last claim we should note how the civilized agent's motive depends on the idea of the quality of the act that is in question. Evidently the notion of having such a motive, a motive that makes reference to this act, together with the norms of reason and reasonableness (small 'r') under which the motive habitually operates, are

8. Hume, *Treatise,* II.iii.3, Selby-Bigge, p. 416 (with interpolations of reinterpretative intent marked in square brackets). On the reading proposed, Hume's polemic against his predecessors' uses of 'Reason' intends no threat either against the idea of the reasons (plural) that agents have for what they do or against the workaday norms of reasonableness in the light of which they might criticize the unreasonableness of someone's preferring the destruction of the whole world over the scratching of their finger.

integral to this form of ethical thinking. They are part of its weft
and weave. Where there is rivalry between competing conceptions
of what matters or is worthwhile, these notions and norms will be
doubly indispensable to us. But such reasons and reasonableness are
already conditioned by the ethical, as they are by the original and
the acquired natures of the creatures who are hosts to these conceptions. Here surely—in Hume's reading his opponents as claiming
to find some higher or more metaphysical reasonableness than this
in morality—is the underlying animus for the denials concerning
reason that have resulted in Hume's being mistaken (perfectly absurdly) for some sort of subversive in relation to morals or read as
one contemptuous of the ordinary sorts of reason that morality supplies to human subjects.

3.7.   In the final analysis, Hume's aetiology of morals successfully
subsumes the artificial virtues, totally different though they are from
'humanity, benevolence, friendship, public spirit, and other social
virtues of that stamp'.[9] But how clean an exit does his idea of convention furnish from the circle that he began by complaining of
within the apparent rationale of acts of justice?

Any careful or complete reply to this question will have to acknowledge that (at least in my construal) Hume's final answer to the
difficulty that he professed to find in the motivation to honesty and
its kindred has depended on his silently revoking the proposition
which, in expounding his infamous circle, he treated as axiomatic:
the proposition about what we look to 'when we praise any action'.
Moreover the reader will already have noted how difficult it would
be, so soon as room was made for the artificial virtues within Hume's

9. Hume, *Enquiry*, III.2, Selby-Bigge, p. 204. The thing we now see is that the
contrast between the natural and artificial is not simply an oddity arising from Hume's
need to defend this aetiology of morals. The distinction can be marked by reference to
the striking way in which the artificial virtues verify and the natural virtues falsify the
general claims that Aristotle enters about virtue and acting virtuously at *Nicomachean
Ethics* 1103a31–2. See my 'Eudaimonism and Realism in Aristotle's Ethics: A Reply to
John McDowell', in R. Heinaman (ed.), *Aristotle and Moral Realism* (London: UCL
Press, 1995), 119–31.

theory, to persist in his original claim that an 'external performance has no merit'. If there can be moral beauty in an observance as such, then any non-accidental performance of some act that is seconded and approved as just or whatever by some convention in force must *pro tanto* have some merit.

At the time when Hume is expounding the circle, it may momentarily appear that moral science should really proceed in an opposite direction and define the justice of an act in a manner derivative from the justice of a person. This is a really most unpromising plan, however. What after all is a just person? A just person is a person with a strong attachment to certain *acts* or *practices* or *outcomes*, namely those singled out in certain ways of behaving which Hume ought to think of the just person as wanting the kind of life he has in community with others to be shaped and constrained by. A just person needs then to be able to have fairly explicit thoughts about the act in question as a requirement of *justice*.[10] (Compare and contrast the work of the natural virtues which carries with it no analogous requirement. See 1.8.) This is an aspect of the artificial nature, in Hume's sense, of justice. If so much is correct, however, then there is simply no room for Hume to persist in the general claim which he makes at the time of introducing his 'circle', that 'virtuous actions derive their merit only from virtuous motives, and are considered merely as signs of those motives'. For according to the completed Humean theory itself, just acts and just motives depend for their merit on their conformity to practices—practices that are beneficial in a special way, practices which have a merit or beauty of their own and could even be subjected to the test of the sacred principle of consent.[11] In its generality, then, Hume's negative axiom

10. This is not to say that they must be thoughts of compact or convention—unless 'compact'/'convention' be given the minimal meaning suggested at 3.3. In a broader framework than the one we are here concerned with, these thoughts take on a new force and urgency: see 9.9 and 9.10.

11. For Hume's thought that principles of consent can attain the status of being 'sacred', see 'Of the Original Contract', para. 20: 'My intention here is not to exclude the consent of the people from being one just foundation of government where it has place. It is surely the best and most sacred of any'. (See also 3.3 above.)

must be withdrawn. Hume's circle, if it had any theoretical merit at all, was at best an expository device.

3.8. Finally, consider the nature of the question we ask on the theoretical level when we ask how beneficial a given convention or as-if-coordinated way of behaving is. Like the question of the merit of an action, this question depends for its answer on our extending moral evaluation beyond states of character and applying it to acts or states of affairs that result from acts being done. Hume, like Aristotle, Nietzsche, and countless other pre-modern moralists, is sometimes classified nowadays as a 'virtue theorist'. But it should now be evident that Hume's system affords a vantage point to look forwards to theories of a different kind—namely theories such as J. S. Mill's, which define acting rightly in terms of the states of affairs that result from doing the act. Hume gives us this vantage point. But he no more belongs with the party of Bentham and Mill than he belongs, in respect of his theory or his explanatory bent, with the party of pure virtue ethics. From the special vantage point of Hume (but here we anticipate the subject of Lecture 9), we may yet conceive of an account of these matters that looks beyond the consequentialist theories that we shall consider in Lectures 6, 7, and 8 and looks beyond the confusion and turmoil that the theories of Bentham's and Mill's inheritors have occasioned. What a fully grown-up moral philosophy might attempt is an account of morality that embraces the full gamut of moral predications, seeing them as mutually irreducible and mutually indispensable, allowing no primacy to character traits *or* virtues *or* practices *or* acts *or* states of affairs—or allowing primacy to all at once. Such a philosophy, being neither consequentialist nor virtue-centred, might take on some of the subtlety of the moral phenomena themselves and of our moral deliverances upon them. We shall return to these themes in due course (and several times between here and the end of Lecture 9); but first we must move closer to an evaluation of Hume's whole account of morals. This is something we cannot do before we lend an ear to the claims of its chief rival. That will be the work of Lectures 4 and 5.

4

From Hume to Kant

The moral law and its Kantian content; the formula of humanity; moral thinking in the kingdom of ends; the completability or incompletability of Kantian ethics

Reasoned accounts of moral virtue . . . are strong enough to encourage the young who are already well brought up or generously and virtuously inclined. They are powerless to induce the mass of human beings to worthy conduct.

Aristotle, *Nicomachean Ethics*, 1179b7-10

If a man have a lively sense of honour and virtue, with moderate passions, his conduct will always be conformable to the rules of morality; or if he depart from them, his return will be easy and expeditious. On the other hand, where one is born of so perverse a frame of mind, of so callous and insensible a disposition, as to have no relish for virtue or humanity, no sympathy for his fellow creatures, no desire of esteem and applause; such a one must be allowed entirely incurable, nor is there any remedy in philosophy. For my part, I know not how I should address myself to such a one or by what arguments I should endeavour to reform him. Should I tell him of the inward satisfaction which results from laudable and humane actions, the delicate pleasure of disinterested love and friendship, the lasting enjoyment of a good name and an established character, he might still reply that these were perhaps pleasures to such as were susceptible of them; but that, for his part, he finds himself of quite a different turn and disposition. I must repeat it; my philosophy affords no remedy in such a case, nor could I do any thing but lament this person's unhappy condition. But then I ask if any other philosophy can afford a remedy.

Hume, 'The Sceptic'

I wish from my heart I could avoid concluding that . . . [morality] regards only human nature and human life . . . If morality were determined by reason, that is the same to all rational beings; but nothing but experience can assure us that the sentiments are the same. What experience have we with regard to superior beings?

Hume, letter to Francis Hutcheson, 16 March 1740

Everyone must . . . concede that the ground of obligation . . . must not be sought in the circumstances in which he is placed but *a priori*, solely in the concepts of pure reason.

Kant, *Foundations of the Metaphysics of Morals* [389]

Part one: From Hume to Kant

4.1. Hume's speculations about the aetiology of morality, however smoothly they show morality as arising from our nature and nurture, seem to leave us with at least one question. Why should one whose nature and nurture was not of the kind that Hume describes accept the standard of conduct that Hume takes to be our standard? Indeed it is still a question to be asked why we who do have that nature and nurture should need to care so much what verdict the moral standard pronounces on our conduct or character. Hume's answer to such questions, read exactly as it stands, can be heavily fortified by taking account of his theory of pride (self-respect) and humility (shame). For this theory brings out how strongly the consideration of our own conduct can engage our idea of ourselves. (See *Treatise*, II.ii.) But such a supplement will serve only to explain how an existing concern with morality can be magnified. It cannot argue into being the thing itself that is to be magnified.

In the *Enquiry*, IX.2, where he undertakes to consider our interested obligation to merit or virtue, Hume gives every appearance of taking questions about why we should care about morality extremely seriously. As if in reply to objections of the kind we are considering, he declares that 'the immediate feeling of benevolence and friendship, humanity and kindness, is sweet, smooth, tender, and agreeable, independent of all fortune and accidents . . . [Besides virtue,] what other passion is there where we shall find so many advantages united; an agreeable sentiment, a pleasing consciousness, a good reputation?' (*Enquiry*, IX.2, Selby-Bigge, p. 282). A page later, after many pleasing expressions of similar points, we find him saying:

> In all ingenuous natures, the antipathy to treachery and roguery is too strong to be counterbalanced by any views of profit or pecuniary advantage. Inward peace of mind, consciousness of integrity, a satisfactory review of our own conduct; these are circumstances very requisite to happiness, and will be cherished and cultivated by every honest man who feels the importance of them. (*Enquiry*, IX.2, Selby-Bigge, p. 283)

How close can such observations carry us to a completion of the Humean answer to the Platonic question through which we have approached the topic designated (B) at 1.1? Answer: either what Hume says here is question-begging, because it speaks to those with an attachment that Hume knows he ought not in this context to take for granted; or else what he says is nothing less than subversive of morality, appealing in its behalf to precisely the wrong motives. If we choose the latter interpretation, it must appear that, having constructed a genealogy of morals that traces its origins back to proto-moral motives that we actually have, Hume then undermines the whole edifice by seeming to reveal that the real foundation is not these but simply some pleasure, a pleasure he would then (if he persisted) need to work very hard to differentiate in a special or distinctive way. (Surely this effort would give him back some variant of the same question that he began with.)

Which of the two interpretations is correct? In my view, the first one. There is the sensible and manageable task of reminding someone who already has some however minimal attachment to morality of its distinctive claims and the distinctive (not necessarily egoistic or complacent) satisfactions of a life that recognizes these claims. But, in the passage cited, this task has been conflated with a different task, namely that of making it plausible that *any and every* human being who has any regard to his own happiness, even a human being not endowed with an ingenuous nature, will 'best find his account [of what he needs to understand about his happiness] in the practice of every moral duty' (*Enquiry*, IX.2, Selby-Bigge, p. 278). Hume ought, by virtue of his own theory, to have been much more leery of undertaking to do this in the way in which section nine of the *Enquiry* attempts the task.

In his essay 'The Sceptic', where different literary concerns are at work from those that motivate him in the *Enquiry*, Hume gives the franker and better response that is prefixed to this chapter, as if abjuring in advance most of what seems so questionable in section IX, part 2 of the *Enquiry*. In 'The Sceptic', Hume signals that a philosopher of morality needs not to contemplate the idea of a non-question-begging *argument* by which to appeal to a villain who is unmoved or too little moved by humanity. For the difficulty with the villain is that he is *callous* and *insensible*. Maybe he is so callous and insensible that even the most persuasive person in the world could not lead him by the hand onto some new scene where completely new possibilities would begin to impinge on him or he could be swept up into a different mode of being. If the humanity or benevolence Hume takes as his starting point is a reasonable mode of being and feeling, if nevertheless it is not the sort of thing that can be rendered mandatory by considerations of theoretical reason or non-question-begging considerations of practical reason, then the only doctrine that needs to see a challenge for philosophy in the persistence of callous and insensible rational villains is a philosophy that insists that humanity *is* extra-ethically or pre-ethically rationally mandatory. Hume himself denies this. He only says that a life founded upon humanity in the ways that he describes is eminently fitting for a reasonable being, well suited to his or her nature as a human being. 'Find another,' he might also say to ordinary non-villainous people. 'Look and see if there is another kind of life that you could seriously choose. In the meanwhile, whatever may be the merits of other ways of living, merits I find obscure but shall not seek to disprove, do not despise the way of life that is securely based in some of the most fundamental facts that there are about you. What better basis could there be for morals than these facts about you? (Could you seriously undertake to extirpate these things from your own nature?) If you persist in the way I am commending, if you follow it through, then you will not want to abandon it.'

Simply on the strength of what he himself says, Hume needs to deprecate all attempts (including his own in *Enquiry*, IX) to go beyond the response just given or try to prove more than it is possible to prove. The most he can show is in what way morality is a reasonable business—but in a sense of 'reasonable' correlative with the already ethical reasons (plural) he might try to show us are good reasons for us to act thus or so, reasons we might then *find* to be good reasons. This is none the worse a sense of 'reasonable' for not being extra-ethical or not simply annihilating all the rival reasons we may have *not* to act thus or so but in some other way. The most Hume can do here is to persuade us to disapprove deeply of our acting in that other way for that rival reason. But why should the rationalists be so sure of the availability of another sense of 'reasonable' or 'rational'?[1]

4.2. Hume was not to know that, within decades of his passing the judgment he passes in 'The Sceptic', a 'more philosophical' and much more ambitious remedy would be offered—in the shape of *Foundations of the Metaphysics of Morals* by Immanuel Kant—to set right the very thing which he had urged his readers to see as irremediable. If Hume had been aware that such a book was imminent, he might not have left the matter exactly where he left it.[2]

The general shape of Kant's answer to the questions Hume had left over can be given as follows. Moral requirements are grounded

1. The logic of 'rational' or 'reasonable' does not suggest that there is another sense. Even where $A \neq B$ or A and B are mutually exclusive, 'It is rational to do A' does not exclude 'It is rational to do B.'

2. Might he even have refined the doubts we see him expressing, however inchoately, in the letter to Hutcheson from which I have taken the third epigraph? If so, it is to be hoped that he would have paused to disentangle the different things that might be meant by 'regards only human nature' as the phrase occurs in that letter.

entirely in reason; and they are categorical requirements, which means that they are not requirements that demand something only conditionally upon the actual desires, inclinations or motives of those to whom they apply. (On *this* point, Hume agrees. The moral requirements whose provenance and authority he explains are directed to everyone and suggest no let-out clauses or exemptions whatever.) Secondly, one and the same thing—namely pure practical reason— is to be *the source* of moral requirements (their grounding and thus the determiner of their content) and *the motive* for paying heed to such requirements. Pure practical reason, unconditioned by anything anthropological, is to be the ground for moral requirements and the best reason that we have to pay heed to them.

> Everyone must admit that a law, if it is to hold morally (i.e. as grounds for an obligation), must imply absolute necessity; he must admit the command *Thou shalt not lie* does not apply to men only, as if other rational beings had no need to observe it. ... He must concede that the ground of obligation here must not be sought in the nature of man or in the circumstances in which he is placed but *a priori* solely in the concepts of pure reason. (*Foundations of the Metaphysics of Morals* [389])

The citation is from Kant's Preface. The claim it makes depends on the rest of the book. The obvious gap that Kant needs to fill stretches between the fact that every moral requirement is *aimed or directed universally* (is directed, fail-safe, to anyone at all who can understand it, is moreover not conditional upon inclination, and is not liable to simple empirical disproof—all points Hume would have strongly agreed with) and something that would be much more contestable, according to Hume's opinion, namely the idea that moral requirements will have a *rational and universal authority that is logically prior to morality itself.* The Kantian thought is that moral requirements are already *in force,* so to speak, among all beings that can so much as understand them.[3]

---

3. Contrast Hume's distinction of two distinct circumstances that constitute the operation of humanity/benevolence (*Enquiry*, IV.1). See below, 5.5.

What will be Kant's way of spanning such a gap? First he creates the presumption that, if morality as we know it has any authority at all, then such authority is not empirical (for nothing that happens in the world can confirm or disconfirm the claim that one should help one's neighbour, not lie to him or rob him) and must be reason. Then Kant draws out from that presumption a principle usually known as the Formula of Universal Law, a law for all rational beings. In various transformations, which will be rehearsed in due course, this formula gives a distinctive shape and a distinctive content to morality. Then Kant argues for an equivalence between the moral laws that the formula sustains and the laws or principles of our freedom. For we attain our freedom *by* willing these laws universally. In the light of that identification, Kant then seeks, by vindicating that freedom, to vindicate the moral law that is underwritten in this way through practical reason. Thus the inescapable commitment that we have to the idea of rational freedom leads back to an equal and equally rational commitment to morality. In sum then, according to Kant, morality is the expression of our autonomous rational nature— just as, according to Hume, morality is the expression of the benevolent (or benevolence-grounded) dispositions of the acquired nature that reason and imagination have founded upon certain constituents of our original nature.

4.3. That is Kant's plan. But now, beginning from the beginning, we must unfold it more slowly over the length of this lecture, which is principally directed at his idea of the content of morality, and of the next lecture, which relates chiefly to Kant's conception of our commitment to morality. (Compare the division of questions (A) and (B) at 1.1.)

Part two: The moral law

4.4. Kant's *Foundations of the Metaphysics of Morals* begins with our ordinary rational knowledge of morality, taken as so far undisturbed by philosophical theory. It seeks to gain our assent for the claim that the way in which we judge acts is by reference to something that Kant calls the good will—where the good will is the standing motive to do an act precisely because the moral law requires the act. When we pass judgment on an agent or his act, the thing that really counts is whether the good will that was present in the agent (if any was) would have sufficed all by itself to motivate him to do that act (would have sufficed whether or not the agent had any prior inclination to do the act). We praise and encourage the shopkeeper who offers the same price to everyone or the friend of mankind who finds inner satisfaction in spreading joy and contentment. It is proper that we should do so. But we withhold from such agents the ascription of 'full moral worth' unless their choices of virtuous acts arise from reverence for the moral law. In moral matters, the very highest accolade is reserved for the person who would help others out of duty even when all sympathy with others was extinguished. (See *Foundations* [398].)

Kant allows that there are all sorts of things that we seek for their own sake, including happiness. Such things are *conditionally* valuable. But, according to Kant, the only thing that is unconditionally or unqualifiedly or intrinsically valuable, the only thing that is *good no matter how other things stand,* is the good will—or that which incorporates the good will, *deserved* happiness, for instance:

> The good will is not good because of what it effects or accomplishes or because of its adequacy to achieve some proposed end: it is good only because of its will, i.e. it is good of itself [intrinsically, as some expositors say]. And regarded for itself, the good will is to be esteemed incomparably higher than anything which could be brought about by it in favour of any inclination or even of the sum total of all inclinations. Even if it should happen that, by a particularly unfortunate fate or by the niggardly provision of a stepmotherly nature, this will should be wholly lacking in power to accomplish its purpose, and if even the greatest effort should not avail it to achieve anything of its end, and if there remained only the good will (not as a mere wish but as the summoning of all the means in our power), it would sparkle like a jewel in its own right as something that

had its full worth in itself. . . . In the estimation of the total worth of our actions it always takes first place and is the condition of everything else. [394]

In making these claims, Kant is only rehearsing the ordinary moral knowledge of ordinary people, or so he would say. (Lest the claim seem altogether unbelievable, it is important to note that neither here nor anywhere else does Kant claim that our deriving pleasure from doing an act excludes the presence of the good will. Pleasure has no part in the test. Choosing the act from reverence for the moral law is the thing that counts.)

4.5. Suppose that Kant has persuaded us of as much as this about ordinary moral knowledge, and suppose our intuitions coincide more or less exactly with his when he confronts us with the various examples he discusses [398]. Then, if the good will is the same as the motive to do the act prescribed by the moral law and do it precisely because the moral law prescribes it, the very next thing we need to know is what the moral law says. Kant's answer runs as follows:

But what kind of a law can that be the conception of which must determine the will without reference to the expected result? Under this condition alone [namely that the will is moved by the thought that it is the moral law to act thus or so] the will can be called absolutely good without qualification. For since I have robbed the will [in my discussion of how we evaluate actions and motives morally] of all impulses [or motivating pleasures] which could come to it from obedience to any law, nothing remains to serve as a principle of the will except universal conformity of its action to law as such. That is, I should never act in such a way that I could not also will that my maxim should be a universal law. [402]

Our difficulty here will be this. In the last sentence but one, Kant is rehearsing the view for which we are supposing that he has already gained our agreement. But such agreement must have been conditional on the prospect of our learning how to determine the text of the moral law. In the last sentence, by contrast, after the *'that is'*, he is giving the very text of the moral law or the principle that generates the text. But where did he find this text? How are we meant to understand this transition?

Here is a suggestion. The section draws professedly upon the ordinary rational knowledge of morality possessed by Kant's reader. Such a reader is expected to allow then that some categorical injunctions are indeed in force. But these injunctions could not be binding unless there was a reason for them. (Followers of Hume will note then that Kant must be assuming that there has to be a general reason, some *one* reason grounding all such categorical requirements.) What then is this reason? Well, supposing that such injunctions are in force categorically and without regard to inclination, this can only be because of some universal law, or so Kant supposes the reader will agree (and here again a Humean will be keeping track of Kant's presuming this), namely some law whose authority is independent of all inclination or contingent fact (e.g. anthropological fact) about human beings. What law is that? The law we are looking for can only be framed in the bare terms that can engage with the good will, the will that any rational creature can have. But this implies that it can only be framed in terms of 'law', 'universality', and 'will'. Surely then the only possible text for such a law is 'Act only on the maxim which you can at the same time will to be a law for all rational beings'. Either that or else think of a simpler or better formulation!

The argument is not conclusive. For those who allow that there *must* be some single principle to be had here and so think that the only question is how it goes, the argument has considerable dialectical force. For those who doubt this, it has less force. Henceforth, we shall call this principle and its variants the Formula of Universal Law or FUL.

4.6. So far then we have this: if you are inside morality at all, then Kant says you are committed (if you think about it) to FUL. But what if you are not yet inside morality? Or what if you are only there because you have strayed into it? The next thing Kant needs to do is to establish FUL as the verdict not of morality simply, but of practical reason.[4]

This task is attempted in part II of the *Foundations of the Metaphysics of Morals*. There are at least two intermediate steps. First, Kant says that everything in nature works according to laws. A reasonable being is special among things in nature by being capable (Kant says) of acting in accordance with a conception of laws, that is according to principles. 'This capacity is will. Since reason is required for the derivation of actions from laws, will is nothing else than practical reason' [412]. What is this practical reason? Well, practical reason is that which determines the practical good on grounds valid for every rational being. But we need to know what else can be said about it.

Further understanding of practical reason will be gained by looking to the work that practical reason is required to do in connection with putative imperatives to act. Imperatives may command *hypothetically,* that is, with a force conditional upon the adoption of some end, or else *categorically,* that is, conditionally upon nothing, that is absolutely.[5] Since a major part of the work of Kantian practical reason is to assess the various ends that condition the force of hypothetical imperatives, it seems that practical reason must know some principle on which to assess claims of unconditional necessity, and thence (given the equivalence between 'It is not obligatory/necessary not to do A' and 'It is permissible to do A') of permissibility.

How then does practical reason adjudicate the ends of action?

4. Christine Korsgaard has usefully emphasized the importance of this transition. For a summary account of her view of it, see her article 'Immanuel Kant' in *The Garland Encyclopedia of Ethics,* ed. Lawrence C. Becker (New York: Garland Publishing, 1992).

5. Even an imperative which refers to the choice of means to an agent's own happiness—a purpose that Kant claims to validate *a priori* by an unconvincing argument from the essence of man [415] and calls a counsel of prudence—is only a hypothetical imperative [416]. Two more points about categorical and hypothetical. (1) Given a *must* with categorical force, we can define *prohibitions* and *permissions* with a similar force. (2) Categorical force may attach to the duty to implement a hypothetical policy such as 'if a child ask bread, not to give it a stone.' (Cp. Matthew 7:9.) Let us distinguish the *must* itself from that to which the *must* is grammatically applied.

And what is the principle 'which alone can be taken as a practical law' [420]?

> If I think of a hypothetical imperative as such, I do not know what it will contain until its condition is stated. But if I think of a categorical imperative, I know immediately what it contains. For since the [categorical] imperative contains beside the law only the necessity that the maxim [or principle on which some-one acts] should accord with the [moral] law, while the law specifies no condition to which it is restricted, nothing remains in [a categorical imperative] except the universality of law as such to which the maxim of the action should conform; and in effect this conformity alone is represented by the imperative.
>
> There is therefore only one categorical imperative. It is: Act only according to that maxim by which you can at the same time will that it should become a universal law. . . . [All] imper-atives of duty can be derived from this one imperative as a principle. . . . [Moreover, by analogy,] the universal imperative of duty can be expressed as follows: Act as though the maxim of your action were by your will to become a universal law of nature. [420–1]

What, if anything, does this add to the demonstration of the same conclusion in [402]? In [402], we were exploring morality from the inside, relying on our ordinary moral knowledge and inquiring what explained our sense that certain moral imperatives do hold or obtain. (In that way, we were determining what the moral law says.) That moral knowledge is something we no longer assume, however, if we want it to be pure practical reason that gives us FUL.

Suppose that someone asks why we should act only according to some maxim which we can at the same time will should become a universal law, or a law for all rational beings? Presumably Kant's answer in part II of *Foundations* is to reply that, if you are to exercise the capacity by which you count as a reasonable being, then you need to act in accordance with a conception of law. You need then to act according to some principle. But what *other* principle could you reasonably act upon than a principle that you can will to become a law for all rational beings? There is no other principle for a rational being to avail itself of. That is what singles out FUL as the requirement of pure practical reason.

4.7. This reply will start two doubts. According to the first doubt, [420–1] is very little advance over [402] because everything depends on Kant's definition of a reasonable being as one capable of acting according to a conception of law. After all the definition itself is a newcomer to philosophy and it incorporates a manifest preconception in favour of FUL. Compare the other reservations the Humean will have placed on the debit side of Kant's account. (A related suspicion: at [420] Kant achieves a determinate text for FUL only by enforcing a dogmatically universalistic and consequentially bare conception of our knowledge of that which is not empirical.)

The second doubt is one expressed by Kant's admirer and critic, Arthur Schopenhauer, in his work *On the Basis of Morality*.

By disdaining all empirical motives of the will in advance, Kant removed as empirical everything objective and everything subjective on which a law for the will could be based. And so for the substance of that law, he had nothing left but its own form. Now this [form] is simply *conformity to law* but such *conformity* consists in its being applicable to all, and so in its *universal validity*. Accordingly, this becomes the substance; consequently the purport and meaning of the law are nothing but its universal validity itself. It will therefore read:

'Act only in accordance with that maxim which you can at the same time wish will become a universal law for all rational beings.'

... I pay a tribute of sincere admiration to the great ingenuity with which Kant performed this trick.[6]

6. Trans. E. F. J. Payne (Providence, R.I.: Berghahn, 1995), pp. 72–3.

In the face of these doubts, Kantians can pause and try to answer them in detail; or they can place them on one side (in order to answer them when all other doubts have been quelled); or else they can soldier on in the hope of showing how well FUL consorts *in its applications* with the findings both of morality and of reason. For the sake of philosophical progress, let us keep going and see ourselves as approving the second or third of these courses. Looking back at 1.12 and the questions (A) or (A') or (A") given there, let us see the Kantians as advancing with Kant towards a more detailed determination of the distinctive substance or content of the morality which they say commends itself to pure practical reason.

The chief issue now becomes this: whether, in its applications, FUL can furnish a content for morality and a content that agents can recognize. And can FUL establish this content on the basis of considerations that correspond fairly closely to the sorts of reason that agents do recognize as reasons to pay heed to moral requirements? Compare now questions (B), (B') and (B") at 1.12. If FUL can achieve this much, surely this will be a very strong point in favour of Kant's whole conception—even if it remains to be inquired whether, in application, FUL really is grounded in a purely *a priori* conception of practical reason. First though, before advancing another step, we need a more exact understanding of FUL.

4.8. 'Act only on that maxim which you can at the same time will to be a universal law, or a law for all rational beings,' FUL says. But what is a maxim? And what is the intended meaning of 'can will'? This matter requires some care.

The clearest explanation may proceed by illustration. One of Kant's examples concerns a person who finds himself forced by acute need to borrow money, but sees also that nothing will be lent to him if he does not firmly promise to repay at a certain time. (See [422].) Suppose this person is resolved to act only on that maxim which he can at the same time will as a universal law. In what terms then must he examine his conscience? We begin with the sincere, relevantly complete statement of his intention:

RCI: Since my need is truly acute and . . . <here the agent is to supply in place of . . . something specific about how acute the need is and why it is so acute>, I shall borrow money regardless of whether I can pay back.

From this statement of intention we now cancel all mention of this particular agent and isolate something that is a proper candidate to be willed universally, thus:

M: To borrow money, regardless of whether one can pay back, when one's need is truly acute and. . . .

Maxim M is a complex verb phrase. It gives us the designation of an act that the agent who examines his conscience might or might not be prepared to will that everyone do. M is a policy, then, which the agent might or might not will that everyone follow,[7] an act or policy formulated determinately by reference to the (actual or putative) sincere, relevantly complete statement of the intention of the agent who is examining his conscience.[8] Let us call any verb phrase

---

7. The policy of not doing the act may also be willed universally. The candidate maxim is 'Not to borrow money regardless of whether one can pay back, when one's need is acute and. . . . ' Prefix this with the words 'let everyone', omit the infinitival 'to', and adjust pronouns, in order to obtain the universalization.

Kant sometimes writes as if RCI were the thing to be universally willed (or not so willed). Compare [422]. But *strictly speaking* this is not what is universally willed. So, as in my text, Kant's use of 'maxim' needs to be regimented a little. See Onora Nell [O'Neill], *Acting on Principle* (New York: Columbia University Press, 1975). Often Kant uses the word 'maxim' to mean the *particular maxim* (in the sense I have explicated above in the text) *that an agent chooses,* the maxim s/he could turn back into a relevantly complete statement of his/her intention. Thus Kant's 'maxim' sometimes means 'the agent's *choice* of maxim or policy'.

8. Unlike the *action* that consists of the agent's doing this act or of following this policy, the act or policy itself does not admit of a whole host of alternative descriptions.

A word more on the act/action distinction. However specific it may be, the act is something universal, a *kind* of action. By contrast, the action is a particular. If act and action are different kinds of thing (for this distinction and our several and various needs for it, see the writings on action of Jennifer Hornsby), then what is the action? The action is an event that instantiates the act. No doubt it also instantiates many other acts. This may be illustrated by an example from G. E. M. Anscombe's *Intention* (Oxford:

that we arrive at in the particular way in which we arrived at the
M in our example a maxim. In that case, the general form of willing
a maxim is displayed in the following application of FUL to the
maxim M:

UM: Let everyone borrow money, regardless of whether s/he can
pay back, when his/her need is truly acute and . . . !

In this universalization of the maxim M, the dots ' . . . ' hold a place,
as before, for the specific sort of circumstances exemplified in the
situation giving rise to some actual or possible RCI.

So much for maxims and so much for willing a maxim as a universal law. Now back to FUL itself. FUL directs us to act only on
a maxim we can will to be a universal law. But now we need to
know what could prevent one from willing a maxim. What might
stand in the way of UM? According to Kant, one of two things. A
person who holds to his resolve, his RCI, may be involved in a
contradiction in conception between his RCI and his UM. That will
be the focus of the very next section (4.9). Or else that combination
of RCI and UM may involve him or her in a *contradiction in the
will*. In due course, we shall come to that case too (4.11).

4.9. In the example we began with, the question that arises is
how the would-be borrower can adhere to his intention to borrow
without regard to paying back *and* will universally something that

---

Blackwell, 1957, 1963). If I am seen pumping water, then this action may instantiate any
or all of the following acts: to pump water, to move one's arm up and down, to exercise
one's biceps, to poison the inhabitants of a neighbouring settlement, to vex by a creaking
noise all of twenty-nine persons nearby. . . . Some of these acts may be done intentionally,
but others will not. Every conscientious agent knows that one can be responsible sometimes for what one does not intend. Every conscientious agent tries to think what else
he is doing besides that which he intends. The agent has, however, to begin somewhere
in his deliberations. He begins, obviously, with his immediate situation and that which
he is to do intentionally—*subject* to a readiness to cancel the plan to do such and such
or so and so, if it later appears that doing such and such or so and so will, in these
circumstances, involve doing acts the doing of which he fears will be damaging, evil, or
dangerous.

is bound (or so Kant supposes) to subvert the very possibility of framing any such intention as his own RCI. Kant's first thought is that, if such a law were willed universally, then no putative creditor 'would believe what was promised to him but would only laugh at any such assertion as vain pretence' [422].

Several problems present themselves (problems that are independent of the particular example, to which we shall shortly return (4.10)). First, can the conflict (the contradiction in conception) between RCI and UM be construed as a conflict at all without our availing ourselves of the ordinary knowledge of morality? Even if there is something *off-colour* about the agent's conjoining this RCI with this UM, is there some *conceptual or logical* inconsistency here? The question arises because on Kant's view, which founds the moral in the *a priori,* the offence needs to be a *pre-ethical* offence against reason.

Secondly, the generality of the claims that Kant is entering is daunting in the extreme. Kant promises a single test for standing intentions that amount to general policies and the same test for one-off intentions that are almost unrepeatably specific.

Thirdly, in the process, is not Kant eliding the middle member of the three-fold distinction that we normally recognize between the mandatory or obligatory, the permissible but not obligatory, and the forbidden?

All three questions are important. Nevertheless, I postpone the first two *sine die* (they belong with the other points we have lodged on the debit side of the account, which the Kantians will have to settle some day before the end of morals or civilization), and the third I relegate to a footnote.[9] The more immediate need is to keep

---

9. For the curious, there follows a way of marking, in tandem with the distinction between the obligatory and the forbidden, a Kantian distinction between obligatory and permissible. Compare Nell, *Acting on Principle.*

In the proposal to be set out below' '(UM) ↑ will abbreviate 'The maxim M is universalizable'. This implies that 'Let everyone do M!' is willable. '(UM) ↓' will abbreviate 'Maxim M is not universalizable'. Similarly '(U not M) ↑' abbreviates 'The negation of the maxim M is universalizable'. This means that 'Let everyone do not M!' is willable. Similarly again, '(U not M) ↓' abbreviates the statement that the universali-

going and look at Kant's own examples. These will show the purport of FUL as the backbone of the whole moral law for rational beings and then they will illustrate the meaning of its proper sequel, a further principle, FH, the Formula of Humanity (or of the End). Once they are understood, FUL and FH will lead in their turn into other principles that reveal yet more of the distinctive ethical coloration of Kant's doctrine.

4.10. *Examples of contradiction in conception.* Kant's first example is of a man who despairs and thinks to take his own life but asks whether the maxim of his proposed act could become a universal law or, equivalently (as Kant supposes), asks whether he could will it to become a universal law of nature. 'One immediately sees a contradiction in a system of nature whose law would be to destroy life by the feeling whose special office is to impel the improvement of life' [422]. The example will take on a new life in due course (see below, 4.12), but at this point it must be objected that Kant's project of founding morality in the *a priori* gives him no licence whatever to introduce teleological notions. Once they were admitted, moreover, teleological notions would surely bring with them conceptions of morality that were deeply unwelcome to Kant.

---

zation of the negative maxim not M is unwillable. So it means that 'Let everyone not do M!' is unwillable. Then for any given M we must rule as follows:

(a) If (UM) $\uparrow$ and (U not M) $\downarrow$ then it is obligatory to do M.

(b) If (UM) $\downarrow$ and (U not M) $\uparrow$, then it is forbidden to do M.

(c) If (UM) $\downarrow$ and (U not M) $\downarrow$ then it is permissible to do M.

(d) If (UM) $\uparrow$ and (U not M) $\uparrow$, then it is permissible to do M.

Cases (a) and (b) are straightforward, though a strict adherence to these definitions would occasion numerous minor revisions to *Foundations*. Cases (c) and (d) may seem unexpected, however.

We have an instance of case (d) where the maxim M is 'to broach a boiled egg at the sharper end'. Nothing forbids either 'Let everyone broach a boiled egg at the sharper end!' or 'Let everyone not broach a boiled egg at the sharper end!'

Case (c) is exemplified by the maxim 'to seek a medical career if one has all the qualifications required for medical school'. With this M it is impossible to will either 'Let everyone do M!' or 'Let everyone not do M!' Every clever person's being a doctor and no clever person's being a doctor seem equally unwillable.

Kant has no great need to dwell on cases falling under (c) or (d), but his not mentioning them has occasioned confusion, in his own formulations as well as in our comprehension of them.

Kant's second example is the one we took to illustrate the meaning of FUL. But now we can discuss it further. According to Kant, one cannot will universally the UM that we formulated. Moreover, one can will its negation,

U NOT M: Let everyone not borrow money regardless of whether s/he can pay back, [even] when his/her need is acute and . . . !

In this way, we certainly arrive at the prohibition Kant desires. (Note that it is important to understand the 'not' as governing the verb phrase that consists of *all* the remaining words.) But someone may object that it is not even true (let alone true *a priori*) that a universal adoption of *this* policy, namely the policy of *borrowing recklessly but only when one is as desperate as this,* would subvert all lending and borrowing. (The system of credit has weathered far worse trials and tribulations, etc.)

The right response to this objection is to concede it. If FUL is all we have to go by, then Kantians ought to admit that, when the RCI is spelled out as just indicated, Kant's argument will not work against the policy the person in the example is thinking to follow. Nor ought it to work. But that does not deprive FUL of interest. For FUL becomes a much more impressive principle as soon as we postpone the simple absolutism that prompts Kant to try to arrive at a general prohibition of any line of conduct whatever that might jeopardize the promise to pay back. Let us use FUL to attack an easier target. Consider the much more damaging policy pursued by those who borrow not only (it proves) falsely, and not only recklessly, but also without any desperate need to borrow. *Against that,* the principle FUL really does appear to work. The only mistake is to claim too wide a scope for Kant's argument or pay too little attention to the reasons and circumstances that figure in many an ordinary agent's sincere, relevantly complete statement of his putative intention to borrow money. (No doubt there is still something amiss with many such agents' line of conduct; but *this* will not appear until we reach the Formula of Humanity (4.14).)

4.11. *Examples of contradiction in the will.* Both the examples discussed so far have purported to rest upon the contradiction in conception. Kant's third and fourth examples illustrate what Kant calls a contradiction in the will.[10]

In Kant's third example, someone systematically neglects their talents. When he asks himself whether this 'agrees with what is called duty, he sees that a system of nature could indeed exist in accordance with such a law . . . but he cannot possibly will that this should become a universal law of nature or that it should be implanted by a natural instinct. For, as a rational being, he necessarily wills that all his faculties should be developed in as much as they are given him and serve him for all sorts of purposes' [422].

Along with the first example, this example can come back into its own (see 4.12). But, if FUL is all we have to hand, it is open to the same objection. The impossibility of willing the maxim rests on a teleological idea from somewhere outside the stated framework.

In the fourth example, a man of capability and independence declares: 'Let each man be as happy as heaven wills, or as he can make himself. I will not take anything from him or even envy him but to his welfare or to his assistance in time of need I have no desire to contribute.' Kant's comment is this:

Now although it is possible that a universal law of nature according to that maxim could exist, it is nevertheless impossible to will that such a principle should hold everywhere as a law of nature. For a will which resolved this would conflict with itself, since instances can often arise in which he would need the love and sympathy of others, and in which he would have robbed himself, by such a law of nature springing from his own will, of all hope of the aid he desires. [423]

---

10. Here is Kant's account of the difference: 'some actions are of such a nature that their maxim cannot even be thought as a universal law of nature without contradiction, far from its being possible that one could will that it should be such. In others, this internal impossibility is not found, though it is still impossible to will that their maxim should be raised to the universality of a law of nature, because such a will would contradict itself' [424].

The example is of considerable importance; for in the whole book it represents our most explicit and worked example of Kant's idea of a contradiction in the will. We need this category. (We shall need it all the more if doubts arise about the idea of a contradiction in conception.) What exactly then grounds Kant's imputation of contradiction in the will?

Kant points to the conflict between the universalization of this fourth man's choice of maxim and the commitment of his will to the purpose of pursuing his own security and well-being. The point that troubles one, however, is how well this line of argument against the reasonableness of self-sufficiency can cohere with declarations of the kind we have recently encountered at [411–12]. Kant said there that it was important

> to derive the concepts and laws of morals from pure reason, to present them pure and unmixed, and to determine the scope of this entire practical but pure rational knowledge ... without making the principles depend upon the particular nature of human reason. . . . All morals must be completely developed . . . independently of anthropology. . . . It is only in this manner that pure moral dispositions can be produced.

Such Kantian declarations might be multiplied at will. They prompt the question: is it not an essentially anthropological fact that many or most human beings need the love and sympathy of others?[11]

In an effort to purge Kant's argument of self-love and merely human need, and in the complementary effort to dispense with the specious and scarcely *a priori* essentialist argument by which Kant attempts at [415] to reconcile his validation of happiness as a moral

11. How can Kant and his followers criticize benevolence-based accounts of morality on the grounds that the motives which they invoke (non-I motives, in fact, according to Williams's classification—see Lecture 2, n. 6) lie outside the ambit of anything which can, 'so far from serving inclination, overpower [inclination] or at least exclude it from being considered in making a choice' [400]? How can the Kantian criticize these Humean accounts if the Kantian duty to give aid and assistance rests on considerations which, at one critical point, invoke not only 'the nature of man [and] the circumstances in which he is placed' [389] but an inclination that is an I-inclination?

end with his own *a priorism,* one might try now to reconstruct the argument. Taking one's cue from the altogether different pattern of argument that one finds at [399] ('to secure one's own happiness is at least indirectly a duty, for discontent with one's condition under pressure from many cares and amid unsatisfied wants could easily become a great temptation to transgress duties'),[12] one might transpose that pattern as follows. The virtuous agent who lives by FUL is committed to do his duty and do it because this is commanded by the moral law. But an agent who would do his duty must recognize that, over and over again, he can only accomplish that duty in cooperation with other rational agents. So he must do anything and everything he licitly can to promote reciprocity and cooperation between rational agents. (This is an *a priori* truth about rational agency.) Therefore the agent cannot consistently will the universalization of the maxim corresponding to the RCI: 'Let each man be as happy as heaven wills . . . I will not take anything from him . . . but to his welfare I have no desire to contribute. [423]' Thus the requirement to give aid and assistance emerges as a requirement of pure practical reason (as well as of ordinary morality).

Whether or not such a reconstruction of the contradiction in the will can bear the whole weight that it needs to bear in suitably constraining the rational agent's readiness to will such and such suitable maxim (or in constraining his readiness to will the negation of such and such other maxim, etc.), it does at least enable us to advance in hope towards the next phase of Kant's argument. When that is complete, we can return to the four examples, and review them in the light of a kind of principle altogether different from FUL, to which it will prove that the *use* of FUL also commits us.

12. Why does Kant argue by these indirect means on behalf of happiness as an end? Well, in the background there is always Kant's tendency towards declarations such as the following: 'All objects of inclination have only a conditional worth, for if the inclinations and needs founded on them did not exist, their objects would be without worth. The inclinations themselves as the sources of needs, however, are so lacking in absolute worth that the universal worth of every rational being must be indeed to free himself from them' [428]. Compare also [396], first paragraph.

Part three: Kant's Formula of Humanity

4.12. Suppose that persons with the good will explicitly or implicitly test by FUL every intention that they ever frame. If they do, then each of these testings is an exercise of pure practical reason. Then, according to Kant, those who are guided by FUL must in their self-subjection to practical reason have some further and larger aim or purpose—some *overriding* concern, over and above the 1001 purposes that they have present to their mind at this, that, or the other time. See [427]:

> The will is thought of as a faculty of determining itself to action in accordance with the conception of certain laws. Such a faculty can be found only in rational beings. That which serves the will as the objective ground of its self-determination is a purpose and, if it is given by reason alone, it must hold alike for all rational beings.

What could this purpose be? At [428] Kant writes:

> Suppose that there were something the existence of which in itself had absolute worth, something which, as an end in itself, could be a ground of definite laws. In it and only in it could lie the ground of a possible categorical imperative (i.e. of a practical law).
>
> Now I say man and, in general, every rational being exists as an end in himself and not merely as a means to be arbitrarily used by this or that will. In all his actions, whether they are directed toward himself or toward other rational beings, he must always be regarded at the same time as an end. . . . thus, if there is to be a supreme practical principle and a categorical imperative for the human will, it must be one that forms an objective principle of the will from the conception of that which is necessarily an end for everyone because it is an end in itself. Hence this objective principle can serve as a universal law. The ground

of this principle is: Rational nature exists [429] as an end in itself. Man necessarily thinks of his own existence in this way, and thus far it is a subjective principle of human actions. Also every other rational being thinks of his existence on the same rational ground which holds also for myself; thus it is at the same time an objective principle from which, as a supreme practical ground, it must be possible to derive all laws of the will. The practical imperative, therefore, is the following: Act so that you treat humanity, whether in your own person or in that of another, always as an end and never as a means only. Let us now see whether this can be achieved. To return to our previous examples.

There is something strange, it must be said, in Kant's using the word 'end' to embrace both a purpose and a human person. But this can be explained. Let us begin by trying, with Kant, to see rationality itself as an overriding purpose of a rational agent's doings—not as their immediate or direct purpose but as a purpose analogous to the indirect but important concerns or purposes that play the role of informing and circumscribing our pursuit of more immediate ends.[13] On these terms, the concern for rationality might then be likened to the concern we have for safety, honour, dignity. . . . (The dots hold a place for the indefinite set of concerns, never fully enumerable, that make up the framework within which we pursue our direct objectives.) The next step is to see human beings themselves as precisely *embodying* rationality, embodying it by virtue of their rational nature. In so far as we see them so, other human beings can constrain our will in the same sort of way as rationality itself constrains it. For our own rationality commits us to seeing other human beings' wills as sovereign wills on a level with our own wills. In this way, as soon as the idea of rational nature is added to the other ideas that agents can have, and as soon as FUL gives rise to the Formula of Humanity, practical reason can possess itself of a

---

13. Cp. Christine Korsgaard, *Creating the Kingdom of Ends* (Cambridge: Cambridge University Press, 1996), p. 108.

substantial content of its own. (N.B. In Kant's Formula of Humanity, henceforce FH, 'humanity' does not have the same sense as it had in Hume, for whom it is cognate with benevolence. In Kant it must be glossed in terms of rational nature.)

Amassing the results of this progress, we shall now find that Kant's four examples (rehearsed already at 4.10 and 4.11) can appear in an altogether new light, at once more convincing and more distinctive in their ethical content.

In the first example [429], suicide can now be seen not as an assault on a mere thing or as a simple means to an apparently innocuous end, but as an assault on rational nature itself and on something of supreme worth. Such an assault on the rational will the rational will cannot condone.

In the second example, a new and ethically quite distinctive objection now appears to the act that is intended, an objection not merely to reckless borrowing but to the very idea of manipulating the sovereign will of the putative creditor as a means to the obtaining of money. We are reminded too that there is a new and different way in which one sovereign will can treat with another. Let the man who is in need say to him or her who might help, 'My need is acute, my circumstances are dire, and I cannot be sure to repay you if you supply me with money. All the same I ask you to supply my need. My circumstances are extreme because. . . . If you supply me with money then, in due course, if ever I can, I shall repay you. Otherwise it will prove that you gave me the money.' When the person in need proceeds in this way (contrast all the ways previously rehearsed) then he *respects the sovereign will* of the putative donor/creditor.

In the third example [430], one may see the talents of a person as an aspect of the rational nature they embody which ought to be an object of reverence to the possessor and to other rational beings alike.

This brings us to the fourth example and the end of [430]. Here Kant's new commentary is as follows:

> Fourthly, with regard to meritorious duty to others, the natural purpose that all men have is their own happiness. Humanity

might indeed exist if no one contributed to the happiness of others, provided he did not intentionally detract from it, but this harmony with humanity as an end in itself is only negative, not positive, if everyone does not also endeavour, as far as he can, to further the purposes of others. *For the ends of any person who is an end in himself, must as far as possible be also my ends, if that conception of an end in itself is to have its full effect on me.* ([430], italics added)

As explicated by Kant in this way under the new auspices of FH, the fourth example is even more central to the content that *Foundations of the Metaphysics of Morals* furnishes for Kantian ethics than it appeared to be when Kant explicated it at [423] under the auspices of FUL. As before, we must make the most of the example. In order to do so, let us enrich FH, so far as we licitly can, by gathering up the further claims that Kant makes on the very same basis as he supplies for FH. From these we learn more about what we can and cannot will under FUL.

4.13. If I use humanity in my own person and in the person of others always as an end, never as merely a means, then I must treat rational nature as what it is. But rational nature distinguishes itself from everything else by its capacity to act in accordance with a conception of law and to express itself in a sovereign will that is subject only to law conceived as in FUL. Such a law, moreover, is not some arbitrary fiat or local ukase and directive. It aspires to rational authority over all reasonable beings. On this basis and the basis of ideas already introduced, Kant is in a position to develop FH into two further principles. These are the Formula of Autonomy (FA): *so act that your will can regard itself at the same time as making universal law through the maxims on which it acts,* and the Formula of the Kingdom of Ends (FKE): *act as if you were always through your maxims a law-making member in a kingdom of ends.* Moreover, FKE has a variant: *all maxims which spring from your own making of laws ought to accord with a possible kingdom of ends as a kingdom of nature.*

In sum, we have this: every rational being who places himself or herself under moral laws must act on maxims s/he submits to the universalization test by inquiring as follows: would I, in choosing to act on this maxim, be treating each other rational being as nothing less than a possessor of a universally legislating will and a member of a systematic union of rational self-legislating beings united through common laws? In the new framework of FH, FA, FKE, each human person, by embodying rationality itself and exemplifying rational nature, needs to be conceived as both *subject to* universal law and *prescribing* a law of which reason can hold itself to be author (cp. [431]). Hence too 'the dignity of a rational being who obeys no law except that which he himself also gives' [434], the dignity whose basis Kant says is the autonomy of the will. (Cp. [436], [445].)

Part four: Moral thinking in the kingdom of ends

4.14.   These formulations pave the way for the account Kant gives of the motivation to morality in part III of the *Foundations*. That is where our next chapter will begin. Our present and first concern, however, is with the content of Kantian ethics that emerges in parts II and III of the book. (For the relationship of these topics of content and motivation, see again 1.12. See also 4.3.)

The first thing to remark is how far Kant's new commentary on the fourth example reaches beyond our original difficulties with Kant's idea of a contradiction in the will. In the new light of the Formula of Humanity, there is a transformation in the ideas of reciprocity, cooperation, and the rest. These ideas, having qualified to be counted among the indispensable means to an agent's pursuit of the end determined by his essence (Kant), or else being seen as the indispensable means (as we have proposed on his behalf) for the agent's cooperative fulfilment of the demands of duty, are now subsumed within an ideal of harmony between one rational being and other rational beings—a harmony which has now become an end in itself. This harmony is not merely negative (even the moderate misanthrope in the fourth example is in full accord with that) but positive, Kant says. Even as it emerges what claim is made upon my own sovereign will by the sovereign will of other reasonable beings, the duty emerges for me to do my part in creating and sustaining the kingdom of ends. It is in this light that we should read 'The end of any person who is an end in himself must as far as possible be also my end if [harmony with humanity, as an end in itself] is to have its full effect on me' [430].

At this point let us return to the citation given last in 4.12 above. When it is filled out with the help of materials we have adduced from the immediately subsequent pages of *Foundations*, Kant's new treatment of the example brings with it something morally and philosophically impressive. It reaches forward to Kantian themes that are not specific to the example and illuminate the full import of the idea of a kingdom of ends. (Briefly, we shall return to that theme in Lecture 9.) There are also perplexities, however.

On the one hand, [430] resolves a troublesome instability in the Kantian conception of happiness. It is no longer necessary for Kant to seek to validate our pursuit of happiness as 'a purpose which we can *a priori* and with assurance assume for everyone [416] because it belongs to his/her essence'.[14] It is no longer necessary for Kant to resort to arguing, as in his second attempt for the desired conclusion, that to neglect one's own happiness may disprepare one for duty itself. (Cp. [399], already quoted: 'To secure one's own happiness is a duty, at least indirectly; for discontent with one's condition under many pressing cares and amid unsatisfied wants might easily become a great temptation to transgress one's duties.') For FH supplies an altogether new way for a reasonable being to see things. Such a being can reflect: 'Other possessors of sovereign wills espouse

---

14. How could such an essence be determined *a priori*? And, even if it could, how could *a priori* knowledge of one's essence validate the purposes discovered within one's essence—give them *a priori* validation as fit purposes for a being whose every maxim is to be tested for its rational willability as a universal law? Where talk of essence makes sense, which all too often it may not, there should be no presumption that true claims about essence will be *a priori*. See my *Sameness and Substance Renewed* (Cambridge: Cambridge University Press, 2002), ch. 4.

and pursue the end of their own happiness or welfare; therefore, in its respect for their will, my sovereign will must second and support their pursuit. It follows that, so far as possible, their happiness must become my end. But then, by the same token, so can my happiness become *their* end—and thus become *my* end.' Compare [430] as cited. In this way, things appear to move discernibly beyond the situation with the 'contradiction in the will' as it stood at [423].

So far so good. On the other hand, there is a new instability. For it is simply a fact that other sovereign wills often pursue evil and nefarious purposes—often enough proceeding against the sovereign will of yet other human persons. Must one, even then, respect their wills and promote such ends out of rational reverence for rational nature? There is a second and kindred instability, which points towards a persisting incompleteness in the fund of ethical ideas that are made available to us by the Kantian construction. Respecting the sovereign wills of others, I can also respect my own. But suppose I fall into doubt about what end to pursue, or suppose I become doubtful of an end that I am ready to espouse. May I then validate the end I am preparing to pursue by a simple appeal to the sovereignty of my own will and the fact that I, the possessor of this will, am drawn to this end?[15] Surely my rational nature and sovereign will need substantially more than the idea of my own rational nature and my own sovereign will to decide the deliberative question, 'What end shall I pursue?' If self-love is to be appropriately contained and constrained, I need to have an independent grasp of the *proper ends* of a rational nature and sovereign will. Such a grasp surely needs to be secured from somewhere outside the bare *a priori* notion of a

---

15. Think of this analogy. Can I (strictly or literally) give myself my word for something? Can I, strictly or literally, resolve the doubt in my mind whether such and such is the case by appeal to the idea that it would not have appeared to someone *of my rational authority* that such and such unless things were indeed thus and so? If the answer to this question is *no*, then is there not a more general difficulty? Consider giving oneself a command. Any authority that I have to give it is matched by an exactly similar authority to disobey it, namely my own. How then does it help for someone to adduce the sovereignty of his own will in his effort to escape from his doubts about what to think or resolve?

kingdom of ends. But how consistent would it be with Kant's starting point or with his *a priorism* to try to develop the idea of a kingdom of ends, or any other Kantian idea, advancing in that way to some point where this deliberative question could be treated effectively, convincingly, and worthily?

There are two doubts here. The second doubt, about the fund of ideas open to Kantian ethics, let us postpone (see 4.17–18). But the first, namely the instability that we imputed to the operation of FH, will certainly provoke a Kantian response. That response merits extended commentary. Moreover the commentary will lead into something that any and every sane moral philosophy will need to measure up to.

4.15. If the proper end of a reasonable being is to create a kingdom of ends and make due contribution to the achievement of this moral ideal, then the simple discovery of evil should be no discouragement. Kant must be right to think that it is short-sighted to allow evil the easy victory that it instantly gains if moral beings respond to evil by withdrawing their contribution to the said Kingdom, or they cease to treat with other reasonable beings on terms that are worthy of reasonable beings.[16] Surely, there are all sorts of moral ends that can only be attained by treating evil persons as if they were not evil. Sometimes, the only way forward is to treat unreasonable acts as if they were intended reasonably. Over and over again, there may be no other way.[17]

16. 'If we value the Kantian ideal of free and non-manipulative relations among rational beings and we want to approximate that ideal in the empirical human community, we must learn to be truthful and straightforward with one another regardless of our imperfect autonomy and the bad results to which it may sometime lead': Korsgaard, *Creating the Kingdom of Ends* p. 358.

17. Compare the concluding pages of Kant's essay 'On the Common Saying: "This May Be True in Theory, but It Does Not Apply in Practice" ' (AA VII, pp. 273–313): 'History may well give rise to endless doubts about my hopes [of human progress], and if these doubts could be proved, they might persuade me to desist from an apparently futile task. But so long as they do not have the force of certainty, I cannot exchange my duty (as something certain) for a rule of expediency which says that I ought not to attempt what may or may not be impracticable. And however uncertain I may be and

There is an indispensable moral insight here. But as is plain from a famous example, things are not at all straightforward. Paul, wishing to kill Peter, pursues him and tries to hunt him down. Peter gives Paul the slip and hides in my house. Suppose Paul comes to my door, asking for Peter. May I lie to Paul and deny that Peter is with me? Kant scarcely wavered from the view that, since truthfulness is a precondition of the kingdom of ends, I may not lie to Paul. It is permissible for me to try to avoid answering. But, if I lie, then I may even become responsible for Peter's death. Suppose, for instance that, unknown to me and even as I lie to Paul, Peter has slipped out through the back of my house and then he encounters Paul at the end of the street. *In that case, I, the householder, am to blame,* whereas 'if I do not waver from the truth, then justice cannot lay a hand on me, whatever the consequences may be'.[18]

In opposition to Kant, Benjamin Constant proposed that 'to tell the truth is a duty only with regard to one who has a right to the truth'. In his reply to Constant, Kant insisted, that the duty of truthfulness is 'an unconditional duty which holds in all circumstances'. Kant claimed that, even though by telling a lie I may not in fact wrong anyone, I still damage the unconditionality and universality of the duty of truthfulness.

Kant's reply to Constant will seem to be question-begging. It will seem as question-begging as Kant's attitude is ultra-rigoristic. Constant might also have complained that Kant was confusing the question of the unconditionality of the duty to truthfulness—however the

---

may remain as to whether we can hope for anything better for mankind, this uncertainty cannot detract from the maxim I have adopted or the necessity of assuming for practical purposes that human progress is possible. . . . Human nature is still animated by respect for right and duty. I therefore cannot and will not see [human nature] as so deeply immersed in evil that practical moral reason will not triumph in the end. . . . On the cosmopolitan level too, it thus remains true to say that whatever reason shows to be valid in theory is also valid in practice.' In *Kant: Political Writings*, ed. H. S. Reiss, trans. H. B. Nisbet (Cambridge: Cambridge University Press, 1991), pp. 89–92.

18. See 'On a Supposed Right To Lie because of Philanthropic Concerns', AA VII, pp. 425–30. The reader will not fail to notice the way in which this remark of Kant's makes Kantian ethics open to the charges (elsewhere less appropriate) of being an ethic of personal sanctity—of sanctimoniousness, even.

content of that duty ought itself to be stated—with the question of the generality or restrictedness of the duty itself. Constant could have insisted that, once we were clear *what* the duty was, he did not want to deny the categoricalness of that duty. These and other complaints might be made on his behalf. But there is something else that Constant would be missing if he thought that that was the end of the matter. In order to see what this is, let us ask on Kant's behalf what it would have meant to replace the requirement to tell the truth by the hedged requirement to tell the truth to those who have a right to the truth. . . . (The dots hold a place for extra conditions that might be supplied if Constant's suggestions were carefully improved.)

The answer to the question just posed is that, if we hedge the requirement of truth, then we lose altogether Kant's statement of the *ideal of truthfulness* between putative members of the kingdom of ends.[19] We also lose the means to say what is bad or a matter for chagrin even in the untruthfulness that is forced upon persons in the same sort of situation as the householder who shelters Peter. If Constant's principle were our sole hostage for the value of truth, and/or for the badness of untruth, then we could not say what is being sacrificed in situations where untruth is forced upon the parties. On the other hand, Kant's judgment about the Peter and Paul case still seems absurd. In truth, if we want neither Constant's hedging about of principles nor Kant's crazed rigorism, which seems at some points to carry the ideal of personal sanctity to almost egotistical lengths, then we shall have to search for a fresh way of thinking.

4.16. Here is a suggestion which can be made within an adaptation of Kant's own framework.[20] FUL provides a scheme of

19. For the absurdity of trying to restrict the duty of truthfulness by exact limitations and advance specifications, see the powerful essay about lying in Leszek Kolakowski, *Freedom, Fame, Lying and Betrayal: Essays on Everyday Life* (London: Penguin, 1999).

20. Compare Christine Korsgaard, 'The Right to Lie: Kant on Dealing with Evil', *Philosophy and Public Affairs* 15.4 (1986): 325–49.

thinking or a formal procedure for an agent who needs to come to terms with all and everything that reason and morality require of him *there and then in a given context.* (Note the provision we have made for this in 4.8.) The principle FH on the other hand and kindred principles do something quite different. The role of the principles we appeal to under the auspices of FH, in order to enjoin truthfulness, helpfulness, etc., is to furnish FUL with matter or substance. FH and its kin supply agents with the substantive values of a reasonable being.

The principle FH, together with its corollaries, has the appearance of a command of utter definiteness and terrifying generality. This as we have seen, is how Kant in his dispute with Constant thinks he has to interpret it. But on that particular point let us part company with Kant. Let us see any moral principles that FH, FA, and FKE imply not as determining *exact instructions* but as staking out the *absolutely general claims* that are made upon us everywhere by certain values and disvalues. As the Peter and Paul example makes evident, these claims cannot always be fully satisfied. That is a source of chagrin and remorse—precisely because FH, FA, FKE, and their consequences express ideals to which reasonable beings are fully committed, and committed even when they are unable to realize them fully at some juncture or when the principles in question conflict with one another. Meanwhile, it is FUL, in abstraction from FH, FA, FKE, that gives the framework within which moral agents have to adjudicate between these unconditional commitments. Compare a legal dispute between parties who make absolute (unrestricted, unqualified, unconditional) claims, where the work of a judge or arbiter is first to test those claims and then, on the basis of all claims s/he finds valid, to allocate to each party that party's (in the context) proper portion.

Back then to Peter and Paul. Suppose the householder describes the situation to himself as one in which he sees a conflict between the unconditional requirement of truthfulness and the equally unconditional requirement to secure the safety of Peter, a reasonable being whom he has taken into his house. Trying to assign each principle its proper portion, the householder might frame his relevantly complete statement of intention, RCI, as follows: 'Since Peter is an innocent person who is being pursued by Paul with murderous intent and since I have taken Peter into my house . . . I shall not answer Paul, if he comes to the door; but, if Paul forces me to answer, I shall have to lie.' The corresponding maxim will have the form M: 'Not to answer if the murderer comes to one's door, but then to lie if the murderer forces one to answer his question, when one is in the situation of a householder who has taken into his house an innocent person who is being pursued and . . . ' (where ' . . . ' holds a place for anything else that needs to be transferred from RCI to the maxim). The question then becomes: can the householder will that maxim as a highly specific moral policy to be followed by all rational beings? Evidently, whether he can will this maxim or not will have to depend upon the values and ideals to which he has committed himself. Let it be clear that the policy in question, the policy which he is proposing to will universally, is highly specific, incompletely articulate, not general at all. It is hardly, then, a candidate to enjoy the generality of a proper law. In its force, however, it is entirely lawlike. And if the householder wills it, then in the framework of FUL he wills the policy universally. Let *everyone* who is in such and such a highly specific situation do thus and so![21]

It may seem that, in siding even to this extent with Constant against Kant, we are preparing to sacrifice that which is distinctive in Kant's outlook upon treating with evil. Have we abandoned his whole aspiration for the kingdom of ends? It would be a bad mistake to think that. For the Kantian aspiration does not really depend on Kant's rigorism. It depends rather on the absoluteness or generality and unconditionality of the claims that FH would enable Kant to

21. There is no chance of this proposal being understood if one confuses the distinction between generality and specificity with the distinction between universal and singular/particular. Something utterly specific can nevertheless be multiply instantiated. Once one sees that, one will see that universality can be combined with utter specificity. Universality is not the same as generality. See here R. M. Hare, *Freedom and Reason* (Oxford: Oxford University Press, 1963), p. 39. See also 11.10, n. 25.

enter on behalf of various values and disvalues. In fact, under the new scheme that we have arrived at, a new resourcefulness becomes possible for an agent who sees himself confronted with an evil that his own moral ideals make it impossible for him to have any part in—the resourcefulness, for instance, of one who utterly refuses to bear arms or kill other people in war yet decides to make his point, *not* by refusing to have anything at all to do with a war that is already in progress or by going to prison, but by volunteering as a stretcher carrier in the Army Medical Corps. That is a compromise, if you like, but it is a creative compromise. It is a compromise not so much with evil, one might say, as against it. It is not a compromise with the categorical, absolute, or unconditional nature of duty.[22]

Part five: The content and completability of *a priori* ethics

4.17. We have developed Kant's scheme in a direction for which it would have been better to have more authority in the writings we have cited. But the redeployment just proposed preserves some distinctively Kantian emphases and it clarifies some important differences between the statuses of FUL and of FH, FA, and FKE. These are the kind of differences that any plausible account of ethics will need to mark in its own way. But, in whatever way we deploy the Kantian scheme, whether in Kant's way or a neo-Kantian way, it will only work if agents who decide or deliberate are allowed some sufficiency of moral ideas on the basis of which to decide which maxims they can will universally and which they cannot. Kant furnishes such agents with the *a priori* ideas of universality, willing, will, law, practical reason, and rational nature (alias humanity) as an end in itself. (See 4.12 above.) But do they not need more? They might think

22. This particular compromise finds living expression in the murals for the Burghclere Memorial painted by the English painter Stanley Spencer, who served as a stretcher bearer in the Gallipoli campaign and depicted on the walls of the chapel what he had himself seen from this vantage point of the experiences of men (and mules) in the First World War.

they need to know what ends are *worthy* of a reasonable being, for instance. But can an ethic purged of all (as Kant would say) merely anthropological content and arrived at purely and exclusively *a priori*, solely on the basis of *a priori* elaborations of the idea of rational nature, give a wide enough basis on which such ends might be tested or proposed or elaborated? There is a related or alternative question. How plausible or acceptable shall we find it that Kant's preoccupation with the development of rational nature, which is his only substantive end for human life, leads him into the teleological thesis that nature's 'purpose' in history has nothing to do with or- dinary workaday happiness?

> Without [the disruption occasioned by] asocial qualities (far from admirable in themselves) . . . men would live an Arcadian, pastoral existence of perfect concord, self-sufficiency, and mutual love. But all human talents would remain hidden forever in a dormant state, and men, as good-natured as the sheep they tended, would scarcely render their existence more valuable than that of their animals. The end for which they were created, their rational nature, would be an unfilled void. . . . Man wishes con- cord, but nature, knowing better what is good for his species, wishes discord.[23]

> Does [Herder] really mean that, if the happy inhabitants of Ta- hiti . . . were destined to live in their peaceful indolence for thousands of centuries, it would be possible to give a satisfactory answer to the question of why they should exist at all, and of whether it would not have been just as good if this island had been occupied by happy sheep and cattle as by happy human beings who merely enjoy themselves.[24]

23. 'Idea for a Universal History', *Kant: Political Writings*, ed. Reiss, p. 43.
24. 'Review of Herder', *Kant: Political Writings*, ed. Reiss, pp. 219–20. Thomas Hill drew this and the preceding passage to my attention.

One possible response to these questions would be to suggest that the content of Kantian ethics needs to be filled out and brought into alliance with a less severely restricted notion of rationality. Must not the rationality of a rational being be given an instantiation in the life of some *particular kind of animate being*, with particular ends and indirect ends? The difficulty that this would make for Kant, however, is that, in so far as it supplements the specifically *ethical* and/or *rational* notions available to Kantian agents, it will subvert Kant's demonstration (in part III of *Foundations;* see Lecture 5 and see the summary given at 4.2 above, the third paragraph in particular) of the identity or equivalence between the moral law and the laws or principles of our freedom within the world of physical laws. This equivalence is central to the strategy by which Kant seeks to supersede all Humean or neo-Humean vindications of morality. It is this that narrows the space in which Kantian ethics can develop further. On Kant's terms, what freedom could a self whose essence was that of some kind of animal being have in a Newtonian world?

4.18. Let it be clear that, in expressing doubts whether 'sovereign will' and 'rational nature' afford sufficient material from which the substantive ends proper to an ethical being might be specified and in complaining against the straitening effect of Kant's insistence that the whole content of morality should be given in a manner purged of all dependence on the animate being of its adherents, one is not holding out for our values to be determined from some new and enlarged science of anthropology or sociology (still less of 'economic science'). One is not returning to the strange idea that moral judgments should be reached by the empirical study of 'human nature'. (This was not Hume's project and nor should it be ours.) The thought is rather that the moral concerns we actually have and approve arise from the acquired nature that we ourselves exemplify. This is not to say that, as agents, we *validate* our standing concerns by the thought that these concerns have this origin. The thing that impresses us as agents is that such and such concerns are *already* our own and that many of them survive our reflection. In the world of first-order thought and action, we explore them and we follow them through. Each object of concern will matter to us either because . . . , where ' . . . ' says in the ethical terms that Hume will say are second nature to us why that thing matters—or else it will matter because its mattering is presupposed to *any* statement ' . . . ' to the effect that some other thing matters. The thing that distinguishes Kant from Hume or Aristotle is that the Humean or Aristotelian philosopher of morals will *acquiesce* in its being some reflection of this second nature how such and such or so and so matters to us ethically, and how it engages with the standard of morals to which that nature has contributed.[25]

4.19. In Lecture 1, at 1.13, we treated as separable but correlative the questions of the content of morality and of the motivation to participate in it. We must advance now to Kant's approach to the second of these questions. In advance of that, let us say that that which is distinctively Kantian in Kant's ethics brings with it fresh insights that almost anyone must recognize as such. So far from being empty or formalistic, Kantian ethics contains insights nobody can dispense with. Yet it seems incomplete. Judging it in the terms on which Kant himself offered it to the world, Humeans will be bound to raise the question whether it is completable—*plausibly* completable—*even in principle.*

---

25. Consider the claim arising from that nature (cp. *Enquiry*, Appendix 1, paragraph five) that ingratitude is a crime. Is this *a priori* or *a posteriori?* The claim is not derived from sense experience or dependent upon it. Nor is it simply derived from or dependent upon some inner counterpart of sense experience. Given that the claim is not *a posteriori*, is it then *a priori?* Philosophical terminology creaks at this point. (Blame the weasel words 'dependent', 'derived'?) If the Humean claim reflects human life or human constitution, then Kant must seek to disallow its *a priority*. But terminology creaks. Is it not enough for the Humean claim to be not *a posteriori?*

Kant will also complain that there is too much contingency in Hume's account of these matters. But it is not contingent that ingratitude is a crime. Nobody who knows what ingratitude is or understands its relation to selfishness—cp. 2.17 and cp. *Treatise* III. ii.v, paragraph 8—will allow that it might have been innocuous. Nor is it a mere contingency that our given and acquired natures are as they are and we disapprove of ingratitude. It is integral to our animate existence and to the significance we give to the language itself in which we speak of the ethical. These and related questions are touched upon further in 5.8; 9.3, n.4; 9.4, n. 7; and 9.8, n. 17.

5

The laws of morality as the laws of freedom and the laws of freedom as the laws of morality

What sort of solidarity in a Kingdom of Ends; the real issue between Kant and Hume

The rational being must regard himself always as legislative in a realm of ends possible through the freedom of the will, whether he belongs to it as member or as sovereign. . . . [The principle of his will] is to act only in such a manner that the will through its maxims can regard itself at the same time as universally law giving. . . . The practical necessity of acting according to this principle, i.e. duty, does not rest at all on feelings impulses and inclinations; it rests only on the relation of rational beings to one another, a relation in which the will of a rational being must always be regarded as making universal law, because otherwise [such a being] could not be conceived as an end in himself . . . [or possessing] the dignity of a rational being who obeys no law other than that which he himself also gives.

Kant, *Foundations of the Metaphysics of Morals* [434]

When we present examples of honesty of purpose of steadfastness in following good maxims . . . even with great sacrifice of advantages and comfort, there is no man, not even the most malicious villain (provided he is otherwise accustomed to using his reason), who does not wish that he also might have these qualities. But because of his inclinations and impulses he cannot bring this about. Yet at the same time he wishes to be free from such inclinations which are burdensome even to himself. He thus proves that, with a will free from all impulses of sensibility, he in thought transfers himself into an order of things altogether different from that of his desires in the field of sensibility. He cannot expect to obtain by that wish any gratification of desires or any condition which would satisfy his real or even imagined inclinations, for the idea itself which elicits this wish from him would lose its pre-eminence if he had any such expectation. He can expect only a greater inner worth of his person. [The malicious villain] imagines himself to be this better person when he transfers himself to the standpoint of the intelligible world to which he is involuntarily impelled by the idea of freedom, i.e. independence from the determining causes of the world of sense. From this standpoint he is conscious of a good will, which on his own confession constitutes the law for his bad will as a member of the world of sense. He acknowledges the authority of this law even while transgressing it. The moral *ought* is therefore his own volition as a member of the intelligible world and it is conceived by him as an ought in so far as he regards himself at the same time as a member of the world of sense.

Kant, *Foundations of the Metaphysics of Morals* [455]

My worth as an intelligence is raised infinitely by my being a person in whom the moral law reveals to him a life independent of all animality, and even of the whole world of sense.

Kant, *Critique of Practical Reason* [162]

5.1.   The second part of Kant's *Foundations of the Metaphysics of Morals* develops the Formula of Universal Law, FUL, and the Formula of Humanity, FH, together with corollaries, into a distinctive (whether completable or incompletable) content or substance for Kantian ethics. Such was the concern of the preceding chapter, which belonged in the province of our topic (A) of Lecture 1. But this stretch of *Foundations* also prepares the way for Kant's account of freedom and his rational vindication of morality. Here we find his response to the question that we assigned at 1.1 to our topic (B). With these new preoccupations before our mind, let us recapitulate this stretch of Kant's book for a second time, in more detail than was appropriate for our overview at section 4.2 and with different interests from those that were in evidence in sections 4.12, 4.13, and 4.14. On this second occasion, the recapitulation must lead into the identity that Kant claims to establish between the laws of morality and the laws of freedom.[1]

In this work of condensation and report, let us begin, as before,

1. Of this part of Kant's argument not even an outline can be above controversy. It will be necessary to make many silent interpretive choices.

with the duty that Kant lays upon each of us to test our every intention by reference to FUL and the further duty that Kant sees FUL as putting upon us to concern ourselves with a larger purpose of absolute worth, a purpose over and above more specific purposes. According to Kant, this overriding purpose on the part of rational beings enforces their respect and reverence for pure practical reason as such. In so far as it is rational, our humanity itself embodies the rationality that pure practical reason exemplifies. From this it follows that, being answerable in the way we are to FUL, we must always act in such a way that we treat humanity, alias rational nature, both in our own person and in that of another, never as a means only but always as an end in itself. On this basis, Kant seeks to show that one who places himself under moral law treats himself and every other human being not only as the possessor of a sovereign and universally legislating will, but as a member of a systematic union of rational self-legislating beings united through common laws. So when we ask ourselves what maxims each of us can will universally, every one of us must consider the suitability and worthiness of our putative maxim to furnish (when universalized) a law for a kingdom of ends. In so far as we act morally, we shall act as if from a conception of ourselves as citizens of such a kingdom and as fellow inhabitants of the standpoint of reason. In so far as we act from such a conception, we manifest our reverence or respect *(Achtung)* for reason and we acknowledge the dignity of the rational nature (or humanity, Kant says) that embodies it. Thus FH, FA, FKE expand the import of FUL.

So much will be familiar from Lecture 4. (See also 9.2 and 9.3.) But now there is a further claim, which is this: our will under moral laws, the rational will of each of us, inasmuch as it treats all rational nature as self-legislative, has as its law only itself. It sets its own end. A rational being who places himself under moral laws is not then a means or instrument at the service of a law imposed on him from without. He must be the sole author of the law that he obeys. No doubt reason in the abstract *proposes* laws to the rational being, but it is for the being himself to ratify them as *his* laws, as the laws for *his* will. And in that case he is not only a moral being under moral laws, but an autonomous being. (For the price that Kantian ethics pays for this sort of autonomy, an autonomy unconditioned by anything merely empirical, see 4.17 and 4.18.) Nor is that all. The autonomy by which a rational will can set its own end furnishes the *only* way by which a being physically constrained in the Newtonian world of phenomena could act according to its own laws or possess a free will. In that case a free will and a will subject to moral laws are one and the same thing (*Foundations*, [447]).

5.2. Does any such freedom really exist? Up to this point in *Foundations* the question has been treated as momentous but it has been carefully left open. But now, if you ask whether true freedom exists, Kant is ready to declare that

> Reason must regard itself as the author of its principles, independently of alien influences: consequently, as practical reason or as the will of a rational being, it must regard itself as free. That is to say that the will of a rational being can be a will of its own only under the idea of freedom, and therefore, from a practical point of view, such a will must be ascribed to all rational beings. [448]

Here we catch sight of the possibility—scarcely dreamt of by Hume—that the concern that we have with morality, the concern of the pure practical reason within us that gives us the Formula of Universal Law and the Formula of Humanity, is not different from the interest that attaches us to the inalienable idea of practical autonomy. We glimpse the possibility that our pre-theoretical submission to categorical requirements is the same thing as our inability to see ourselves as other than autonomous beings.

At this point, however, Kant sees the risk of a kind of vicious circle. If it were only morality itself that assured us of our freedom, then such freedom could scarcely be that which vindicated morality. In order to avoid this circle, he then invokes two different standpoints, the standpoint of one who is subject to the phenomenal or sensible world and the standpoint of one within the intelligible world, the world of things in themselves, things possessed, as he thinks we take the real *you* and *me* to be possessed, of the pure spontaneity of rational beings. Rational being are beings whose nature and destiny it is to face the deliberative question, 'What shall I do?'

> As a rational being and thus belonging to the intelligible world, man cannot think of the causality of his own will except under the idea of freedom. For independence from the determining causes of the world of sense (an independence which reason must always ascribe to itself) is freedom. The concept of autonomy is inseparably connected with the idea of freedom and with the former there is inseparably bound the universal principle of morality, which is the ground in idea of all actions of rational beings, just as the laws of nature are the ground of all appearances. . . . When we think of ourselves as free, we transport ourselves into the intelligible world as members of it and know the autonomy of the will together with its consequence, morality. [452-3]

So now we have the answer to Hume, or so it is supposed. Recognizing myself as subject to the law of reason which contains and encloses within the idea of freedom the law of the intelligible/noumenal world [454], I have to regard the laws of the intelligible world, FUL, FH, FA, as imperatives for me.

There is much more to say in exposition, interrogation, and defence of this argument of Kant's. It has provoked hundreds of scholarly and philosophical books. But here in bare outline is the rational remedy that Kant supposes philosophical inquiry must discover to a person who has no relish for virtue and humanity (in Hume's sense) and no benevolent sympathy with his fellow creatures.[2] Here too, along with familiar insights that almost any philosophy of mo-

---

2. In this bare outline, as in other Kantian expositions in this book, I have sought to dispense with that which I see no hope, despite Korsgaard, of my understanding, or even imagining myself understanding. I have striven all the same to put together a line of exposition that is argumentatively complete.

rality and action coming after Kant will be tempted to try to appropriate for itself, is Kant's hope of making rationally evident to a
malicious villain, and much more evident than it is supposed Hume
could have done, the nature of the mistake that the villain is making.
See now the second epigraph, which is the point of departure for
the next section.

5.3. What is the phenomenology of the process that Kant would
describe as that of a villain's imaginatively attending for a moment
to a moral demand that is really a demand *upon his reason?* In
conceiving of himself as a noumenal being endowed with a will and
a causality other than that which he has as a phenomenal being (cp.
[457]), or in daydreaming (if he does) of a better self, how does the
villain connect together his empirical self and his noumenal self?
And what is the temptation or the necessity for the villain to look
at matters seriously, even for one moment, from the point of view
of the noumenal self? Finally, one last question: supposing that the
villain does look at things in this way, how will the 'intelligible world
itself' furnish to him a rational concern that becomes a specifically
moral concern with his own conduct? (Compare [462], end of first
paragraph.)

   We might suppose that the villain is meant to think: 'My villainy
does not belong to the real me. The real me is my rational will as a
noumenal being. That is the will I must heed.' But a Humean will ask
how the villain could really believe the first of these two claims. How
can he believe this consistently with taking responsibility for the acts
that he does? And how is the thought of his own rational will meant
to work upon him? Meanwhile, on the level of theory, the Humean
may ask to have it recapitulated for him how exactly the rational will,
Wille, and the will's own other-than-phenomenal causality, was introduced. The answer to the last question is that Kant defined *Wille* as
the causality of living beings *in so far as they are rational* [446].
Wille is that by which such beings determine themselves to action in
accordance with a conception of law [427]. Kant's mode of definition

here is surely creative,[3] however, and that invites the first and basic question, whether there is really such a thing as this *Wille,* this will that is *distinct* from the malicious villain's ordinary will.

Reverting now to the Humean question of how the villain's thought of his own rational will is meant to work on the villain, we can imagine Kant's saying that the villain can be invited to reflect that, by renouncing morality as Kant sees morality, he (the villain) is renouncing freedom and, with it, rational agency itself. The villain's way of life is a perpetual offence against reason. Here though, a clear-minded villain might wonder how *exercising* the freedom to choose either one or the other of the options open to him could represent a *renunciation* of freedom? It could, no doubt, if this were analogous to the free choice of slavery (one's last free act, so to speak). But how could the villain's choice be assimilated to a choice of slavery? At this point, Humeans will have to complain that, in his vindication of morality as freedom, Kant relies upon the most implausible and question-begging features of Kant's conception of a life without morality. Kant is simply repeating his view that such a life represents a servitude to desire, desire itself being conceived as an alien force. The Humean, who is of course no ally of villainy and holds no brief for the choices the villain makes, will doubt whether Kant can make an effective but *not specifically moral* objection to the villain's way of being. He will insist, moreover, that an ordinary, carefully considered, reflectively ratified desire is not an alien force. The only convincing criticism of the villain's choices will be a specifically ethical criticism; and *that* kind of criticism, the Humean will say, cannot bring the kind of firepower that Kant aspires to bring against a villain's claim that his way of being is carefully considered, free, and reflectively ratified. (For a neo-Humean option in the matter of freedom, see n. 11 below.)

Should Kant say then that, in renouncing morality, the villain renounces *true* freedom, the freedom that can only come to him from arbitrating his choice of act by the empirically untainted principle *act only on the maxim which you could will as law for all rational beings?* Yes. Of course, Kant can say that and he can call renouncing that a renunciation of the condition of rationality. But such a declaration provokes the question whether that is the only freedom, or the only rationality. Why is Kant so sure that every argument from freedom will lead to FUL in particular? For instance, why is it not possible for one to qualify as escaping from the tyranny of desire who acts, not from FUL + FH + FA + FKE, but from principles which emerge from gradual refinement and intersubjective accommodation of the passions that Hume describes? Is there really no freedom to be had in the morality, neither theoretically nor effectively coextensive with Kantian morality (though equally opposed to villainy), which Hume describes as arising out of the nature of human beings? Is there no freedom to be had in that altogether new creation, rooted in human nature not in pure practical reason, that is human civilization itself?

Let it be clear that there is no question here of Hume or his apologists' taking the villain's part, defending his choice or celebrating his freedom to stick to his chosen way of being. Their stand is rather this: that a Humean criticism of the villain's choice and his reasons for it cannot be pre-ethical. Hume can point to distinctive felicities and consolations of ways of being the villain disdains, but not in a way that will make the alternatives to villainy (pre-ethically) rationally mandatory.[4] The Humean appeal is to the ordinary sorts of reasons the malicious villain has already abandoned.

5.4. At this stage in the argument, where it seems less and less clear exactly how the identity between the laws of freedom and morality is meant to furnish a reprobate with a convincing criticism of the rationality of his own way of being, we shall sense the need to find some new idea in the third part of Kant's book.

---

4. Of course, if you are neo-Humean rather than strictly Humean, you may want to count the ethical as *already* a part of the rational. There are grounds to say that. They are no help to Kant, however.

Is this the new idea? That in persevering in villainy, in turning his back on the noumenal, the villain turns his back on a *compelling ideal*—an ideal so compelling that it can reach out and recruit anyone who knows reason at all:

The idea of a pure intelligible world as a whole of all intelligences to which we ourselves belong as rational beings (though on the other side we are at the same time members of the world of sense) is always a useful and permissible idea for the purpose of a rational faith. This is so even though all knowledge terminates at the boundary of a pure intelligible world. For through the glorious ideal of a universal realm of ends-in-themselves (rational beings) a lively interest in the moral law can be awakened in us. To that realm we can belong as members only when we carefully conduct ourselves according to maxims of freedom as if they were laws of nature. [463]

If this passage is a reliable indicator,[5] then morality conceived as Kant finally conceived it is not founded in an incontrovertible necessity comparable in force to that of formal logic or of the necessity to think that, if all men are mortal and Socrates is a man, then Socrates is mortal. The passage from reason through FUL to FUL + FH + FA + FKE is not like that. Rather, pure practical reason brings into being a special sort of solidarity, the glorious solidarity of beings that partake in the noumenal world and participate there in a kingdom of ends, a systematic union of wills under shared objective laws. For a reasonable being, how could it be reasonable not to aspire to live with other reasonable beings in the accord that is worthy of reasonable beings? For reasonable beings, surely solidarity in reason is mandatory.

Such a plea is certainly impressive. But, equally certainly, it elides the difference between its being reasonable to aspire so and the

---

5. Having always since 1990 or so imputed to the passage this indispensable role in the argument of *Foundations,* I was reassured to discover the kind of emphasis placed upon it by Christine Korsgaard in ch. 6 (dating in fact from the 1980s) of *Creating the Kingdom of Ends* (Cambridge: Cambridge University Press, 1996). See especially p. 170.

stronger claim that it is unreasonable not to aspire so. And one cannot help but wonder about the position of a philosopher who rests morality in rational solidarity if its chief rival rests morality in a rival solidarity—not the solidarity of rational beings *qua* rational, but the solidarity that Hume describes of human beings *qua* human. How well is Kant placed to dismiss or criticize a theory that seeks to account for morality as the complex elaboration and diversification, in the hearts and minds of the 'party of humankind' (see *Enquiry*, V.2, Selby-Bigge, p. 224), of the weak but disinterested sentiment of benevolence? When we pursue the question of rationality all the way through to the last part of *Foundations* and seek to hunt it down there, it seems that the thing that makes all the difference between Kant and Hume—between the idea that it is Reason (construed as [463] suggests we construe it) that gives us a motive to act from the good will and the idea that it is something subtly elaborated from benevolence that can give members of the party of humankind durable and sensible ordinary reasons to act against the promptings of self-love—well, this thing that makes all the difference, this difference between different solidarities, suddenly appears to have the width of a knife-edge.

Kant tried to identify one thing that might be both the foundation of morality and the motive to morality, a thing that might span the gap between the idea of a constituency to which categorical requirements are addressed and the idea of such requirements' having effective normative authority among all those to whom they are addressed. In opposition to Kant, Hume will claim that the form in which Reason finally settles down to play its systematic role of connecting content and motive is not a form in which Reason, even Reason as Kant conceives it, can make anything quite *mandatory*—even among human beings. Simple solidarity—even rational solidarity of the sort Kant is concerned to advocate—may point towards good ethical reasons, but it will not render anything Rationally compulsory.

5.5. As part of our effort to adjudicate between two systems so impressive and so different as Hume's and Kant's, let us now return to the gap that we spoke of Kant's unsuccess (or only partial success) in bridging with the idea of Reason. (See at 4.2, second and third paragraphs.) Of course, there is a somewhat similar gap in Hume, creating a somewhat similar problem. It is signalled by Hume's acknowledgement of the clear distinctness of the 'two circumstances' that constitute jointly the operation of benevolence (*Enquiry,* IV.1). These are, first, the existence of a sentiment that 'renders the actions and conduct of the persons the most remote an object of applause or censure, according as they agree or disagree with that rule of right[6] which is established' (compare the uncircumscribed aim of the Kantian commandment not to lie); and, second, the existence of a 'sentiment common to all mankind which recommends the same object to general approbation and makes every man or most men agree in the same opinion or decision concerning it' (compare the postulated universal rational authority of the Kantian commandment). If these circumstances are *two* circumstances, what accounts for the existence of each and what links them together, albeit in distinctness?

Kant's answer is Reason, or his whole system. Hume's answer is humanity (humanity = benevolence) and its diversifications within the scheme that he describes. Hume's answer cannot be correctly understood, however, if it is construed as coordinate with the Kantian answer or as simply competing with it to close a gap in the way in which it is represented that Kantian Reason can fill such a gap. For humanity (= benevolence) is not one thing in Hume's construction, but the source of a whole multiplicity of moral sentiments associated with a multiplicity of natural and artificial virtues, each of which furnishes a distinctive consideration stateable in the indicative mood in favour of certain modes of conduct. It would be *cruel* not to help our friend, ally, or country cousin, Timothy William, or *dishonest* not to tell him what we have done, or *disloyal* not, at this

---

6. The rule of right Hume speaks of here is (I have claimed) a standard of assessment (of personal merit as expressed in actions, etc.) applied by an onlooker and studied further by a moral scientist or moral philosopher. The rule, then, is first and foremost a rule for judging rather than a precept commanding such and such an act (or commanding abstention from such and such an act).

point, to defend his name and reputation vigorously. Each of these claims is backed by some consideration that is backed by a sentiment that Hume aims, as a moral scientist, to explain as arising from the common nature of human beings, or aims to explain as arising from the second nature that results from the collision between ordinary human nature and whatever facts and conventions its possessors encounter in human society. And then in most cases—if not in every case, then in normal cases—this same sentiment is something that Hume aims in his capacity as moralist to commend to us. To understand the aetiology of the sentiment is usually (but not always) to understand its very indispensability to us, collectively speaking. (Not, of course, always. As we have seen, Hume is careful to condemn the monkish virtues, which 'harden the heart', and thereby subvert what he takes for the whole basis of morality.) And, finally each of these considerations that is backed by sentiment affords us a reason—a reason we can make our own, however often we *fail* to make it our own—to conduct ourselves in a certain way.

5.6. If we are to decide between these proposals we need to clarify yet further the real contrast between Kant and Hume. The chief true contrast, when one has tried to make some philosophical judgments about what new moves each of them can or cannot make consistently with his brief, appears to turn on the contrast between Reason and ordinary reasons (plural). This contrast is not helpfully described as the contrast between a philosopher who founds ethics in Reason and one who claims that it is not contrary to Reason (or reason) to prefer the destruction of the world to the scratching of his finger (*Treatise*, II.iii.3, Selby-Bigge, p. 416). That way of describing the contrast rests on an ambiguity in 'reason' and assimilates Hume to one of the parties between whom he announced in the opening sections of the *Enquiry* that he would arbitrate. Nor is it even right (though it is certainly an improvement) to describe the contrast as holding between Kant, who would found ethics in Reason, and Hume, who would found ethics in reason and passion, where reason is the slave of the passions. It would be silly to deny that Hume commits himself to this last thing. But even here there is room for doubt about what exactly he means. For here (as in the first famous dictum) the reason that Hume speaks of is really theoretical reason, something whose province is stipulated to be relations of ideas and matters of fact. Like the text of Aristotle (*Nicomachean Ethics* 1139a30) that Hume is echoing (or echoing an echo of) when he says that reason is inert (a text bearing on *sophia* not *phronesis*—theoretical reason not practical wisdom), Hume's claim leaves it open whether there can be a distinctively non-theoretical species of reason or reasonableness. I do not mean that it is Hume's intention to leave this possibility open. I mean that that is what results from the things that he says. Given Hume's silence about practical reason(s)—a silence only fully intelligible in the context of the polemic he is conducting against his rationalist predecessors (see here 2.11 and 3.6, n. 7; also 2.4, n. 4) but open, given that particular context, to benign construal—the temptation is to say that at root the real contrast is between Kantian *a priori* practical reason and some Humean practical reason of *reasons* (in the plural) that are conditioned by the sentiments that it is part of human beings' first and acquired natures to be moved by.

At this point, having already noticed in Lecture 4 the temptation to release Kant from his insistence on the *a priori* purity of the proper content of morality, and having yielded to the temptation to explain away some of Hume's denials about the role of reason—denials as gratuitous for his system as they are outrageous in their apparent import—one may be tempted to find some convergence on the part of each of Kant and Hume with the conception of ethics and *logos* that is presented in the *Nicomachean Ethics* by Aristotle. The adjustments it would be necessary to make to Kant's thinking in order to achieve this are hard to contemplate.[7] But there is a stronger temptation to make a comparison between Hume and Aristotle.

Aristotle defined the end of human action as happiness. Happiness

---

7. Once (for instance) we prescind from Kant's polemic against the philosophers who transgress the sort of a priority that Kant insists upon for the subject matter he is concerned with, so much of the rationale will disappear for Kant's distinctive justification for FUL and for everything that flows from that principle. See also 4.17-19.

itself he defined as activity of the soul in accordance with virtue, where virtue includes both the ethical virtues and the intellectual virtues, among them *phronesis* or practical wisdom. For Aristotle, practical reason itself is not something pre-ethical, or ethically un-conditioned, or something free from all the human sentiments and predispositions of our first and acquired natures. On the contrary, practical reason *presupposes* the ethical virtues, without which it would fail to possess itself of any right practical end; and the ethical virtues are themselves *mesotetes,* or intermediates, that is, choices of the right measure between having too much or too little to do with this, that, or the other way of acting or feeling.[8] For this reason, Aristotle's notion of practical reason develops as if in tandem with his piecemeal specification of the better and worse ways of being, feeling, and acting. And so for Hume, well after he has said his piece against 'eternal fitnesses' and other curiosities and vacuities of polite moral theology, we can even be on the look-out in reading him for unpolemical, unsystematic, ethically conditioned, idealizing uses of the word 'rational' such as the following:

> This constant habit of surveying ourselves, as it were, in reflec-tion, keeps alive all the sentiments of right and wrong, and be-gets, in noble natures, a certain reverence for themselves as well as others, which is the surest guardian of every virtue. The animal conveniences and pleasures sink gradually in their value; while every inward beauty and moral grace is studiously ac-quired, and the mind is accomplished in every perfection, which can adorn or embellish a *rational* creature. (*Enquiry* IX.1, Selby-Bigge, p. 225, my emphasis)[9]

Is not this the very same use to which sensible, passably good people put the word 'rational' in ordinary workaday life? (Such questions will recur at 9.20.)

---

8. The difficulties of the 'too much' and 'too little' need not concern us here. All that matters is that, within the Aristotelian account of morality, the doctrine of the mean plays a crucial role in connecting practical reason with the thing Hume calls passion. See the beginning of book VI of *Nicomachean Ethics*.

9. Note incidentally the passing anticipation of Kantian *Achtung*.

5.7. So much for the gap that Hume closes with (Humean) humanity and all its progeny and that Kant closes with Reason. It may still seem unnerving that Hume's recommendation of morality can only be relative to a contingency, the contingency of humanity, benevolence, or fellow feeling. But for us at least, for human beings I mean, this is not a contingency like just any old other contingency. Could we seriously undertake to change ourselves in order to remove our own (Humean) humanity? Or in order to remove our simply workaday reasonableness (with a small 'r')? Without these, should we even recognize ourselves?

Is that enough? Even for a Kantian who said he was fully prepared to take seriously all the Humean reservations about Kant's theory, these pleas will scarcely suffice as a reply to the complaint of contingency. He will remind us that

> Whatever is derived from the particular natural situation of man as such or from certain feelings and properties . . . can give a subjective principle by which we might act only if we have the propensity and inclination, but not an objective principle by which we would be directed to act even if all our propensity, inclination and natural tendencies were opposed to it. [425]

To this I think that all the Humean can reply is as follows. Hume's theory allows for the possibility of an obligation's making a claim against our self-love, and it allows for the possibility of the claim's *prevailing*. It does not *guarantee* that the claim will prevail or even that it will prevail on the level of what can non-question-beggingly be called reasonable reflection. Not even Kant's theory could claim to do that. But in the Humean account (the reply continues) the claim against self-love can be strongly *reinforced* (as we found Hume intimating in the passage last quoted from him) and reinforced in various ways that will renew the reason to act. It can be reinforced, for instance, as we pointed out at 4.1 above, by the consideration of the 'humility' (or shame) that would result from the omission of something we know to be required of us. Whatever may be the promptings of our inclination or natural tendencies, our reflection and practical deliberation can carry us to the point where we can see that we have no alternative but to grant or concede the claim that is made upon us—where we see that it would go against too much that we find in ourselves if we denied that these reflections and deliberations give us a real reason to act. Hume has furnished everything we need in order to understand how this can come about.

5.8. The Kantian may now ask how close this can carry a Humean to accounting for the practical necessity that is created by moral obligation. How is the Humean to account for what the agent himself means when (or if) he arrives at the finding that at this point he *must* (say) defend the name and reputation of his friend and country cousin Timothy William? How is a Humean subjectivist to make intelligible the hardness of this 'must'? What sense can he make of its phenomenology? Suppose that the agent finds that, in prospect, the failure to defend Timothy William's good name and reputation displeases him, after a certain manner, strongly (see the Humean dictum quoted at 2.10, p. 49). Suppose he finds that such a failure falls far short of the public standard by which we judge such things. That standard is rooted no doubt, in humanity, benevolence, self-love, and the rest. But why should the fact that an act or character conforms to this standard have an autonomous motive force, a force not reducible to any of the motives from which it historically originates?

The Humean answer must still be that that which the agent feels is that he must defend the country friend; that *he has no alternative but to defend him*,[10] however intractable the circumstances may be, and however little inclination he has to do this; that it would be disloyal and cowardly not to do so, etc.

What sort of thing are we saying, when we say this? Kant's answer is on the table. But where is the subjectivist's? The Humean subjectivist, concentrating on *the subject himself,* will have to declare that what we are saying is something irreducibly psychological (in

10. On this expression and the psychological interpretation that it invites, see Bernard Williams's discussion 'Practical Necessity', in *Moral Luck* (Cambridge: Cambridge University Press, 1981).

part)—namely that the circumstances have combined with what we now are, with our now actual second nature and the concerns that go with that nature, to force a certain act upon us. This act is our duty. The duress we feel is as strong and unyielding as the duress that Reason can impose upon us. But, at least in the first instance, it is not the promptings of a Kantian Reason that we feel. The duress we feel is simply the collision of inclination with something potentially far stronger than inclination. This no doubt is a most important difference from Kant. For the Humean subjectivist, it is the force of something in ourselves (something that we have allowed into ourselves) that *gives* us a reason, or completes our reason, to defend our friend and ally's name and reputation, namely the disloyalty that attaches to the failure to do so. Maybe this disloyalty will only be visible to an intelligence that shares certain sentiments with us. Hume furnishes little or nothing to make it possible to say anything stronger. But that which is bad about the disloyalty is no less real for that. We feel the force of the disloyalty that would attach to the failure; and we feel the authority of the sentiments that force this disloyalty upon our attention. What is this authority? Well these are *our* sentiments. (They define our moral identity, some will want to say. Slightly less obscurely, I should prefer to say that they are something in us without which we could scarcely recognize ourselves or might prefer not to. Cp. *Treatise,* II.ii.) How then, the Humean will ask, can we ignore them? What good reason could there be for us to ignore or despise the standard of morals that these sentiments—along with Humean reason and imagination—give to us.

5.9. Having reached this point, let us refer back now to Lecture 1, and sections 1.1 and 1.12 in particular. Having set out and gradually elaborated a Humean response to questions (A') and (B'), we have also compared and contrasted a rival response to the same questions, namely Kant's. In further discussion, we have tried to record what answers Hume owes to Kant and Kant owes to Hume. It would be tedious to collect up every debit. It is neither here nor there if at some point a verdict may have seemed to be forming itself in favour of Hume (on the condition maybe that Hume be construed in a

manner better emphasizing his numerous concealed or further con-
structible affinities with Aristotle). That which really matters is one's
sense—which will be enhanced by all the difficulties and disadvantages of all the philosophical options and alternatives to be rehearsed
in Lectures 6, 7 and 8—that the main truth about the two questions
we set ourselves in Lecture 1 is out there, ready and waiting to be
hunted down in the space that lies between Hume, Kant, and Aristotle.[11]

11. Here, though, I enter one caveat. I do not want to say that a satisfactory view of
human freedom is to be arrived at by any process of mutual accommodation between
Kant and Hume. For the reasons why I say that, see ch. 8 (with p. 381 ff.) of *Needs,
Values, Truth* (amended 3rd ed., Oxford: Oxford University Press, 2002) or the version
of the same essay reprinted in Gary Watson (ed.), *Free Will* (Oxford: Oxford University
Press, 2003), where something less strange is said than that which either Hume or Kant
want to say. It is said that the empirically given world can be at once *orderly* and *non-
deterministic*, allowing reasonable beings to act for good reasons without anything's
always narrowing down to unity the alternatives that are physically/empirically possible
for them.

6

Classical utilitarianism

The arguments by which it is advocated and some variants in which it is reformulated

I have planted the tree of utility. I have planted it deep and spread it wide.
Jeremy Bentham

Let no one think that it is nothing to accustom people to give a reason for their opinions, be the opinions ever so untenable, the reason ever so insufficient. A person accustomed to submit his fundamental tenets to the light of reason will be more open to the dictates of reason on every other point. Not from him shall we have to apprehend the owl-like dread of light, the drudge-like aversion to change, which were the characteristics of the unreasoning race of bigots.

J. S. Mill, *Essay on Coleridge*

6.1.   There was much for Kant and Hume to disagree about. But there was at least one way in which they agreed, both with one another and with many of their predecessors. They wanted to ground their ideas about what it is to act rightly in *prior* ideas about something else which had to do with the agent—be it his virtue, his personal merit, his intentions, his good will, or whatever. 'All virtuous actions derive their merit only from virtuous motives and are considered merely as signs of these motives,' was the Humean formulation. (See Lecture 3. For Kantian formulations, which are more intricate, see the immediately preceding lectures.)

Consider the claim that an act is right at the time t in circum-

stances *c* just in case it is the act that would be chosen at *t* in *c* by
a person with the good will/possessed of 'personal merit'. If questions of conceptual priority are put on one side and space is made
within such a formulation to allow agents of imperfect merit or virtue
to seek for the act that is appropriate for *them,* few will find an
actual falsehood here. But Hume and Kant will go further. They will
defend such claims against the charge that they suggest a dependence that is *the wrong way round.* They will approve the spirit at
least in which the proposal is drafted. For the official explanation
that each of them envisaged of what constitutes the rightness of an
act turned crucially on the way in which the choice of act expresses
the good will or personal merit of the agent. ('Personal merit' is a
Humean variant on 'virtuous formation'.)

There is a connection between this way of thinking of theirs and
the strategy by which Hume and Kant contrive to develop in tandem
their accounts of morality's content and of morality's motive. In the
case of Hume, it will be remembered, the virtues are seen as the
culmination of ramifying reasoned benevolence. In the case of Kant,
the good will is a manifestation of pure practical reason. In so far
as Glaucon's and Adeimantus' problem is the focus, there are signal
advantages in these accounts; but there is a serious incompleteness.
For among our moral notions, there have always been some that
suggest an exactly opposite dependence, namely the dependence of
the idea of virtue on the idea of the right act. Along those lines,
why not define a good or virtuous person as one with a dependable
disposition to do an act that is right and that qualifies as right
independently of the disposition? And why not see the dependable
disposition itself as a disposition to try to produce by action certain
sorts of *outcome?* According to one natural development of this alternative, it will then appear that the prospective goodness of an
outcome must be able, unprompted, to *speak for itself* to anyone
who wonders what has to be done; in which case the state of the
agent will not have any logical priority at all, in matters of acting
well or rightly, over either an act or the doing of an act or the
outcome of the doing of an act.

Suppose that, at some moment in the first half of the nineteenth century, we walk down a city street, past a stinking urban hovel. Shoeless, half-naked children run in the street. A glance into an open doorway reveals a listless scene of near starvation and despair. Our first reaction to this scene of immiseration might be to press questions in which we are briefed by English literature of the nineteenth century. 'Whose doing is it that these families are living here in such desolation and squalor? Did these families come to the city of their own accord, led on by some false expectation? Or is their presence here to be compared to the presence of water on the ground to which it has simply been pumped uphill? That is, did some land-owner see greater profit in sheep, say, than in the benignly labour-intensive farming that he had practised previously? Was he cynically indifferent to the fate of people who had no other prospect of earning their living? If so, was the eviction nevertheless legal? At a higher level of generality, what might have been said of the constitutional aspects of Acts of Enclosure or of the various interpretations of Common Law relating to land tenure that made it possible for land-owners to act as so many of them did? Could not the evictions to which all this gave rise have been challenged in the courts?'

These are all perfectly good questions, however 'utopian' their practical connotations may appear to the down-to-earth economic historian. Framed as we have begun by framing them, however, our interrogations have focused so far on virtues and vices of the actors as these are expressed in their acts within the drama being enacted. Other kinds of question clamour for attention. Independently of the vices and virtues manifested or not manifested in the course of events that has turned out in this way, what are the generality of moral subjects to make of the resulting state of affairs itself? Do no moral duties at all flow for anyone from the *simple existence* of so piteous a scene *except* in so far as it can be seen as owed to questionable acts of people whom it is fair to hold answerable for the effects of their actions? Do no moral duties at all lie on anyone except those thus answerable? That is hard to believe. It is harder still to believe that, where the badness of such a scene is not matched by the badness of what was done intentionally by those whose actions have led to such immiseration, the outcome intimates to us the positive will of God.

6.2. There were always pressures within the subject matter of moral philosophy to take seriously the thought that the best place for the subject to begin is with a manifest situation and the act that the situation 'calls for'. We saw in Lecture 3 how Hume had a special reason to recognize that *not* all moral evaluation can be regarded as bearing directly upon human character traits—if only because he needed in his theory of the artificial virtues to recognize the direct evaluation of the states of affairs in which this or that coordinated practice normally resulted, as well as the direct evaluation of the acts that it demanded. But independently of Hume's unreadiness or readiness to acknowledge that point, it was inevitable that his incipiently generalized conception of the foundational and natural virtue of benevolence should open the way to act evaluations that are not really virtue-centred at all. Suppose we begin by asking what one with this virtue is to be expected to feel or think about the piteous spectacle we began by describing. Such a person, we imagine, 'would resent the misery' of these unfortunates. Being not callous or insensible, he or she could scarcely help but consider what ought to be done by *whoever* can do anything—done *not* in the name of virtue as such but simply because of the plight of the victims. A virtuous thought of this sort waits solely on the moral quality of the situation itself. One who has played some part in the events that led to the terrible scene will owe more, no doubt, but every benevolent person—or every person (shall we say?), for it scarcely seems to matter whether 'benevolence' is mentioned or not—has to be ready to combine with others, or so it appears, in *some* alleviatory and/or preventive response.

This trend of thought, lying latent in Hume's moral philosophy, comes fully into its own with the emergence in the later eighteenth century and the early nineteenth century of a strong sense that the time has arrived for human society to seek to control all sorts of things not previously regarded as open to human control. At the same time, there is a new impulse to consider the law of one's country not as a given or as the settled background against which an agent's deliberation takes place, but as something with a social purpose that needs renewal and redirection:

> By the early institutions of Europe, property in land was a public function, created for certain public purposes and held under conditions of their fulfilment; and, as such, we predict, under the modification suited to modern society, it will again come to be considered. In this age . . . [it is impossible] to maintain an absolute right in an individual to an unrestricted control, a *jus utendi et abutendi,* over an unlimited quantity of the mere raw material of the globe, to which every other person could originally make out as good a natural title as himself. It will certainly not be much longer tolerated that agriculture should be carried on (as Coleridge expresses it) on the same principles as those of trade: 'that a gentleman should regard his estate as a merchant his cargo, or a shopkeeper his stock', that he should be allowed to deal with it as if it only existed to yield rent to him, not food to the hands that till it; and should have a right, and a right possessing all the sacredness of property, to turn them out by the hundred and make them perish on the high road. . . . It will soon be thought that a mode of property in land which has brought things to this pass has existed long enough. (J. S. Mill, *Essay on Coleridge,* 1840)

6.3. At the inception, in terms such as these, of various sorts of movement for social reform, a close student of Hume would have seen Hume's special, opportunistic, and explanatory use of the idea of utility, and the theoretical or genealogical aim that utility subserves in Humean 'moral science', transformed to subserve a newly systematic and prescriptive purpose. The student would also have seen Hume's account of what might be expected from possessors of the natural and artificial virtues merged with quite other thoughts,

thoughts which had their roots in Rousseau and Kant, in Kant's development of the Formula of Humanity, and in new ideas (loosely designated Romantic) that had closer links to idealism than to any empiricist philosophy. In a new framework of speculation, such ideas took on a practical importance that would have astonished social critics who were of Adam Smith's generation. In so far as this new practicality touches moral philosophy, the most distinctive feature of the new thinking was this: it strove to give an operationally applicable account of right action that would be *prior* to any characterization of good will, of virtues of character, or of other agent-centred things—an account that was to be set out entirely in terms of observable and secular consequences. An action or a policy or a measure (or whatever) will be deemed right if and only if it is conducive to the greatest happiness of the greatest number (Bentham); or else (losing the embarrassment of having a two-factor criterion, adverting both to quantity of happiness and to its distribution) an action will be deemed right if it is simply conducive (as J. S. Mill always said) to the greatest happiness, the happiness of each person being something that it is chiefly for him or her to work out and determine.[1]

Being less speculative than Hume's or Kant's philosophy and conditioned by a far greater sense of practical urgency, the new moral philosophy of Jeremy Bentham, James Mill, and James's son, John Stuart, came to be linked with a stupendous programme of social and political reform. As a result, moral philosophy became party to propaganda, persuasion, and political intrigue and agitation. At barely one remove, it involved itself (intimately at first and then simply by virtue of its conditioning influence) in campaigns for law reform, prison reform, adult suffrage, free trade, trade union legislation, public education, a free press, secret ballot, a civil service competitively recruited by public examination, the modernization of local government, the registration of titles to property in land, safety

---

1. These thoughts are variously prefigured in Hutcheson, Beccaria, Helvetius, Priestley, Godwin, and Paley, and various others, no doubt.

codes for merchant shipping, sanitation, preventive public medicine, smoke prevention, an Alkali Inspectorate, the collection of economic statistics, anti-monopoly legislation. . . . In sum, philosophical utilitarianism played a leading part in promoting indefinitely many of the things that we now take for granted in the modern world. Thus, both for good and for ill, and in a way that is almost as alien to our times as it would have been to the earlier eighteenth century, mainstream moral philosophy was brought into close contact with the reflections of practical jurists, economists, colonial administrators, civil servants, entrepreneurs, bankers. . . . Indeed John Stuart Mill and his father James Mill are figures in their own right under several of these heads—as earlier was Jeremy Bentham. Each of them spent a long period of his adult life in the employ of the East India Company.[2]

In having John Stuart Mill succeed Jeremy Bentham and James Mill as their advocate, the utilitarians were singularly fortunate. He had every gift that was needed to communicate into the main stream of English-speaking intellectual life the utilitarian version of new ideas and ideals of individual autonomy, creativity, and self-development. There were, of course, precursors for all of these ideas; but they are remade by Mill for his own age in an awareness of their romantic transformations that is at once anti-obscurantist, practical, and constantly alert against absurdity or metaphysical excess. Partly by virtue of the Mills' efforts, such ideas and ideals are another thing that we take for granted in the modern world. There will be something ungrateful, then—and unjust too when so many insights of John Stuart lie practically and even theoretically unheeded[3]—if we

2. For an account of the Indian connection, see Eric Stokes, *The English Utilitarians and India* (Oxford: Clarendon Press, 1959). See also *J. S. Mill's Encounter with India*, ed. M. I. Moir, D. M. Peers, and L. Zastoupil (Toronto: University of Toronto Press, 1999).

3. Not least among these are his ideas about work, ownership, and social and industrial organization, for instance, on which see *The Principles of Political Economy* (1848), bk IV, ch. 7, and his predictions of the abuses to which the less well-considered forms of democratic government will be especially prone, on which see *Considerations on Representative Government* (1861).

take for granted that which the utilitarians achieved in thought and action and subject certain foundational aspects of their moral philosophy to meticulous scrutiny. There will be yet more injustice in making so little further reference to the works already cited, especially to Mill's masterpiece *The Principles of Political Economy*, and in turning our attention to his minor work, *Utilitarianism*, which was not originally a book, still less a manual, but a sequence of three articles for *Fraser's Magazine* (October, November, and December 1861).

So far as concerns moral philosophy, there is no real alternative to such injustice. Mill's singular eloquence in the service of ideals of creativity, liberty, and self-development forcibly compels us to wonder what to think of that which has flowed in the real world from utilitarian philosophy's becoming our public philosophy. Do not the practical evils of the world now correspond rather closely to the theoretical deficiencies of the utilitarian creed? There are similar questions to ask about that which has resulted from past and present applications of the various disciplines of economics and social accountancy to which philosophical utilitarianism once gave its theoretical encouragement. Indeed, the more questionable some of these applications may begin to appear, the greater and more urgent is the necessity to scrutinize the first and most elementary steps by which utilitarianism sought to justify itself. How good a case has ever been made for these steps? Surely the emerging content of the position needs to be assessed in the light of the values that Mill himself drew upon in argument and persuasion. Even now, at the beginning of the twenty-first century, utilitarianism, with all its difficulties and equivocations, is still our public philosophy, however complicated or overlain by a new problematic of individual rights. If Mill saw now the overbearing acts and attitudes of some of the new 'partisans of utility' or if he were moved to try to diagnose utilitarianism's failure to identify and consolidate some proper basis for the longer-term defence of the interests of the destitute to which we see him paying heed in our second citation from the *Essay on Coleridge* (the defence of these interests against the very forces that utilitarianism has *itself* mustered or consolidated), then how could he disapprove of such an inquiry? How is it (one wonders) that, after the longest and most extensive practical test any philosophical principle has ever been granted, the principle of utility, once promoted as uniquely suitable for public, non-coercive moral and political debate, so far from bringing an end to the despotism against which Bentham railed, seems now to have replaced that despotism by new forms of 'oppression in the name of management' previously unheard of?[4] Mill would not distance himself from that question.

6.4. Because almost every doctrinal detail of Mill's *Utilitarianism* has been patiently and exhaustively commented upon elsewhere (not least the famous distinction of higher and lower pleasures by which he seeks to restore credibility to his starting point), we shall focus here almost exclusively on the foundations of Mill's theory—and then, in the next two lectures, on various new foundations that have been proposed for theories of a similar type. So we begin with Mill's account of what makes it right for someone to have done this or that at such and such a moment in such and such circumstances:

> The creed which accepts as the foundation of morality, Utility or the Greatest Happiness Principle, holds that actions are right in proportion as they tend to promote happiness, wrong as they tend to produce the reverse of happiness. By happiness is intended pleasure and the absence of pain; by unhappiness, pain and privation of pleasure. To give a clear view of the moral standard set up by the theory, much more requires to be said; in particular what things it includes in the ideas of pain and pleasure; and to what extent this is left an open question. But these supplementary explanations do not affect the theory of life on which this theory of morality is grounded—namely, that plea-

---

4. The phrase is Simone Weil's. For documentation of the anti-despotic Benthamite argument for the principle of utility, see Stephen Darwall's illuminating essay, 'Hume and the Invention of Utilitarianism', in *Hume and Hume's Connexions*, ed. M. A. Stewart and J. P. Wright (Edinburgh: Edinburgh University Press, 1994), pp. 74-6.

sure, and freedom from pain, are the only things desirable as ends; and that all desirable things (which are as numerous in the utilitarian as in any other scheme) are desirable either for the pleasure inherent in themselves or as means to the promotion of pleasure and the prevention of pain. (*Utilitarianism,* ch. 2, second paragraph)

Roughly speaking, the rightness of acts (their obligatoriness or permissibility) is explained in terms of the good, which turns out to be the goodness exclusively of outcomes as more or less pre-ethically described. Thus the Utility Principle is *teleological,* as some put it; it founds rightness in some goal that is taken to be the direct or indirect *telos* of each or every act.[5] In Hume, by contrast, the explanatory-cum-genealogical account of morality leaves him room to see moral terms as *sui generis,* allowing the right and the good to be mutually irreducible.[6] (In Lecture 3, we commended this as the proper conclusion for a mature moral philosophy.) In Kant, deontological notions were elucidated by reference to the good will; but the good will consisted *inter alia* in a certain attitude to the

5. Cp. John Rawls, *A Theory of Justice* (Cambridge, Mass.: Harvard University Press, 1972), p. 24, where he defines teleological theories as theories in which 'the good is defined independently from the right and then the right is defined as that which maximizes the good. More precisely, those institutions and acts are right which produce the most good'.

6. Regimenting things a little, we might say that for Hume an act will be right if either it is permissible, because it is the sort of act a virtuous person might do, or it is obligatory, because it is the sort of act a virtuous person would not fail to do—an act of fidelity, kindness, or whatever. In a modern ethics of virtue that puts the person and his moral attributes at the theoretical and practical centre of all other ethical attributions, such a formulation might be intended to explain obligation in terms of virtue. But the reader will recall that, in Hume's own account, all reference to the person with virtue or personal merit and to that person's conduct involves some essential reference back to the pleasure or displeasure that others will feel at the 'view' of an agent doing or not doing such and such an act. Nothing prevents such a feeling of displeasure or pleasure from involving us in thoughts about what an agent *ought* or *ought not* to abstain from doing. These connections, in so far as conceptual, will obstruct any project of reduction or subsumption. (As for the pleasure or displeasure that is in question, what is at issue here is not a project of maximizing pleasure and minimizing displeasure, but only Hume's concern with the thing that the pleasure or displeasure arises from the thought of.)

moral law and its *requirements*. An act is right or in accord with the law either by virtue of being required by the moral law or else by virtue of its non-performance not being required by the law. Here too nothing is reductive of the morally right. In the sense of 'teleological' just introduced (the sense first regularized in moral philosophy by John Rawls), Kant's account of rightness concedes even less to the teleological than Hume's does.

So Bentham and Mill really do mark something new in our story. Furthermore, because the rightness of an act now depends on the goodness of its outcome, and the goodness of outcomes depends on happiness, and happiness depends on pleasure and pain, rightness is tied now to something testable or would-be operational. The 'principles of morals', which Hume had sought to render intelligible, nineteenth-century utilitarianism seeks to demystify entirely—only continuing, it should be said, the trend already evident in such dicta of the later Enlightenment as Helvetius': 'ethics is the agriculture of the mind.'

Every sane moral philosopher since the beginning of the subject has had regard for outcomes and consequences. Few have needed to be reminded how many ordinary verbs of action depend for the elucidation of their sense upon allusion to the aim or purpose and/or the intendable outcome of doing the act that the verb stands for. The thing that is new about Utilitarianism is not to have dwelt on consequences—consequences really are nobody's monopoly—but to have sought to fix the extension of the predication 'acts rightly' *purely in terms of consequences,* and the sort of consequences that we find enumerated in Mill and Bentham. It is this heritage that it bequeaths to its modern inheritor, namely consequentialism. (See Lecture 8.)

From the outset, let us be as clear as we can about this point. If an ethical argument appeals to outcomes, that need not make it into a utilitarian or a consequentialist argument. It is only utilitarian or consequentialist if it *disallows* substantive reference to unreduced ethical and agential ideas. It is only utilitarian or consequentialist if it is the kind of argument you would be apt to put forward if you thought that all rightness was to be determined *exclusively* by reference to the valuation of outcomes. To appeal in the ordinary way, deploying the full range of ethical notions to all the effects that doing such and such an act will have, or to point out what if anything is so good or bad about these effects will not, in itself, commit us to anything utilitarian or consequentialist at all. There is widespread and needless confusion about this. You will have to forgive me when, in subsequent lectures, I point this out again and again.

6.5. The second matter that Mill's official formulation draws to notice is a question of interpretation. In our citation from chapter 2 of *Utilitarianism*, what is it that 'tends to promote happiness. . . . or produce the reverse of happiness'? Strictly speaking, it might seem that anything that can *tend* thus or so or can have such and such a tendency must be something of which there can be instances, namely a *kind* of action, or, as I should say, an act. (As they figure in strict English parlance, acts are universal things, things that can be done by different people at different times and places. Persons' doings of these acts are their actions. See Lecture 4, n. 8.) If we go by these indications, it may appear that the creed that Mill speaks of must say something like this: an action is right in so far as actions *of that kind* tend to promote happiness. . . . So is that what Mill meant?[7]

As an interpretation of the particular sentence cited from chapter 2, we shall not sustain this suggestion. But this kind of reading would have fitted well with the classic statement by the jurist John Austin of a position now called rule utilitarianism: 'Our rules would be fashioned on utility, and our conduct on our rules.' There is much

7. Or else, grappling with the indeterminacy that results from the fact that there are indefinitely many acts (kinds of action) that any one action or doing may exemplify (far more than could be singled out for encouragement or discouragement by a single rule), the creed which Mill speaks of should say that an action is right in so far as all the acts that the action is the doing of are in accordance with rules whose general adoption produces more happiness than does the adoption of any rival rule. Does anyone want to say that *that* is what Mill meant? I am not sure. Would the attribution be made more credible if the word 'intentional' were inserted before 'doing'?

For further material that might seem to enlarge the case for such interpretations, see Mill's essay, 'Whewell's Moral Philosophy', in *Collected Works,* ed. John Robson (Toronto: University of Toronto Press, 1961–91), vol. X, pp. 165–70.

in Mill that would accord with this reading, but that does not prove that this is the correct interpretation of the foundational sentence we quoted. And it is precisely where Mill comes closest to writing in the spirit of John Austin and insists on the importance of what he (Mill) called 'secondary principles' that we see best how he must have supposed he was directing us to interpret the key sentence. See the last three paragraphs of chapter 2 of *Utilitarianism*. Here Mill says that even the rule of veracity ('sacred' though it is and 'transcendent' as it is 'in point of general expediency')

> admits of possible exceptions. . . . But in order that the excep-
> tion may not extend itself beyond the need . . . it ought to be
> recognised and its limits defined; and if the principle of utility
> is good for anything it must be good for weighing these con-
> flicting utilities against one another and marking out the regime
> within which one or the other preponderates.

Here it seems that the principle of utility we began by quoting must arbitrate this question of exceptions. It also seems that, in order to do that, the principle of utility needs to apply directly to the actual or putative doing here and now of such and such an act of deception or unveracity or whatever, taken together with all the consequences of *that* doing. This is confirmed, moreover, by the claim in the last paragraph of *Utilitarianism* to the effect that 'if utility is the ultimate source of moral obligations [the obligations, that is, which may be supposed to result from the application of subordinate/secondary/ Austinian principles], utility may be invoked to decide between them when their demands are incompatible. Though the application of the standard may be difficult, it is better than none at all'. If this statement is anything to go by, then it is to actions that Mill intended the principle of utility which we began by citing to be applied. It follows that, whatever else it says, Mill's official position is action utilitarian or (in the cant phrase, which confuses acts with actions, but it is much too late to do anything about that now) *act utilitarian*.

What then about the Austinian or rule utilitarian tendencies that are visible in Mill, and what about the passages where he seems to be in accord with John Austin's formulation? The explanation for these passages is that Mill proceeds as if, in addition to propounding a principle of utility for the rightness of actions, he is *also* proposing a principle of utility for the evaluation of all sorts of other items, namely policies, practices, measures, reforms, rules, etc.—a principle that is confined neither to rightness nor to actions. Indeed this was precisely what Bentham had done in his *Principles of Morals and Legislation*, section 9:

> A man may be said to be a partisan of the principle of utility *when the approbation or disapprobation he annexes to any action or to any measure* is decided by the proportioned tendency which he conceives it to have to augment or diminish the happiness of the community.[8]

Mill proceeds as if his own rule of rightness were simply the central case of the more general principle, ranging more widely than doings in the here and now of particular acts, which Bentham calls the principle of utility.

If this is the correct interpretation of his intention, then what status would Mill ascribe to rules that passed the test of utility? Their status must be that their adoption assists in the whole business of promoting utility. If these or those rules are adopted, then their adoption will create expectations that it is beneficial to promote. The value of these expectations and the cost of their disappointment will itself register upon that total utility in the light of which judgments are passed on particular actions. It will promote utility to create and safeguard expectations of this kind; but the status of the expectations does not exceed their status as inputs to the calculation of utility.

---

8. Here, where the partisan is a legislator, the idea of action embraces 'measures' and their indefinitely numerous enforcements, which last can create a tendency, in the ordinary sense of 'tendency'.

6.6. I believe that this is the correct interpretation. But here begins a double-mindedness about rules that has simultaneously fascinated the spectators of utilitarianism and enraged its critics. For every moral norm or moral expectation can now present itself under two aspects. There is the aspect it presents to a committed adherent of the norm, who will *not* reflect that the principle in question is only a 'secondary principle' or a principle subordinated to the principle of utility. There is also the aspect it presents to the 'partisan' of the principle of utility. In the eyes of the partisan, the point of the rule comes down to the fact that its adoption serves a utility-promoting purpose which will impinge on outcomes. Sometimes though, under this aspect, utility (which is the rationale for the rule) will be so appreciably diminished by the disutility of not here breaking the rule that the consideration of utility must *override* the normative meaning that an ordinary agent will attribute to observance of the rule. The thing that counts with the act-utilitarian theorist is a comparison between the overall utility that will result from the agent's sticking to the promise and the overall utility of his not doing so, including within the computation of the second, as one item among others, such things as the net cost, all told, of the disappointment of expectations. Contrast with this the thought of one who is an adherent to the norm: if he promised and the person to whom he promised, has a corresponding expectation, then the thing that matters is the *legitimacy* of the expectation.

6.7. So much then for the content of the principle of utility; so much in bare outline for the kind of framework Mill proposes to erect upon it; and so much for double-mindednesss (to which we shall return). The first question we face is why as moral philosophers, or as moral subjects, *we* should become partisans of the principle. Why should we think that the principle is true or prepare ourselves to accept it? And why should we expect such a principle to have the slightest rational sway over ordinary rational beings or moral agents? What claim does it make on either their reason or anything else? Compare question (B) at 1.1.

Mill has several ways of seeking to persuade us. First, he tries to represent in his chapter 4 that our commitment to our own happiness commits us to the principle of utility. Secondly, Mill can echo the sort of thing Bentham says, for example: 'When a man attempts to combat the principle of utility, it is with reasons drawn, without his being aware of it, from that very principle itself' (Bentham, *Principles of Morals and Legislation*, sect. 13). Whether or not we *believe* that we believe the principle, Bentham and Mill will say we do in practice believe it already. It is implicit, they will seek to claim, in the way in which we waive or qualify the operation of moral rules.

Thirdly, Mill has the thought that, when it is taken together with its Benthamite gloss, 'each to count for one and none for more than one', the principle represents a definitionally truistic application of an arithmetical truism.[9]

6.8.   The first of these lines of argument runs as follows:

If the end which the utilitarian doctrine proposes to itself were not in theory and in practice acknowledged to be an end, nothing could ever convince any person that it was so. No reason can be given why the general happiness is desirable except that each person, so far as he believes it to be attainable, desires his own happiness. This being a fact, we have all the proof the case admits of that happiness is a good, that each person's happiness is a good to that person, and that the general happiness therefore a good to the aggregate of persons.

Where an argument is sought for the conclusion that the general happiness is something each of us should see as the good or see as the source of everything it is our duty to strive for, the argument in question ought not to depend on an inferential transition from the

9. See here the claims Mill makes in the footnote to ch. 5, where he says that 'happiness and desirable are synonymous terms' and that 'the truths of arithmetic are applicable to the valuation of happiness, as of all other measurable quantities'.

For Bentham's actual words, see the text referenced at n. 10.

concern that each of us has with our own happiness to a concern that is had by an entity that one concerned with his or her own happiness might not yet care about, namely 'the aggregate of persons'. It is true that Mill's argument does have the great virtue of attempting to connect the concern each of us has for our own happiness with the general happiness—something Bentham had never really attempted (speaking, as he always did, only for the legislator). Without Mill's reference to the said aggregate, however, there would not even be the appearance of an argument. Worse yet, even that appearance is dispersed so soon as we adduce a Benthamite explanation (*Principles of Morals and Legislation,* sect. 4): 'the interest of the community then is what?—the sum of the interests of the several members who compose it' (and *only* the sum of those interests).

Mill might say to a convinced Humean: 'You were prepared to accept it as fact that human beings have benevolence. Why then do you seek to confine my position to a starting point in self-love?' Reply: your argument seems to start from self-love. You could begin again from benevolence. Nothing prevents. But then you would need to show something that is far from obvious, namely that adherence to the principle of utility is what benevolence amounts to. But that will be hard to show. Look at what your principle demands. Note also that it is inconsistent with the first-order Humean morality that Hume founded in benevolence and redirections of same.

6.9. The second argument is implausible. When we explain why we should refrain from keeping a promise where keeping it will bring harm, our explanation does not need to extend to considerations of 'the happiness of the community' or to the augmentation of utility. It suffices for the explanation to invoke our relation to the beneficiary and the beneficiary's presumed wishes, or else to invoke the independently evident duty of everyone (including the putative beneficiary) not to cause various specific kinds of harm. The act-utilitarian thought which Mill thinks we invoke in our justification for not keeping a promise offers only a wildly inaccurate version of a sane person's attitude to a promise. You do not need to be a partisan of the principle of utility to be against harm! You do not need to be such a partisan to be prepared to appreciate the cumulative effect of several harms. (See again 6.4, third and fourth paragraphs.)

Consider now Mill's attempt, under the same general heading, to ground justice in utility or happiness, taking the claims of justice for perfect obligations under moral and social rules and taking the rules in question to be rules that pass the test of utility. It may be claimed that, even if Mill's purpose is different from Hume's (as we already have said), Mill's account of such matters simply corrects and supplements Hume's.

Taking Hume's account in Hume's terms, that might be accepted or contested, but Hume cannot help Mill here. For the question here is whether Mill's account constitutes a *successful reduction* (something Hume would not offer) of the rightness of acts of justice to their contribution to utility—that is, a successful subsumption of the first under the second of these things. And surely it does not. At best Mill reduces justice to rules, utility, and the attributes that rules need to have in order to qualify as rules of justice, e.g. that of being such that they can be seen by their putative participants as rules they can consent to. Even if we may hope for Mill's sake that this being 'such that participants can consent to them' does not demand (or simply come down to) their being 'fair' or 'just', Mill comes nowhere near to subsuming our concern for justice under the simple concern for utility or reducing the rightness of an act of justice to its claim to be the act that it is most felicific to do. He comes nowhere near, then, to demonstrating that the concern itself that we have for justice is revealed as some alias for our concern for the greatest happiness. Justice is not *absorbed* without residue into utility in the way that is required for the defence of Mill's account of rightness.

Mill was no stranger to such worries. His usual way of disposing of them is to say that, when we choose under some other head than happiness, we are choosing the thing in question as a *part* of human happiness:

If human nature is so constituted as to desire nothing which is not either a part of human happiness or a means of happiness ... then happiness is the sole end of human conduct and the promotion of it the test by which to judge of human conduct ... If this doctrine be true, the principle of utility is proved. (*Utilitarianism*, ch. 4, para. 8)

Here, however, as is well known, Mill makes a fallacious transition of the form 'W desires X (money, virtue or whatever) and X is a part of Z (e.g. happiness); therefore W desires Z and W desires X *as part of* Z'. His argument also has the effect of stirring up obscurer questions, about whether everything that is a part of happiness is even consistent with everything else that is. If not, then it seems doubly wrong to represent everything that is desired for itself as desired in the name of happiness.

6.10. The third argument remains. This is to the effect that it is a definitional truism, an analytic truth or analogous to an arithmetical truth, that 'actions are right in proportion as they tend to promote happiness'. What else (people are apt to say) could make an act right? But to this question one will be tempted to reply by asking where to find a non-question-begging analysis of the various terms involved which would vindicate the claim. Adapting the famous 'open question' argument by which G. E. Moore hoped to show that good was not equivalent to any natural property of things—his *Principia Ethica* (1903) may be read as a conceptual, as well as moral, protest against the all-consuming scientism into which utilitarianism conspired with Darwinism (not Darwin) to lead so much nineteenth-century ethics—one will be moved to insist that, even if an act promotes happiness, that leaves it an *open question* whether the act is right. Suppose that the action consisted of exterminating, to universal relief, some hideous person who was widely feared and detested (on plausible-seeming grounds) by all other human beings even though (as was never going to be known) he or she was in fact totally harmless. Would such an extermination be right? Is it not strange to suppose that *this* could be consequence of an analytic truth?

If the utility or greatest happiness principle is not an analytic or conceptual truth, is it then the summation of something that we already believe or a principle that makes such a new and enlivening sense of such a mass of things we already believe that we can embrace it as correcting and systematizing those beliefs? Well, even if we decide that this sort of status would suffice, the prospects of utilitarianism appear quite bleak—as the last example cited seems already to illustrate. It is true that Bentham insists that, in the reckoning of happiness, 'Every individual in the country tells for one; no individual for more than one'[10] but all that this ruling secures, once we read it literally and as it was intended to be read, namely tautologically, is that, in any reckoning of happiness, it makes no difference whose pleasure is in question. That does not prevent the widespread pleasure that is experienced at the disappearance of the harmless but hateful person from vastly outweighing the victim's objections to being hunted down and exterminated or vastly outweighing the loss of his or her pleasures to the sum of pleasures.[11]

6.11. The principle of utility is very far then from being a summation of our convictions. If the principle's status is no more than that of such a summation and its achievement is in fact much less than such, and if it casts little or no light on the nature of those convictions, then the case for accepting it is very weak. Indeed there is no case. After all, Kantians have their own way of understanding those convictions, and, nearer to home, so do the adherents of

10. *Rationale of Judicial Evidence,* bk 8, ch. 29, *The Works of Jeremy Bentham,* ed. J. Bowring (Edinburgh, 1843), vol. VII, p. 334.

11. It is strange, but the loss of the victim's pleasures to the sum of pleasures *is* one of the things the theory is obliged to count as relevant to the matter. Let the reader hold fast here to his or her sense, if s/he has such a sense, that *that* loss cannot be the real objection to the extermination of the victim. Who, by the way, is going to feel that loss?

Hume. Kantians and Humeans can do far better justice to them. The Humeans, for instance, taking one cue from Aristotle and another from the secularism of the Enlightenment, are at liberty to rehearse in their own way their own version of the belief, not inimical to Bentham or Mill, that considerations of human happiness, human need, and human harm and flourishing do indeed shape in divers ways the divers norms of feeling and action that make up the whole formation of a person possessed of the natural and artificial virtues. It will not follow from this, a Humean will say, that the whole import of that formation can be spelled out in terms that can be vindicated before the bar of utility, this being conceived as the utilitarians conceive it. Nor does it follow that that import can be spelled out into a principle, or finite set of principles, to determine rightness in acting simply by reference to happiness or satisfaction or need, or flourishing, or whatever—still less into a set that can be correctly summarized by a principle of utility.

6.12. In the face of examples and difficulties such as we have appealed to, the modern utilitarian is certain to respond by insisting that, when he advances the principle of utility, he has always been prepared to include within the outcome of an action the *quality of the act* that is done in producing the result that is in question. First, let the rule against intentional killing (for instance) be tested before the bar of utility. It will surely pass that test, he says. Then let the disutility of breaking that rule and the bad character of the act of doing this be counted among the consequences of exterminating the harmless but hateful person. Under these conditions, he may say, the chances are that troublesome examples such as the one we have instanced will disappear altogether. On these terms, he may insist, there is a very good chance of restoring something like Mill's official position—even the position that is set out in the footnote to chapter 5 of *Utilitarianism:*

What is the principle of utility if it be not that 'happiness' and 'desirable' are synonymous terms? If there is any anterior principle implied, it can be no other than this, that the truths of arithmetic are applicable to the valuation of happiness, as of all other measurable quantities.

There is more than one way of implementing this defence of act utilitarianism. But the difficulty with the one in front of us is that, so soon as some definite value is given to the utility of the rule against killing not being broken here (where it is entirely certain, suppose, that the harmlessness of the person will never be ascertained and never bring public discredit upon the decision to exterminate him), it will be easy to imagine that so many people will be overjoyed at the victim's death that the mass of their pleasures swamps the disutility of breaking the rule.[12] Utilitarianism not only lacks any convincing answer to our question (B). Its conceptual impoverishment condemns it to fail also under the heading (A) set out at 1.1. The trouble is that its conceptual impoverishment was (and still is) all of a piece with its iconoclastic appeal. If a fuller range of moral concepts were restored to the position, how could it defend any simple principle of utility?

By way of illustration of such difficulties, and for the sake of having an example that is not very contentious, I return over and over again to the same sort of case. Needless to say, not all examples need to be of this kind. In fact there are indefinitely many different kinds of example that bring out the pitilessness and remorselessness of the position that 'moral theory' has seen itself as constructing upon the foundation of benevolence (of all things).[13] But my thought is that,

12. Are we being pedantic here? Well, if it amounts to pedantry to object in these terms to a rule whose simplicity and obviousness was meant to be part of its appeal for anti-obscurantist persons, yes, it is pedantry. But blame this pedantry on that which created the need for it.

13. There are numerous examples by which to illustrate: utilitarianism's almost undiscriminating endorsement of the imperatives of industrial development, for instance, or its endorsement in practice of the harsh usage of indigenous or nomadic people who are denied their title to the use of the lands on which their life depends. Implicitly or explicitly it has been endlessly involved in the eviction or resettlement of peasants or others who have been judged to stand in the way of economic progress, etc., etc. Such

in dissuading the reader from espousing utilitarianism, I have first to persuade him or her to read Mill's proposal literally, then to expose the dearth of grounds to accept the proposal, then to pit uncontroversial examples against it, and *only then* to urge the reader to purge his/her convictions of that which is owed to the legacy of utilitarian thinking. That legacy is not (I claim) coeval or coextensive with morality itself. Rather it is at odds with the rest of our pre-philosophical ethical inheritance, which will suggest that, where there really is an economic or other necessity to do some evil thing, the evil should be avowed as such an evil, and the necessity for it (where this really exists) *vindicated* (if it can be) *as a necessity.*

6.13.   Back now to where we were before it seemed necessary to digress about examples. There is another and quite different way in which the utilitarian can defend his position. On the basis of a new appreciation of the strength and durability of the sort of example that is being opposed to him, the defender may search for some *extra principle* which (unlike tautological claims to the effect that each is to count for one and none for more than one) shall enforce a proper attention to the question of *who* is to bear the burdens of the pursuit of utility or receive the benefits that are to be maximized.

It would be hard to exaggerate the disruption this move would inflict upon the position we began with. The first difficulty would be to draft this extra principle as one principle. Shall the new principle follow the sort of slogan that makes one notable appearance in Karl Marx's *Critique of the Gotha Programme* (1875) and stipulate 'from each according to his ability, to each according to his need'? If so, then one trouble will be that it is not clear how to characterize

---

examples are as invaluable in illustration of the content of utilitarianism as they are revealing of the width of the lacuna over which it is still hoped, no doubt, to extend some new conception of rights. But *persuasively* or *dialectically* these other examples are usually ineffectual, because such a considerable proportion of readers will lack any basis in thought or feeling to resist the 'sad necessity' to sacrifice various vital human interests—well, indigenous, nomadic, or peasant interests, anyway—to 'economic' imperatives. (But see 9.8, 9.9.) That is the only reason why I return over and over again to an uninteresting but more or less uncontentious example.

the full ethical significance of 'needs' in strictly utilitarian terms. Even if this was achieved, however, at some considerable conceptual cost, there would still remain the chief difficulty, namely the problem of mediating between this extra principle and the principle of utility, which would otherwise, in the absence of the extra principle, have called for happiness (or welfare or the satisfaction of desire . . .) to be maximized. In a trice, we are back with the intuitionism that Bentham and the Mills so openly despised in the moral philosophy of so many of their predecessors.

If the abilities/needs principle will not help, shall the principle of utility be regulated instead by a principle of equality? And, if so, how is this to be drafted? Are things to be set up in such a way that everyone is to end up with the same disposable income (say)— or the same effective income (say)—regardless of their criminality, their laziness, their unbenevolence, or their undeservingness? And regardless, too, of their particular responsibilities? If not, if something subtler is demanded, then how can the second principle help but subdivide itself into a whole cluster of principles that are intended to recapitulate all the divers ideas of need, entitlement, or desert over which every human civilization has contended? These are ideas which Aristotle, Hume, Kant, and countless other moral philosophers have attempted to systematize. Their efforts have not been in vain, but the outcome has not been a principle that can run alongside the principle of utility. At best, 'equality' or 'equal concern for each person' can only be a place-holder. If such an open-ended collection of notions is to regulate the working of the principle of utility, however, then we are back once again with the difficulty that we found before. Worse, some among these notions actively subvert that utilitarian principle. In fact, it is becoming more and more evident that the curtain is coming down, not only on Bentham's and the other utilitarians' contemptuous dismissal of the pluralism and intuitionism that characterized the creeds of the 'unreasoning race of bigots', but on the very idea of such a position's counting as a serious rival for Humeanism or Kantism.[14]

_____

14. It is no wonder then, that sensing the threat of any such pluralistic disorder,

6.14. We shall look in the next two lectures at two other sources of argument for positions akin to act utilitarianism. But up to now no sufficient reason at all has appeared for us to consider moving across to embrace that which act utilitarianism offers under the heads (A) or (B) of 1.1 (or their variants at 1.12). It is not a summation of our convictions and it offers us no reason to alter our convictions. Moreover, by its double-mindedness, already complained of, this position, which purports to concern itself with the welfare of human beings, prescribes a moral regime that threatens agents of virtuous formation with an uncomfortable alienation between their moral sentiments and the acts that are expected of them by the utilitarians. In a variety of ways and a diversity of connections, the point was made with force and brilliance by Bernard Williams.[15]

In conclusion, I shall emphasize in 6.15 and 6.16 two differences between utilitarianism and the position of Hume. Bentham and Mill seem to have taken Hume for an amiable friend and forerunner of their own position—a sort of proto-utilitarian. But this is yet another reflection of these philosophers' and their successors' settled incapacity to keep track of the ideas or conceptual resources to which different positions in moral philosophy must either preserve their entitlement, or else (in the case of reductive and teleological positions such as the utilitarian one) establish their entitlement.

6.15. Let us return to the double-mindedness we adverted to in 6.6. The Humean norm for promising (or fidelity or repaying what is owed or . . .) proves itself, where it does prove itself, by the good results of the system that consists in observance of this norm. It is approval of the results of its operations that explains the persistence

---

exponents of the art of economic evaluation always prefer to stay with the principle of utility and give some special 'weighting' to the benefits that they calculate will be awarded to 'the poor', however arbitrary this method of weighting may be, rather than to qualify the pursuit of a maximum in ways that will respect patterns of slum-dwellers' or peasants' or indigenous people's life, dwelling, or land-holding that experts or consultants see as standing in the way of whatever they denominate progress.

15. See Williams in J. J. C. Smart and Bernard Williams, *Utilitarianism: For and Against* (New York: Cambridge University Press, 1973); Amartya Sen and Bernard Williams, eds., *Utilitarianism and Beyond* (New York: Cambridge University Press, 1982).

of the norm. But, by *this* account, the norm remains what it is—namely the norm inherent to promising—even for those who theorize about its origin. Those who live by such a norm live by it as *their* norm. Attributing moral beauty to it, they are not open to afterthoughts about utility. They do not need to consider different and rival norms that might result in different demands upon them. Even where they do have ideas about the aetiology of their own norm, their aetiological thoughts will not and need not affect their account of what they expect of themselves as agents.[16]

This is not to say that Humeanism will take no interest in the case where the thing that will result from following the norm seems on a given occasion disastrous, and where agents are unable to persist in the norm as a proper thing for them to do. Even here, however, where a moral dialectic enters the scene, there will be no concession to Utilitarianism. When the virtuous agent fends off the disaster that might flow from his keeping his promise, he simply allows consideration of that disaster, potentially of his own making, to eclipse in a piecemeal way the ugliness of his breaking his promise. At the same time, he resolves to do whatever else he can do in recognition of the legitimacy of the beneficiary's expectation that the promise would be kept. In this matter, he does not need to appeal to the sum of utilities. Indeed he needs not to attempt such a thing, because a non-utilitarian philosophical account of promising does not encourage the agent to see promise-keeping as depending for its force on the utility of the system of observance. Rather, it encourages the agent to see the norm for what it is, namely a norm by which he conducts ordinary life with others, one whose infraction he sees as morally base and ugly. Such a norm will also give to the agent the thought that it, the norm, is not meant either to harm the person for whose benefit it here applies or to contravene the concerns that it is fair to impute to that beneficiary him/herself if s/he is to be a worthy beneficiary of the norm. Among these concerns will be the

16. Unless of course the aetiology reveals a norm or custom to be absurd—which is not the case with the norm of promise-keeping. Rather, the aetiology places the norm in the life that agents are living already and justifies it *there*.

concern that the life that these norms uphold be not maimed or subverted.

In so far as the Humean account attempts more than to describe the origin and nature of our moral ideas, it refuses any one-off determination of what it is to act rightly and, in effect, it bids the agent to follow the second or acquired nature that his ethical formation has imparted to him—something he can perfectly well do even if he is led by Hume to see that his second nature is a historically conditioned development of his original nature. In short, Hume is not a proto-Benthamite or a proto-J. S. Mill. He is a genealogist who is, in addition, *committed* to that which he explains—prepared that is, when enough of the pieces are falling into place, to try to vindicate most (but certainly not all) of the attitudes and convictions he seeks to explain. I repeat it, Mill's and Bentham's purpose is something altogether new in our story.

6.16.   The other contrast between the Humean view and utilitarianism concerns the notion of utility. For the utilitarians, 'utility' leads straight to the idea of the greater or greatest good overall. In Hume, by contrast, the term 'utility' simply refers at any given point in his genealogical story to the *good that is in question in a given set-up or situation,* the set-up or situation that he is describing. In a sense, this is an all-purpose or general notion: the notion of *the good that is at issue.* It is applicable, that is, to *any* given set-up. (Compare the expressions 'one's father', 'one's family', 'an agent's purpose in acting'.) But it is only a *determinable,* one might say, which stands ready to receive determination in a context, once such a context is specified. In that context, Humeanism will commend the deployment of the full range of moral ideas that are applicable there.

If this is right, then it is evident that we must distinguish between the Humean, unproblematic, universally available notion of *the good for a given context* (context to be specified) and the would-be universal notion of *the good for any context,* alias *the good for each and every context,* alias *the greater or greatest good* or *the universal good.* In any given context, we can easily find what falls under the first (or determinable) notion. It is far from obvious, however, that any-thing at all must answer to the second. Nothing like that is guar-anteed. It is the second, moreover, that utilitarian doctrine needs to bring into consideration. Once a general rule for right action is to be propounded, and happiness or pleasure or satisfaction . . . is used to give content to the rule, it is only to be expected that the prescribed outcome should become the aggregate of all happiness or the sum of all pleasures had by anybody or a sum of satisfactions—and never mind if this seemed, before the theory came onto the scene, a most un-likely object of moral striving.[17] Has not the time arrived (I keep on saying) to abandon the project of having a general rule?

The utilitarian's new conception of utility leads out into other problems. Starting with human happiness, pleasures, and pains, as if in general, he finds himself compelled, little by little, by the force of that which he discovers himself saying, to extend his conception to embrace the pleasures and pains of all the people who will exist or who may come to exist *if* such and such happens. (Taking fright at that, he will probably try to discount these, on principles that create mysteries of their own, according to distance in time.) He is also forced by the maximizing project into questions about the dif-ference between the pleasures or pains of human beings and those of other creatures. Equally inexorably, or so it seems, he will be forced into questions about the standards for comparing the huge mass of pleasures of a population just above the bread line with the mass of pleasures that is made up of the larger pleasures of a much smaller population. From the outset it then seems that he finds him-

---

17. No doubt it will be open to the utilitarian to try to build up from Hume's conception of utility to successively larger conceptions of utility for larger and larger contexts arrived at by enlarging initial contexts and aggregating the interests that are at stake in each. That would be a sound enough procedure—not least because it would force the would-be enlarger to face over and over again the question whether any such aggregation of interests can home on a relation with the formal properties of 'better than'.

For a rehearsal of some of the groundless assumptions that tempt those who think that such a relation *must* be available or who lose sight of the onus of proof (which rests with those who aver in each case that the relation is available), see my 'Incom-mensurability: Four Proposals', which figures now as ch. 10 of *Needs, Values, Truth* (amended 3rd ed., Oxford: Oxford University Press, 2002).

self confronted with questions about *how many people there ought to be.*[18] That question, indefatigably explored by Derek Parfit in his book *Reasons and Persons,*[19] can be avoided by insisting that what should be summed is not total happiness but average happiness. But proceeding in the same style of ratiocination brings problems of its own. As Ronald Dworkin has pointed out, it means that, where there is a population comprising a number of people who have less than average happiness (e.g. by virtue of lapsing into later middle age or old age), their death will raise the sum of well-being! The moral I draw is that we do better to draw back and retreat to Hume's notion of utility.

Apart from these issues, there is another kind of problem. In trying to consolidate Mill's foundational conviction that utility is something measurable, the theorist is forced by the whole discipline of devising general theories of value and valuation—or so the history of utility theory suggests—to replace the notion of pleasure by that of benefit, and then to gloss benefit in terms of the satisfaction of desire. The original idea of utility is supplanted by the easier and apparently more promising idea that there is some as-if mathematical function which each given 'consumer' seeks to maximize in his personal pursuit of his 'tastes' and which can be given the characteristics it needs to have in order to define an ordering of more and less. In the first instance, this function is posited (we are told) because the hypothesis that it exists is meant to have implications that observation can support or contradict. It is meant to yield predictions about observable behaviour.

In practice, however, very little thought has gone into setting out the empirical or other credentials *of the claim itself* (the dogma, I

18. I do not say these are not questions at all. But surely they lie a million miles from the ethical concerns that one might have thought to lie at the first foundation of the subject. Every question of this sort deserves to be taken on its merits. But if that is to happen, the subject matter of moral philosophy needs to have been understood as a going concern, possessed of its own, autonomous modes of reasoning, well in advance of questions of these kinds coming into consideration or seeking to draw upon its conceptual resources. The thing that is hard to bear is for the sense of the would-be first principles to have to *wait on* the answer to population questions!

19. Oxford: Oxford University Press, 1984.

venture to call it) that there *must,* for each consumer, be some such function embracing not only his transactions in the market place but *everything* that he values.[20] Evidence is not sought for that—because it is the thing that is simply assumed. Far more consideration has been given to the empirical or other credentials of the idea that, provided that the utilities of different persons can be compared, there must be some overarching function the maximization of which integrates the welfare functions of each and every consumer. Apparently, though, it no longer matters whether there is or there isn't such a thing as utility, or whether there is or isn't such an overarching function. It no longer matters whether the definitions of these things are creative (either in the accountants' sense or in the logicians' sense, each sense being fully pertinent in its own way).[21] It no longer matters how well or badly newly received notions of utility can engage with a well-considered philosophical position of utilitarianism and whether such a position can be put back together and defended. For an intellectual industry has come into being which produces tens of thousands of pages every year and has refined a myriad subtle thoughts about how to maximize this or that measurable whatever-it-is and how to trade off quantities of it against quantities of something else which is also available in the market place.

The role of the moral philosopher is not (I should suggest) to butt his or her head into these transactions or perpetuate the intellectual phantasmagoria to which they relate, but to keep his distance and point to the *sheer arbitrariness* of the thoughts from which all this has originated (the total failure to consider other conceptions of deliberation and choice). The philosopher's office is to point to the human and conceptual cost of disfiguring and thrusting into the said

20. The claim suggests, among other things, that each and every thing is commensurable with any or everything else. Beware of making such a claim vacuous by saying that its truth follows from the bare fact that always, if he has to, the agent chooses. See sect. VI of my 'Nature, Respect for Nature, and the Human Scale of Values', *Proceedings of the Aristotelian Society* 100 (2000–1).

21. See 1.13, n. 12.

market place precious, intuitive, ethical notions that are immanent in the practices of an ordinary life which might, for all the utilitarians and their inheritors care, have been happier and more contented if it had been organized around the fireplace (this can stand or fall as an empirical claim, once a less mechanical effort is made than the utilitarians' to understand or remind ourselves what happiness is)—or, as Voltaire urged, the garden or allotment—or, as Socrates might have urged, the agora.

7

A fresh argument for utilitarianism

Universalizability after Kant, and an excursus on the limitations of the constructional method

Let us ask what it is about the moral concepts that makes it inevitable that, when we understand the moral questions, we shall adopt certain moral principles and not others. . . . I say that moral judgments are prescriptive because in their typical uses they are intended to guide our conduct; to accept one is to be committed to a certain line of action or to prescribing it to somebody else. I say that they are universalizable because a moral judgment made about one situation commits us, on pain of logical inconsistency, to making the same judgment about any precisely similar situation. . . .

Because moral judgments and moral principles have the features of prescriptivity and universalizability, the person who adopts one is in effect prescribing universally for all situation of a certain (perhaps minutely specified) kind. These situations will include not only actual ones, but hypothetical qualitatively identical situations in which the roles of the agents are interchanged. When, therefore, I ask what I ought to do in such and such a situation, I am in effect asking for a prescription for a situation of a certain kind, on the understanding that it is to apply to *all* situations of that kind, no matter what role I myself am to play in them (for example that of murderer or of victim).

This does not mean that any of the roles carries a veto. That is to say, [even if], considering some one distribution of the roles in isolation from the others, I may be disposed to reject the prescription, because in that role I would be the victim, this does not commit me to rejecting it [now] *simpliciter* [for application there and then]. For it may be that the disadvantages to the person in that role are outweighed in sum by the advantages to the others. If this is the case, I may be willing to accept [now for then] the disadvantages . . . , as the price of the greater total advantages to the occupants of the other roles, any of which I might occupy. There are various ways of dramatizing this choice, the most illuminating of which, perhaps, is that suggested by C. I. Lewis, who bids us suppose that we know that we are, in a series of worlds, to occupy in succession, and in random order, all the possible roles of those affected by such a choice, and then choose.

This way of putting the matter, as has been generally acknowledged, leads to a form of utilitarianism; the person who chooses under these conditions will give equal weight to the equal interests of all the affected parties and will therefore seek to maximise the satisfaction of those interests in total. [This is the Principle of Equal Interests.] Thus, if moral principles were chosen in the awareness that they are universal prescriptions or prohibitions, everyone would choose these same utilitarian moral principles (or maxims realizing, in the actual world, the single utilitarian principle), providing that they were fully apprised of the consequences of accepting or rejecting them. We have to ask, in the light of this thesis, and of what I have said above, whether the adoption of such principles is a rational process. . . .

. . . It is because, in adopting a moral prescription, we are implicitly prescribing that anyone in an identical situation should do the same, that there is a discipline imposed on moral decisions . . . The person who adopts a moral principle knowing what the principle is, and what its acceptance concretely involves, is being as rational as he could be. The universality of moral principles secures in addition . . . that there will be, in practice, agreement between all those who rationally adopt moral principles, at any rates in cases (that is, the vast majority of cases) where the implementation of a principle affects the interests of many people, or even of more than one. . . .

No part in rationality is played by a requirement that one should first ascertain what the right principle is, and only then adopt it. . . . While the adopting of a principle is one and the same thing as coming to think it right, there is no place, antecedent to coming to think it right (i.e., adopting it), for a separate earlier task of ascertaining that it is right, which could be the province of some further cognitive activity beyond that of understanding what the principle is, and what its implementation would concretely involve.

R. M. Hare, 'What Makes Choices Rational'

7.1. Philosophical utilitarianism did not stand still with Mill's redeployment of Bentham. In response to doubts and objections, English-speaking philosophers refined and reorganized the position, recruiting reinforcements for the task from among Australian, American, Swedish, and other nations of philosophers. Meanwhile economists, social theorists, anthropologists, evolutionists, jurists, and others took from the theory whatever they could make use of.

This is a mass of work. It is hard, though, to discover in it any accumulation of convincing reasons that are further or better than the reasons already assessed in Lecture 6 to move across from the essentially different framework of Hume's genealogy of morals or of Kant's conception of morality to the utilitarian way of thinking. Moreover, Humean genealogy has among its further merits an apparent concinnity, already remarked in Lecture 2, with Charles Darwin's own account of the origin of human morality—even as Hume's account of the way in which the natural virtues will usher in the artificial virtues effortlessly upstages most of the single-layered and/or neo-contractualist reconstructions of morality we are offered in sociobiology or the theory of games. (See Lectures 2 and 3.) Given also the moral counterintuitiveness of philosophical utilitarianism, there is a temptation to conclude that either it will muster new arguments or else it must sink into oblivion, taking with it (one might hope), if only this could be contrived, everything else (by way of doctrine, presumption, or outlook) that has passed from this source into western consciousness.

7.2.   Beyond those already considered two arguments stand out. Each demands close attention. The clearest version I know of the second argument, putting back into service what may appear to be a residue from Mill, will be the subject of Lecture 8. In the present lecture we shall discuss an earlier and more distinctive form of argument, untried by earlier utilitarians, which is due to Richard Hare.[1]

Hare's argument starts from a place that was well within reach at

1. I want to thank Professor John Hare for the permission he has given me to make the lengthy citations with the help of which I have hoped to discuss Hare's contentions so far as possible in his own formulations.

The epigraph to the chapter is from *Review of Metaphysics* 32 (1979). In my citation I have supplied some square-bracketed explications. The authority for these is the collateral writings of R. M. Hare.

The epigraph draws upon a plenary articulation that Hare gave of his position, namely 'Ethical Theory and Utilitarianism', which may be found in the 3rd volume (ed. H. D. Lewis) of a series of decennial reports on the state of philosophy in the British Isles, entitled *Contemporary British Philosophy* (London: Allen & Unwin, 1976). See also the reprint of this in Amartya Sen and Bernard Williams, eds., *Utilitarianism and Beyond* (New York: Cambridge University Press, 1982). The exposition of the theory given in Hare's *Moral Thinking* (Oxford: Oxford University Press, 1981) is continuous with these texts.

the beginning of Lecture 6; but, after this initial stage, his line of reasoning depends on further ideas, some of which (however alien they may be to true Kantian autonomy) will remind one of Kant. The argument is set out in the epigraph to this lecture, in a text we shall shortly elaborate and interpret. In advance of that elaboration, it will be well to say something about the position of Hare in the century of philosophy that divides him from John Stuart Mill.

7.3. Over the numerous decades of its development, utilitarianism not only forced new agenda upon moral and political philosophy, not only influenced thinkers outside the strict confines of the position, e.g. William James and Herbert Spencer. It provoked the passionate opposition of others. As Coleridge resisted Archbishop Paley and William Whewell opposed Bentham, it fell to F. H. Bradley to assail John Stuart Mill. This last onslaught was made from the British idealist standpoint, reviling both Mill's conclusions and what the idealists saw as his condescension towards the ordinary moral convictions of ordinary agents. At the next phase, in succession to Bradley and in contrast with him, G. E. Moore and his successors assailed something else, namely the scientism or 'naturalism' in relation to ethical and aesthetic values which they imputed to the utilitarians (as well as to other positions).

These two kinds of opposition are worth distinguishing. The line of opposition which is most prominent in Coleridge and Bradley amounts to a radical rejection of what we should now call consequentialist conceptions of agency, of acting as one ought to act, and of responsibility. This is the matter of Lecture 8. The Moorean line of objection against utilitarianism defends the *sui generis* character of moral and other non-instrumental values. By tracing this later line of opposition against Mill into the part of moral philosophy that has come to be known as 'metaethics' and approaching Hare's revival of utilitarianism along this route, the present lecture will rehearse in barest outline one part of the history of moral philosophy in the twentieth century, advancing from Moore's *Principia Ethica*[2]

2. Cambridge: Cambridge University Press, 1903.

well into the second half of the century. (Thus questions about consequentialism and agency are postponed so far as possible to Lecture 8.)

7.4. The charge G. E. Moore urged against utilitarianism (as against several other positions we are not here concerned with) was that it committed the *naturalistic fallacy*. To understand this accusation, we first need to know what Moore meant by 'nature'. 'By nature,' Moore writes, 'I do mean and have meant that which is the subject-matter of the natural sciences and also of psychology.' (See *Principia Ethica*, pp. 40–1.) Naturalism in ethics not only seeks to define the indefinable. By approaching good in the sort of terms Bentham and Mill had employed, naturalism approaches ethics *in the wrong kinds of terms*.[3] Moore's strongest line of argument against the fallacy he finds in the account of 'good' that is offered by utilitarian and kindred positions (a target he constantly expands, it should be said, as he moves further and further from his original starting point) is the so-called *open question argument*. We may simultaneously display this form of argument and illustrate its application to utilitarianism as follows: even if x promoted or constituted or partially constituted the greatest happiness (say) or the greatest sum of pleasures, it would still remain an open question whether x was good (or indeed obligatory, one might think).[4]

This and similar arguments are brought to bear constantly in *Principia Ethica* in defence of good as intrinsically conceived.[5] (The

3. Cp. Aurel Kolnai, 'The Ghost of the Naturalistic Fallacy', *Philosophy* 55 (1980): 5–16; Casimir Lewy, 'G. E. Moore and the Naturalistic Fallacy', *Proceedings of the British Academy* 50 (1964): 251–62. Moore did not properly avow his debts in this area to Henry Sidgwick, author of the neo-utilitarian work *Methods of Ethics* (1877). Partly as a result of this, twentieth-century ethics and metaethics focused almost exclusively on Moore. In sketching this narrative, I have had to follow their reading of the origination of his objection to naturalism.

4. For an attempt to find more force in the open question strategy than is normally attributed to it, see my 'Cognitivism, Naturalism and Normativity' and 'A Neglected Position?' in *Reality, Representation and Projection,* ed. J. Haldane and C. Wright (Oxford: Oxford University Press, 1993.)

5. The clearest and most useful component of the notion of intrinsicness implicit in Moore is made fully explicit in W. D. Ross, *The Right and the Good* (Oxford: Oxford

utilitarians are only one of Moore's targets.) Curiously though, once Moore has secured the non-natural character of ethical value and shown that it is absurd to think that 'good can be defined as a natural object' or defined at all, Moore then relaxes his guard. It is a striking fact that his account of *ought* or *must*—equally vulnerable, one might have thought, to the open question challenge—is not different in principle from the utilitarian one:

> Our duty, therefore, can be defined as that action which will cause more good to exist in the universe than any possible alternative. And what is 'right' or 'morally permissible' only differs from this as what will *not* cause *less* good than any possible alternative. (*Principia Ethica,* p. 148)

This feature of Moore's position, which is tantamount to a reduction of the right to the good,[6] exposed Moore himself to telling criticisms by W. D. Ross. This is part of the background to Lecture 8, however, and we must digress no further from setting out the early development of twentieth-century metaethics.

We began with Moore's idea of intrinsic good as a non-natural property. At the moment in *Principia Ethica* of Moore's introduction of the distinction between natural and non-natural, it seems plain that the author will defend the second of these categories, the non-natural, against crude scientism. Two decades later, however, we find Moore suggesting in his *Philosophical Studies*[7] that natural properties 'describe what possesses them in a sense in which non-natural properties do not'. Here the idea of a non-natural property is already in decline. Then, thirty years after that, we see a similar line of reflec-

University Press, 1930), p. 68, as follows: 'The intrinsically good is best defined as that which is good apart from any of the consequences it produces.'

6. There is something entirely fitting in the fact that Moore's position, imperfectly emancipated as it is from some of the trends he set out to oppose, was often referred to as Ideal Utilitarianism or Ideal Consequentialism. It has also been called *agathistic* (focused on good) and *ethical neutralist* (not so much concerned with the ethics of agency as with a net upshot of good).

7. London: Kegan Paul, Trench, Trübner, 1922.

tion issue in R. M. Hare's *non-descriptivist* conception of 'good'.[8] According to the conception that we find at this terminus, 'good' is a term whose meaning one grasps not by learning some unitary contribution of sense or reference that the word makes to the description of things or situations, nor yet by learning the accepted criteria for grading this or that kind of thing, but rather by learning that 'good' is simply the most general term of commendation, where commending is the speech act that is expressive of considered approval and/or choice.

How can Moore's brave intrinsicalist beginnings of 1903 have issued after so few steps in such an austerely anti-metaphysical account of value and valuation? Well, even at the outset, there were signs of what was to come. It is true that, at the beginning of his polemic against naturalism, Moore deprecates 'substituting for "good" some one property of a natural object or of a collection of natural objects . . . , thus replacing Ethics by one of the natural sciences' (*Principia Ethica,* p. 40). At that point, the conclusion we reach is that good is a non-natural property. But even there, instead of being content to continue the first passage that I quoted ('By nature, I do mean and have meant . . . ') into some careful and simple elaboration of the distinction between properties that do and properties that do not pull their weight in the natural sciences (including empirical psychology), Moore immediately advances to a further contention which is in no way licensed by his definition of 'nature'. This is that the natural sciences should 'include all that has existed, does exist or will exist in time' (p. 40). This in its turn, gives rise to a doubt about good: 'I have said that "good" itself is not a natural

---

8. Hare says that a sentence is not descriptive unless its meaning is *wholly determined* by the designated conditions under which it will count as true. He holds that the presence in a sentence of an 'evaluative' term such as 'good' stands in the way of its being properly descriptive. See 'Descriptivism', *Proceedings of the British Academy* 49 (1963). Since the nature of the good will not be pursued further in these lectures, let me commend an exposition of these questions much closer to that which I myself should follow, an exposition largely exempt (I should judge) from many or most anti-cognitivist doubts and difficulties, namely that of G. H. Von Wright, *The Varieties of Goodness* (London: Routledge, 1965).

property. . . . Can we imagine "good" as existing *by itself* in time?" (p. 41). (One wonders why Moore aims this question particularly at *good*. In so far as it impugns any property, it surely impugns all.) So, even at that early stage of his exploration of the ideas of nature and the natural, Moore's doubt looks forward to the further idea, which is Moore's too, that good only *supervenes on* natural properties.[9] This is an idea that has wavered fatally (and still wavers fatally) between the unexciting claim (scarcely distinguishing good from other properties) that the goodness of any particular thing in its particular state of being *rubs shoulders* with the way in which it possesses other properties (because the extent to which the thing has one property limits the extent to which it can have others) and a much more contestable claim, either false or vacuous I think, namely that the natural properties of a thing are what *determines* its goodness.

7.5. Some such confusion was surely one factor in the diminution, bit by bit, of the idea that 'good' stands for a property—as it has been in the tacit dismissal of the less discussed and much less problematical idea that *each* of the several varieties of good represents a cognitively accessible, however essentially contestable, property.[10] But confusion was only one element of the story. Another element was the twentieth-century preoccupation with meaning and meaningfulness, a preoccupation prefigured in the writings of Ernst Mach, a physicist and theorist of science, and then, in a subsequent generation, by L. E. J. Brouwer, the intuitionist mathematician, and Ludwig Wittgenstein, who had turned to the foundations of mathematics and to philosophy from the physics of flight. For far too long (they might have said) it had been unthinkingly assumed that there is no particular problem in determining what the *cognitive meaning* is of the various things people are moved to say in the business of pursuing their philosophical or non-philosophical theo-

9. As if all there *really is* is nature?
10. See again Von Wright, *The Varieties of Goodness.*

ries or expressing their convictions about the nature of the world. It was not to be denied that Leibniz, Hume, and Kant had each expressed in their own way doubts of their own about the bounds of significance or sense; but too little had been made of their doubts. Under the influence of Mach, Wittgenstein, and Brouwer, *inter alios*, the logical positivists then developed a theory of their own about these matters. They proposed that grasping the cognitive meaning of a sentence was a matter of grasping the 'method of its verification'. If there was no prospect of such a method, then there was no prospect of the sentence's signifying anything.[11]

Where did that leave moral and aesthetic judgments? Brushing aside any claim to the effect that such utterances propose their own contextually determinable standards of verification, the early positivists declared that ethical utterances, taken non-naturalistically (as it was agreed that Moore had shown they must be taken) and lacking any palpable or cognitively enforcible method of verification, were simply meaningless. They represented the same kind of nonsense as metaphysical utterances.

The philosophical moralists' response to the last claim was understandable enough: not all meaning was cognitive meaning. Sustained perhaps by the report that the Cambridge philosopher C. D. Broad had given in *Five Types of Ethical Theory*[12] of the work of Axel Hägerström, the Swedish jurist, they advanced the so-called 'emotivist' theory of ethics, which likened ethical utterances to 'expressions of attitude'. What sort of attitude? The sort of attitude one could express by saying, 'I approve/disapprove of this!', where

---

11. What about the meaning of a word? If the meaning of a word is its contribution to cognitive meaning, then grasping the cognitive meaning of a word must be a matter of understanding how to verify the satisfaction of whatever it is that the word's presence in a sentence demands within the verification conditions of the sentence as a whole.

It should be recorded that, in the event, the positivists involved themselves at this point in endless difficulties, difficulties we still have in seeking for some principled philosophical exclusion of that which really is nonsense. For a magisterial brief survey of the positivists' attempts to delimit the factual, see Hilary Putnam, *The Collapse of the Fact/Value Dichotomy* (Cambridge, Mass.: Harvard University Press, 2002), pp. 21ff.

12. London: Kegan Paul, Trench and Trübner, 1930.

the force and quality of the approval/disapproval could be further specified (A. J. Ayer suggested)[13] by a whole notation of differentiated exclamation marks, and the utterance itself was to be construed, not of course as a report of the speaker's state of mind, but as *evincing* or *expressing* it. According to theoretical inclination, one might give further colour to the expression of attitude by seeing it, with the American emotivist C. L. Stevenson, as carrying it with it the implicit command, 'Do you too approve/disapprove of it!'[14]

Such was the scene that awaited Hare's reaction when immediately after his service as a soldier in the Second World War, he resumed his studies and set out on moral philosophy:

> Moore's non-natural qualities proved elusive as objects of moral thought. . . . There seemed to be no solid moral questions or moral facts in the world for our moral thinking to grasp. . . . I came to see that what was needed, instead of [Moorean] moral facts, was a way of thinking rationally about what one ought to do . . . the rational ordering of our prescriptions for action . . . H. J. Paton [the Kant scholar] . . . first drew my attention to the similarity between Stevenson's 'attitudes' and Kant's 'maxims'. If one could find, as Kant thought, a way of criticizing these maxims or attitudes rationally, then one could accept most of what the emotivists were saying, and, without needing any moral facts, establish moral reasoning on a secure basis. In short, what was needed was a rationalist kind of non-descriptivism to replace the irrationalist kind. . . . [This rationalist theory] borrows from emotivism the negative idea that moral judgments are not essentially statements of moral facts, and from imperativism a positive idea about what they might be instead, namely prescriptions. For there are other kinds of prescription besides imperatives; moral judgments might belong to the genus prescriptions, but not belong in the species of it called simple imperatives. One

13. See A. J. Ayer, *Language, Truth and Logic* (London: Gollancz, 1936), p. 107.
14. See Stevenson, 'The Emotive Meaning of Ethical Terms', *Mind* 46 (1937).

has to look for [the] differentia; and I found it. . . . A speech act's being prescriptive was no bar to its standing in logical relations. . . . [There is] a logical inconsistency [for instance] between 'shut the door' and 'do not shut the door', and in general between prescriptions. . . . It is by showing . . . 'contradictions in the will' that moral reasoning has to proceed. . . .

[A] differentia is obviously needed to distinguish moral prescriptions from simple imperatives. . . . This differentia I found . . . in the feature of universalizability.[15]

7.6. Two or three further details will be supplied in the next chapter and in the Introductory Note for Part III to fill out one further part of this scandalously brief and selective account of the work that promoted 'metaethics' so called to such a position of prominence in moral philosophy. But present purposes do not require very much more. For it was in metaethics that Hare wanted to lay down new foundations for moral philosophy. In more of Hare's words, the epigraph for our chapter continues the Harean part of that story. Among the several questions these words prepare us to ask is the question to which this chapter is devoted, namely whether Hare, in joining forces with the Kantian tradition, found a new and better argument for utilitarianism than those which we encountered in Mill or Bentham.

Let us begin upon this with something which, in some form or other, almost everyone will agree to and which Hare treats as constitutive of rationality in ethics. When someone thinks or speaks in moral terms, he has to depart from his private and particular situation, as Hume says, and choose a point of view that shall be common to him with others. (Cp. 2.9, 4.5.) Here is another formulation: it flows from the essential purport of a moral utterance and is part of its content that it looks for consensus and appeals to a point of view that is not only the maker's but something shared—or so the utterance seeks to establish—and common to the utterer with other per-

15. R. M. Hare, 'A Philosophical Autobiography', *Utilitas* 14.3 (2002): 287–90.

sons.[16] Yet another aspect of what may appear to be the same ethical phenomenon shows itself in the precept of Pittacus, the Greek tyrant of Mytilene in the sixth century B.C. 'Don't do yourself what you disapprove of in others.'[17] It is hard not to understand all these utterances as groping for one and the same thing, even if there are almost as many statements of this thing in philosophy itself as there are moral philosophers. (The full significance of the thing that is not in itself controversial is far from incontrovertible.) Meanwhile though, for Hare's own approach, the reader must consult again the first paragraphs of the extract that is prefixed to this lecture.

7.7.   In the epigraph, as in the extract I have given from his 'Philosophical Autobiography', Hare begins with certain linguistic phenomena. In proceeding so, he looks backwards at the course of analytical philosophy after Moore. But he also looks forwards to the role that his rational reconstruction of the content of morality assigns to a special kind of impersonality or impartiality between conflicting interests. This impartiality can be achieved, Hare thinks, by our

16. Compare Aurel Kolnai, 'Moral Consensus', *Proceedings of the Aristotelian Society* 70 (1969–70), reprinted in B. Klug and F. Dunlop, eds., *Ethics, Values and Reality* (London: Athlone Press, 1978). Note that this formulation is drafted not to exclude the insincere or exploitative employment of such a form of words. Since such employment precisely misuses the very same content, Kolnai's account predicts those employments.

17. For fuller discussion of these matters, see my *Needs, Values, Truth* (amended 3rd ed., Oxford: Oxford University Press, 2002) ch. 2, especially pp. 82ff. (The subject matter of that chapter extensively overlaps the subject matter of the present lecture, but I have tried to focus here on some different criticisms of R. M. Hare.)

For *New Testament* formulations of the so-called Golden Rule, see *Matthew* 7:5 and *Luke* 6:31.

With Pittacus' precept compare and contrast Leonard Nelson's *Principle of Balanced Consideration:* 'never act in such a way that you could not approve of your conduct if the interests of the other party were also your own.' Compare also Thomas Reid: 'what we approve in others, that we ought to practice in like circumstances, and what we condemn in others we ought not to do.'

Outside the western tradition and outside the formalism of analytical philosophy, something similar surely resonates in Confucius' *Analects:* 'Tzu Kung asked, "Is there any single saying that one can act upon all day and every day?" The master said: "Never do to others what you would not like them to do to you." *Analects*, trans. A. Waley (London: Allen & Unwin, 1938), XV.23.

submitting all our acts and attitudes to judgments of right and wrong and submitting our judgments of right and wrong to the test of universalizability. By virtue of being a *moral* judgment, a moral judgment (if we venture upon that) *commits* us, and commits us on pain of logical inconsistency, to making the same judgment about any precisely similar situation regardless of which role we play in the situation and regardless of our own particular interests. Or putting the point more usefully and more exigently than Hare does in our epigraph, and drawing on Hare's other writings, one may say that a moral judgment commits us to making a *similar* judgment about any situation which is *relevantly similar*.[18]

Hare gives notice that his version of the universalization test will in the end commit us to utilitarianism. But *so far,* let it be clear, no Aristotelian, Humean, intuitionist, phenomenologist, or other pluralist need find anything here at which to demur. Why should any of these moralists doubt that, when I need to arrive at a moral judgment concerning what I should do under such and such circumstances, it will be good for me to ask whether there is a line of conduct or, as Kant might say (see 4.8), a maxim, that I should counsel[19] to anyone placed as I am placed? ('Placed as I am placed' means 'placed in the same sort of circumstances as these circumstances of mine, included within these circumstances being all relevantly similar commitments, etc.'). The reason why this is not controversial is that what maxim I choose can depend entirely on my metaphysics, on the revelations of my religion, on my sentiments, on my intuitions, or on whatever. Only by constraining somehow the choice of maxim can the universalizability approach enjoin anything that is distinctive or substantial for moral philosophy as such.

One familiar constraint is to stipulate that, in considering what I can prescribe universally, I have to limit myself to choices of maxim

18. It is to come out in dialogue between the maker of the judgment and his/her critics, one of whom can surely be the maker, what s/he intends to be the criterion of relevant resemblance.

19. Or a line of action I should find morally fitting. Not everyone will think they have to *analyse out* the content of morality into the ideas of prescription and universality.

corresponding to the deliverances of my rational will and to maxims that respect rational nature as an end in itself. (Cp. 4.12.) Of course, this is not the only possibility. Maybe there are as many ways of constraining the choice of maxim as there are moral philosophies. The thing that is as important for Hare as it was for Kant is that the choice of maxim be constrained incontrovertibly by unadorned practical reason.

Following that path, Hare first models the rationality of a rational universalizer upon *individual prudence,* a prudence that is corrigible by reference to fact or logic and is rational with respect to the deliberator's own interests and/or preferences. In the second instance, he models the universalizing rationality of the rational person who is within morality upon *prudence with respect to all interests and/or preferences.* Hare's contention is that the only way in which generalized prudence can give its proper due to each preference or interest while seeking to do the best for all collectively is for it to proportion whatever it awards to each interest to the strength of the preference— as rationally adjusted, if necessary.[20] This is called the Principle of Equal Interests, and Hare contends that it is equivalent for all relevant purposes to classical utilitarianism.[21] Thus classical utilitarianism graduates to the status of a rational requirement.

20. You might suggest that it be proportioned to the degree of importance of the interest, but this distinction does not figure large in Hare's construction.

21. To get an exact fit with utilitarianism it has to be all right to suppose that there is no mismatch between the strength of a (rationally corrected) desire and the efficiency with which it can turn into the effective satisfaction of desire any benefits the universalizer's choice of maxim may award to it. Unluckily, such an assumption is not generally true (see here my *Needs, Values, Truth,* p. 86 *ad fin*). We also need to suppose that there operates a uniform law of diminishing returns, to the effect that the nearer any preferences comes to satiation the less effective satisfaction is achieved by each extra unit awarded to the preference.

Suppose we make these assumptions. Then, wherever we depart from the Principle of Equal Interests, something will have been awarded to one preference that could have yielded more effective satisfaction if allocated to some other preference—one which was further from satiation. The most efficient distribution is that which makes equal awards to preferences of equal intensity. Thus the Principle of Equal Interests, the demand supposedly of generalized prudence, is the same as the ethical demand of classical act utilitarianism, to maximise happiness or satisfaction.

7.8.   That is an outline of the position Hare develops. But several
intervening points call for closer comment.

The first thing to note is that, in Hare's sort of search for a practical maxim that is fitted to further all interests and/or preferences,
generalized prudence is required not to appeal to anything beyond
preferences/interests and their strength or degree. The thought is
that, if morality is to reveal itself from the workings of the deliberative search for a maxim, then morality must not itself be presupposed to that search. To the extent that this may be possible, the
deliverances of morality may of course be *reconceived* as interests or
translated into interests. But, pending the completion of the construction, interests or preferences with this provenance have no special standing or pre-eminence. See especially the sixth paragraph of
the epigraph at the head of the chapter. Let us call this first principle
the *Constructionalist* or *Constructional Assumption.* It is the first of
the three principles Hare's construction depends upon. It is a highly
non-trivial assumption.

7.9.   *A second principle.* If I had generalized prudence, then, it
would prompt me to generalize the procedure which individual deliberation follows with regard to my own interests. It would prompt
me to follow a principle that has come to be called *the Prudential
Principle.* In the case of individual prudence, I am advised, other
things being equal, to try to maximize the satisfaction of preferences—my own preferences or any others that I myself care about.
Generalized prudence simply omits these references to me and my
own preferences.

Here, though, a doubt arises. Is 'maximize the satisfaction of my
preferences' really the thing an individual deliberator, even an entirely self-interested rational deliberator, actually intends in practising
individual prudence? Surely a rational deliberator asks himself constantly not so much how to maximize his preference satisfaction as
what to prefer, what to desire, or even *what it would be best or most
fitting here to desire.* Moreover, one might think that it will be foolish
for him not to interest himself constantly in the question *what do I
vitally need?* If Hare's object is to show what makes choices rational,

then it is a pity for him to ignore these questions and begin from so attenuated a conception of the ordinary rationality of ordinary first-person deliberation. Presumably this attenuation is among the first results of the Constructional Assumption. Let us put this doubt into reserve, however, and simply leave it on the record.

7.10. *A Third principle.* Moving onward to consider how generalized prudence treats with interests/preferences other than the deliberator's own, we come next to something that has come to be known as the *Conditional Reflection Principle.* One with the generalized prudence enjoined by a deliberator's aspiration to speak from the moral point of view needs to know how things are for others. More generally he needs to know their motivations/preferences/interests; and according to Hare, he has to do this by seeking to put himself imaginatively into others' positions with *their* motivations/preferences/interests. Hare insists that one who is seeking impartially or impersonally for the maxim to universalize will not count as having achieved this kind of knowledge in any particular case, unless he acquires *a motivation now for then* equal to the motivation *that he would have then for then* if he were in the position of the person whose situation he is seeking to ascertain.[22] One who chooses a maxim that does not award some interest or interests a treatment proportional to the strength of the corresponding preferences is either *imperfectly informed* at a point where his commitment to the point of view of morality commits him to be properly informed, or else he is *imperfectly rational*—which explains his failure to follow through his supposed commitment to the moral point of view.

7.11. Let us put all this together now. If I am to make a moral judgment, I must universalize: if I am to universalize I must identify a maxim I am sincerely prepared to endorse, now for then, for all

---

22. For an illuminating discussion of this principle and its difficulties, see Bernard Williams, *Ethics and the Limits of Philosophy* (London: Collins, 1985), pp. 89–91. See also his contribution to D. Seanor and N. Fotion, eds., *Hare and Critics: Essays on Moral Thinking* (Oxford: Oxford University Press, 1988).

possible situations, endorsing it on the basis of simultaneous epistemically best possible consideration of all positions (regardless of which position is mine), doing the best for all in all positions (regardless of which one is mine). The only thing I can consider in seeking to endorse a maxim or prescription is the satisfaction of preferences/interests (the Prudential Principle). All other considerations are excluded. That is the effect of the Constructional Assumption. And with regard to preference satisfaction, if the Conditional Reflection principle holds, and if it is a necessary truth that whoever is a rational person following through his commitments will identify fully with each preference he properly understands (and he needs, if he is seeking the standpoint of morality, to try to understand all), then it would be irrational for me to have regard for one preference over another if they were of equal strength. (Cp. 8.3.) But, if so, then the only way in which I can proceed en route to my moral judgment is to look for a maxim that will have equal regard for equal interests. This, however, is practically equivalent (Hare claims) to utilitarianism. Anyone who rejected it (a fanatic, an idealist, or whatever you want to call him) would be *irrational* in his choice of which maxim to universalize. Such is the argument.

7.12.   The non-compressed way of saying that one with generalized prudence gives equal weight to equal interests is to say that generalized rationality is in search of the maxim that proportions the award which it makes to each interest to the felt import of that interest for the person who has it and/or to the efficiency with which the interest can convert whatever is awarded to it into the achieved satisfaction of the person who has the interest.[23] But what does it

23. So far as I know, Hare never addressed the possibility of these things diverging or the implications of this for the claim that universal prescriptivism coincides exactly with classical utilitarianism.

The possibility of divergence is illustrated (too dramatically perhaps, for the difficulty is general) by the situation of the handicapped. Their needs and preferences are very demanding, but some of these are disproportionately expensive to satisfy. For that reason,

involve to look for a maxim that meets these requirements? It is not always realized that this question bifurcates. There is the question of what it requires in the practice of individual agents. But there is also a question about our theoretical understanding of generalized prudence. What does it amount to, what is it constitutively, for a maxim to be one that deserves by Hare's criteria to be universalized? How are we to grasp fully and properly what that involves?

7.13. Let us take first the first and easier of these questions, concerning what is to be expected of individual agents.

Hare distinguishes the level of *critical thinking*, which we have been concerned with so far, from another level of moral thinking called *intuitive thinking*, which will not concern itself with the abstractions so far rehearsed. How can he justify this? Well, moral thinking conceived as critical thinking can be applied to moral or ethical policies, to principles, to dispositions . . . , and to moral thinking itself. According to Hare, the result of thinking critically about critical thinking is to conclude that most everyday thinking had best not be critical thinking. It had best be conducted on the different level which Hare calls the level of intuitive thinking. This is to say that it is much the best for most everyday thinking to be the intuitive exercise of those moral dispositions that critical thinking would recommend as best calculated to maximize by their joint effect the satisfaction of preferences. In other words, Hare claims that what we need is a two-level theory, a theory that not only recognizes critical moral thinking, but also recognizes intuitive moral thinking. Intuitive moral thinking is to be exercised in the here and now, on the basis of dispositions imparted in the ordinary way and promoting the ordinary ethical awareness which such dispositions require. The strength of such intuitive thinking is that it can look out constantly, in a way that these dispositions moralize, at the interests of those parties directly affected in every situation in which action may be

---

classical utilitarianism would have to be much less generous to them than it seems universal prescriptivism must.

called for. For practical purposes of ordinary agents, whom the Constructional Assumption need not trouble, the idea of 'persons affected' will readily stir up questions of rights or legitimate expectations.

This is Hare's resolution of the question that appeared first in 6.5 and then reappeared at 6.12. As regards the philosophy of the virtues and of ethical education, it might seem that, in its final content, the result will agree well enough with the doctrines of Hume or, if you prefer, those of Aristotle or of many another ordinary moralist. But that is less straightforward than it seems, if only because the theoretical framework is so utterly different. At the root of Hare's two-level theory lies universal prescriptivism or classical utilitarianism, *not* an account of virtues such as we set out in Lectures 2 and 3. In the two-level theory that Hare proposes, critical thinking is the final authority and critical thinking seconds classical utilitarianism. *The deliverances of intuitive thinking have such authority as they have only by being approximations to the deliverances of ideally well-informed critical thinking.* The two-level conception will certainly enable Hare to defend his utilitarianism against the simple charge that it is simply unliveable, or destructive of all trust and virtue, etc. Moreover, the restoration of ordinary morality to the scene becomes principled and systematic in a way that such restoration was not in some earlier defences of act utilitarianism. This is a real gain for the inner coherence of Hare's two-level theory. But it does little or nothing where the question is one of choosing between Hare's position and its non-utilitarian rivals.

A word more on the last claim. It is one thing to allow that the ordinary morality promoted by intuitive thinking is consistent after all with the utilitarianism that is promoted by critical thinking. It is another to allow that this should increase our philosophical confidence in critical thinking or the universal prescriptivism that it implements (or in utilitarianism, for that matter). For the said consistency will not put to rest all the earlier doubts we have raised about the principles by which Hare arrives at his position. To find that intuitive thinking and critical thinking are consistent falls well short of our allowing that intuitive thinking is *founded* in critical thinking.

If intuitive thinking is attractive, then the credit for that belongs elsewhere, as we have seen already.

Suppose we embrace the ends that are implicit in the ordinary morality which Hare wants to interpret and second or uphold as precisely sustaining the greatest possible satisfaction of preferences. Suppose we think that, in embracing these ends of ordinary morality, we can achieve such a good answer to the question (B) of 1.1 and answer Glaucon and Adeimantus so effectively on that basis that, in our engagement with question (A) of 1.1, we shall be able to confirm and recover, there and then, a whole substantial content for morality. It will still be controversial whether our attachment to the ends of ordinary morality, newly supported (however conditionally) by Hare, will generate or recover anything that coincides with Hare's version of philosophical utilitarianism. It will be controversial and, in Lecture 9, we shall identify an implicit end for ordinary morality which is positively at variance with every distinctively utilitarian or consequentialist position.

7.14. This reservation has the effect of stirring up other reservations relating to the two-level structure.

How perfect can the segregation be between intuitive and critical thinking? Is Hare's proposal simultaneously to inculcate ethical dispositions, to ingrain them into the formation of moral agents, and yet *subordinate* them to a way of thinking (the critical way) that is a stranger to them? If they are *not* to be subordinated, then intuitive thinking comes loose from critical thinking in a way that Hare cannot consistently contemplate. If these dispositions *are* to be subordinated, however, then there is trouble of another kind, namely the alienation of moral agents from that which critical thinking will butt in to require of them. Moreover, it will do so *in defiance* of the canons of intuitive thinking in which Hare's critical thinking has ruled that they should be formed.[24]

---

24. Bernard Williams made this point with great force. See again footnote 15 to Lecture 6. In this summary statement of his position, I seek to show that one may dispense with the strange and special sense that Williams seeks to confer on the word

A complementary point: suppose that intuitive thinking is not to come loose altogether from critical thinking but take orders from it. Then would not intuitive moral thinking be constantly unnerved and discomfited by anything at all that it heard of the way in which the theoretical reflections of critical thinking treat all interests, the interests of the wicked who intimidate and oppress other moral beings and the interests of the simply and intuitively virtuous, as if they had equal weight and equal importance, regardless of the content of these preferences/interests and regardless of what kind of persons they are the interests of? What at the critical level becomes of the ethical idea that human beings must be treated never as means but always as ends in themselves? How can a doctrine that studies only the intensity of preferences furnish any guarantee for this?

7.15. At 7.12 we asked two questions. The second question, so far left hanging, was what it amounts to *constitutively* for a maxim to be a maxim whose implementation will proportion what it awards a given interest to the strength of the rationally corrected preference that defines it.

Hare makes things seem much easier than they are by representing that, when generalized prudence looks for a maxim to universalize on behalf of all interests, the only thing that is at issue is the interests *of those affected* by the choice of this or that maxim. If one takes this ruling in the way in which it would be taken by ordinary intuitive morality, it will seem clear enough in principle. 'Those affected' will comprise those with some sort of *right,* if such and such is the maxim to be universalized, to have had their interests taken into account. Better perhaps, it comprises those with some *legitimate expectation* of being protected from certain outcomes. (The details are not immediately relevant. It is enough if, in any context, such details will be available to be spelled out.) Once the Constructional Assumption is correctly and consistently enforced, however, such a

---

'integrity'. The ordinary (or almost ordinary) use of the word 'alienation' makes it possible to register the same point in a way that seems more natural.

reading is ruled out. 'Affected' can only mean 'causally affected'—which means that, in advance of the choice of a maxim and its being put into practice, *there is no circumscribing* the totality of preferences/interests to be borne in mind.[25] This is to say that there is an open sea of present interests that will be causally affected by anything at all that one does. Beyond that, there is a whole ocean of future interests, either actual or hypothetical. At best, this is a mathematically intractable totality. At worst it is conceptually and operationally intractable—something we surely ought to find to be a paradox if we bear it in mind that, historically speaking, Hare's universal prescriptivism was the (however long delayed) by-product of an extreme, almost puritanical, doctrine of cognitive meaningfulness.

At this point, Hare might complain that the objection is rigoristic: '*In practice,* it is perfectly clear what "those affected" means.' But the place for *this* point is the place where we have already been, namely Hare's distinction of the intuitive and the critical levels of thinking. The intractability we are now complaining of is different. It is a constitutive difficulty, one imported by a kind of theory that Hume or Aristotle would say we do not need at all, namely Hare's theory of critical thinking, a theory not animated (they would say) by the right kind of conception of the internal aims of morality. See 9.10 and 11.2.

7.16. The problem here is the Constructional Assumption. It seems obvious that there must be better ways of managing this.[26]

---

25. Indeed there is no circumscribing the set of people or of times. How long there will go on being people, moreover, and which ones there will be, will partly depend on what maxims *are* universalized.

26. Might there be a procedure (reminiscent of recursive definition in logic) that generated a first set of moral ideas relating to the choice of a maxim to universalize, then generated (partly by reference back to the first set) a second set . . . , then generated a third set perhaps, by referring back to the first and second sets . . . ? Such a procedure might be expected to generate a first approximation to the maxim desiderated, then a second approximation, then . . . , and, in the end, a final choice. (Slightly similarly, are not Hume's natural virtues an input to his theory of the artificial virtues? Natural virtues such as love of kith and kin certainly effect a first identification of 'persons affected', which reasoned benevolence widens and the artificial virtues then modify . . .)

What is much less obvious is whether any of these other ways would generate classical utilitarianism, rather than some regimentation of (say) Hume's conception. Even if we persisted in Hare's governing idea (which we shall seek in Lectures 9 and 10 to question and replace)—namely the idea that that the one aim which morality and its minister, the universalizer, must seek to achieve is a mediation of the conflict between competing interests/preferences, a mediation thus maximizing the satisfaction of preferences—it would still be uncertain whether utilitarianism would be the outcome. So much depends on what ideas, what ideas more manageable and intuitively acceptable than the Principle of Equal Interests, the universalizer will be permitted to bring to bear upon his search for a maxim. (This last is, of course, a philosophical or constitutive question about the deliberative procedures of the entirely notional universalizer whom Hare has to invoke in his theoretical development of the idea of critical moral thinking. It is not a question about the ordinary agent who practises intuitive moral thinking.)

Suppose Hare's notional universalizer were to look afresh at individual prudence and have regard for the key role that is played there by the idea of vital need in clearing away a whole battery of unimportant desires or preferences. (Compare the objection we placed on the record at the end of 7.9.) Suppose the universalizer then transposed this new observation to generalized prudence and was led in this way to dispense with the Constructional Assumption. With or without further modifications of Hare's method (designed, say, to recover the hierarchy of moral concerns referred to in 1.3), the result might qualify as a post-Harean version of universal prescriptivism. It might come closer and closer perhaps to a position once delineated by Leibniz:

> Virtue is the habit of acting according to wisdom . . . Wisdom is the science of felicity, [and] is that which must be studied above all things. . . . Justice is charity or a habit of loving conformed to wisdom. Thus when one is inclined to justice, one

tries to procure good for everybody, so far as one can, reasonably, but in proportion to the needs and merits of each.[27]

There might be a great deal to be said for such a view, but it would not be utilitarianism. (If anything, is it not slightly closer to the socialistic maxim cited at 6.13?)

7.17. *Conclusion.* In this lecture no diminution has been intended of the philosophical significance of one ordinary moral agent's capacity to act on the basis of sympathetic identification with the situation of another. The targets of attack have been other.

The first target was the idea that *metaethics* (the third of the four theoretical subjects enumerated in Lecture 1, and first broached in the historical sketch given at the beginning of this lecture) can play the part that Hare and so many others have wanted it to play in preparing the ground for a brand new determination of the content or substance of ethics. In truth, metaethics, as practised under constructionalist assumptions, has simply translated the bareness of the positivist conception of ethical thinking back into a first order moral thinking of unrecognizable bareness. (The bareness it compensates by becoming a parasite upon intuitive moral thinking.) Or so I have asserted. Meanwhile the positivistic conception of ethics reflects no careful study of ethical thinking itself.

The second target was the equally unjustifiable idea that utilitarianism in particular is the presumptive beneficiary of the best-judged metaethical approach to morality. It is far more likely, I think, that the best-judged metaethics will be the metaethics of the best-judged (metaethically more or less innocent) account of the substance of ethics itself. See Lectures 11 and 12.

Excursus

7.18. For a short while, let us put aside the concern with utilitarianism, as such, or its title to displace Hume or Kant, in order

---

27. G. W. Leibniz, 'Felicity', trans. in P. Riley, ed., *Leibniz: Political Writings* (Cambridge: Cambridge University Press, 1988).

to say a word more about putting oneself in the place of another. Real moral agents (at the level Hare calls the intuitive level) will often do this to remarkable effect—as moralists and other preceptors of mankind have perceived. In this way, human beings sometimes enlarge the scope of the ethical and correct its findings, as if to home closer and closer upon moral truth. This has excited a host of constructionalists and model builders in philosophy. But how far can this capacity for identification with others, either taken by itself or else generalized in a seemingly self-evident way and afforced with whatever is incontrovertible and *a priori* in logic and prudential practical reason, carry philosophy to the determination of a proper content for a first-order ethical outlook? How close will the models and constructions that are inspired by the thought of changing places take us to a good account of morality itself? Since Hume first introduced the form of words 'the point of view that shall be common to one man with another', philosophy has seen Kant's theory of the categorical imperative, Adam Smith's theory of the impartial spectator, the twentieth-century revival of Smith in the theory of the ideal observer ('omniscient, disinterested, dispassionate, but otherwise normal'),[28] Hare's Universal Prescriptivism, and several other proposals too, no doubt. How conspicuous, one might ask, is their convergence?

The last question may seem unfair or misconceived, if only because (as it may be said) there are so many other differences between the authors of all these theories. So a further and better test might be to compare the actual conclusions that are reached by two members of the same philosophical generation, working in more or less the same analytical tradition and at more or less the same temporal distance from the utilitarian tradition, namely Richard Hare, the chief subject of the present lecture, and John Rawls, the author of *A Theory of Justice*.[29] It is true that the professed aims of these two philosophers are at variance, Hare being chiefly concerned with

28. For this, see Williams, *Ethics and the Limits of Philosophy*, pp. 84–5.
29. Cambridge, Mass.: Harvard University Press, 1972.

'right' and Rawls with 'just', and true again that their choice of methods of construction are different. Hare, operating a Constructional Assumption foreign to Rawls, favours the ratiocinations of a notional practitioner of generalized prudence who is indifferent to the identities of those whose interests he is to arbitrate between. Rawls, on the other hand, prefers to model 'just' on his reconstruction of the findings of a group of representatives of a whole citizenship at large, a small group of free and equal persons each of whom is to exercise the thinking of ordinary prudence and from this basis to debate and deliberate with his colleagues, under a common veil of ignorance, the conditions of fruitful cooperation in a well-ordered society. The veil of ignorance is to prevent these deliberators from knowing anything at all concerning either the part it will fall to each of them to play in this society or the content of their own conception of the good—except to the extent that they can determine this content by thinking of themselves as free and equal deliberators or by reflecting that there are some good things, the *primary goods,* that anyone will want whatever else they want. (Primary goods comprise certain rights, liberties, opportunities, powers, income, wealth.)

Evidently, Hare's and Rawls's methods are wide apart. Yet their procedures have the appearance of being different means to one and the same sort of philosophical end. Not only do they appear as rival elaborations of a common enduring intuition. Since Hare's topic in a sense subsumes Rawls's topic, it will want explanation that the results that they reach are not merely different (that is to be expected) but *inconsistent.*[30]

In Hare's construction, everything depends on the application of the Principle of Equal Interests. The practitioner of generalized prudence proportions that which he awards to any interest to the strength of the corresponding preference or desire. For Rawls, on the other hand, no principle so insensitive to the content or moral import of a desire could be acceptable. He proceeds in another way.

---

30. Hare has discussed Rawls's theory in his critical study 'Rawls's Theory of Justice I/II' in *Philosophical Quarterly* 23 (1973).

Stressing the separateness of distinct persons, the first focus of his construction must be each deliberator's need to assure himself in the spirit of 'maximin' (in the spirit, that is, of making the worst possible outcome be as benign as possible) that, whatever may prove to be his own lot and however unlucky he may turn out to have been, his prudence will have secured for him the least bad outcome possible. Each deliberator will have as his remit to ensure that everyone he represents in the deliberations he is taking part in can benefit, if the results are translated into practice, by this same ratiocination.

The results of these two implementations of the changing places idea are strikingly different. It is true that we may lose sight of the differences between Hare and Rawls when Hare bids the practitioner of generalized prudence to suppose, with C. I. Lewis, that he knows that he is 'in a series of worlds, to occupy in succession, and in random order, all the possible roles of those affected by [the] choice, and [on this basis to] choose [the maxim he is to universalize]'. But, in so far as this way of putting the matter emphasizes the separateness of persons rather than the equal standing of all desires (or interests) of equal intensity, it is oblique to Hare's wishes. For Hare's purpose is to vindicate utilitarianism. Rawls's conclusion is professedly anti-utilitarian.

What has happened here? Has Hare begged the question somehow in arriving at his utilitarian conclusion? Or has Rawls illicitly allowed his anti-utilitarianism into the place where it does not belong, namely the implementation of a common insight that is nobody's particular preserve?

Answer: neither of these. If, following Hare, we impose the principle that we called the Constructional Assumption, then there is no room for the normative idea that one who is prudent is more than a maximizer of preferences—or ought always to ask himself, 'What *ought* I to want?' 'What do I *need?*' Into the vacuum thus created, in the wake of the Prudential Principle and along the route designated by Hare's characterization of the moral point of view, rushes the Principle of Equal Interests. On the other hand, if we find no merit in the Constructional Assumption, or we discern there a highly questionable philosophical thesis, then we shall see it as a real virtue of Rawls's model that it makes room for all sorts of moral and normative notions—'free and equal deliberators' and so on. In their implications, all such ideas entering the construction must be essentially contestable, no doubt; but that does not mean that the ideas are illicit or out of place. It means that their force and their merit needs to be debated outside the construction that is to implement the changing places insight. Once the question becomes how much room there ought to be for this or that substantive notion within constructions such as Hare's or Rawls's, well, everything really depends on what is being attempted in any particular case. Or it depends on the quality of the explication of the notion that is in question. In itself, the bare idea of changing places settles practically nothing.

7.19. In further illustration of such points, it may be no bad thing to conclude, as if in anticipation of the subject of Lecture 10, by attending for a moment to certain further but related matters concerning the prospects and limitations of the constructional method itself. Everything that needs to be said will appear well enough if we allow it to arise in comment upon a more recent summation by Rawls of his own conception of justice:

> A conception of justice must incorporate an ideal form for the basic structure in the light of which the accumulated results of ongoing social processes are to be limited and adjusted.
>
> Now in view of the special role of the basic structure, it is natural to ask the following question: by what principle can free and equal persons accept the fact that social and economic inequalities are deeply influenced by social fortune, and natural and historical happenstance. Since the parties regard themselves as such persons, the obvious starting point is for them to suppose that all social primary goods, including income and wealth, should be equal: everyone should have an equal share. But they must take organizational requirements and economic efficiency

into account. Thus it is unreasonable to stop at equal division. The basic structure should allow organizational and economic inequalities so long as these improve everyone's situation, including that of the least advantaged, provided these inequalities are consistent with equal liberty and fair equality of opportunity. Because they start from equal shares, those who benefit least (taking equal division as the benchmark) have so to speak a veto. And thus the parties arrive at the difference principle. Here equal division is accepted as the benchmark because it reflects how people are situated when they are represented as free and equal moral persons. Among such persons, those who have gained more than others are to do so on terms that improve the situation of those who gained less. These intuitive considerations indicate why the difference principle is the appropriate criterion to govern social and economic inequalities.

To understand the difference principle, several matters have to be kept in mind. First, the two principles of justice [given below, as (a) and (b)], as they work in tandem, incorporate an important element of pure procedural justice in the actual determination of distributive shares. They apply to the basic structure and its system for acquiring entitlements. Within appropriate limits, whatever distributive shares result are just. A fair distribution can be arrived at only by the actual working of a fair social process over time in the course of which, in accordance with publicly announced rules, entitlements are earned and honoured. These features define pure procedural justice. Therefore, if it is asked in the abstract whether one distribution of a given stock of things to definite individuals with known desires and preferences is more just than another, then there is simply no answer to the question.

Thus the main principles of justice, in particular the difference principle, apply to the main public principles and policies that regulate social and economic inequalities. They are used to adjust the system of entitlements and earnings and to balance the familiar everyday standards and precepts which this system employs.[31]

For the record I set down here Rawls's two principles of justice in the revised formulations from *Political Liberalism:*

a. Each person has an equal claim to a fully adequate scheme of equal basic rights and liberties, which scheme is compatible with the same scheme for all; and in this scheme the equal political liberties, and only those liberties, are to be guaranteed their fair value.[32]

b. Social and economic inequalities are to satisfy two conditions: first, they are to be attached to positions and offices open to all under conditions of fair equality of opportunity; and second, they are to be for the greatest benefit of the least advantaged members of society. [The difference principle.]

7.20. *Comment.* The first question that Rawls has the deliberators ask here is by what principle they, the deliberators, who are free and equal persons and know that they are free and equal, can accept the fact that social and economic inequalities are deeply influenced by social fortune and natural/historical happenstance.[33] It may seem altogether strange, however that Rawls's first question should take this particular form.[34] For the very idea of the conditions of fruitful co-

31. John Rawls, 'The Basic Structure as Subject', in his *Political Liberalism* (New York: Columbia University Press, 1993), pp. 281–3; originally published in *American Philosophical Quarterly* 14 (1977).

32. For 'fair value' see Rawls, *Political Liberalism,* pp. 356–63.

33. It assists in the interpretation of the question to collate it with a sentence from the same essay (p. 271 in *Political Liberalism*): 'what the theory of justice must regulate is the inequalities in life prospects between citizens that arise from social starting positions, natural advantages and historical contingencies.'

34. It is almost as if in the background there is a conception of human beings who *will* become members of a society but exist in and of themselves in abstraction from their place in that society, exist equally untrammelled and equally omnipotent (metaphysically speaking) but then become *bogged down,* so to speak, in natural and historical happenstance. But is it not obvious that Rawls cannot have toyed with so absurd a conception?

operation will prompt those who think of themselves as realists about
contingency to think that there is another, much more obvious first
question for the deliberators to attend to. The question is this: given
that, *whatever* principles may be instituted by human beings to regulate the social and political spheres, the human world will always
be replete with contingency, good luck, bad luck, and the rest, what
guarantees of what strength must we place among the conditions of
our cooperation in order to ensure that the worst of the bad luck
that anybody encounters will be alleviated, along with its consequences, by concerted social action? After all, the realist will say,
the first and foremost thing that affects and harms the dispossessed
or destitute is dire, unsatisfied need. Wherever there really is dire,
unsatisfied need, it will be an absurd euphemism to refer to it as
'inequality'. Or so you might think, listening only to the meaning of
the English word. ('Never mind what others have, whether less or
more, there is *not enough* here for us.') How seriously (if at all) will
inequalities of income or wealth *simply as such* detract from the
freedom, the citizenly/participative equality, or even the happiness
of the free and equal persons whom the deliberators represent? Not
seriously, the realist will say, unless they issue in serious deprivation.
Surely, then, freedom, participative equality, and happiness are the
first things for a cooperating society to protect against contingency—
these things and the other things *without which* these things will
not be.

Is there something within Rawls's construction that makes Rawls's
own preferred question the point of departure? If there is not, then
what else makes it the first question? Does some issue lurk here of
legitimacy? What else lurks? To judge from the wording of Rawls's
own question and the presence there of the words 'free and equal',
an assumption is at work there concerning the connection between
freedom and equality on the one hand and equality of income and
wealth on the other, or else between citizenly equality and equality
of 'life chances'. This assumption, however it runs, is evidently momentous. It flows from this whether the deliberators proceed in the

direction we see Rawls move in, towards the difference principle, or they proceed by the more direct route against contingency and natural happenstance. If they take the second of these courses, then they will have to see to it that the principles of cooperation be drafted to enshrine, in the spirit of maximin, certain well-considered principles relating explicitly to the vital needs of members of a well-ordered society. These principles will be designed to safeguard their freedoms, to preserve or enhance their opportunities to make the best they can of their situation, and to offer protection from avoidable immiseration, from personal disaster, or from any other avoidable thing that obstructs their active life within the society. Such an approach might, of course, coincide at some points with Rawls's, but in general it is quite alien to him.

For the deliberators to prefer the realists' question over Rawls's own question and formulate principles of cooperation along these essentially ameliorative lines—for them to react chiefly to the prospect of *misfortunes* or *disabilities* that issue in what Rawls prefers to call 'social and economic inequalities or differences'—will surely lead them in the direction of a partly remedial and partly enabling conception of justice designed for a society of participative or citizenly equality. For the deliberators to prefer Rawls's question leads to Rawls's carefully qualified general egalitarianism.

One who lacked preconceptions in political philosophy, but found deeply interesting and promising the idea of arriving at a substantive conception of justice by working out the principles for fruitful co-operation among the members of a well-ordered society, could not help but wonder why the notion of vital need does not figure in the text of either of Rawls's principles of justice.[35] As before, however (compare our previous discussion of the changing places idea), the answer to the question seems to lie outside the business of construc-

---

35. How can Rawls suppose that the difference principle will do the work of principle relating to need as such? An illuminating answer to this question is furnished by Brian Barry, *The Liberal Theory of Justice* (Oxford: Oxford University Press, 1973), pp. 55–8 and 114–15.

tion and beyond bare ideas of legitimacy and conditions for fruitful cooperation. If the construction itself does not draw up the agenda to be pursued by its means, then something else must.

7.21. I have claimed that the constructive agenda are influenced by assumptions that ought to have been laid out to view and were not. But one other possibility is worth mentioning, having to do with an unintended by-product of the idea of a foundational contract for a well-ordered society. There is something to be learned from considering this possible answer, even if the suspicion it is founded upon is baseless.

Once the contract idea is given and it is seen as conditioning the business of construction, a tendency is noticeable for this contract to be thought of as concluded *as if at some particular moment*—albeit a notional moment when there is as yet no history of the society which the contract is to make possible, no pattern of holdings, and no past events of any moral or social significance. So soon as we accept the contract idea as an innocuous 'aid to intuition', or as 'priming the pump' for a procedure of construction, it may be that the full implications of the contract idea are not clear to us. Can it be that the notional contracting idea lulls us into acquiescence in a second meaning of the expression 'starting point' as that occurs in Rawls's sentence 'the obvious starting point is . . . to suppose that all social primary goods, including income and wealth should be equal'?[36] (Compare also: 'Because they start from equal shares, those who benefit least . . . have so to speak a veto.') If *from the outset everyone has the same* social primary goods, then from the outset their shares are equal. The charm of the second meaning is this. It makes the idea of equality seem entirely clear—because having *identical* primary goods gives us a perfect and completely transparent

36. Perhaps this obviousness ought to be compared with that of the notorious Principle of Indifference of Laplace, to the effect that, in the case of complete ignorance, the *a priori* probability of a given proposition is 1/2. For the gruesome fate of this principle, cp. the discussion in J. M. Keynes, *A Treatise on Probability* (London: Macmillan, 1921), ch. 4 and *passim*.

case of equality. (For *this* case all rival theories agree.) The trouble is though that this may not give us much idea of what it will take, *constitutively*, to measure the equality or inequality of persons six eventful months (say) after the notional starting point. Identity only furnishes a sufficient condition of equality. If any other dispositions of primary goods, besides everyone's having exactly the same primary goods, are to count as sufficient for Rawlsian equality, what are they? What is the metric for equality? What are the necessary conditions of this sort of equality? These are not easy questions at all. It is far from obvious, moreover, that there is here some vast fund of speakers' inexplicit knowledge or moral/political/linguistic understanding that philosophy can draw upon to explicate this notion of equality. Contrast the fuller and more numerous intuitions that lend some pre-theoretical support to 'just' or 'free' or 'fair' or 'owed', say. Is it really all right for this sense of 'equal' to be a free construction of the theorist's mind?

It is at this moment that someone with a different take from Rawls on the problem of legitimacy (and much less patience perhaps with the as-if) may want to protest that it is only the contractualist picture and the direction in which it pushes the Rawlsian construction that obliges us to find better than rhetorical use for the invented notion of equality; that the invented notion stands in no certain relation to 'equal' as 'equal' occurs in the relatively clear phrase 'free and equal persons' (which was where we started); that it is only this invented notion that commits us to the possibility of a *metric* of social primary goods. So far as justice and the allegiance of citizens are concerned, can we not make do with the notion of equal that figures in 'free and equal deliberators' and *follow that through properly?* Why not leave the troublesome invented sense to wither on the vine and let the notion of vital need limit the gravity of the effects of contingency? Why not dispense with the contract idea altogether by seeing the deliberators as debating, preferably from the starting point of some 'us' that they understand of free and equal citizens, the conditions of *perpetuating* or *renewing* or *improving* social cooperation itself in an ongoing society whose workings they know well enough? Will

not a more a selective amnesia do duty for the thicker veil of ignorance prevailing in Rawls's original position? On these terms the
deliberators will surely not begin with the question that we have just
seen Rawls begin with. In this way, might not philosophy now prepare to close the enormous file it has amassed from two or three
hundred years' work devoted to the supposedly fascinating question
of the epistemology and metaphysics of sovereignty and the endlessly
inconclusive answers mustered for it? Might it make do with the
alternative to contractualism that comes to our attention in Hume's
essay, 'Of the Original Contract'?

7.22. Too many questions! This is not the place to try to decide
between Rawls and this critic or take sides between egalitarian justice
and the protective-cum-restorative-cum-meliorist justice of free and
equal citizens. (That is one part of the business for Lecture 10.) The
point that chiefly interests us here is only this: that, in themselves,
constructions or models such as Hare's or Rawls's will never settle
such matters. At their best they will illustrate and illuminate the
purport of semantical elucidations and philosophical considerations
that come from without, considerations about legitimacy, allegiance,
reasonable expectations, the best construal of equality, the soundness
or unsoundness of this or that idea of equality, and (as we shall see
in Lectures 9 and 10) the roles of human constitution, habit, and
ethical formation. It is inquiries such as these that determine what
question the deliberators are to put first and what positive conception of justice they are to make for the people on whose behalf they
deliberate. All the real action lies there, outside the construction.

There is no such thing as an (autonomous and self-containing)
moral mathematics. But even if there were, it could settle nothing—
and least of all the point, sense, or significance of what the moral
or political philosopher finds himself saying.

8

The consequentialist argument

There is but one unconditional commandment, which is that we should seek incessantly, with fear and trembling, so to vote and so to act as to bring about the very largest total universe of good we can see.

William James, *The Will to Believe*

The ardor of undisciplined benevolence seduces us into malignity and whenever our hearts are warm and our objects great and excellent, intolerance is the sin that does most easily beset us. . . . I rather think that the distant prospect, to which [Robespierre] was travelling appeared to him grand and beautiful; but that he fixed his eye on it with such intense earnestness as to neglect the foulness of the road.

Samuel Taylor Coleridge, *Conciones ad Populum*, 1795

I think that particular events are what they are, and do not become different by absorption into a whole. Each act is eternally a part of the universe; nothing that happens later can make that act good rather than bad or can confer perfection on the whole of which it is a part.

Bertrand Russell, *History of Western Philosophy*

8.1. We come now to the second of the two further arguments that were promised for espousing some form of utilitarianism. This will be the occasion to focus on a particular way of thinking in which the utilitarian tradition and G. E. Moore shared: 'Our duty . . . can be defined as that action which will cause more good to exist in the universe than any possible alternative'.[1] (See 7.4 above.) In English-speaking philosophy, the thing *Principia Ethica* had in common

---

1. *Principia Ethica* (Cambridge: Cambridge University Press, 1903), p. 148.

with ordinary utilitarianism was to sustain and perpetuate the tendency of twentieth-century ethics (see 6.4 and 7.3) to see the good
as determining the right. *Principia Ethica* assisted in this tendency.
It assisted even as it lent utilitarianism an intrinsicalist character up
to that point foreign to it. In England, both author and book exercised a preternatural influence on the thoughts and creative endeavours of generations of Bloomsbury writers and artists who would
have found ordinary utilitarianism entirely unconvincing or worse.
The chief critic of the consequentialist tendency in Moore's thinking
was W. D. Ross, author of *The Right and the Good*,[2] the philosophical moralist and Aristotelian scholar whose thoughts we encounter
later in the lecture.

8.2.   Roughly, the consequentialist argument we are to expound
and anatomize is this: use any criterion, ethical or extra-ethical, that
convinces you for determining the goodness or badness of the outcomes of actions. It is neither here nor there, for instance, whether
this criterion includes or excludes the nineteenth-century utilitarians'
customary reference to happiness.[3] Then, once that issue is decided
and you count the doing itself of the act among outcomes, the only
sensible or rational way to determine what ought to be done is for
you to ask this: the doing of which act is likely to have the best
total outcome? 'If such an argument has any merit at all' (and 'how
can it be altogether mistaken?', a proponent will say), 'then, despite
all the subtle moral and other objections that the position always
provokes, there *must* be some defensible version of utilitarianism.'
   The idea that propels this argument probably subsisted in the
consciousness of utilitarians almost from the outset. But it was rarely
or never made explicit. The clearest and most succinct version of

---

2. Oxford: Oxford University Press, 1930.

3. In practice, after nineteenth-century beginnings, happiness is usually drained off
altogether from canonical statements of utilitarianism, along with other mentalistic com-
ponents. There have been reasons for this, see 6.16; but, if the result is for the position
to float free altogether from all constraints upon the content of the ethical, then is not
something important thrown away?

the argument that we have in the literature is due to Samuel Scheffler.[4]

Scheffler begins his exposition with an account of the disputes aroused by arguments of the kind just expounded:

> The dispute between consequentialism and its opponents grows out of a deep puzzle about our moral ideas. The puzzle that fuels the dispute concerns an apparent conflict between the canons of rationality that we most naturally apply and the moral values we most confidently affirm.

There are two points to make about these opening remarks.

The name 'consequentialism' neatly isolates one feature of classical utilitarianism and it connotes the commitment not simply to hold that consequences matter (everyone thinks that, see 6.4), but to hold that right and wrong are to be determined without the independent deployment of distinctively ethical, deontological, or agential ideas and on the sole basis of the merit or demerit of consequences. It is hard to imagine dispensing with so useful a name, but it has a relatively recent provenance. It was introduced into philosophy by G. E. M. Anscombe in a famous article entitled 'Modern Moral Philosophy'.[5] The word has a particular felicity for our purposes, suggesting as it does that one who is a consequentialist will believe that our notion of outcome must be expanded in order that the rightness or wrongness of doing a particular act should be grounded completely or exhaustively in consideration of all the consequences (in some extended sense) of doing the act (including any consequences there will be of others' doing things relevantly similar to this thing); grounded in outcomes, that is, *without regard under the aspects of agency or responsibility to what the act itself is or what it is to do that act.* Thus in the consequentialist ranking of alternatives, con-

---

4. The citations to follow will be taken from the first page of Scheffler's editorial introduction to his anthology, *Consequentialism and Its Critics* (Oxford: Oxford University Press, 1988).

5. 'Modern Moral Philosophy', *Philosophy* 53 (1958): 1–19.

siderations of the obligatoriness or forbiddenness of an act are assimilated to other features of the goodness or badness, all told, of
outcomes. In arguing in the way in which we shall see Scheffler
argue, the consequentialist precisely celebrates this subordination of
the right to the good.

A second point: Scheffler speaks of a conflict between the moral
values we ordinarily affirm and canons of rationality. But it may be
that the chief reason for such a conflict's appearing to us is an
assumption philosophy ought not to make: namely that, in advance
of morality itself, the notion of rationality is already complete, together with all sorts of canons or norms of rationality that one might
have learned to apply in advance of all considerations of ethics or
value. Is that a plausible bifurcation? One might think, for instance,
that rationality embraces the logic of inquiry, which must from the
outset have embraced the value of truth. (Must it not?) Nor is that
reason's only involvement with value. The logic of inquiry also needs
to embrace an ethics of belief; but the ethics of belief needs to
acknowledge the indispensability (as well as the defeasibility and
openness to disappointment) of trust in the testimony of others.[6]
Here again rationality is no stranger to the ethical, and has no alternative but to acknowledge the non-hypothetical (categorical, that
is) permissibility of procedures or attitudes to which it is committed
by the pursuit of the intrinsic good that is the value of truth and/or
committed to by avoidance of the intrinsic bad constituted by the
false or the inaccurate. (For the categorical and hypothetical see 4.4–
6.) If reason must embrace within itself non-hypothetical values or
concerns such as these, then what else (one might ask) must reason
embrace within itself? By what right can it circumscribe itself against
the categorical concerns of the ethical?[7] In advance of the ethical,

6. Charles Sanders Peirce claimed that logic, including the logic of inquiry, was a
social art. Here he had chiefly in mind a further contention of his own: that one who
embraces good procedures for non-deductive inference has to accept that sometimes not
s/he necessarily, but only the community of researchers as a whole, will be the beneficiary
of these procedures.

7. That may be another way of saying something that is said sometimes about a
paradox called the Prisoners' Dilemma. For this dilemma, see the excellent account of

surely rationality is incomplete.[8] If there really is the conflict Scheffler says there is, may it not lie within reason itself?

8.3.   Scheffler writes next:

> Consequentialism in its purest and simplest form is a moral doctrine which says that the right act in any given situation is the one that will produce the best overall outcome, as judged from an impersonal standpoint which gives equal weight to the interests of everyone.

If you are party to any of the misgivings expressed in the preceding lecture, you will wonder how much store Scheffler ought to set by the 'impersonal standpoint' as a place from which to judge the 'best overall outcome'. In its passion to find a starting place that is as yet ethically non-committal, does such a standpoint have to give equal weight to the equal interests of Mafiosi, of gallant soldiers disabled in war, of scrupulous accountants, of child molesters, of conscientious road sweepers, of kidnappers and torturers, of honest sempstresses . . . ? Maybe there is a better way of characterizing the impersonal; but it is equally possible that the very idea of such a starting point is misconceived.

Now though, simply remembering the substantive and questionable role played in the last chapter by the Constructional Assumption and noting how strangely committing the search for neutrality becomes (does true even-handedness really require us to be neutral between good and evil?), we need to move closer to the central part of the argument itself:

> Somewhat more precisely, we may think of a consequentialist theory of this kind as coming in two parts. First, it gives some

---

such matters given by J. L. Mackie, *Ethics: Inventing Right and Wrong* (Harmondsworth: Penguin, 1977), pp. 115–20.

  8. Unless Kant is right, of course, and pure rationality can give to us the whole of the ethical—in which case, it may be said, Scheffler's 'apparent conflict' must again be only apparent.

principle for ranking overall states of affairs from best to worst
from an impersonal standpoint, and then it says that the right
act in any given situation is the one that will produce the
highest-ranked state of affairs that the agent is in a position to
produce. Obviously, there can be as many different theories of
this type as there are criteria for ranking overall outcomes. One
thing they all share, however, is a very simple and seductive
idea: namely, that so far as morality is concerned, what people
ought to do is to minimize evil and maximize good, to try, in
other words, to make the world as good a place as possible.

The last sentence prepares the ground for the conclusion of the
argument, which comes in our next instalment. Meanwhile, though,
we may find something unnerving in the form of words 'to make
the world as good a place as possible'. Who will dare to scorn or
diminish heroic acts that have been inspired by aims given in such
words? But who will want to forget that the perpetrators of some of
the most extraordinary crimes in history have felt moved to use
words no different from these?

One more remark about the passage from Scheffler in front of us:
theorists are apt to set great store by the capacity they find we have
to rank given states of affairs in the manner that Scheffler describes.
But it is important to remember here that the choices by which we
make rankings are narrowly constrained by the circumstances of the
choices. Once we appreciate this, real life feats of ranking will appear
to fall short of licensing the idea of any extrapolation to an underlying *general* ranking (or a context-free 'indifference map', as I think
I should say to colleagues in economics). A further and distinct point
is this: that the choices or rankings of ordinary agents need not
necessarily be *founded in* or *based on* comparisons in respect of
'more' and 'less' of something or other. It may be that, in real life,
it is the choice itself of A over B that gives the ranking 'A is better
than B'. Where this is so, the judgment of right or wrong may be
more basic than the judgment 'A is better than B'. In the world that
we know—contrast some world of valuation and action conceived in

accordance with the Constructional Assumption or with consequentialism—it may be that ideas of right and wrong, obligatory and forbidden/taboo, and ideas of good and bad stand in no general relation of priority and posteriority.[9] A careful study of the varieties of goodness might confirm that, in many uses, 'good' and 'bad' (or 'evil', as Scheffler goes on to write) *presuppose* or *already involve* 'must' and 'must not' or 'ought' and 'ought not'. It is a substantial assumption of Scheffler's—one reminiscent of the Constructional Assumption and no more to be acquiesced in than that was—that there *can be* rankings of states of affairs of the kind that the consequentialist will need in order for him to advance in the manner he desires from good to right.

8.4.   Prescinding from all the doubts so far expressed, let us now have the final instalment of Scheffler's argument:

> On the face of it, this idea [namely to minimize evil and maximize good], which lies at the heart of consequentialism, seems hard to resist. For given only the innocent-sounding assumption that good is morally preferable to evil, it seems to embody the principle that we should maximize the desirable and minimize the undesirable, and that principle seems to be one of the main elements of our conception of practical rationality. Anyone who resists consequentialism seems committed to the claim that morality tells us to do less good than we are in a position to do, and to prevent less evil than we are in a position to prevent. And this does not sound nearly as plausible.

Here Scheffler's exposition well encapsulates the underlying intuition which almost all consequentialist arguments have been designed to translate into persuasive argument. It presupposes a generalization of the notion of consequence, but the generalization is not open to

---

9. See my *Needs, Values, Truth* (amended 3rd ed., Oxford: Oxford University Press, 2002), pp. 360–1.

the accusation of making the position true vacuously. Rather, the position is controversial, but it is controversial in a way that Scheffler's argument appears to transcend. How will a reasonable or ethical being who refuses to act in the manner that Scheffler commends live with himself or herself when confronted with the evil s/he could (it will be said) have prevented or forestalled?

Faced with arguments like Scheffler's, people either rush to embrace the conclusion or else struggle to refute it. It is remarkable (if not almost comical) how often those who choose the first celebrate their new-found consequentialism by attending on this basis to the long-standing need to find some way to grant a waiver to one who has made a promise but realizes that its execution would be disastrous for all concerned. We already have a better way, however. (See 6.4.) Those who respond to Scheffler in the second manner will have recourse to counterexamples, and counterexamples certainly have the virtue of making clearer what is at issue. But they will not show what is wrong with the argument; and our chief concern will need to be with the argument. Let us never forget the dialectical situation. We are Humeans or Kantians (or else agnostics) who are holding ourselves open to be persuaded by some simpler or better or more developed position descending from the utilitarianism we decided in Lecture 6 not to prefer over those positions. In that role, we must cross-examine the argument closely (8.6). First though, in deference to those who want to think about examples, let us illustrate its workings in a case where other philosophies would find it harder to sanction the same conclusion as the consequentialists.

8.5. Let us suppose that ethnic non-quarrelsomeness is a species or subspecies of moral virtue and let us suppose that this virtue is itself an intrinsic good—in a sense of 'intrinsic' equally available to a utilitarian and to G. E. Moore, namely that of being good apart from any of the results that it produces.[10] Let us suppose further that, in the Balkans somewhere, some reflective, self-conscious

10. Cp. Ross, *The Right and the Good*, p. 68.

person, a patriot of some sort, possessing both determination and armed power, deliberates as follows:

> The only way out of the present situation is to bring into being communities which do not see themselves as ethnically divided and in which the issue of ethnicity can be allowed to go to sleep. That is the essential prerequisite of their becoming communities in which questions of race can be discounted and the positive virtues can eventually be cultivated of ethnic non-quarrelsomeness and non-factiousness. That is for the long run. But now, in the world of 1997, the only way in which even the first step can be achieved is at cost of a rearrangement . . . even at cost of measures of partition or of ethnic cleansing, as some call it. And that, alas, is what must happen now. . . . I can see no alternative.

Suppose that this deliberation appears markedly *more thorough* (at least) and takes into account *more facts, political and historical,* than any other deliberation that looks steadfastly for some way out of some present impasse. Suppose also that some duty of 'beneficence' requires that we should produce as much intrinsic good as we can.[11] Then agents who have this thought must inevitably face the altogether insidious question of how many of their virtuous concerns it is right for them to sacrifice in the present in order to fulfil their duty to promote some larger and more widespread future virtue, the virtue of ethnic non-quarrelsomeness or non-factiousness, which they claim to see continuing, and continuing within less troubled communities, into an open-ended future. If there really is a duty to maximize good and there is no mistake in the ratiocinations of the patriot, then agents who have the thoughts just expounded will have to answer the question of what could ever *release* them from the

---

11. In due course it will be important to distinguish this construal of beneficence from the ordinary or the Humean construal. See Stephen Darwall, 'Under Moore's Spell', *Utilitas* 10.3 (1998).

positive duty, by the patriot's or any other effective method, to maximize future virtue.

If the example seems totally flawed or does not carry conviction,
let the reader apply the same recipe again and find another. But the
patriot's idea (let us suppose) is not simply silly—the idea that some
cloistered virtue of racial non-quarrelsomeness will exist wherever
everyone is of the same race (or everyone sees everyone else in this
way). His idea is that, in the short-term future of certain torn communities, the question of race and culture must be put therapeuti-
cally to sleep, so that, in the longer term and among new generations
to come, the ordinary questions that will arise of race and racial
difference can be managed more calmly and reasonably. (Compare
the counsel of an allergy specialist who advises that for a considerable period the patient should withdraw from all contact with an
irritating agent to which he has become hypersensitive—*before* resuming ordinary life on a better regime.) The patriot's idea is not
even simple-minded. Anticipating the moment to pass judgment on
it, I should say rather that the magnitude of the distant prize and
the special character of the framework in which the patriot permits
himself to deliberate distract his attention from the true nature of
the acts which he is preparing to countenance. (Compare Coleridge
in the second epigraph.) Whatever prospect his idea may hold out
for human peace and virtue stretching into an open-ended future, it
may give cover in the present to other and far more disquieting
intentions and acquiescences.

For just these reasons, some consequentialists will draw back and
express doubt that the patriot has shown that it would be right to
do what he is proposing. Fair enough. (I have only described the
case here in order to show what is at issue, not in a spirit of refutation.) If we modify the example to make the costs small enough,
though, or the prize large and certain enough, then there is no such
obvious escape by this route. The only escape seems to be to give
up consequentialism and, with it, the last residue of utilitarianism.
If that were the result of someone's rehearsing the considerations set
out here, then that would be a noteworthy development. Even then,

though, I should not say that consequentialism had been refuted. The most that can be refuted is the argument *for* consequentialism.

8.6. The time has come to interrogate Scheffler's argument more closely. First, let us spread things out a bit:

> *x* acts rightly if and only if *x* does the best thing to do.
> *x* does the best thing to do if and only if *x* produces the best state of affairs.
> *x* produces the best state of affairs if and only if *x* produces the state of affairs that is ranked highest among those *x* is in a position to produce.

In these three equivalences we have four things, namely: (1) acting rightly or doing the right thing; (2) doing the best thing; (3) producing the best state of affairs; (4) producing the highest ranked state of affairs that *x* is in a position to produce. Between these four things, we have three links, set out in the table below.

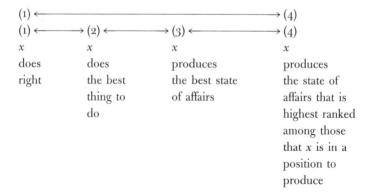

Now the claim that there is a two-way link, (1) ↔ (4), between (1) and (4) is scarcely obviously truistic or analytic or platitudinous. In Lecture 6, we were unable to credit anything like J. S. Mill's claim that we believe in this link already. On the other hand, someone *may* be able to show how, through other and shorter links, if we forge them correctly and we align them properly, it can be rendered *unobviously* truistic or analytic or platitudinous, and thus as deserving our credence, that (1) ↔ (4).

By virtue of the doubts given above in 8.3 about the significance of ranking, the (3) ↔ (4) link may seem doubtful. But (2) ↔ (3) is the linkage that should provoke more misgivings. Let it be clear that, if (2) is something that we can derive from (1), if it is (1) that helps fix the relevant sense of 'good', and if the link (1) ↔ (2) is meant to be analytic or uncontentious in each direction (neutrally acceptable, that is, between all parties to the argument in hand), then the goodness of the best thing to do—the goodness of choice of the specific act itself, I mean, which we are supposing to be required of the agent in the circumstances that he finds himself in—will have to be owed to the act in question's meeting the relevant criteria for such an act. Its goodness will be goodness among possible acts or responses to a given situation. Such goodness, reflecting the claim (1) ↔ (2), lies downwind of rightness. (This has to hold if (1) ↔ (4) is to link right with good.) What then is the relation of that goodness, as per (2) ↔ (3), to the act's producing the best state of affairs? The consequentialist will be stealing the conclusion that he intends to pay for by argument if he answers these questions by simply assuming that the criteria for assessing such goodness as this must be formulated exclusively in terms of consequences. How then is the consequentialist positively to persuade us? Our own position is of course that consequences matter hugely, but that the way in which they are to be taken into account depends on the deployment of ideas *including* ideas of responsibility and agency that are ethical and more than simply valuational. (See 6.4.) The dialectical situation is that, on our side, we do not lack for an account of the nature of morality—Kant or Hume can supply that and neither of them would positively affirm (2) ↔ (3)—but that the way still remains open for us to be persuaded, in ways we have not yet imagined, that there is some better account of morality to be had and that *this* entails (2) ↔ (3).

Here it becomes important for it to be clear that the transformation that makes (2) into (3) and (3) into (2) is not a purely grammatical or logical one. Sentence (2) records an agent x's choice of the best act. Sentence (3) records the state of affairs that results from an agent's doing that act. These are different; and (2) $\leftrightarrow$ (3), read right to left, makes the substantial claim that we can find the best act, *the best thing to do,* by the method of valuing the states of affairs that result from doing that act. In other words, we are to judge the act done by the outcome of doing it. If we are in any doubt what that commits us to, then the Balkan patriot's solution to the problems of the country that he is concerned for will serve to remind us of one part of the meaning of (2) $\leftrightarrow$ (3). If bloodshed, destitution, and a host of refugees are the almost invariable result of the sort of 'rearrangement' the Balkan patriot has in mind, for instance, then the consequentialist judgment upon the said acts of rearranging simply sets the 'moral cost' of bloodshed, destitution, and a host of refugees (this 'loss of intrinsic value') against the 'moral or intrinsic costs' of the present situation and then sets the difference between these against the longer term intrinsic benefits (including 'moral gains') that we are to imagine as plausibly assured for the future.

8.7.   It is easy to anticipate that at this point a consequentialist or sympathizer will break in with some impatience: 'If the situation really is as you allow and the Balkan patriot's historical and political appreciation of the situation is correct, then who are you to be so slyly moralistic about what he is proposing? Who are you to try by your seasoned pessimism to upstage his assessment of what it is right to do here?'

The answer to the question is that, for such purposes, I am nobody—not even a person trying to refute consequentialism or trying to refute every imaginable consequentialist argument. As I have already indicated, the strongest verdict I see any prospect of reaching on Scheffler's argument is 'not proven', though I think that that would be enough to clear up the dialectical situation. In the interim, the chief thing that I aim for is to understand better what it would be to believe in consequentialism and what kind of argument it would take to persuade someone to go over to it—or else to understand what it could be to lose all interest in its prospects of convincing us that (2) ↔ (3). In this matter, most of what I have said so far is that it has proved that there is less help than one had at first hoped to find in the extracts I have quoted from Scheffler—if only because closer examination shows that, when it comes to it, his reasoning assumes rather than argues the logical interchangeability of considerations about acts and considerations about outcomes. Consequentialism, it now appears, is not something to be defended under the aspect of a merely grammatical transformation or a platitude or a truism of moral mathematics and or moral reasonableness. It is a striking and controversial proposal—the proposal, in the name of the ethical rationality of value maximization, to find a single rule for the determination of overall rightness that will replace the multiplicity of ways that are sanctioned by practices that recognize the realities and limitations of human agency and are sanctioned by notions of morality and reasonableness that take it for granted that morality itself fills out our idea of reasonableness in the manner suggested at the end of 8.2 above.

8.8.   What then are the prospects for such a single rule? Are they any better now, at the turn of the millennium, than the prospects were a hundred years ago for the Moorean principle that we cited in section 8.1 of this lecture, or better than the prospects that existed for the earlier form of consequentialism, namely utilitarianism, which Moore sought to convict of the naturalistic fallacy?

In *The Right and the Good,* W. D. Ross maintained that Moore and the ideal utilitarians had fallen into the grave mistake of thinking that 'the only morally significant relation in which my neighbours stand to me is that of being possible beneficiaries of my action'.

They do stand in this relation to me, and this relation is significant. But they may stand in the relation of promisee to promiser, of creditor to debtor, of wife to husband, of child to parent, of fellow countryman to fellow countryman, and the like, and each of these relations is the foundation of a *prima facie* duty. (p. 19)

Lest we suppose that there is one underlying principle which, in one swoop, can render up all of these things, Ross further anatomizes the differences between six broad categories:

1. Duties resting on previous acts of my own, either (a) promises or implied promises, entailing duties of fidelity, or (b) wrongful acts, entailing duties of reparation;
2. Duties deriving from the acts of others, such as duties of gratitude (or, as one might say with greater generality, of reciprocity);
3. Duties of distributive justice;
4. Duties of beneficence;
5. Duties of self-improvement;
6. Duties of care not to injure others or non-maleficence, rightly perceived by Ross as not reducible to duties of type (4) or beneficence.[12]

In sum, 'the essential defect of the 'ideal utilitarian' [or consequentialist] theory is that it ignores, or at least does not do full justice to, the highly personal character of duty'. The duty of one who has made a promise to keep his promise is not the duty to promote or enlarge the totality of intrinsically valuable promise-keeping. He might do that without keeping his promise. Similarly, the duty of a parent with respect to their children is not a duty to promote the intrinsic value that consists in parents' providing for their children or a duty to promote the intrinsic value that is augmented by more and more parents' cultivating and exercising the virtue of which

12. 'Even when we have come to recognize the duty of beneficence, it appears to me that the duty of non-maleficence is recognized as a distinct one, and as *prima facie* more binding. We should not in general consider it justifiable to kill one person in order to keep another alive, or to steal from one in order to give alms to another', p. 22.

looking after their children is a characteristic exercise. It is the duty that any parent has with respect to their own children. Indeed, so far from being its foundation, the value attributed to this virtue's being cultivated and exercised seems to *presuppose* the said duty.[13] Is there not something strange, moreover, in taking this duty for granted at first and then subsuming it within a single or overarching rule of right action that will sometimes be at variance with this same duty?

8.9. However archaic modern consequentialists may profess to find Ross's way of expressing himself or his typology of 'duties', and whatever problems Ross made for himself in the course of developing his own account of everyday morality,[14] the sheer intractability of the material with which everyday morality confronts modern consequentialism is not different from what it was at the time when Ross undertook to criticize ideal utilitarianism (and utilitarianism) in these terms. There is a strong ethical case against any single principle's replacing the multiplicity of principles by which we ordinarily determine right and wrong. I shall not deny that there is something worthy to be considered further in Scheffler's insistence that what matters is the *rationality* of the ethical point of view. I undertake to return in Lecture 9 to the issue of rationality, only remarking in the meanwhile that consequentialism has problems of its own here (see 8.2 above). First, though, I hasten to complete the rest of the case against Scheffler's presentation of consequentialism, remarking to begin with that the line of objection will not depend on any sweeping rejection of absolutely all the consequentialists' verdicts on cases.

13. Would it not verge on absurdity—the ultimate in the right hand's not knowing what the left is doing—if someone became so preoccupied with the business of promoting the cause of parents' properly looking after their children that they neglected the care of their own children?

14. There is matter bearing on this in David Wiggins, 'The Right and the Good and W. D. Ross's Criticism of Consequentialism', *Utilitas* 10.3 (1998), and in Darwall, 'Under Moore's Spell'.

So far, the case against Scheffler's argument has focused on that which is special to the consequentialist *procedure* for considering cases. But next it must concentrate on the assumption, implicit in such procedures, that to act in accordance with the ethical is one and the same as to realize as much value as possible. Do all ethical concerns relate to matters of value? It is very much to the point that Ross doubted this (albeit for reasons of his own). One of his ways of expressing his objections to Moore was to say that 'right does not stand for a form of value at all'.[15] Moreover, the proposal of the Balkan patriot shows a way for us to illustrate, generalize, and enlarge on that Rossian dictum.

8.10. Suppose someone reacts to the patriot's plan with deep misgiving. Suppose they draw back in horror from the suggestion that problems of race, hatred, and prejudice can only be solved by acts of genocide. Let us call this person the waverer. Let us suppose that the waverer had warmed at first to the patriot's vision of some future virtue of ethnic non-factiousness, before being brought up short in the act of envisaging in realistic terms the means necessary for the realization of that vision. How would a consequentialist have to describe the waverer's state of mind? As follows, it seems:

The waverer began by placing the agreed high value N upon the end E consisting of racial non-quarrelsomeness. On this, waverer and patriot were at one. Then, when the means to E became clearer, the waverer insisted that, in prospect, he placed the negative value $(-M)$ upon the implementation of these means. At this point the patriot reminded the waverer of the agreed high and positive value placed upon E, which was a good perpetuated into an open future. He pointed out that N was so big that $(N - M)$ was really quite close to N. Even if you doubled M, it made little difference. For $N - (M \times 2)$ was

15. *The Right and the Good*, p. 122, and cp. p. 133.

still very close to N. For some reason, though, the waverer still
found it impossible to continue in the patriot's cause.

Using the terms to which he is entitled, can a consequentialist improve this description to make better sense of the waverer's reservations, or even to become party to them? Perhaps. But, if he is to
make sense of waverer, the difficulties he confronts are serious. For
the thing that shocks the waverer is surely not the simple contem-
plation of genocide. (The waverer knows enough about the real
world to know that human history can put on show tens of
thousands of outcomes even worse that that which the patriot is
contemplating.) What shocks him is the prospect of the patriot's
doing and *his* (*the waverer's*) *acquiescing in the patriot's doing* the
act the patriot contemplates. It must surely be a mistake to try to
explain the waverer's reservations as attaching to the difference between the sizes of N and (N − M). That is just a quantity, very
much like any other quantity. What he is shocked at is the idea of
his doing the terrible act itself that is said to be disvalued at − M
or of anyone's doing it whom he might influence. Surely, though,
'disvalued' isn't the right word. When he starts and draws back, the
notions that our waverer is deploying are already ideas of right and
wrong, forbidden, *nefas*, etc. The thought that brings him up short
is the thought of doing something *like that*—the thought, that is, of
doing or acquiescing in the doing of an act that is as appalling as
that! Of course, once consequentialism had been argued for in a
persuasive and *non-question-begging way*, it could be argued that
such responses were to be discounted. But that is not the present
situation.

   In practice, we deploy all sorts of ideas that appear to fall under
the *right* as well as the *good*, namely ideas of the forbidden, of the
taboo, of the unspeakable, of the *nefastum* or the *atasthalon*, *apor-
rheton*, *arrheton*, and of the sanctity of practices that respect and
safeguard human life and its purposes. By their nature, *such* ideas
are already involved with thoughts of that which it is morally impossible or morally imperative for agents to do. But, if that is so,

then what sense is there in the project of converting ideas like these into ideas of mere value and disvalue? Inevitably, one who pursues this project not only misunderstands ethical language. They overlook that which the linguistic facts reflect or prefigure, namely the foundational facts about human agency and the responsibility that agents take for what they specifically contribute to the sequence of events and for acts they intentionally do. (For the rationality of having regard for these things, see Lecture 9.)

8.11.   A simpler case than that of the Balkan patriot may be useful. A terrorist of some kind demands (for reasons scarcely more complicated, mad, or obscure than those the world has recently become used to) that I lean out of the window of the room in which he has surprised me and shoot two rounds into a crowd of persons below— or else (he says) he will blow up Waterloo railway station (London) at rush hour (as he convinces me that he has already prepared to do). In this way he seems to force me, as a putative agent, to make a comparison between the badness of a handful of casualties and the badness of thousands of casualties. If the comparison so described is as easy as that, then a remarkable thing becomes visible, which Philippa Foot has pointed out:[16] namely that, according to the canons of consequentialist reasoning, there will be nothing so terrible that an agent cannot be required to do that very thing in order to dissuade/prevent others from doing more of it, on a grander scale, with yet more dreadful outcome.

Here, it may be said, in cases such as the one you are citing, you are disregarding all the *further* outcomes that need to be borne in mind. Consider the long-term effect of giving in to blackmail, etc. All right, I reply, let us, just for the sake of simplicity, change or complicate the example in order to insulate the case in question from having any effect or influence upon subsequent cases where wicked and/or unreasonable demands will be made. At least on these

16. Compare Philippa Foot, 'Morality, Action and Outcome', in T. Honderich, ed., *Morality and Objectivity* (London: Routledge, 1985).

terms, the consequentialist will find nothing else to guide the agent but a comparison between the bad effects flowing from each of the only choices that the terrorist leaves open to him as agent. These outcomes are simply deaths and injuries, passably comparable totals.

What fails to register on this ratiocination? This it seems: that if the agent lets off two rounds into the crowd, then that is what the agent has done. That is the choice he will be responsible for—which is not to deny that he may explain or justify himself. That is a question to be addressed later. The present point is simply that that is what he has done. If on the other hand Waterloo is blown up, then that is what the terrorist has done. There is more to say, of course. But there is also this to say.

8.12. Yet again, I emphasize that the present reason for setting out instances of consequentialist reasoning is not so much to demonstrate that consequentialism is wrong as to illustrate its nature, to remind the reader of the gap already remarked in the only positive argument given for it, and to point to the ethical ideas that the position has the effect of excluding. Our aim is not to condescend to consequentialism—if only because consequentialism seems to furnish a mode of reasoning that may yet appear indispensable to the treatment of extreme moral emergencies. We shall go into that in the next lecture. (See 9.15.) In the meanwhile, let us say that, regardless of whether consequentialism might at this late hour come to the rescue of some improved form of utilitarianism, it does point to a mass of unfinished business. Non-consequentialists need to explain what sort of reasonableness ordinary morality partakes in and how our ethical ideas cohere with our ideas of agency and responsibility, as well as to measure up to the question of reasoning in emergencies. In the interim, though, four remarks suggest themselves about the state of the argument.

First, when someone, an ordinary person who is not necessarily a consequentialist, points to some emergency so great that a beneficent agent will have to do something simply terrible in order to avert a disaster of almost unthinkable proportions, is the person who offers this advice really in the business of telling the beneficent person what it is *right* for him to do? Surely not, a non-consequentialist might say. He is in the business of showing our agent there is *nothing else* for him to do—that there is nowhere else that anyone can turn if total catastrophe is to be averted. He is trying to show the beneficent person that that awful act is what he *has* to do, not what he 'morally ought' to do. This is a new discipline and a new dialectic, lying altogether outside the remit of 'deontology' as that was traditionally conceived. Surely, though, where such a thing is shown—and the difficulty of showing it is always extreme—questions of right and wrong, of obligation, or of acts the doing of which would be morally praiseworthy because they were done from a sense of duty . . . all these things will long since have gone out of the window. Their place will have been taken by dire (alleged) necessity.

The second remark is that it will deserve careful examination whether the ordinary casuistry of emergency really is consequentalist in character. We shall inquire into that in 9.15. (The fit, we shall say, is very bad.)

The third remark is that consequentialism, in coming to the rescue of utilitarianism, announced itself as appealing to an incontrovertible norm of rationality. But we have seen no reason as yet to accept this claim. We have expressed serious doubts which will be strengthened as soon as we explain the *competing* rationality of ordinary morality. In so far as the consequentialists claim to be in a rationally and ethically incontrovertible business of maximizing ethical value, we have claimed that they misconstrue ethical language in seeing the thoughts we express in it as exclusively concerned with valuation. It will be plain, moreover, that, at this point, we are only rediscovering something that passed without much notice in Lecture 1. For at 1.2, in our first fix on the content of morality, we claimed that there were four phenomenologically salient kinds of ethical concern. It is the very first of the four kinds that we have now rediscovered, the kind comprising primitively prohibitive aversions against such things as wounding, injury, murder, the harming of innocents, or the repaying of good with gratuitous evil. If anything stands in the way of philosophy's taking such concerns as *sui generis,* as non-valuational and as obstructive of claims made on behalf of consequentialism, it is only the outstanding question (to be addressed in Lecture 9) of the rationality and rationale of the whole structure of ordinary morality that declines to treat them as simply valuational.

8.13. *Coda.* It will be manifest that the three utilitarian or quasi-utilitarian positions we have considered in Lectures 6, 7, and 8 are constrained in very different ways with respect to the characterization of outcomes.

For Mill what counts in an outcome is the quantity, quality, and intensity of pleasures and pains. For Hare what counts is the quantity and intensity of desire satisfaction. The disadvantages of these two positions stem in part, or so I have claimed, from their failure to accord the right importance to the ethical ideas we actually have, including ideas of agency and responsibility. Or else they stem from the failure to accord importance to them in the right way.

With Scheffler, and with other modern consequentialists who advance in effect from the place where Moore left off, criticism cannot take this form. For they have wanted to position themselves so that they can deploy almost any ethical idea they wish—except in so far they are prepared to refrain from using the idea that they aim to define, namely the idea of the verdictive rightness (all told) of an act or thing done.[17] We have opposed this position in another way.

The criticism we have urged against Scheffler and his allies is this: that, whereas ordinary ethical thought considers consequences, considers the quality of acts that issue in those consequences, and forces agents to think deontologically or praxeologically about those acts as acts they might or might not involve themselves in and have responsibility for doing, the kind of thinking that the consequentialists commend to us telescopes all of this into a new and extended

---

17. For the observations made so far on these matters, see Overview 0.1 (second paragraph); 6.4; 6.12; 7.8; 7.15–16; 7.18 (last paragraph); 8.1; 8.2 (fourth paragraph); 8.3; 8.10. See also, yet to come, 9.11; 9.12.

kind of evaluation of outcomes. Ignoring or misunderstanding ordinary practical thinking and the language in which that thinking finds its natural expression (see 8.10), it assimilates the bindingness of that which one must do to the mere (overall) goodness of an outcome and the excludedness of what one must not do to the mere (overall) badness of an outcome.

In setting out an altogether different diagnosis, it is sometimes suggested that we should contrast the modern imperatival conception of ethics, which finds its most characteristic expression in Kant, with an ancient conception of ethics that finds its expression in the Greek philosophers' foundational emphasis (it is suggested) upon the *eudaimonia* of an agent. It is not clear that this is quite accurate, however. In modern times, the imperatival conception is only one of several conceptions. In ancient times, the original awfulness of *nefas* is rooted outside the agent who blunders into it, before it pollutes him or blights his being. *Nefas* is imperatively rooted, one might say.

Of course different philosophers at different times have emphasized different things, but the foundational autonomy and distinctness of the valuational and the deontological is equally marked in English and in ancient Greek. For the categorically forbidden in ancient Greek speech and thought, see Aristotle, *Nicomachean Ethics* 1116a27, Sophocles, *Oedipus Tyrannus,* line 465.

Before concluding, one further point ought perhaps to be made about consequentialist modes of defining rightness. In so far as they exploit analytic-cum-semantical relations (nowhere denied in Lecture 8 or this coda) linking the deontic with the valuational, and in so far as they read these relations as enabling them, when en route to a deontic conclusion ('such and such is the right course of action'), to subsume deontic notions within the valuation of consequences, they are open to a variant of Frege's forceful critique of piecemeal definition. In characterizing the deontic *in one way* consequentialists take advantage of properties (such as implying something valuational) that the deontic only has by virtue of having been semantically founded—how not for contexts of doing, or of not doing, and of being answerable?—*in another way*. Thus the right hand undoes that which the left hand needed already to have done. There is an incoherence here.

8.14. Consequentialism (one might say) is a philosophy not so much of human agency and responsibility as of better and worse happenings—counting actions simply as happenings, of course. We have not refuted this philosophy. The question is how much reason now remains (save only its modern familiarity) for us to accept it. The reader is well within his or her rights to adjourn answering this until Lecture 9 has filled out the alternative to accepting it.

9

A first-order ethic of solidarity and reciprocity

Notions of agency, responsibility, and emergency as they figure within such an ethic; the rationality of embracing the internal aim of morality

[Hobbes] did not agree that man was designed for society, and imagined that we have merely been forced into it by necessity and by the wickedness of the members of our species. But he did not take into account that the best of men, free from all wickedness, would join together the better to accomplish their [aim], just as birds flock together the better to travel in company.

Leibniz, *New Essays*, III.i.1

Formation in ethical virtue comes about as a result of habit, which is why the word 'ethical' itself derives from the word for habit *(ethos)*. From this it is plain that none of the particular moral virtues arises in us simply from our given nature. For nothing that is there simply by nature could be trained to act otherwise than in that given way—just as a stone that by its nature falls downwards could not be schooled to fly upwards, not even if you threw it upwards ten thousand times to train it. In the same way, fire cannot be trained to burn downwards nor can anything else that is one way by nature be trained into some other way. The conclusion we reach is that the particular virtues arise in us neither *from* our given nature simply nor yet in a manner *contrary to* that nature, rather because we are *fitted by nature* to receive them and then drawn into them and perfected in them only by habituation.

Another thing we should notice is that, where things come to us simply by nature, we start with a potentiality for whatever it is and then comes the actual activity (as we see with all the five senses); but, in the case of the particular virtues, we first embark on them by undertaking the very acts they call for, as also happens in the case of our getting other kinds of know-how. For, in the case of the things we have to learn before we can do them, we learn these *by* doing them. For instance, we become builders by building and lyre-players by playing the lyre. So too we become just by undertaking just acts, temperate by undertaking acts of temperance, and brave by undertaking acts of bravery.

This is borne out by what happens in the *polis*. For law-givers make citizens good by forming habits in them, and this is the purpose of the law-giver. Law-givers who do not bring this about are falling short. This is one of the ways in which a good constitution differs from a bad one.

Aristotle, *Nicomachean Ethics*, II.1

It has been suggested [by the author] that one criterion for a good moral system is that it should be possible [just by virtue of what it gives and takes] to demand [some recognizant return] from every individual because of the good the system renders to him. . . . It has also to be such that anyone can conform to it and still live well enough in the ordinary, non-moral, sense. This condition may well be what limits the demands of altruistic action [or aggregatively justified] action; and a whole new non-utilitarian enquiry should open here.

Philippa Foot, 'Morality, Action and Outcome'

9.1.   We have now passed in review three philosophies of morality and the answers that each suggests to the twin questions ((A) and (B), (A') and (B'), etc.) that we formulated in Lecture 1. These were interdependent questions relating to the content of morality or to the nature and strength of the motivations that support it. In the process of our making this review, which has committed us not to forget certain matters so far unresolved (see the end of Lecture 8), Hume's explanatory naturalism has emerged not as flawless in his presentation of it, nor as complete, but as hugely plausible. It will be all the more plausible to the extent that it holds itself ready to discover what else will come forth from the springs of feeling and thinking that Hume identifies. Hume's genealogical scheme lies equally open to true insights of other provenance, not least to ideas from Aristotle concerning justice, for instance, or the shape of a life that is worthwhile. In further exploitation of the scheme, there is room for Kantian insights too, in so far as they do not depend for their whole validity or force on Kant's ethical system. More evidently, the Humean framework is hospitable to the early utilitarian effort, crude, reductive, and unpropitiously theory-driven though it was, to put human morality into some relation with human happiness (an effort unwisely abandoned later, when the concept of happiness was itself despaired of or dispensed with). It matters, but it does not matter for purposes of this résumé, how seriously, from its inception onwards, utilitarianism misconstrued this relation.[1]

Such are the advantages, not of eclecticism, for Humeanism is not eclectic, but of seeking in Hume's way to understand the phenomenon of morality instead of rushing into that which goes under the name of moral theory. Such too are the advantages of seeing the phenomenon itself for the severally rooted thing that it is and of waiting as long as necessary to let it appear which moral ideas (if any) will come to seem inseparable from a first-order ethic by which creatures like human beings are fitted to live.

9.2. In the spirit of openness already mentioned, let us begin with the most controvertible of the several claims just entered on behalf of the Humean schema, namely that relating to Kant. Let us take up once again the Kantian conception of a kingdom of ends:

> Rational beings stand under the law that each should treat him/herself and all others never merely as a means but always at the same time as an end in himself or herself. In this way, there arises a systematic union of rational beings under common objective laws—that is a kingdom . . . a kingdom of ends. (*Foundations of the Metaphysics of Morals* [433], end)

For present purposes, two features stand out here. First, the members of the kingdom act or judge according to a maxim that can be a law for all beings that are ends in themselves and possessed of a sovereign will. (Cp. second paragraph [434]. Cp. also 4.12 ff.) Sec-

---

1. See below, 'Concluding Overview.'

ondly, every law to which a member of the kingdom is subjected is one to which his or her sovereign will can assent.[2]

The kingdom of ends, even as so technically described, holds a strong pre-philosophical appeal. Independently of all philosophical theory and independently of special conceptions of sovereign will, morality as we know it can recognize here an ideal that seems to be its own[3]—just as it recognizes something that is already its own when Hume speaks of the sacredness of the principle of consent (see 3.5) or recruits us to the 'party of humankind'. (See *Enquiry*, XI.1). It is true that Kant himself, going along the route by which he reaches the kingdom of ends and then elaborates the idea, exploits special exclusions that threaten (according to 4.17 ff.) to make a first-order Kantian ethic incomplete and incompletable. Even the idea of a sovereign will or an end in itself has to take on an animate shape and needs empirical instantiation (or so we have asserted in opposition to Kant) if it is to command its proper ethical import. But those criti-

2. Cp. [438], second paragraph. The Kantian exposition of this claim would typically advance through the idea that the laws to which a rational being is subjected are laws of which that being can regard him/herself as actually or potentially a maker. But outside the Kantian framework that is not the only way of supporting the claim. Compare the third epigraph to the lecture. See also my *Needs, Values, Truth* (amended 3rd ed., Oxford: Oxford University Press, 2002), pp. 64–8. And see below, 9.7 ff.

3. Among those party to some such conception are Tim Scanlon, see his 'Contractualism and Utilitarianism', in Amartya Sen and Bernard Williams, eds., *Utilitarianism and Beyond* (Cambridge: Cambridge University Press, 1982); Philippa Foot, see her 'Morality, Action and Outcome', in T. Honderich, ed., *Morality and Objectivity* (London: Routledge, 1985); and John Rawls in *A Theory of Justice* (Cambridge, Mass.: Harvard University Press, 1972). More obscurely and faintly, see the exploration of intersubjectivity attempted in my essay 'Universalizability, Impartiality, Truth', which is ch. 2 in *Needs, Values, Truth:* and see also the development of the Limitation Principle commended in 'Claims of Needs', which is ch. 1 in the same collection. For that principle (compare, in the same collection, pp. 319 and 324) arises from a not dissimilar inspiration.

In the citation from Foot's essay that we have taken as the third epigraph at the start of this lecture (a citation adjusted in consultation with Professor Foot), we find a constitutive condition for a first-order ethic that will *deserve* to secure a certain kind of loyalty from its adherents. There is no compulsion, however, to see the citation as outlining some sort of contract. The point made—which is put into a new light at 9.7 ff.—is available to contractualists and anti-contractualists alike.

cisms are already behind us. Rather than abandon the conception of a kingdom of ends or deprive the neo-Humean scheme of insights which can only fortify it, it will be better to try to undo some of Kant's exclusions and vindicate the conception in a further way.

9.3. A place from which one might begin on the first part of this work, resuming at the same time some of the contentions of Lecture 5, is a passage not very far away, where Kant writes as follows:

> Empirical principles are always unfitted to serve as a ground for moral laws. The universality with which these should hold for all rational beings without exception—the unconditioned practical necessity which they thus impose—falls away if their basis is taken from the special constitution of human nature or from the accidental circumstances in which it is placed. [442]

One of the several things we must preserve here is the claim, not denied by Hume, that that on the basis of which we judge our own or others' acts or decide our own policies is not something open to ratification or rejection by reference to empirical experience.[4] The idea that it is that kind of thing is as implausible as the idea that ethical requirements can be bypassed by a revision of one's desires or interests.

Another point of Kant's we must never let go is that, once we have the proper interpretation of a moral requirement, that which emerges must be addressed equally to all who are capable of understanding it. Here too there is nothing peculiarly Kantian. In effect Hume says the same, declaring at *Enquiry,* IV.1, in a passage we

---

4. This is not to deny that something can happen that brings us up with a start and makes us see that there was something wrong with our convictions. But what we *then* have is not so much a counterexample to a moral generalization as an improved understanding of what we might have realized before. (Might *in principle* have realized before? *Always* might in principle . . . ? There is unfinished business here. On 'conversion' see John McDowell, 'Are There External Reasons?' in J. E. J. Altham and R. Harrison, eds., *World, Mind, and Context* (Cambridge: Cambridge University Press, 1995).

have already cited (see 5.5), that one of the two circumstances which constitute the ethical operation of benevolence is the existence of a 'sentiment that renders the actions and conduct of the persons the most remote an object of applause or censure, according as they agree or disagree with the rule of right [way of judging questions of what is right] which is established'.

In our citation from [442] there is a much more doubtful exclusion. There is ground or basis in the sense of 'reason' or 'basis in reason'. But there is ground or basis also in the sense of 'source' or 'origin', meaning that thing within us, that element in our given and acquired natures, which (the Humean can say to Kant) makes some decisions or choices ethically possible for us and rules out others. Followers of Kant claim that facts about human constitution cannot figure among the grounds for foundational principles of morality.[5] A follower of Hume may reply to this as we did in 4.17 and 4.18. He will also insist that it is our given-cum-acquired nature that inclines us to our own specifically human conception of what it takes for an animate being to qualify as an end in itself and a fitting subject for the special mode of interpretation that human beings direct towards other human beings.[6] (See below, 9.8 ff.)

9.4. Can the position we have now reached be explained in its own terms rather than by way of opposition to Kant's exclusions at [442]? I believe so. To this end, let us have recourse to the second of the two distinct 'circumstances' that Hume mentions in the passage we have cited already from *Enquiry*, IV.1, about the operation of benevolence. The second circumstance is the existence of a 'sentiment common to all mankind which recommends the same object to general approbation and makes every man or most men agree in

5. In this attempt to mediate and identify points on which Kant and Hume can agree, let us be careful to withhold assent from the idea that morality is a superstructure raised on a basis of *foundational principles* in Kant's sense of 'principles'.

6. Indeed, unless some common thing within us so prompts or inclines us, it seems we may have to go without a first-order ethic or a set of moral concerns to call our own. (Compare 4.17.)

the same opinion or decision concerning it'. In the absence of a fund of shared sentiments of *this* sort, there would be no such thing as a shared first-order ethic. *Pace* Kant, it will be a matter of the anthropology of the shared life of human beings (the gregarious creatures Leibniz portrays in our first epigraph) which particular dispositions or states of character come to be recognized and upheld as the natural virtues and what further 'conventions'—importing what artificial virtues—enter into the fabric of the shared life of these creatures. In such a contention—or so it was argued in the second half of Lecture 5—there is no threat to the determination of a proper content for human morality and no threat to the 'unconditioned practical necessity' that attaches to its requirements.[7] The as-if anthropological basis for the judgment 'I must' neither restricts the categorical purport of this *must* nor weakens the force it exerts with those who understand the claim that it makes.

Back now to the place where we were at the end of 9.2. The kingdom of ends conception, even when it is shorn of the Kantian restrictions that 9.2 and 9.3 have been seeking to remove, brings vividly to mind an ideal for human life as well as a distinctive ethic. This ethic is at odds with recognizably utilitarian or consequentialist conceptions of morality, but it is all of a piece with certain invariants that more eligible conceptions of morality (see 9.2 above, *ad fin.*) will need to recognize. Indeed it is all of a piece with a Humean conception of morals—or so I shall argue in 9.6 ff. First though, in

7. For a response to further reservations under these heads, see 5.7 ff. For further responses to further objections, see *Needs, Values, Truth,* pp. 205–7.

If it is an empirical fact that that anthropology is as it is, what is to be said about the possible world in which the anthropological facts are otherwise? Well, *within that world* conscious creatures will care about different things and talk about different things. *From outside that world,* we whose nature conforms rather to the given or actual anthropology, and who operate a conceptual scheme keyed to the actuality of that anthropology, can react to reports of that other world in our own way (that is, adversely, except in so far as we try to make allowance somehow for the fact that in that world the conscious beings in it do not have our take on things or our discernments of them). Neither of these answers (if we keep them apart) licenses the critic of the contentions in the text to claim that they imply that it is *a posteriori* that ingratitude (say) is reprehensible, or imply that it might have been not reprehensible.

advance of that effort, the Humean-cum-Aristotelian stage needs to be set.

In philosophy as it is, there is a tendency for a first-order morality to be conceived as a structured array of propositions or judgments. But it will cohere much better with the purposes we now resume and extend from Lectures 2 and 3 to conceive of such an ethic more dispositionally, as a nexus of distinctive sensibilities, cares, and concerns that are expressed in distinctive patterns of emotional and practical response. As instantiated in the formation of those who live by a given first-order ethic and see their way of being and acting as answerable to some particular standard or norm that they hold in common,[8] such a nexus will be conceived by a neo-Humean genealogist or aetiologist as something with a prehistory and a history, as well as a present and a possible future. The dispositions that realize the ethic he will see as arising neither uninvited from the given nature of human beings nor in a manner contrary to that nature (see here the second epigraph), but as establishing themselves in creatures who are well enough suited to receive them and are rehearsed, practised, or habituated therein by those who already have and exercise such dispositions.[9] The dispositions in question are not only dispositions to feel and care and think and act in certain ways, to refrain from acting in certain other ways,[10] or to take more notice of certain features of situations and less notice of that which has

8. The word *norma* meant for the Romans a T-square that a carpenter or mason carried about with him for making right angles. My use of the English word 'norm' looks back at that meaning. It works *metaphorically*, at one but only one remove from *norma* thus literally understood.

9. Another name for what is at issue here is *formation*, in German *Bildung*. For a masterly recent account of this idea, though not from a Humean point of view, see Sabina Lovibond, *Ethical Formation* (Cambridge, Mass: Harvard University Press, 2002), chs. 1–3.

If someone wonders how it can ever have come about that, within historical time, each generation was preceded by an earlier generation which would rehearse, practise, or habituate the next generation in this way, then I refer here to Lecture 2, especially 2.12, and the familiar facts of which we are reminded by the first epigraph.

10. Compare the sketch of these matters attempted at pp. 64ff. of ch. 2 of *Needs, Values, Truth*.

lesser ethical import. One who shares in such dispositions and follows them through will also be committed, according to the moral phenomenology for which the next section must complete the preliminaries, to look upon other persons in the ethically distinctive way we have seen Kant sum up in his own special way and his own phrase 'ends in themselves'.

9.5. On the formational and essentially practical view, which is the view of Aristotle but fully harmonious with that of Hume, what is the relation of a person's ethical dispositions to his or her moral convictions? A rough answer might be that, however incompletely or inexplicitly, a person's spoken convictions express the state of being that is realized in these dispositions. An agent's spoken utterances are a part of his practical response to the situation in which he find himself. Or else they are a provisional response to the as-if practical envisaging of a whole class of such situations. In the typical case (or so the formation theorist will aver), the person who gives voice to a moral conviction thereby manifests a state of practical understanding of a certain context—an understanding whose title to correctness does not depend on its degree of articulacy or the immediate availability to the moral subject of propositional grounds adduced for it. Its correctness will depend on the soundness of the subject's perception, the experience and the practical intelligence applied, and the quality of the ideas and expectations brought to bear in the context. In chapter 11 of book VI of the *Nicomachean Ethics*, Aristotle says that, within the sphere of the ethical and the practical, it is the capacity for appreciation of what matters in this or that situation *as given* which is the starting point for understanding the 'that for the sake of which' the practically wise person acts. Then Aristotle says that this capacity for appreciation is the sole basis of any grasp of the universal in the practical sphere (1143b5). Then he says that maturity will tend to bring with it the capacity for such practical appreciation and judgment: 'This is why we ought to attend to the assertions and declarations of experienced people or of people of practical reason, not less than to arguments or proofs. Because experience itself has given them an eye, they see aright' (1143b11–14). They see what to aim for in *this* situation or in *that*. The assertions of such people, taken in context, will help others to grasp what a practically wise person should be concerned with under these circumstances—what they should attempt when things are *like this*. With respect to this specific sort of circumstance, their claim is universal but not very general. These assertions do not constitute general instructions[11] because they are made in a specific context *for* that context. From the midst of such a context, the things said by the practically wise and virtuous will indeed point towards a more general 'that for the sake of which'; but it is not by following verbal instructions so much as by living and doing and engaging with the practically wise and virtuous that anyone can enter into the whole spirit in which these precepts of experience are to be understood. Only by drawing on some such understanding of the 'that for the sake of which' will anyone subjugate the indefiniteness of the subject-matter of the practical or impose upon any part of it a shape[12] that is faithful to an ethical aim. It is an understanding of the *spirit* in which the agent is to act.

According to this formational (or, as one might say, mental dispositional) view of morals and morality, which will be explored further in Lecture 10 and applied there to the special virtue or virtues of justice and deployed over again in Lecture 11 in connection with questions about the supposed relativity of morality, the propositional or declarative element in morality rests in part on the practical. But, once you take the practical fully seriously, the question is not foreclosed whether the correctness or incorrectness of moral judgments can amount to substantial truth or falsehood.[13] (See further Lectures 11 and 12.)

11. Hare's distinction of universal and general is still in force here. See Lecture 4, 4.16 and n. 21. See also 11.10.

12. I owe to Lovibond, *Ethical Formation*, this deployment of the idea of 'shape'.

13. This is to say that, taking the practical seriously, we should expect practical wisdom itself to issue in expressions of propositional knowledge, e.g. that it is the part of a *spoudaios* or virtuous person placed precisely thus (. . .) do to such and such

9.6. Now at last we reach our question. Consider an arbitrary first-order ethic, as lived by people who act freely and act as they do because they see their acts and thoughts as answerable to it. Why should we suppose that, wherever its content is made articulate in the ways described in 9.5, this content will correspond to a universal legislation that *each* participant, seeing himself as a member of a future kingdom of ends, could regard himself as not dissenting from?[14] What is it about an ethic with real participants—and what is it about the ideas that contribute to the content of such an ethic—that secures this? In non-Kantian terms, why must the purport and tendency of the norms enforced by a first-order morality approximate more and more closely, point by point, to something no party to the morality could regard as giving him or her reasonable grounds for taking flight or defecting from that morality? (Compare 9.2 above; compare Scanlon as cited in the last footnote.)

It is a fair guess that one part of the answer to such questions is

---

(——). Practical truth (*tou praktikou kai dianoêtikou alêtheia*, 1139a29) is not a special and weird kind of truth. Why should not the ordinary kind of truth be the kind of truth that is aspired to in an agent's making certain judgments pertaining to an essentially practical matter? Someone might aspire to attain ordinary truth, it now appears, if they know how things are here . . . , if they have participated in *ethismos* or ethical formation, if their aim here is the right one to have (their *orexis* is *orthê*, 1139a30–31), if 'experience gives them an eye by which to see correctly', and, deploying all this upon the situation here, they find that the thing to be done is the act——.

Here, in effect, I reiterate the claim in the text about taking the practical seriously. It is folly to rush to the conclusion that, even as practicality enters, real truth must find its exit. If it takes a practical experiment to satisfy oneself that the best way to chop an onion is to hold the top, cut off what remains of the root at the other end and chop away from there . . . if such practical experimentation be indispensable, why must that dependency undermine the truth status of the claim that this is the best way? Inevitably, Lecture 12 will carry us back to this matter. Meanwhile, let us not despise practical questions that would need to be answered on the basis of the practical in action or despise answers whose vindication depends indispensably upon that.

14. Cp. Scanlon, 'Contractualism and Utilitarianism', p. 110, who uses an analogous thought to offer a definition, 'an act is wrong if its performance under the circumstances would be disallowed by any system of rules for the general regulation of behaviour which no one could reasonably reject as a basis for informed, unforced general agreement'. It is important to remark that the importance of the original Kantian (and Humean) insight that Scanlon thus elaborates does not stand or fall with Scanlon's success or unsuccess in any strictly *analytical* or *definitional* project.

connected with the need for a first-order ethic of the kind we have been describing to retain its participants by something stronger and more reasonable than force. It is true that, at the outset, an ordinary non-sceptical person who feels no temptation at all to side with Glaucon and Adeimantus, and is fully satisfied with the critique that Lecture 1 offered of their preconceptions, may demand to know why any such answer should be needed at all. We might have needed that answer (such an unsceptic may say) if, in the world as it is, human beings who were living out in the wild (so to speak) were now being herded or corralled into morality—as if taken aboard a man-of-war by a press-gang and subjected there to the alien rigours of naval discipline. But the gentler induction of infants into morality can hardly provoke the same revulsion as impressment: 'It brings children to that which is already their own, to their birthright, namely an outgrowth of human constitution itself that has come into being under the normal conditions of human existence and precisely enables its recruits to realize the potentialities with which they are endowed.'

Such a plea must count for something. But does it count for enough, when there is in morality something so pervasive and so potentially intrusive into every last detail of human life that its power has begun to merge with the power of the law? Does the plea count for enough in so far as morality now shares in the monopoly of force by which society claims to protect itself from those whom it perceives either as defaulters or as enemies? If that is the company morality has started to keep, we need more than the non-sceptic will have found in Lecture 1.

9.7. At this moment, help is to be had from the third epigraph, coming from Philippa Foot. There is one utterly distinctive benefit which a first-order ethic with the right kind of content can offer to each and every one of its participants. From the same author and the same text, here is a further development of the same thought:

The existence of a morality which refuses to sanction the automatic sacrifice of the one for the good of the many . . . secures to each individual a kind of moral space, a space which others are not *allowed* to invade. Nor is it impossible to see the rationale of the principle that one man should not want evil, serious evil, to come on another, even to spare *more* people the same loss. It seems to define a kind of solidarity between human beings, as if there is some sense in which no one is to *come out against* one of his fellow men. In both cases, the good of the rule is a good that comes from having a system. But the justification is not [simply], as with rules that limit the direct pursuit of the general good in utilitarian systems, that those who accept them will be most likely actually to bring about [most welfare].[15]

In this neighbourhood there are at least two points. The first point is that morality not only plays a part in supporting that which shields us and the fruits of our collective labours from all sorts of menaces from within and without. In the form of a true ethic of solidarity, it offers to its putative adherents (creatures deprived by evolution of any reservoir of salutary instincts of the rather specific kinds that preserve most other sorts of creature) something that is so extraordinary that it can hardly be *unfair* for infants to be brought up as if in ignorance of every alternative.[16] (Would it not be more unfair not to?)

The second point one might discern in our citation relates to the

---

15. 'Morality, Action and Outcome', p. 86.

16. The full extraordinariness of this thing can only be appreciated by reflecting that the thing it provides is utterly at variance with every public philosophy that is prepared (as most are, the democratic and the egalitarian no less than the autocratic) to sacrifice the vital interests of the few to the aggregated less vital interests (the mere desires and preferences indeed) of the many. (See the later pages of Lecture 11.) Neither this discrepancy between ordinary morality and public morality nor the perception of it is a new thing. It is in no way special to the era of claim-rights—an era which infringes against this ideal of solidarity just as frequently and multifariously as every other era, still exercising a confidence and self-righteousness equal to that which made possible the collectivization of the Russian peasantry or the clearances of the Scottish Highlands. It would be a part of the unfinished business of a truly post-utilitarian philosophy to regulate our public philosophy by reference to the ordinary deliverances of ordinary morality and carry forth into the field of the practical and the political the ideal we are concerned with in the argument of the text. See J. S. Mill, *Considerations on Representative Government*, ch. 7. Constant and Tocqueville make similar points.

content of anything that can answer to the role of an ordinary ethic for ordinary life. We misrepresent and undervalue this thought, however, if we understand it as specifying nothing more than an enabling condition for an ethic to recruit or retain its participants. For that collapses all too easily into something that the selfish theorists will belittle as yet another appeal to simple egoism—as, at best, the offer of a fairer-seeming contract to its putative participants' self-love. That is not good enough, you may say. A much more interesting and compelling point will emerge, however, if we can begin with the idea of a first-order ethic (cp. 9.5 above), discover next, attached thereto, the idea of solidarity that Foot mentions, and *then from this* derive some version of Foot's requirement. That which we are to discover need not of course be something that the adherents of a first-order ethic will *call by the name* 'solidarity' or some synonym. It will be enough and more than enough if, in trying to understand the spirit that needs to animate a way of being that is sustained and perpetuated in the manner we have already described in 9.5, we find, as I shall declare (in 9.8) that we do, that the idea or expectation of solidarity must either be *at work* there—or else placed there in some temporary and special *abeyance*.

9.8.   The first-order ethic we are concerned with incorporates a human scale of values and a human deontology.[17] It arises out of our human sentiments and predispositions. It is perpetuated by human beings who bring into it succeeding generations of human beings. Such facts and the facts that are coeval with them are so familiar that they are usually deprived of the philosophical attention that they deserve. But let us try for a moment not to take them for granted.

---

17. This is not to say that, when articulated, it says 'for human beings only'. It addresses and it purports to affect any consciousness that can grasp or understand it—as we have said already. (See 9.2 and 9.3.) For the claim that *subject of consciousness, rational being, being possessed of a sovereign will* are determinables—concepts awaiting further specification such as that which we catch on to by recognizing human persons before they can assume the full duties of a sortal concept—see my *Sameness and Substance Renewed* (Cambridge: Cambridge University Press, 2001), pp. 194-5.

In confrontation with the human form, we immediately entertain a multitude of however tentative expectations, relating to the possibility that presents itself there of converse or colloquy, of interaction, or of treating with a personal being. In recognizing another person, we recognize not merely a subject of consciousness but a being who will seek to interpret *us* even as we seek to interpret *him* or *her*, each of us deploying more or less the same minimal expectations, a similar perception of our immediate surroundings, a similar norm of the reasonable, and a similar, however weak, proclivity to reciprocity. We recognize also the possessor of a will *not necessarily at one with our will*. To gesture in the direction of these things, to separate them, and to enumerate them in the work of philosophy takes a great effort of discernment and of description, because in reality, they are inseparable and pre-intellectual. Their everyday aspect has deprived them of the full recognition they deserve. Here, though, is Simone Weil:

Anybody who is in our vicinity exercises a certain power over us by his very presence, and a power not exercised by him alone, that is the power of halting, repressing, modifying each movement that our body sketches out. If we step aside for a passer-by on the road, it is not the same thing as stepping aside to avoid a bill-board. Alone in our rooms we get up, walk about, sit down again quite differently from the way we do when we have a visitor. . . . But this indefinable influence that the presence of another human being has on us is not exercised by men [such as one's adversary in warfare] whom a moment of impatience can deprive of life, who can die before even a thought has a chance to pass sentence on them. In their presence people move about as if they were not there.[18]

---

18. 'The *Iliad,* or the Poem of Force', as translated by Mary McCarthy in *Pendle Hill Pamphlet* no. 91 (Wallingford, Pa.: Pendle Hill Press 1956), p. 7. Here I venture to record my experience in the 1970s of happening on this extraordinary work for the first time. A xerox copy of it had been left behind in a London intercollegiate lecture room where earlier in the day (I discovered) Peter Winch had been lecturing. Once I had read the prize I took away with me and been overwhelmed by Weil's essay, I always

At the end of the citation, Weil begins to describe, in accordance with her main purpose, what it is for the expectation of recognition to be in suspense. At the beginning, she draws out in a remarkable way the consequences of the same facts we have been reaching for, concerning the 'indefinable influence' it must have upon one person to find in another (whether we like or dislike them) a subject of interpretation, to find a subject of the kind of consciousness that we ourselves know, or to find 'one of us'. To treat a person like a billboard, on the other hand, I have to make myself ready to suspend all the impulses that make possible the recognition of a person *as* a person.

Consider wilful killing, an extreme of unsolidarity. Consider what we have to lay aside even to contemplate the actuality of doing this. In combat and where there is present danger from a mortal enemy, someone will kill the enemy intentionally and without a further thought. There will be no time to have a further thought. The to-and-fro of ordinary interpretive intercourse in which we are normally caught up has already been conspicuously suspended. Even here, though, there are some for whom it takes a great deal to put into abeyance the 'indefinable influence' that Weil speaks of. How slow some are with a gun precisely shows how much it takes to *make* them put that influence into abeyance—a fact clearly recognized in all systems for the training and drilling of military recruits and con-scripts. Where nothing at all has put the to-and-fro of ordinary in-terpretive intercourse into abeyance, consider how much you then have to put aside—how many habits of mind and feeling—in order coolly to contemplate simply cutting off, simply 'taking out', another person. Obviously, these numerous things can all be suspended. The point is not the impossibility of suspending them, but the psychic and visceral cost—and the affiliated moral unreasonableness—of doing so. (This is a strictly neo-Humean variant of a Kantian con-tention—or so one might contend.)

---

wondered what Winch had been wont to say on the subject. With the publication of his *Simone Weil: 'The Just Balance'* (Cambridge: Cambridge University Press, 1989), all is revealed.

An explanation that started from here of what is wrong with wilful killing, or wanton cruelty, or repaying good with evil, might seem to be unable to rise above the superficial. But, if anything is superficial here, it is the opinion that this sort of explanation is *bound* to be superficial. Fully set forth, if only that could be achieved, the explanation would be as deep as the moral facts are.

9.9. The suggestion for which 9.8 has prepared is this. We should see Foot's solidarity requirement as spelling out one non-negotiable corollary of the transition that human beings make from mutual recognition under the aspect of personal beings to a social morality that requires personal beings to *live out* that recognition in a solidarity that is all of a piece with the recognition that requires each personal being to recognize the other one as participating in that morality and equally requires the other one to recognize him or her as a participant in it.[19] *This* is the source of the supposition (all too easily disappointed, but that is neither here nor there) that one who participates in an ethic expressive of that recognition will be disposed (in the way Foot describes) to refuse to contemplate the automatic sacrifice of one personal being for the good of the many or to sanction the exchanging of the serious suffering of the one personal being for the lesser sufferings of a larger number. How *could* the transition to social morality traduce in this way its original basis in mutual recognition, the recognition at once of human affinity and of the alterity and the otherness of the will of the other? In so far as aggregative considerations gain admittance to a social morality that rests on the solidarity of recognition, such considerations must enter only on terms that respect the ethic itself and sustain its basis. From the same solidarity, moreover, it is another short step to the idea of reciprocity between personal beings, and to Hume's idea that gratitude is a natural (not an artificial) virtue. (See here 2.17.)

From this vantage point there are other things we can see (if we want to call them 'other'). We see the rudiments of Humean benevolence, for instance, and we see sympathy, rooted in the more natural

19. See ch. 2 of my *Needs, Values, Truth*, especially pp. 61, 64, 65.

than voluntary attunement of one personal being to the mental or bodily state of another. In Hume's picture, benevolence has its further development in other social virtues, but the same vantage point that makes primitive benevolence visible also reveals that which ought to qualify or control or regulate the transformation of benevolence into public spirit, beneficence, generosity, and the rest. For many or most of the concerns proper to the social virtues—those aimed at aggregative ends, for instance—belong on an altogether lower level of priority than the level at which we experience our primitive aversion from acts that appear as a direct assault by one personal being upon another, acts such as murder, wounding, injury, plunder, pillage, the harming of innocents, the repaying of good with gratuitous evil, false witness. . . . Compare Aristotle: 'There are some acts in regard to which there is no such excuse as the excuse of "having been forced" to do them. Rather than do the thing in question, one must even be ready to die after suffering the most terrible things' (*Nicomachean Ethics,* III.1 1110a26–8). Compare also the category (1) of 1.2, where we claimed to establish, in a phenomenology equally accessible to author and reader, the clear priority of the aversions falling under this category over the concerns of ordinary benevolence, of fellow feeling and of the readiness to cooperate with others (category (2)). We also claimed the priority of these aversions (category (1)) over engagement with the public interest (category (3)).[20]

In the same section of that first lecture, whose preliminary findings I hope I am now vindicating, we also maintained that, in ordinary ethical thought, there is a marked tendency for concerns belonging to category (1) not only to trump the concerns belonging to category

20. In 'Morality and Practice II', a chapter in Brian Klug and Francis Dunlop, eds., *Ethics, Value and Reality* (London: Athlone Press, 1979), Aurel Kolnai speaks in a related connection of the 'thematic primacy of evil': 'There is no archetype of benevolent action on a par with archetypal crime of murder' (p. 108). There is an exaggeration here. (Consider the brave and benevolent actions of the Swedish diplomat Count Wallenberg in Budapest during the Second World War and then consider some downtrodden victim's criminal murder of her persistent oppressor.) But the dictum points in the direction of the same *sort* of truth as the one that my text is seeking to pin down.

(2) and category (3), but also to constrain the preoccupations that go with artificial virtues such as loyalty, veracity, or fidelity to promises. These last we assigned to a category (4), remarking also that there is a tendency for concerns of category (4) to trump those of categories (2) and (3). To default in loyalty, veracity, or fidelity to promises moves us towards something in certain ways analogous to the kind of criminality from which we are deflected by aversions falling under category (1).

9.10.   How then to situate that which belongs to category (4) and has its basis in the artificial virtues? How are we to place them within the phenomenology that Simone Weil and David Hume help us to arrive at? Well, as soon as personal beings recognize one another as personal beings, open themselves to the claims of solidarity, and become party to prohibitive aversions of the kinds already described, as well as to sentiments of reciprocity, gratitude, and the rest, there is *also* room for such beings to enter into closer relations of trust and mutual dependence. At this point, then, there is room for the rudimentary and more personal forms of the developments described in Lecture 3. But these, in their turn, make room for an extension (an artificial extension, so to say) of the inventory of acts that have the semblance of a direct assault by one personal being upon another. Beyond Hume's natural crime of ingratitude, but in analogy with it, we discover the artificial crimes—some but not all of them directly comparable to assault by one personal being upon another— of betrayal, false promise, fraud, slander, and the rest. Where a comparison with assault can be sustained, such acts pass beyond the valuations *bad, disappointing . . . , most unfortunate* or *regrettable, disgraceful, lamentable,* and trespass onto the ground marked *forbidden, nefastum, verboten, atasthalon, arrhēton.* (Compare 8.10.)

In contemplating this last extension and comparing category (4) with category (1), we are back at the point where we were in 8.9, when we cited W. D. Ross from *The Right and the Good.* Whatever truth lurks in Ross's dictum 'right does not stand for a form of value at all', a similar truth will lurk in the contention that 'wrong does not stand for a form of disvalue'. This is not a plea to the effect that no disvalue resides in acts of criminality, only to the effect that the original and first work of 'right' and 'wrong' (as of 'must', 'must not', 'ought', 'ought not') lies at some distance from value. It lies within the deontological as such. The distinctiveness of the deontological itself will appear much less strange altogether if it is approached first, as here, from the side of the phenomenology of that which is utterly forbidden—the original paradigm of the utterly forbidden or *nefastum* being taken to be that which menaces the very fabric of the ethical by threatening to destroy the basis of the ethical in solidarity.[21] It is one thing for the doing of an act to deserve the adverse criticism of the ethical. It is another for the doing of an act to subvert the ethical itself—or to promise to combine with a multiplicity of similar doings to subvert it.[22]

If such ideas lie at the core of the deontological, then maybe we can make sense of what is special about it. But the forbidden has been typified so far by a personal being's mounting a direct assault on another personal being. In widening this conception—as it will have to be widened—it would be a delicate matter to maintain the distinctiveness of the deontological while tracing its relation to the simply valuational. But that is work for another occasion. On pain of our failing to meet existing commitments, something else must now be extracted from our phenomenology.

9.11. Lecture 8 depended on our taking seriously the ideas of agency and responsibility—ideas not made much of by those who espouse consequentialism. But I think that next door to the expectation of solidarity we shall find some of the other ideas that we

---

21. Compare Hume, already cited, on 'the party of humankind' (*Enquiry,* IX.1).

22. If we use the *forbidden* as a primitive notion, we can take that which is *required* as that which one is forbidden not to do and the *permissible* as that which one is not forbidden to do. As adapted to *ought* and *must* (there is unfinished business here, not least in connection with making necessary distinctions between these), such an account will explain and predict the *bluff* that has to be practised by those who seek to enforce the more doubtful among requirements that are announced to us in the words 'You ought to . . . ' and 'You must . . . '.

need in order to vindicate our original notions of agency and responsibility. If solidarity conditions our whole outlook, then we shall want to know whether the intention with which a fellow being acted did or did not bespeak the outlook towards *other* personal beings that is proper to one who does not fail us in solidarity. And once this idea of *intention with which* is added to the idea of the quality of a thing done, we cannot help but find here the *responsibility* of a person for a particular outcome that can be fairly attributed to *his or her agency*. Once a first-order ethic reaches this point in its ordering of the concerns we have categorized (1), (2), (3), and (4), it cannot help but attach importance to the place that these categories hold and the priorities they enjoy in the mental formation of its participants. It matters to those who are living by an ethic of the kind we are trying to depict not only what acts a person does, not only what results from their doing what they do, but also in what spirit, and with what intention, they and other agents act. It matters what they do and intentionally do, but also, in abstraction from the act they do, it matters what the quality is of a person's will. (Compare Foot.) These are the terms on which it seems that, at our best, we treat with one another—and the terms we think we have reason to allow to control and constrain our own agency.

9.12. The ideas of agency, quality of will, and responsibility having been roughly and readily situated and made sense of (or recovered, so to say) within the first-order ethic of solidarity and reciprocity, it is now time to fulfil the promise given at the end of Lecture 8 and attend to the proper treatment of situations of emergency. Within the non-consequentialist thinking that anathematizes acts infringing the obligations in which agents are fixated by type (4) considerations or that offend against the type (1) inhibitions that spring from their formation as ethical beings, there will be many acts that are forbidden. Yet circumstances will often arise that call eloquently and imperiously, as if in recognizably ethical terms, for such acts. How can non-consequentialism respond to these circumstances?

9.13.   In Nicholas Monsarrat's novel, *The Cruel Sea*,[23] set during
the war in the Atlantic, 1939–45, the commander of a British cor-
vette, *The Compass Rose,* is escorting a convoy of merchant ships
headed to Gibraltar.[24] Towards the end of a voyage endlessly ha-
rassed by torpedoes and air attack, yet another cargo is sunk by a
German U-boat. Numerous survivors are in the sea, swimming in
the hope of being picked up. This is bad enough. But worse, the
commander knows from the Asdic (a sonar device) that still 'the U-
boat was there, one of the pack which had been harassing and
bleeding them for days on end, the destroying menace which *must*
have priority'. Unless it is destroyed, the U-boat will go on to tor-
pedo ship after ship. It can only be destroyed, however, by dropping
a depth charge, a weapon which acts by making a huge explosion
under the surface. Well aware that none of the people in the water
can survive such an explosion, but convinced that this is his opportunity to destroy the U-boat that is underneath them, the commander closes on the place to which the Asdic traces the enemy
submarine and delivers the depth charge. He does what he has to
do to save the rest of the convoy. But among those in the water, not
a single human being survives.

If we take the standpoint of ordinary morality, what shall we say
about this case? First that what the commander did was a terrible
thing to do. It was not intentional, of course, on the commander's
part to kill the survivors. Nor did he save the convoy by killing the
survivors. He saved the convoy by dropping the depth charge, and
his dropping of the depth charge killed the survivors. He fulfilled

23. London: Cassell & Co., 1951.
24. The example was suggested to me in connection with the Principle of Double
Effect by Dr Sophie Botros, to whom I express here my signal gratitude. For Double
Effect, see below, 9.15. See also Philippa Foot, 'Morality, Action and Outcome'; Joseph
T. Mangan, 'An Historical Analysis of the Principle of Double Effect', *Theological Studies*
10 (1949): 41–61; and see Sophie Botros, 'An Error about the Doctrine of Double Effect',
Philosophy 74.287 (1999): 71–83; Sophie Botros, 'Response to W. Kaufman', *Philosophy*
76.296 (2001): 304–11. Sophie Botros is the only author I have read who has seen that,
in and of itself, Double Effect can generate no prohibitions, only (heavily qualified)
permissions. (See below.)

his duty in this way; but no sane person could envy him that terrible role. ('No one [on the ship] looked at Ericson as they left that place.') It flowed from his agency that the lives of many of his compatriots were sacrificed in just the way in which ordinary morality seeks to exclude *anyone's* being sacrificed. For that sort of reason, it is hard to say 'the agent did right' or even 'the agent did what it was right for him to do'. Rather, the commander did what he *had to do*, which was defend the rest of the convoy by dropping the depth charge. He had to do a terrible act.[25] So we pity him—even as we exonerate him or withhold all criticism of his moral character.

The difficulties we are concerned with, the chagrin agents feel when they have to take account of *what* they did as well as of their blameless direct intention—are these a by-product of habits of mind that humanity should have grown out of when it abandoned ancient ideas of pollution? Surely not. They are a reflection of the conception of acts and agency that we simply have to have (or so I recently argued) if we are to participate in the conception of the ethical by which persons like us, persons who are separate but radically interdependent, *have* to live and have their being. It is in that conception of the ethical that the typology of forbidden and not-forbidden acts has its roots. It may seem strange that one who is party to the ethic

25. Even where there is blameless ignorance, there is little consolation: 'Morally innocent though [Oedipus] is and knows himself to be, the objective horror of his actions remains with him. . . . Is that simply archaic superstition? I think it is something more. Suppose a motorist runs down a man and kills him. I think he *ought* to feel that he has done a terrible thing, which nothing can restore even if the accident is no fault of his: he has destroyed a human life, which nothing can restore. In the objective order it is acts that count, not intentions. A man who has violated that order may well feel a sense of guilt, however blameless his driving.' E. R. Dodds' 'On Misunderstanding the *Oedipus Rex*', *Greece and Rome* 13 (1966).

This seems almost exactly right, but I venture one remark about 'the objective order'. The kind of ethic I have been concerned with looks to what Dodds calls the objective order. We have seen why it must. At the same time, though, we have seen why, *pace* Dodds, that ethic must also concern itself with agents' intentions and the will that these intentions betoken. There are *objective reasons* why it must concern itself with *all* these things, public reasons having to do with the anchoring office of solidarity. (I concede that, if *the sole* concern were the avoidance of *miasma* or pollution, then things might be different.)

of solidarity and makes it his own has sometimes to be harder on himself than others are on him. But this too flows from his internalization of the norms of ordinary morality.

9.14. Suppose this is a correct account so far of the findings of ordinary morality. Then where is the system? What are the non-consequentialist principles for judging the doing of acts such as the commander's?

In answering such questions, defenders of the ordinary first-order ethic we have described will want to distinguish the commander's case from a much harder sort of case (readily imaginable, no doubt) where it is represented that someone had to save the convoy *by* sacrificing four hundred of his own countrymen. For we distinguish passionately between the *Cruel Sea* case and this new kind of case. For the new one would have involved someone's forming the intention to *sacrifice four hundred people*—an intention for which there can certainly be no justification, at least of the kind we have so far allowed. In making sense of the exoneration-cum-justification so far allowed, we cling to the point that Kant has insisted upon in one way and Foot in another way, Foot being supported by the neo-Humean speculations we set out at 9.7 ff. We cling, that is, to the precious remnants of solidarity—and thus to the precondition of the ethical itself. Despite emergency, there is still something we can truly say we could not do or condone in these sorts of circumstances. For instance, we could neither justify nor exonerate on the same terms a naval commander who gained a safe passage for the convoy by (say) offering to the enemy the same number of people to be killed or be set to work as slave labourers. For here *the means themselves* will offend against the solidarity constraint. There is no useful and *in itself blameless* act the agent can form the intention to do in order to avoid the great evil that is in question.

How much ordinary non-consequentialist agents can hold on to—and how much they have to abandon in cases like the *Cruel Sea* case—will be easier to measure when conditions are set out for judging acts done on in the kinds of situation we are concerned with. We shall give four conditions. First, though, some clarifications and/or precautions against misunderstanding.

(a) Let it be clear that the principle of justification/exoneration[26] will not *itself* provide an account of acts that are forbidden. It presupposes such an account. (Just such an account is sketched in 9.8 and 9.9.)

(b) Let it be clear that, in distinguishing the agent's direct intention from that which the agent knows is likely to happen if he carries out his direct intention, we do not commit ourselves to frame any general permission to do just anything provided that one's intentional relation to it is not direct but is oblique in the way in which the commander's relation to the prospect of the survivors' death in the sea is oblique. All sorts of act are simply forbidden (cp. 9.8, 9.9) and this requires that agents should do *everything they can* to avoid doing them (even unintentionally). If the principles we are looking for are to save whatever can be saved of solidarity, then they will have to be both exigent and specific.

(c) The justificatory/exonerative principle that is to be furnished helps agents to come to terms with certain kinds of emergency. About other kinds of emergency it will simply be silent. In itself it will say nothing for or against any other accommodations agents might make to other kinds of emergencies calling for the intentional doing of awful acts. As always, the intrinsic awfulness of these acts is secured *independently* of the principle that we shall need and applied in advance of it. Compare (a).

9.15. This is the moment to mention the so-called Doctrine of Double Effect. So far from being something special or proprietary

26. For the choice of word, see again the references to Sophie Botros at n. 25. But even 'justify' sounds one false note, if we ought to prefer to say 'the agent did what he had to', rather than to say 'the agent acted rightly'. As for exoneration, this relates to the act done knowingly in destroying the U-boat.

to moral theology, this principle appears to muster the resources of ordinary morality for circumstances of hazard, emergency, and dire necessity. It adds relatively little to ordinary morality except a certain redeployment. The doctrine goes back to a brief passage of Aquinas (article seven of question 64 of Secunda Secundae of St Thomas's *Summa Theologicae*). It was further spelled out over subsequent centuries in numerous works of moral theology. Adapting one such account[27] to the terminology of these lectures as well as to our example, we have it that:

> it is lawful for an agent to actuate a morally good or indifferent cause [i.e. to do an act, such as drop a depth charge in the waging of a just war] from which cause will follow two effects, one good and the other evil, if there is a proportionately serious reason, and the ultimate aim of the agent is good and the evil effect is not the means to the good effect. . . . First of all, [the act the agent intends to do] is not unlawful on account of the end intended, because the end [e.g. to save the convoy] is good. Secondly, [doing the act in prospect] is not [in itself] unlawful . . . because [dropping a depth charge] is . . . at least indifferent. [The captain does not have to reason as follows, for instance: 'I shall kill the survivors and *thereby* I shall save the convoy'; for killing the survivors is not the means, dropping the depth charge is.] Thirdly, [doing the act the agent intends to do] is not unlawful on account of the foreseeing of the evil effect [the evil effect being here the death of the survivors from the ship already torpedo'ed]. For [in our example] the evil effect, though foreseen, is not intended but merely [endured]. Fourthly, there is a proportionately serious reason [the safety, here, of the rest of the convoy] for permitting [better, for enduring] the evil effect.

The scholastic language, such as remains after my alterations, elaborations, and excisions, is clear enough, I hope. The result can be

---

27. The account I adapt is given in Mangan, 'An Historical Analysis of the Principle of Double Effect', see pp. 60–1.

fully generalized in more complete conformity with the crucial distinction we have tried to respect between acts = things done and actions = doings of acts.[28] The doctrine is only improved if it is divorced from the conventional deontology from which we have been seeking to escape. (Cp. 8.10–11.)

It is predictable that a consequentialist will fasten here onto the fourth condition and the words 'a proportionately serious reason for the agent's permitting [or enduring, or countenancing] the evil effect'. I expect he will say, 'So in the end, you too invoke utilitarian reasoning.' I do not know how many expositions of Double Effect have laid it open to this move on the consequentialist's part, but the exposition just given is not open to this move.

In the account of the matter that we are following, the commander's reasoning is not a search for the course of action with the overall best outcome, where that is identified by computing a sum of utilities or of goods minus evils. (Nor is it a search for the course of action with the highest expected utility—the course of action that scores highest when a comparison is made on the following basis: for each possible course of action, the value of each good thing it may lead to is multiplied by the probability of that good thing's being achieved; and from this positive sum of these products is subtracted the sum of the disvalues of each evil it may lead to, each evil being multiplied by the probability of that evil). No, the commander is reasoning causally about means to the particular end with which it is his duty to concern himself. Every morality and theory

---

28. Here, for purposes of more detailed discussion, is a suggestion. A person is not acting contrary to morality if he performs an act of X-ing that he foresees will have a good and a bad effect provided that four conditions hold:

(1) X-ing is itself good or indifferent.

(2) the good effect of X-ing is intended and the evil effect of X-ing is not intended (though it may be foreseen)

(3) the good effect of his X-ing is not *produced by means of the bad effect* of his X-ing. Suppose he W-s by X-ing. Suppose this is the good effect. Suppose he also Y-s by X-ing. Then his Y-ing is the bad effect. But he does not W by Y-ing. (The commander does not save the convoy by killing the survivors in the water.)

(4) There is a proportionately grave reason for permitting the evil effect. That is to say that there is a proportionately serious reason for the agent to X even though he cannot X without Y-ing.

of morality commends causal reasoning to an end already determined.[29] Causal reasoning itself—let it be remembered—is not proprietary to consequentialism. The commander is looking for some
way out of a terrible situation—the degree of that terribleness bearing
upon the degree of evil that can be countenanced in any remedy
under consideration. In the *Cruel Sea* example, the overwhelming
evil to be avoided is the loss of the whole convoy, an objective that
the commander can confidently refuse all utilitarian or consequentialist help in identifying or appraising. Nor can he make very much
use of such help in considering the question of proportionateness.
For the judgment of proportionateness depends on the deployment
of distinctively ethical ideas. With regard to the act chosen, the agent
must be able to say truly that he *had* to do what he did, that the
evil to be avoided was as terrible as . . . , and that there was nothing
else he could do that was not worse.

'But *why* does Double Effect place such emphasis on the primary
content and the quality of an agent's intentions?—and why does it
dwell so much on the fact that, in our example, the captain of the
destroyer does not save the convoy *by* killing the survivors?' someone may ask. Because, in an ethic of solidarity anathematizing the
kinds of act already identified and focusing on the quality of the
wills and the motives of participants, thus focusing on their readiness
to treat other participants as *equally* participants in this way of acting
and being, it matters exceedingly what sorts of act an agent can
properly intend if he is to participate in this ethic and to participate
in the ethic by living it. Double Effect does not *place* the emphasis
on these things. In ordinary thought, it is there already. Double
Effect tries to preserve everything it can while seeking to accommodate contingency and emergency. The thing that makes the doctrine of Double Effect so distinctive is that it seeks to recognize
emergency and dire necessity and *simultaneously* to hold onto that
which is special in the ethical outlook of solidarity and reciprocity.

29. That causal reasoning towards an objective is not a utilitarian monopoly is a point
we have made several times already. See 6.4.

If, when the going gets rough or choice is narrowed unbearably, there is no question of reverting to the mentality of sheer instrumentalism or bare consequentialism, then Double Effect must distinguish *with a nicety that would be out of place in other contexts* between what an agent intends and what he or she reluctantly acquiesces in.

9.16. For a whole range of emergencies, Double Effect may suffice. But it is perfectly obvious that there are many other kinds where no such exemption can be got from Double Effect.

If the tyrant has taken my wife and children and is threatening to kill or torture them unless I act as his assassin, Double Effect does not license me to save my wife and children by killing the tyrant's enemies. If I do that, the only help I shall get from anyone or anything, where eventually I am judged, is for my reasons to be borne in mind when the verdict is pronounced and for my moral character to be assessed in the light of the circumstances. Double Effect adds nothing to the adverse judgment on acts of assassination and it subtracts nothing either.

Double Effect does not license the midwife or the doctor to save the life of the mother by crushing a foetus's head if the head is too big for the foetus to pass from the uterus. Again Double Effect is silent. The awful aspect of the act is a given, and the doctrine offers no escape from that awfulness. Independently of Double Effect, it may be argued that the midwife's or doctor's primary duty of care is to the mother, whose position is really not symmetrical with that of the child. Others may want to try saying that the child has yet to attain to the status of member of the community of human persons. No doubt, all sorts of other opinions are possible. Double Effect says nothing.

Double Effect does not license us to buy off the terrorist who threatens to kill three thousand innocent people by giving in to his demand that we execute an innocent person. Nor, though, is it Double Effect that forbids this. In the case of these demands, it is other teachings that will encourage the agent to reflect that terrorism only breeds terrorism; and other teachings that encourage him to think that, if the terrorist's threat is carried out, it will not be he, the agent, who was responsible for the doing of the thing threatened, but the terrorist.[30] If the agent has a duty in the matter, it may be said it is the same as everyone else's, namely to add his own voice to any clamour that demands that, as soon as possible, the underlying conflict be imaginatively and magnanimously resolved. This counsel does not derive from Double Effect, however. The act of killing an innocent was already condemned by ordinary morality. As always, Double Effect simply leaves us with ordinary morality. In the cases just described, it leaves us wondering whether there are other and more powerful waivers or exemptions than that which it furnishes to dire emergency—or else looking for other ways of qualifying the terrible dilemmas that agents have to face.

9.17.   At this point, the non-consequentialist will always be offered cases that put an even greater strain upon the system of ideas which we have tried to describe and explain.[31] But what is the existence of such extreme cases meant to show? They will scarcely show the bankruptcy of ordinary morality, on which we precisely depend to

---

30. This claim does not rest on the idea that your responsibility always depends on whether you are the human agent physically 'most closely involved' in the sequence of events. If I have undertaken a duty to look after a child for an afternoon and, through someone else's agency, the child falls into the canal, it will be my responsibility to rescue the child.

Another point about terrorist blackmail: consequentialists will be apt to say that one who demurs at his demand *permits* or *allows* the terrorist to do whatever it is. Such language is ambiguous and inappropriate. The agent who refuses does not tolerate or acquiesce in the outrage, but it is out of the question for him to do the act demanded. He morally *cannot* do the act demanded of him. That does not mean that he 'allows' the outrage. On this kind of 'cannot', see Bernard Williams, 'Moral Incapacity', *Proceedings of the Aristotelian Society* 92 (1992–3).

31. A case that Scheffler mentions of this kind is one where it has been contrived somehow that if you do not torture one child to death, everyone else in the world (including the child) will be tortured to death. See *The Rejection of Consequentialism* (Oxford: Oxford University Press, 1981), p. 86 n. See also William James's essay, 'The Moral Philosopher and the Moral Life', in *The Will to Believe* (London: Longmans, Green & Co., 1897), especially p. 188.

help us spell out what *is* extreme and what is at issue in extreme cases. They scarcely show the correctness after all of consequentialism. As literally understood, consequentialism, even if it represents itself as embodying the logic of emergencies, rarely even points in the general direction of something we can recognize as the right calculation! And that is what you would expect of a position which arises neither from a non-question-begging argument nor yet from ordinary moral conviction.

Maybe the extreme cases show something quite different—namely that a fifth kind of moral concern, a category (5) concern, needs to be added to the four kinds we singled out in Lecture 1 and rehearsed again in pp. 246–9. This new category might be thought of as subsuming the ordinary passably virtuous agent's concern *to preserve the very conditions* under which human civilization will survive and/ or ordinary morality can make its characteristic demands on normal human life. Less imprecisely, maybe the fifth sort of concern is the concern to preserve the very conditions under which ethical choice itself is possible. Perhaps this type (5) concern, once added to those we sketched in 1.3, once properly formulated and sternly enough interpreted, can be seen as trumping all kinds of other concern, including even category (4) concerns and category (1) concerns. Again though, as with actions that invoke the doctrine of Double Effect—but how much the more so!—there will be no question of the agent's emerging from the terrible situations in which he has had to take part with the claim that he did the morally good act or the act that it was simply right to do. The whole question of the strict 'permissibility' and 'impermissibility' of various acts, already many miles away, is far out of sight. All that remains is the dire necessity that presses on an agent, and the question of what is possible for a human being in that situation.

9.18. In this lecture, we have resumed the Humean position that was set forth in Lectures 2 and 3 and was defended further in Lecture 5. Once enlarged around the idea of solidarity, an idea drawn from the same fund of materials that Hume drew upon, the position *reappropriates* pre-theoretical ideas of responsibility, quality of will, and agency that lose their contours within consequentialist thinking. The account we have been led to give of reasoning in emergencies is closer to pre-philosophical conviction than anything that another position can offer. In 9.13–15 that which was postponed under this head in Lecture 8 has now been concluded; or else, if it is not concluded, sufficient indication has been given of the lines on which the residue might be completed. But under another head there is one last piece of unfinished business.

In the face of the non-consequentialist explanations now provided, Samuel Scheffler can still ask: 'How *rational* is this reasonableness that you seem to yourselves to be practising by living within the framework which has now been described?' Again, ignoring the protest that I entered so many pages ago (see 8.2, eleventh paragraph) about the attempt to invoke some *pure* and *pre-moral* notion of rationality, Scheffler would still have us ask ourselves: how well does the practical rationality of this ordinary morality of ours, this reasonableness of ordinary reasons that we recognize as good reasons for acting or feeling thus and so, consort with 'the canons of [strict, genuine, ordinary] rationality that [Scheffler says] we most naturally apply'?

9.19. Let us take first the second of these questions. Surely it is nothing like so clear as Scheffler supposes whether the canons of rationality that we most naturally apply really are consequentialist criteria.[32] Surely 'the canons we most naturally apply' will precisely refer the question of the rationality of a proposed act to the reasons that already count as such with ordinary people or hold sway over workaday life, namely the body of reasons that we recognize already (and constantly subject to ordinary criticism) for acting or feeling or being thus or so. When distinct and opposing reasons of these fa-

---

32. Unless Scheffler means by *us,* us philosophers. But *that* would scarcely carry any weight at all in an argument such as Scheffler's. His argument loses most of its force if it has to appeal to canons of rationality which are already philosophical or stem from the same source as consequentialism itself.

miliar kinds compete for an agent's attention, those who live by the notions we have been describing in the preceding sections can only draw on the same understanding by which they live already in order to determine which is the stronger or better reason.[33] In this picture, rationality is conceived as the sum of the reasonable, where the reasonable is determined piecemeal by reference to the most carefully considered of the said reasons. Such reasons themselves will have arisen from considerations that have their force with persons possessed of the given and acquired natures of human beings, *among* such considerations being those that minister already to the balance which human beings' participation in the ethical prompts them to try to find between their self-love (which is indubitable) and their dispositions to follow through their sentiments (equally indubitable) of benevolence and of solidarity.

Scheffler appeals to a distinction between ordinary morality and the canons of rationality 'we most naturally apply'. There certainly is a separation to be made between reasons arising exclusively from self-love and other ordinary reasons, but that is not the distinction Scheffler is appealing to. There is the distinction between worse and better considered non-egoistic reasons. But that is not the distinction he wants either. Only those who are already consequentialists—for some reason that Scheffler has left off the page—will be immediately content with the distinction that he is appealing to.

9.20. We imagined Scheffler's asking two questions. By the first of those questions, which we reach now, we are asked to *vindicate* or *validate* the real rationality of the sum of the reasonable as that is determined piecemeal by reference to the whole heterogeneous plurality of our workaday reasons.

Even if this is the right question, I wonder how it can ever be agreed what is going to count as an answer. In order to encourage

---

33. Where the matter is very difficult, no doubt they will look for some explicit unifying account of rationality; but their looking for such a thing cannot guarantee that it is there for them to have.

us to attempt such a validation, a detailed critique could be offered, I suppose, calling on us for some piecemeal defence. I fear though that the challenge and the response would simply recapitulate the arguments already rehearsed. A different and more global critique could be offered, making reference to how miserable human beings have made themselves up to now. But that would invite in its turn some historical examination of what consequentialist reasoning itself has contributed to human misery. It is not as if human beings have given constant heed to the ordinary ethical notions despised by consequentialists. (Compare the epigraphs from Coleridge and Russell at the head of Lecture 8.) It is not as if they have cultivated scrupulously the ordinary reasonableness that is immanent in our non-consequentialist morality.

Over the reasonable conceived as the sum of our best considered reasons Scheffler prefers (as we have seen) an alternative that finds rationality in the pursuit of states of affairs that have the largest possible value (intrinsic and extrinsic values all being correctly accounted, none omitted and none double-counted). The trouble still is that, at the point where he seems to furnish an argument for this conception of rationality, the case for it seems to presuppose that we already have an argument for something else—something that is not self-evident at all. Or so it will seem unless we have *already* conflated the valuational and the deontological. But Scheffler's argument needed to reach out to those not yet convinced by such an assimilation.

Suppose a transcendental cost-benefit analysis aimed at the maximization of intrinsic values really were the source of 'the canons of rationality that we most naturally apply'. Then it would be no wonder that we are so often assailed—in a world already partially remade in the light of the canons Scheffler has in mind—by the thought that true contentment is only the terminus of an infinite process, the non-existent endpoint of an endless aggregation. It would be no wonder then if it should sometimes appear, as J.-P. Sartre remarked in another connection, that 'l'homme est une passion inutile' ('man is a futile passion'). It is not to be denied that intrinsic values matter. Human well-being counts among them. But the true importance of such things is marked by the place they hold *already* in the whole mass of good reasons that count as good reasons in ordinary ethical and practical thinking.

9.21. In the end, I conclude, the issue about the question of the nature of rationality is not as disjoint as the consequentialists hoped it could be, or as Glaucon and Adeimantus assumed it could be, from the issue we have been concerned with all along, namely the merit or demerit of the divers reasons there are to adopt and to persist in—even where we offend against it over and over again— the moral outlook. Along with that question, however, comes another question: namely, whether that outlook is more reasonable than the outlook of sincere indifference to the canons of morality.

Strictly speaking, the reasonableness of each of the outlooks of moral concern and of moral indifference needs to be explored not merely in words but imaginatively and experientially. If the answer to Glaucon and Adeimantus requires an even-handed comparison between both kinds of lives, then philosophy has somewhat neglected one half of its duty. Even literature, being much taken or preoccupied with active wickedness and the fate of those who draw attention to themselves in this way, has focused too little on sincere indifference. These lectures prolong that dereliction, but they do so in the conviction that, however theoretically important such an even-handed comparison might be, there is something utterly unrealistic in the very idea of trying to contemplate, even in theory, some exactly balanced frame of mind to which the comparison could make unquestion-begging (prudential?) appeal. The lectures have been animated by a further conviction, however—that the most important thing for philosophy to do here is to allay the misconceptions that constantly obscure the reasonableness that inheres in an ordinary person's attachment to the first-order ethic by which they and other persons live at a given place and time. Let the philosophy of morality dissipate the preconceptions that render needlessly mysterious the inward significance or internal aim of the norms that everyday morality so unmysteriously proposes to us.

9.22. If, on the sum of good reasons approach, morality will count as at least as rational as this, then oughtn't something to be sayable about some sort of overall aim that morality does achieve? We have opposed the claim that the aim or point of ordinary morality comes down to the sovereign will's discovery of maxims it can will universally; or comes down to the promotion of a single-minded generalized pursuit of happiness or desire satisfaction; or comes down to the (however double-minded) pursuit of intrinsic value; or comes down to the discovery of a device for mediating between conflicting interests (cp. Lecture 7). The conclusion we have already embraced is that ordinary morality is something that is not even describable or intelligible externally to the whole life of which it, morality, forms one central (albeit only fitfully or intermittently evident) constituent.[34] If that is right, though, and we shall return

---

34. It is some such insight that has prompted moral philosophers to propose yet another possibility, namely that the organizing focus of morality is *virtue itself.* Even here, however, there is something to be resisted. If Kantianism were right, then agents who deliberated well would have constant regard to the sovereign will; if utilitarianism were right, then agents who deliberated well would have regard to happiness or desire satisfaction; if ideal utilitarianism were right, then they would have regard to intrinsic value, etc. These implications are not counterintuitive or unintended. What then if virtue ethics were right? Agents who deliberated well would have regard to virtue. That sounds wrong, however, for it suggests a general preoccupation on the part of agents with virtue as such, a preoccupation that few 'virtue ethicists' can have intended. Contrast our preoccupation with the purposes proper to virtue—the purposes themselves, not their connection to virtue. Either then 'virtue ethics' is wrong or else (much more likely) it is not really coordinate with Kantianism, utilitarianism, intrinsicalism, etc. Something virtue ethicists can truly say is that a person who deliberates well will have regard to anything or everything that the virtuous person would concern himself or herself with. There is a real point in saying that. Indeed it emphasizes in its own way something we have already insisted upon in another Aristotelian way. But it leaves the virtuous person *himself* or *herself* where s/he was with the question, 'What shall I have regard to here?', and it does not advance the question about the point or aim or morality; and here we are brought back to the idea that the point or aim of morality is not only internal to the life of which moral concerns are a constituent but almost equally inseparable also from the other constituents of that life. If this is right, it helps to explain the difficulties that we claimed to see in Kant's theory at 4.17.

It should be remarked that Humeanism too is not coordinate with Kantianism or utilitarianism or intrinsicalism. But Humeanism, by furnishing an account of the nature of morals and morality on the basis of which we can understand better why morality

to the point in the first half of Lecture 11, then it would be wrong for us to expect that we could arrive at an assessment of the success of a first-order ethic of a given place and time by measuring its success in implementing some independently determinable 'aim' or 'object'. In the end, we determine the aim by understanding the spirit that animates the ethic, and we come to understand the spirit by means of the piecemeal elucidation of the ideas and preoccupations in the light of which one who is party to that ethic will be wont to feel, act, and live. There will always be those who despise the piecemeal. Maybe they will always revert to the scepticism that Glaucon and Adeimantus affect in their interrogation of Socrates. But in despising the piecemeal they cut themselves off from all sorts of truths that bear closely on the questions that they ask. By means of the piecemeal and the defeasible, taken in tandem with the ae-tiological, there can be displayed a slow, ever-evolving, but multiply constrained mutual adjustment between the content of morality and the moral motive and of motive. (Cp. 1.12.) In so far as the case for morality can be stated briefly, all that can be said is that, in a way already illustrated, it is the most enterprising and durable expression that a human being will find for the benevolent dispositions he or she can discover within himself or herself.

9.23. Even at the outset, it seemed unwise in the extreme to try to answer Glaucon's and Adeimantus' challenge just as it stood. Only slightly less quickly, it became clear how difficult it is, how essentially contestable it is, what this thing morality is—what its motive-determined content is and what its content-determined motive is. Closer now to the end, a third point begins to appear: that it is almost as essentially disputable what reason is and what reason requires of us as it is essentially disputable how we should live. To show how we should live must surely involve the demonstration or exhibition of convincing ideals, ideals of a life that human beings

---

has the content it has, plays a role that virtue ethics could not aspire to usurp or to fulfil in a better sort of way.

could find worth living and defending. But why did we ever suppose that there ought to be some *uncontentious* notion of reason—some morally neutral or logically-cum-metaphysically invincible notion of reason—which would eventually yield up to philosophy a theoretically incontrovertible ideal of the life worthy of a human being, either an answer to the question whether it is reasonable to cleave to morality or an answer to the distinct question whether it is unreasonable not to cleave morality? Not only does it seem essentially contestable what morality is. It is not even clear whether the notion of practical reason can furnish an *uncontentious sense* for Glaucon's and Adeimantus' questions. The sense of the answer and the sense of the question will tend to communicate contentiousness to one another. It seems sufficiently evident, though, that, along the way we have already traversed, a *good enough* sense has been assigned to the questions posed in Lecture 1. That sense is well enough matched to the substance of an answer that is, for many purposes and contexts, good enough to pause upon, better anyway (though longer and more discursive) than anything that is offered by clever scepticism or lazy cynicism.

Does that leave over the possibility of establishing a different sense and a different answer? Well, if so, then let these things be shown forth too—after due pause for rest and recreation.

II

Justice

Introductory note

Part II consists of Lecture 10. In this part we advance from the ethical ideas of formation, reciprocity, and solidarity, as they emerge from Lecture 9, and we seek to bend them towards more political ideals. We reach for distinctively political thoughts that are all of a piece with something that J. S. Mill called 'the principle of cohesion among members of the same community or state'—a principle Mill gives further expression in the words 'our lot is cast together'.[1] Such cohesion is natural in its basis and origination. But the cohesion of human association is not the cohesion of just any ordered aggregation of beings, such as one finds among ants or bees. It is political, Aristotle says:

> Man is the only animal who has the gift of speech. And whereas mere voice is but an indication of pleasure or pain, . . . , the power of speech is intended to set forth the expedient and the inexpedient, and likewise the just and unjust. It is a characteristic of man that he alone has any sense of good and evil, of just and unjust, and the like. An association of living beings who have *this* sense makes a family or makes a *polis*. (Aristotle, *Politics* 1253a10–19)

Where so much has been written in our times about justice and so much of it has already been epitomized so many times, Part II

---

1. See *A System of Logic,* 10th ed. (London, 1879), vol. II, p. 522. I owe this reference to Roger Scruton, *The Need for Nations,* Civitas, Institute for the Study of Civil Society, London, 2004, an article I commend to the reader. See pp. 4–5.

opts for an alternative: to contrast a prevalent conception of these matters, one particular liberal conception, with an earlier view of justice, one whose continuing interest is that it is so closely aligned with ethical and proto-political ideas and sentiments that are still natural to us and still available to us. (Indeed nothing has prevented liberalism itself from drawing freely upon this same fund of ideas and sentiments.)

The strategy of Lecture 10 is to stage a dialogue between a pre-liberal conception of justice, represented by Aristotle as revived with the help of ideas of John Lucas, Bertrand de Jouvenel, and (later on in the argument) G. A. Cohen, and a liberal conception that was founded in Kant and refurbished, renewed, and worked out in John Rawls's *A Theory of Justice*[2]—a conception ever since much discussed and epitomized. Among the questions at issue will be the roles of habit, disposition, and formation, already made much of in Lecture 9; the nature of the dependency (whether one way, the other way, or back and forth) between the justice and the ordinary natural and artificial virtues of the citizen of a just polity and the justice of the constitutional, ethical and legal norms of that polity; the preferability of a piecemeal, bottom-up approach to justice or of a top-down, contractual approach; remedial/restorative conceptions of justice versus more than merely remedial/restorative conceptions; tolerance of contingency; the reason why liberal regimes tend to replace by managerial procedures more and more of the older arrangements that entrusted all sorts of important matters to the practical judgment of individuals; the multiplicity and distinctness of the neo-Aristotelian requisites for a good polity versus the rather simpler demands of liberalism, which relate mostly to legitimacy; and the idea of equality best suited to a just and good polity.

Part I comprised a connected sequence of lectures all dedicated to the moral motive and the content of morality. From Part II onwards, the lectures will be rather more self-contained. At some

---

2. Cambridge, Mass.: Harvard University Press, 1971.

points, the texts will overlap with the texts of lectures 1–9 or with one another. For the overall shape in which all twelve lectures are intended to lie, see again the Preface, fourth paragraph. For other signposts, see the Overview for Part I, the Introductory Note for Part III, and the Concluding Overview.

In this whole design (it may be asked), what place is there for the kind of right that accrues to a person simply by virtue of his or her being recognized as a human being? The first germ of this idea, and the first intimation of our need for it, appeared at 3.4. Compare also 6.12. Well before 6.12, at the point in Lecture 4 where we reached Kant's Formula of Humanity, it may have seemed that everything was almost ready for such an idea to emerge full blown—except that the humanity at issue in 4.12 proved to be a humanity of pure rational nature, 'independent of all animality' (cp. p. 122, epigraph). This is not the humanity that comes to mind when Simone Weil reminds us (as in 9.8) of the way in which one human being can instantly know the presence of another such being, and under an 'indefinable influence' recognize them as such. It is under the care of the animate conception and the collateral ideas that it imports of the nature and vital needs of such a being that the first staging post is to be found for any substantial elucidation of the idea of a human right. As regards the rest of that work, well, the closest we shall come is to one part of it. See 11.12.

Despite appearances and despite its importance, the idea of a human right seems not to be a primitive or a simple notion, or a secure foundation for a convincing philosophy of morality. Better to think of it as a coping stone for further philosophical labours that lie somewhere beyond the aspirations of this book.[3]

---

3. Beyond present-day work on human rights, it will profit the reader to consult Allen W. Wood, *Hegel's Ethical Theory* (Cambridge: Cambridge University Press, 1990), pp. 71–93. For the shortfall between *vital need* and *human right* and the hazards incurred when we give too little work to the former and load so much upon the latter that we jeopardize its would-be absoluteness and indefeasibility (cp. 9.17), see David Wiggins, 'Claims of Need', in *Needs, Values, Truth* (amended 3rd ed., Cambridge: Cambridge University Press, 2002), pp. 1–2, 31–49.

10

Neo-Aristotelian reflections on justice

10.1. In the second supplement to 'Perpetual Peace', Kant wrote:

Hard as it may sound, the problem of setting up a state can be solved even by a nation of devils so long as they possess understanding. . . . A problem of this kind must be soluble. For such a task does not involve the moral improvement of man; it only means finding out how the mechanism of nature can be applied to men in such a way that the antagonism of their hostile attitudes will make them compel one another to submit to coercive laws.[1]

A few lines later, Kant says:

we cannot expect [a people's] moral attitudes to produce a good political constitution; on the contrary, it is only through the latter that people can be expected to attain a good level of moral culture. . . . We may say that nature *irresistibly wills* that right should eventually gain the upper hand.

This lecture was written for a conference on law, political morality, and human nature held 11–13 July 2002 in the Faculty of Law, Cambridge University, England. It was drawn from an earlier text that had once benefited from the comments of Pierre Manent and Monique Canto-Sperber, and had been given thereafter as a lecture at the Sorbonne, Paris IV, in March 2002.

1. Kant, *Political Writings,* ed. Hans Reiss, trans. H. B. Nisbet (Cambridge: Cambridge University Press, 1970), pp. 112–13, translation here slightly modified.

These are striking declarations. But how kind have the ensuing centuries been to the last claim, of inevitability? And how plausible is (or ever was) the strong assertion of one-way dependence conveyed by the penultimate sentence cited? If the claim of asymmetrical dependency—the denial even of back and forth between political constitution and the expectations, dispositions and virtues of citizens— seems not plausible, in what ways (if in any) does this matter to political theory? Kant refers to 'coercive laws'. Is that sinister or perfectly benign? It is questions such as these that have prompted me to try to arouse a fresh interest in a neo-Aristotelian or pre-liberal approach to justice which lays greater emphasis than Kant and his inheritors do upon the roles of formation, mentality and habit. (Cp. Aristotle, *Politics* 1269a20.) The most immediate aim is to put Aristotle and/or his inheritors into some kind of dialogue with our own generation's inheritors of Kant and with present-day theories of justice. One thing that encourages such a dialogue is that, despite their overwhelming differences, and despite the passage of two and a half millennia, the two parties apparently agree in at least one thing, namely in conceiving of justice as the maintaining virtue of a well-ordered society/a good polity.

10.2. If a dialogue such as this is to treat of things that are comparable to any significant degree, the first effort of reformulation must fall on the Aristotelian side. In this work—in the radical renewal of Aristotelian conceptions—we shall heavily depend (or depend on those who depend) on the possibility of resuming Aristotle's dialectical, or as one might say, phenomenological method. This method is not altogether new to our times. A remarkable instance of the fusion of it with the particular insight of linguistic philosophy may be found in my colleague J. R. Lucas's short book, *On Justice*.[2] Another example, even more Aristotelian (and downwind of much else besides in the philosophical and economic speculations of the

2. Oxford: Oxford University Press, 1980.

west) but scarcely linguistic at all, may be found in Bertrand de Jouvenel's book *On Sovereignty: An Inquiry into the Political Good*.[3] There are surely others. But Jouvenel's is the only neo-Aristotelian work I know that engages quite explicitly—and engages in ways that at least put one in mind of mid-twentieth century realities—with the very questions that I mentioned at the beginning. That is chief among the reasons why (at risk of representing Jouvenel as yet more Aristotelian than he is, and representing Aristotle himself, however anachronistically, as having some affinity with a defender of what Rawls has called the system of natural liberty) I have chosen *On Sovereignty* as a stepping stone towards a neo-Aristotelian or pre-liberal proposal. In the French original, Jouvenel's book appeared before Rawls's *Theory of Justice*. For reasons owed partly to the lapse of time, Jouvenel requires some of the same good will on the part of the reader as does Aristotle. But never mind. Let neo-Aristotelianism begin (at least) by presenting itself as something exotic and strange. Why should you not take seriously—in the end— the exotic and strange?

10.3. In the fifth book of the *Nicomachean Ethics*, Aristotle first conceives particular justice—contrast justice identified with general righteousness towards others—as involving the justice of allocations (proportioning to the worthiness of the recipients the award of office, booty, or anything else, presumably, of which the *polis* can dispose) and the justice of rectifications (restoring the *status quo ante* after a civil wrong has been done). A bit later on in the book, Aristotle adds (in effect) commercial justice or justice in exchanges. Then, closer to the end of the book, Aristotle adds *epieikeia* or equity, which he sees as a certain kind of correction of justice. This is a family of notions, or a family in the making. At one point, Jouvenel

---

3. Trans. J. F. Huntington (Cambridge: Cambridge University Press, 1957); originally published as *De la souveraineté: à la recherche du bien politique* (Paris: M. T. Genin, 1955). Page references below are to the 1957 Huntington edition.

proposes to see the members of the family as divers variations on the Aristotelian idea of proportionality. But let me assert immediately that proportionality as such—roughly, match the award of anything to the strength of the claim for it, a truism to be treasured as such, but scarcely more than a reminder—cannot contain within it each and every one of the various forms of justice. (In and of itself, it demarcates no specific claims.) There is no serious question of deducing any one of Aristotle's kinds from any of the others or of deducing all four from a more fundamental idea.

The Aristotelian details of the first three kinds of Aristotelian justice are archaic. Far more important for our purposes is Aristotle's general strategy. The strategy is enumerative and bottom-up, the apparent inverse of attempts to deduce justice or the principles of justice, top-down, from the deliberated fairness, the fairness once and for all, of some system of cooperation. Another thing I should stress is that a neo-Aristotelian approach does not exclude other kinds of justice beyond those designated by Aristotle. Rather it strongly invites them: the justice of penalties, for instance (for the whole business of Aristotle's rectifying justice belongs within civil justice), economic justice (in so far as it is not treated under justice in allocations and justice in exchanges), fiscal justice, administrative justice. . . .

As such a list grew longer and longer, you would demand to know why a neo-Aristotelian thinks that these things all belong together. Such a question is of the first importance if one proposes to follow an enumerative method with any semblance of system. Moreover, the answer we shall propose will even subtract a few inches from the width of the divide between neo-Aristotelianism and present-day accounts of justice. (See below, 10.5 and 10.7, last paragraph.) First though some preliminaries. Let us forget, despite its manifest presence in book V of the *Ethics,* the Aristotelian theory of the mean. Let us forget Aristotle's tendency to think of injustice as arising essentially from a specifically unjust motive, which needs then to be greed or cupidity (*pleonexia*). That was a bad mistake, for ordinary acts of injustice will often arise from the simple lack of any positive concern for justice.[4] Let us also forget (if we can) the fact that, in the *Politics,* Aristotle thought he had to justify slavery and excluded women, artisans and craftsmen from citizenship.[5] In further acts of conceptual depredation, let us forget a thousand and one other details one encounters in that text, and try to situate neo-Aristotelian justice by reference to neighbouring concerns of Aristotle's—not least (a) his interest in the human fulfilment and participative satisfaction that come from the sequential experiences of submitting to others in office and then holding office, and (b) Aristotle's concern that those who participate in the *common thing* (*to koinon, res publica*) should both desire to perpetuate its existence (contrast its each and every attribute at a given moment in its historic development) and will the common good.

10.4. In taking further the question of how to make a neo-Aristotelian account of justice and identify the organizing point of the idea, let us turn first to a positive declaration of Aristotle's that is crucial for the philosophical rationale of any piecemeal and/or quasi-phenomenological method. The declaration (*Nicomachean Ethics* 1137b18-19 conjoined with 1137b29-32) is that the subject matter of action (the province where it operates and the field of things it is concerned with) is inexhaustibly indefinite. Or, as one might say in further developing this declaration, the matter of the practical cannot be treated with, handled, mastered or managed by

4. See Bernard Williams, 'Justice as a Virtue', in Amélie Rorty, ed., *Essays on Aristotle's Ethics* Berkeley: University of California Press, 1980). I am indebted to this article. Justice is conspicuous among the artificial virtues. For an account of these that explains how Williams's finding coheres with what is to be expected of such virtues, see my vindication of Hume's scheme in R. Crisp, ed., *How Should One Live?* (Oxford: Oxford University Press, 1996).

5. We must also postpone, without date, the task of adjusting Aristotle's definition of a citizen at 1275a2 as one who participates in judgment and in the holding of office. In the interim, let us try to think of the citizen body as demarcated after the fashion of a western democracy. The price we pay for saying no more than this here will be a certain faintness of outline in our account of justice$_{[C]}$ in 10.8 below.

means of principles or precepts that are at once general and unrestrictedly correct. It follows that for an agent properly to grasp a practical thing such as justice, he must be ready to enter into the spirit of its requirements.

The claim that the subject matter of the practical is indefinite is entirely general in purport, but it comes from book V, chapter 10, the famous chapter on equity, to which we shall return. In due course, it will put us into a position to answer the question we have asked about the organizing point of the idea. But now, for the duration of three long paragraphs, we need to connect the chapter and the claim of indefiniteness of the matter of the practical with a general view of the practical that is all over the *Nicomachean Ethics*.

Somehow, despite the said indefiniteness, any agent who has practical wisdom and everything presupposed to practical wisdom, namely the ethical virtues, will understand how to determine a practical end that is pertinent for a given context of action or decision and hit on the right decision for that context. In that context, he will exercise perception *(aisthēsis)* of ethically salient circumstances, make judgments about which virtues the context calls upon, and determine what this or that virtue requires there. But if this finding or determination has to be specific to the context, then what is its source? From whence does the agent arrive at it? Answer: the specific finding will be the product of ideals or principles concerning how to be and how to act which impinge *independently of any context* on those who are possessed of the ethical virtues and who grasp thereby the general, however inexplicit, aim in life (the *hou heneka*) which, by their presence in the agent, these virtues singly and collectively impart (1144a6 ff.). Considered thus independently of context, these ideals or principles can prescribe only for the most part *(hōs epi to polu)*. (See 1094b21. See also *Nicomachean Ethics* II.2.) It takes *phronēsis,* practical wisdom and the conception of the good that is secured by ethical virtue, to shape, determine, and validate their application in this, that or the other set of circumstances. (See 1143a35–b17).

Why *should* such validation require practical wisdom and every-

thing that practical wisdom itself requires? Well, the first thing to
be said to one who sees the contentions just made as peculiar to
Aristotelianism (as not making any other claim for serious attention
in their own right) is that, if you try to transpose ideals or principles
that the *phronimos* appeals to into self-sufficient injunctions, instructions, or prescriptions of the form 'It is always right, or it is always
just, when so and so (when . . .), to do such and such act (the
act——)'—if you forget the outlook or mentality itself and concentrate instead on verbal expressions in which those subject to some
non-Aristotelian system of moral education might supposedly be cat-
echized or trained—then the resulting form of words will be false
and will remain false (open to counterexamples) however lengthy
you make the specification of the so and so (. . .) or the such and
such (——).[6] You may try to save the injunction by tying it down
to one particular situation that is deictically identified. But if you
save it in that way you lose the last shred of the generality attaching
to the ideal or principle you began with. In another way you can
try to save the injunction you are aiming for by leaving the words
as they stand and adjoining a *ceteris paribus* clause. But, according
to Aristotle as I reconstruct him at this point, only one who deployed

6. Nothing follows from this about prohibitions. Or rather, the matter is obscure. If
we try to formulate prohibitions on Q-ing in the pattern 'It is always right when . . . to
do the act of *not* Q-ing', we obtain universal but specific instructions to do the act of
abstaining from Q-ing where such abstention is supposed to be the whole answer to the
question 'What specifically shall one do?' In so far as there are universal prohibitions
of this sort, offering the answer to a question of what act to do, and they are excep-
tionlessly correct (see *Nicomachean Ethics* 1110a25-7), the claim in the text must be
qualified. But most prohibitions are not demands for specific acts of abstention. They
relate rather to doing *no* act of the type in question, no act of Q-ing. Here there is a
different sort of asymmetry between injunctions and prescriptions in their unrecon-
structed states. Prescriptions promote the choice of one particular act among acts it is
possible to do. Sometimes they tip the balance. Most prohibitions on acts are intended
not so much to tip the balance strongly against these acts as to exclude them altogether
from the space of ordinary deliberation. That is what *Nicomachean Ethics* 1110a25-7 is
really about. No doubt this was the real, mainly negative, purpose of catechism in its
original setting within benign Judaeo-Christian *ethismos*. That, however, is not the thing
under discussion in the text—rather the ideas that would have to be proposed by those
who seek to supersede or upstage the way of *ethismos*.

the cardinal, always incompletely explicit knowledge afforded by the practical wisdom in which the ethical virtues culminate would ever be able to determine whether *cetera* were *paria* (or what this meant)—in which case it will seem to have been a mistake for any-one, theorist or agent, even to contemplate the business of a would-be approximative process of qualification which was bound to tail off into *ceteris paribus*.[7]

In the second place, it is not a mere contingency about the prac-tical, or so anyone will maintain who takes the Aristotelian view, that it is impossible to draft for all contexts or conjunctures of circum-stances explicit statements of action-specific principles that will be found in each context to be correct, reasonable, or what one in-tended. It testifies to the plurality and complexity of our concerns—and of the dispositions that sustain them—and it shows something of the vast and expanding scene where we have to act them out. Nevertheless—and this prepares the way for a third point—the im-possibility claim concerning explicit statement does not need to be coupled with the denial that, for every context, there will be some way of resolving how to go forward. One might hope that, by de-termining, in their practice and by the ideals to which they hold their practice answerable, what things matter, how these things co-here, and in what spirit they are to be brought into being, an as-sociation of human beings could furnish itself with enough to ensure that there will always be some basis for an agent to resolve how to go forward. By the same token, might one not hope then for some general and teachable method applicable to all contexts? No. The fear of falling into the oldest or second oldest fallacy there is (the fallacy of moving without further premises from 'for all x there is a y . . . ' to 'there is a y such that for all x . . . ') forces us here, with the third point, into a positive discovery. The only unitary thing

7. On this point, I should like to refer to the remarkable and importantly sensible essay on lying and truth-telling in Leszek Kolakowski's book *Freedom, Fame, Lying and Betrayal: Essays on Everyday Life* (London: Penguin, 1999). For the best account I know of the Aristotelian idea of formation that underwrites practical reason, see Sabina Lov-ibond, *Ethical Formation* (Cambridge, Mass.: Harvard University Press, 2002).

there *has* to be here apart from the permanent concerns of the ethically initiated agent (contrast with these the residue left by any
process of internalizing some catalogue of principles), and the only
constant resource that needs to be looked for, is the irreducibly
practical grasp of the good (*hypolepsis tou telous*, 1142b34) possessed
by one who has practical wisdom and the ethical dispositions that
are prerequisite to practical wisdom.

10.5. The thesis of the indefiniteness of the practical and the
claim that it suggests about a non-propositional and an incompletely
articulable element in all our practical knowing how to go on is an
entirely general thesis. It is in no way special to justice. But it returns
us to our appointed subject. For one of the most striking applications
of the thesis is illustrated at book V, chapter 10, in connection with
equity, justice, the law, and the legislator, where Aristotle writes:

> all law is universal but about some things it is not possible to
> make a universal statement which shall be correct. In those
> cases, then, in which it is necessary to speak universally but not
> possible to do so correctly, the law takes the usual case, in full
> awareness of the possibility of error. And it is nonetheless right
> to do so; for the error will not be in the law nor in the legislator
> but in the nature of the thing, since the matter of practical affairs
> is of this kind from the outset [i.e. indefinite, cp. 1137b29–32].

Where a *psēphisma* or special decree is needed as a supplement to
the law, as a correction of the law, or as an interpretation of the law,
you arrive at this (Aristotle then suggests) by entering into the
thoughts of the (notionally wise, just, and benevolent) legislator. You
ask what he would have said about the case.[8] What *telos* or *skopos*,

---

8. Compare Jacques Brunschwig, 'Rule and Exception: On the Aristotelian Theory
of Equity', in Michael Frede and Gisela Striker, eds., *Rationality in Greek Thought*
(Oxford: Clarendon Press, 1996). See also Henry Maine, *Ancient Law* (London: John
Murray, 1906), chs. 2, 3; F. W. Maitland, *The Constitutional History of England* (Cambridge: Cambridge University Press, 1919), pp. 221–6, 466–71.

we then find ourselves asking, would the legislator have held himself answerable to? In book V, chapter 10, Aristotle does not say. But in the *Politics*, Aristotle maintains that the end of a *polis* is that of an association for sharing or *koinōnia* whose purpose is for its participants to live the ethically perfect and self-sufficient life; and he says that justice is that by which this *koinōnia* is maintained. And here would have been the key to the spirit in which a contextually definite determination was to be arrived at for the act that justice demanded. Adapting Aristotle to the conditions of the modern world, however, Bertrand de Jouvenel would prefer to answer our question by saying that the *telos* the legislator should have in mind and communicate to citizens and their magistrates as signalling the spirit in which they should act is the common good, *le bien politique*, considered not as the perfection of citizens (still less as the whole sum of particular interests of citizens), but as a certain condition or *sine qua non* of the good for any or every person, and for the human condition as such, namely the condition for social friendship, *l'amitié sociale*, or the social tie,[9] which Jouvenel envisages as holding, actually or potentially, between people who may be complete strangers. (Again, at this last point, contrast the account Aristotle gives of such matters in the *Politics*.)[10] Jouvenel would also say that, like Aristotle, he sees

9. For some of Jouvenel's several reasons for preferring this goal over Aristotle's, see n. 15 below. 'Social friendship' sounds oddly. But 'social tie' sounds obscure. So I have used the one, the other or both. To grasp the full intended resonance of either, it will be best to have the experience of reading *On Sovereignty* as a unified book.

10. There is here a certain spectrum of possible positions which may be suggested by the ordering (1) Aristotle, (2) Jouvenel, (3) Rawls in *Political Liberalism* (Cambridge, Mass.: Harvard University Press, 1993), (4) Rawls in *A Theory of Justice* (Cambridge, Mass.: Harvard University Press, 1971). Jouvenel subtracts explicitly from the enclosing ideal of communality represented by Aristotle. In (4), Rawls's ideal of fraternity (see below, 10.7, second paragraph, and 10.15) arises chiefly in connection with citizens' sense of justice, of justice as interpreted by Rawls's principles of justice. In (3), which was published after Jouvenel's death, Rawls emphasizes further elements of the public political culture and the degree to which there can be a morally substantial bond between fellow citizens, despite potentially threatening differences in their conceptions of the good. Of course, this diminishes the distance between Jouvenel and Rawls, leaving us to speculate what Jouvenel would have said about (3). He might perhaps have raised the question whether, starting originally from (3), Rawls would have reached the same

justice as emerging from citizens' observance of specific norms—as from magistrates' satisfaction of citizens' expectations of their magistrates. (Jouvenel uses the word 'magistrate' in the Roman sense to mean officer of state.) In the absence of any of these things, the proper *telos* of legislator and statesman may go unattained. In sum, justice is the keystone of the social edifice.

10.6. I do not know if Jouvenel, who lived till 1987, ever came to read Rawls. If he did, I doubt that he will have objected to the use Rawls makes in *A Theory of Justice* of the idea of cooperation. He will have protested, rather, that the thing that deliberators behind Rawls's veil of ignorance most badly need, if they are to draw up good principles for their cooperation, is to find a way to make positive use of their lived or practical experience of the world, as well of their recollection of cooperative ideals they have never so far been able to realize; that within Rawls's framework, this experience will have to be distilled, if that be possible, from some anonymized version of their own life in the world and any propositions of suitably anonymized human history that Rawls will grant them liberty to consult. But anyone who proceeded in this way, Jouvenel might then have declared, anyone that is who managed somehow to translate such a version of his or her experience back into practical knowledge, would have to despair of translating their findings into anything so abstract or general or professedly complete as Rawls's principles. Here Jouvenel might ask why, rather than struggle against all the odds in this effort, the deliberators do not redeploy their practical understanding of the business of fruitful cooperation into an open-ended project of enumeration and elucidation. Let them try to

---

principles of justice as those he had drafted in (4). Pursuing further the question of formation with which the present essay begins, he might have quoted Aristotle, *Politics* 1310a20 ff.: 'The greatest of all means to secure the stability of a polity is one that at present people despise. It is a system of education suited to the polity. For there is no use in the most valuable laws ratified by the unanimous judgment of the whole body of citizens if these are not educated in the constitution.' If it is effective at all, will such an education tend to diminish somewhat differences in conceptions of the good? Kept within reasonable limits, is that altogether lamentable?

list the divers specific concerns that anyone will have to have if they are party to the norms, the sense of obligation, and the expectations (of self, of others, and of public magistrates) which all cooperators and participators will need to be party to: (a) in order to uphold and preserve their cooperative association as a shared thing with a past, a present, and a future; and (b) in order to protect their modes of cooperation from participants who will otherwise pursue practices or policies that disregard or slight the interests of other participants, thereby provoking them to see in such acts a cause for disaffection. Let would-be cooperators have no cause to complain indignantly that for such acts not to be singled out for public disapproval and remedy is for their own interests as participators to be held of no account.[11] If Rawls's philosophical strategy is anywhere near correct, the neo-Aristotelian will say, then it ought to be possible to refine such an enumeration of concerns, norms and expectations into the beginnings (as the neo-Aristotelian equally hopes) of an account of the various forms of justice. (For the primarily restorative, remedial, and only thereafter enabling conception of justice that may be drawn from such a development, see further the citations from Jouvenel given in 10.9 and 10.12 below.)

One more remark about this contrast—this contrast and comparison, rather—between Jouvenel and *A Theory of Justice*. On a neo-Aristotelian view, this active understanding of the aims and aspirations of a political association, this understanding held in common, being something essentially practical, need not be susceptible of full, finite, or more than partial articulation. (Only under the myth of a

---

11. Lucas, *On Justice*, p. 70 (cp. Lucas' pp. 7, 69, 154, 184, 246 . . .), cites approvingly the words of Janvier: 'La justice est essentiellement altruiste. Par la justice nous sortons de nous mêmes, nous brisons avec le souci de notre étroite personne pour nous occupier de nos semblables. La justice est en chacun de nous le défenseur des êtres distincts de nous; elle est dans l'individu le défenseur des autres individus.' ('Justice is by its nature altruist. By justice, we go out from ourselves, break with our narrow concern for self and have care for our fellows. Within each of us justice is the protector of beings distinct from us. Within the individual it is the protector of other individuals.' *La Justice et le Droit* (Paris, 1918), p. 15.) Cp. Giorgio del Vecchio, *Justice*, ed. and trans. A. H. Campbell (Edinburgh: Edinburgh University Press, 1952), pp. 173-4.

contract and a notional moment of contracting is there need for very much more.) Such an understanding is something one comes to possess, and then develops, but only spells out at need and in the business of living.[12] On the neo-Aristotelian view, it is a part of the work of political philosophy to prolong this effort of articulation into the further work of explaining and developing the same understanding—not necessarily in a shape that present-day exponents would dignify by the name of a theory, but in the form of a nucleus of ideas or notions that at once reflect and enlighten practical reflection.

So much to be going on with for the philosophical foundation and the organizing rationale, and so much for some of the distinctiveness, of the piecemeal, enumerative, dialectical, or phenomenological treatment of justice.

10.7. Jouvenel begins his account of justice in chapter 9 of *On Sovereignty* with the remark (p. 139) that preoccupation with justice is 'the political preoccupation par excellence, and it is no bad thing that "social justice" should be the obsession of our time'. But then he warns us that justice acts as a principle not of concord but of discord. Pointing to 'the spectacle of a society splitting and crumbling in the name of the justice which should harmonize it and cause peace to reign', he harks back immediately to Justinian's definition, 'justice is a constant and unceasing determination to render everyone his due'.[13] Jouvenel then declares:

---

12. Under this aspect, neo-Aristotelianism is the natural ally of the Leibnizian preoccupation with ideas that are both clear (and as such good) and also indistinct. See Leibniz, 'Meditations on Knowledge, Truth and Ideas', in G. W. Leibniz, *Philosophical Papers and Letter,* ed. and trans. Leroy E. Loemker, 2nd ed. (Dordrecht: Reidel, 1969).

13. See Justinian, *Institutes* I.ii.1, which is based on Ulpian, which is based on Cicero, which derives ultimately from the sort of thing Polemarchus says in Plato's *Republic.* Justinian's definition embodies the same thought which was developed by Aquinas at *Summa Theologica,* Quaestio LVIII, in the claim that 'justice is a habit of mind which maintains in us a firm and unceasing determination to render everyone his due'. Of course, Justinian's definition is also downwind from *Nicomachean Ethics* 1129a8, but this sentence of Aristotle's is innocent neither of confusions we have set aside about

Whereas it used to be thought that social relationships are improved by justice in men, it is now thought, contrariwise, that the installation in institutions of a thing called just promotes the improvement of men. (p. 140)

The justice now recommended is a quality not of a man and a man's actions but of a certain configuration of things in social geometry, no matter by what means it is brought about. Justice is now something which exists independently of just men. (p. 140)

The last sentence marks a contrast, oppositional (we remark) to Kant's asymmetry claim, that is very important for Jouvenel. But the possibility lurks here of a simply terrible confusion (latent also, one might fear, in some would-be Aristotelian works of virtue ethics). Look at Justinian's definition, approved by Jouvenel. This suggests two senses of 'just', two good senses, [A] and [B], where [B] is defined in terms of [A]. The personal virtue of someone who is just in a sense [B] is a constant and unceasing determination to do what? To do the just act. Here, in this last, 'just' occurs in a separable and apparently prior sense, one which we have no alternative but to label sense [A]. (Sense [B] depends on a prior determination of a sense [A], but sense [A] does not depend on sense [B].) Moreover there is simply no room, if we follow Justinian, for Jouvenel's programmatic scepticism about predicating 'just' of things other than persons. Justinian's definition precisely depends on such predication—even as it depends on the possibility of a collateral and prior account's being provided of how *that which is due* is itself to be determined.

According to Justinian, we have it then, that:

An act is just$_{[A]}$ if it secures to another that which is due to him/her.

___

injustice (see n. 4) nor of the idea, which we shall criticize, of the semantic primacy of 'just person'.

The virtue of one who is just$_{[B]}$ is a disposition which both (i) maintains a firm and unceasing determination to do acts that are just$_{[A]}$, that is, acts which secure to each what is due to each; and <(ii) maintains the determination to second and support just$_{[A]}$ acts on the part of others and prompts a corresponding concern for each and every person to come to have what is due to them>

The words placed in the angle brackets are intended to enlarge on the thought one has that the character trait in question with just-ness$_{[B]}$ comprises not only a certain kind of conscientiousness in acts of one's own, but also a concern for that which just acts are carried out *for*, and a measure of preoccupation too with the doings of other agents. For one can scarcely concern oneself with just acts unless one is also preoccupied with the states of affairs that these acts are directed towards—namely each person's actually *having or obtaining* what is due to him. Evidently then there is a logically anterior provision to which any neo-Aristotelian must also be committed

An outcome or state of affairs is just$_{[A]}$ if it consists in some person's or persons' having what is due to them.

Here, as before, 'what is due to them' is a place-holder for something which can only be determined within the larger picture that will be revealed when we broach the questions that come into view with the justice of the *polis*. That will be justice$_{[C]}$. (See below.) In a semantically more complete treatment, pursued for its own sake, these two uses of 'just$_{[A]}$' might be further disentangled. Provided that we are aware of the real complications that lurk at this point, they need not be pursued here.

There is yet one more thing to complain about in this beginning of Jouvenel's. (How can so modest an exordium provoke so much criticism?) Jouvenel is mistaken in finding fault with modern philosophy for disregarding justice in sense [B]. Rather he is a bad prophet. See Rawls:

Human beings have a desire to express their nature as free and equal moral persons, and this they do most adequately by acting from the principles that they would acknowledge in the original position. When all strive to comply with these principles and each succeeds, then individually and collectively their nature as moral persons is most fully realized and with it their individual and collective good. . . . In a well-ordered society each person understands the first principles that govern the whole scheme as it is to be carried out over many generations; and all have a settled intention to adhere to these principles in their plan of life.[14]

However faintly, both of Justinian's two justices still echo in this passage. Whether they echo loudly enough is a question I shall come to much later, when I shall ask whether either Rawls or his critic, G. A. Cohen, have got justice$_{[A]}$ and justice$_{[B]}$ and justice$_{[C]}$—the justness of a *polis,* to which we shall come in due course—into the right alignment.

In the interim, the most immediate question is how to say the thing that Jouvenel ought to have said. Perhaps he should have said this (I put words into his mouth): 'Apart from justice$_{[B]}$, as D.W. labels it, the disposition of a just person, there is of course the justice, the justice$_{[A]}$, as D.W. labels it, of a just norm or a just practice directed at a just$_{[A]}$ outcome. Justice$_{[A]}$ then is that which is exemplified by the act that is just$_{[A]}$ and the state of things that such acts are aimed at. The view I was taking in *On Sovereignty* was that—*pace* the sentence of Kant's 'Perpetual Peace' adduced by D.W.—justice$_{[B]}$, the justice of the just person, is basic and foundational. Justice$_{[A]}$ is unthinkable without justice$_{[B]}$. In sheer logic, though, I see that I must agree that these kinds of predication are distinct. I must also agree then that justice$_{[B]}$ looks outward to the norms, practices, and outcomes that are just$_{[A]}$. Justice$_{[B]}$ needs justice$_{[A]}$. That too I must not deny. But the thing justice$_{[B]}$ must see there in justice$_{[A]}$—must see as if through a transparent medium—is not, *pace* Professor Rawls, some abstraction of social geometry or

---

14. *A Theory of Justice,* sect. 79, p. 528.

some property "of the basic structure of society", but rather this sort of thing—: the need for the act that restores, to Peter, Peter's proper portion; the need for an act that restores Paul to the condition where he was before he suffered the injury or loss that he suffered; the concern any just person will have that Paul's aggressor be punished; the concern any just$_{[B]}$ person will feel that meritorious effort not go unrecognized; the concern any just$_{[B]}$ person will feel that the main burden (but not every part of that whole burden) of taxation should fall on citizens least badly placed to bear it, etc. The thing the person with justice$_{[B]}$ sees in justice$_{[A]}$ is a sum of obligations, concerns, expectations (from self, from others, and from magistrates) only comprehensible as such to one with justice$_{[B]}$. The underlying unity of this sum of things is that, singly and collectively, the satisfactions and fulfilments of these divers requirements are in part constitutive of the social tie or practical prerequisites for it. Acts and outcomes can be just$_{[A]}$ only to the extent that they can be recognized by those with the virtue of justice$_{[B]}$ *as* such prerequisites. It may appear that the fulfilment of this sum of citizenly obligations, expectations, and concerns, lacking the formal beauty of some larger configuration in social geometry or the basic structure of a well-ordered society, is nothing very uplifting or heroic or magnificent. But it is nothing dispensable, either. There supervenes on the justice$_{[B]}$ of citizens, if this be properly trained on justice$_{[A]}$, an order of thing that is intelligible enough from within by those who have any sufficiency of this virtue.'

10.8. So much then for neo-Aristotelian justice of acts, their aim and intentionality, and so much for the justice in a person or citizen that is manifestable in his individual acts and in his private and public preoccupations. So much too for the correction to Jouvenel's opening contentions. But at least one semantic question remains to be tidied up about 'just'. What should one say about 'just' in a 'just regime', a 'just political constitution', or a 'just *polis*'? Simply in order to bracket all questions of size and scale (questions which, elsewhere in *On Sovereignty*, Jouvenel advances beyond the speculations of Aristotle or Rousseau and some considerable way into the world we now live in),[15] let us frame the question by using the strange word *polis* (richly resonant of 'polity' and the older use of the French word 'police', as it occurs in Montaigne and Rousseau). What ought to be the Jouvenelean account of 'just$_{[C]}$' as applied to the *polis?* Maybe this:

> A *polis* that is just$_{[C]}$ is a *polis* that arrives at (and by its constitution expresses) an understanding of the just$_{[A]}$ and at norms and practices of acting justly$_{[A]}$ which—by dint of a settled disposition of just$_{[B]}$ citizens to act according to justice$_{[A]}$ and/or to second in all relevant ways public acts or policies that are just$_{[A]}$ or issue in outcomes that are just$_{[A]}$—sustain social friendship and secure the social tie.

Sense [B] was explained in terms of sense [A]. This exemplified the focal (or *aph'henos*) paradigm of semantic linkage mentioned at *Nicomachean Ethics* 1096b28. Now, in a complication of that paradigm (see also *Metaphysics* 1028a20–30), sense [C] is explained in terms of senses [A] and [B] together.

There is much else to say about this proposal, most conspicuously that it shows plainly why the philosopher of justice cannot prescind

---

15. In the ancient conception, Jouvenel says, the city is small, culturally homogeneous, and tries to resist innovation and foreign ideas. Under those conditions the government of the city was in a position to play a rather specific *animating* role. Under modern conditions, government can only pursue the purposes of perpetuating the *polis* and of promoting the social tie and the social good by *abdicating* the role of animator and acting in the new role of umpire and regulator. (If it goes too far in seeking to resume the animating role, it moves the *polis* in the direction of totalitarianism.) See the difference marked at the beginning of 10.4 between Aristotle's legislator and Jouvenel's.

Jouvenel's legislator is absolutely not the liberal economists' legislator. The 'wisdom of the market', once extended beyond the market itself, is a natural ally of a new kind of totalitarianism. Moreover, once extended beyond its proper limits, the market will in the long term subvert patriotism and other local loyalties. Jouvenel might have added, if he had lived to see the prospect now visible to us, that the wisdom of the market, once extended outside the sphere where it belongs, will in practice subvert education, ethical formation, public spirit, and concern for environment.

from questions of formation and education, from questions of human nature and endowment, or from the needs and capacities to which Aristotle seeks to minister by allowing the prospect of office to those who must *in the interim* obey. The most immediate thing to say is that, in the effort to arrive at the proposal just made, one happens on a further thought. If a philosopher of justice were to try to specify the three distinct justices [A] [B] [C] as coordinated in the way in which the proposal coordinates them, then the problem of the philosopher would be to understand the business of repeated adjustment and readjustment, of trial and error, of approximation back and forth. It would involve a recapitulation of the ideas and processes by which [A] [B] [C] are coordinated and recoordinated in *poleis* fortunate enough to govern themselves wisely and temperately.

Let us accept these conclusions and formulate the question which would then arise. Under the new conditions of here and now, is there any specification at all of the just$_{[A]}$ which will *in practice* realize the just$_{[C]}$? Under present-day conditions, does the simultaneous equation that corresponds to our proposal have any solution?[16] Or has the preoccupation with questions of power and legitimacy carried some western societies beyond the point where justice$_{[C]}$, so defined, is realistically even conceivable? But here, leaving that gloomy question on the record—together with the neo-Aristotelian counterparts of the political questions pursued by Aris-

16. Del Vecchio, *Justice* (see his index) reports that Dante defined justice as *proportio hominis ad hominem quae servata servat hominum societatem.* That is to say that Dante defined it, roughly speaking, as a proportion or ratio between human beings, or a relation of human to human, namely the proportion or ratio or relation whose preservation preserves human society. On these terms, the question becomes which *proportio* would now do that. Is there such a *proportio?*

An interesting and easier question is whether I am right to suppose, as I do, that an Aristotelian can both maintain the focal meaning account and insist on the simultaneous determination of [A] [B] [C] by back and forth. But this is not the place to stop to justify that claim. One further thought presents itself about the question in the text. Once we catch sight of the possibility that justice$_{[C]}$ may be unrealizable under certain conditions of expectation and certain material and institutional conditions, the question will arise whether realizability can be regained if there are adjustments to the size or self-governing autonomy of units that are candidates to be treated as *poleis* (or if there are adjustments to the constitutional arrangements that determine the powers of those whom citizens elect to govern them).

totle without conclusive outcome: namely, what form of monarchy, what middle constitution, what moderate democracy without mob rule, what mixture of oligarchy and democracy will best achieve the stated end?—let us now go back to where we were at the point when we ventured to criticize Jouvenel.

10.9. Under the constraints given, what is to be said, if only for the sake of illustration, about the content of justice$_{[A]}$? Putting the question in the terms of the definition offered by Justinian, what ought to belong to each person? In his chapter on justice, Jouvenel begins with two traditional forms of justice, the rectificatory and the commutative. Given that way of beginning with the *status quo,* there are all sorts of things I wish he had done. I wish especially he had extended rectificatory justice to involve itself in situations such as this: the existing capability of some group to earn their own living by their own labours is undermined by the commercial or industrial decisions of other people or other sections of society that promise to render this group economically superfluous. It is important that, at one point in *On Sovereignty,* we find Jouvenel drawing near to this area of concern.

> [The authority] acts as a more or less discriminating filter to innovations in behaviour and diversions from the norm; necessarily, too, it is on guard to remedy the resulting uncertainty. It is in this process of filtering and remedying, in this unceasing work of repair to an equilibrium, that the question of the Political Good is most often posed. (p. 55)

In the chapter on justice, however, he fails to return to this duty of the authority. He does not connect this earlier thought of his with his remedial or protecting conception of justice. There are wasted opportunities here. Indeed, Jouvenel's chapter on justice needs to be two or three times as long or else to be supplemented from other works in the same tradition. But rather than complain of that now, let us focus on some more of what he does say.

Jouvenel remarks gloomily in the next phase of the chapter that:

The notion that justice consists in the upholding of existing
rights finds little favour with our time, which considers that it
is to be found in the creation of new rights. But what new rights
will be just? . . . [E]ven today demands for new rights are styled
'claims', a word which, in the phrase 'statements of claim', de-
notes actions in law for the recovery of something which was
yours and has been taken from you. . . . Nothing is more necessary to intercourse between men than the justice which preserves—which asks no other title for what is than that it has
been. But, it is certain, this [justice which preserves] is not the
justice at which innovators aim. The justice of their seeking is
a more perfect kind, in which rights are founded, not on long
possession, but on reason. (p. 142)[17]

Here, though, Jouvenel sees a problem of theory and of practice.
We repudiate rights based only on the extension of past usage. But
we do not agree about the next stage. Jouvenel rehearses and rejects
several useless and well-known options, simple stability and simple
conformity to the established order, for instance. Then he makes a
suggestion, namely the principle of proportionality, as contextually
applied. He illustrates the suggestion by imagining a dispute between
three advisers, Red, White, and Black, over the relative rates of pay
of the workers Primus and Secondus. Should the pay for each be
proportional to work achieved, or to need, or to hours worked?

The identical aim of all our three disputants [Red, White, Black]
is to treat equal things equally and proportional things propor-
tionally; only the proportions which serve as starting-points are
different for each of them. Light has been thus thrown on the
relations between equality and justice; justice, as Aristotle said,
is an equality of proportions. Every allocation of reward which

17. Compare *On Sovereignty,* p. 55 and Conclusion, paras. 20–3; see also Bertrand
de Jouvenel, *Power,* trans. J. F. Huntington (London: Batchworth Press, 1952), ch. 19,
sect. 2.

is, as it must be to be just, founded on equality under a certain aspect, will be hierarchical and contrary to equality under another aspect. (p. 151)

I have complained already that Jouvenel lays too much store by the idea of proportionality—that, stripped down to its essentials, the bare idea is truistic. Here, though, the chief thing is that, as Jouvenel says, proportionality leaves over the question: how is the *relevant* aspect, whether need, effort, contribution, or whatever, to be identified and determined? Jouvenel's answer will by now be familiar. The one unitary conceptual resource that there is to appeal to at this point consists in the thoughts, perceptions, notions, and ethical formation of one who knows and understands a given context well enough to determine what *ought* to be at issue there.[18] But how is such practical wisdom to be *deployed?* Well, if justice is to remain at the level of human cognition and human practicality, then, according to Jouvenel, such questions of aspect need to be divided and fragmented.

Men are very unevenly taken up with distant ends necessitating collective action; thus a minority of promoters with a lively sense of ends requiring action, who therefore regard resources as first and foremost means of action, is naturally bound to come into conflict with a majority whose nature it is to regard resources as means of existence. The result is that tension underlies every process of share-out; it is the more serious with every rise in importance of the blocks of resources to be divided. That is the reason why it is wise to break up the general process of share-out into as many small disconnected share-outs as possible. The more comprehensive the process the more serious the tension.

The simplest method of effecting this fragmentation of share-

18. Aristotle, *Nicomachean Ethics* 1132a21–2: 'To go to the judge is to go to justice. For the nature of the judge is to be a sort of *animate justice*.' To say that it is the nature of a judge to seek to personify justice suggests equally that it is the nature of justice to seek to be personified here or there or wherever by a judge.

out is to attribute every new element of resources to its owner
as it appears. . . . [Under fragmentation of share-out] contrary
influences are forever at work in combination. The work teams,
which provide society with resources, affect it, so far as equality
is concerned, like some hot spring which breeds inequalities,
whereas society, which uses the resources, functions like a cold
spring which attenuates these inequalities. The state of inequality, photographed at any given moment, is the product of
a crowd of phenomena, on each of which certain actions can no
doubt be brought to bear; it is, however, utopian folly to seek
to annul *en masse* all their consequences with a view to creating
a condition of share-out which is the result of mental choice and
transcends the phenomena of social life. (p. 162)

10.10. Jouvenel's advice to fragment will provoke a whole variety
of responses, among them my own, then the old-fashioned utilitarian's, and then the Rawlsian response. In the dialogue to which
the rehearsal here of these responses will eventually give rise, one
new voice will be audible, that of G. A. Cohen. However unex-
pectedly, that voice will draw us back to Aristotle.

10.11. My own reaction: if the fragmentation that Jouvenel coun-
sels (and four paragraphs hence we shall purge the term 'fragmentation' of connotations that he did not intend) is to issue in anything
recognizable as justice, then everything depends on the deployment
by practical wisdom of a richer variety of ideas and a larger gamut
of forms of justice than Jouvenel makes explicit. Here Lucas's book
is a copious and invaluable supplement.[19] Jouvenel's scheme, like
Aristotle's, is wide open to such enrichment. Other enrichments
would further specify the aspects and contexts under which justice[A]
requires impartiality. Yet other enrichments might propose that un-

---

19. See, for instance, Lucas's ch. 14 on fiscal justice, and the wealth of considerations
by which Lucas shows how contributive justice has a rationality of its own not deducible
from general principles you could honestly say your theory of justice already encom-
passes.

satisfied vital needs, even needs over and above those resulting from the kind of disruptions that Jouvenel refers to in the passage that we cited first in 10.9 above, represent some sort of claim in justice upon the *polis*.[20] For there is no possibility of providing in advance against the indefinite variety of circumstances in which the vital need of citizens will have to obtrude on public attention. In the particular case of the life-threatening disruption of reasonable economic expectation, the *polis* may see an injustice$_{[A]}$—or if not an injustice still a special situation that it must count as unjust$_{[A]}$ for a polis that is just$_{[C]}$ not to rectify. In other cases, the reason for intervention may relate to the preservation of the political *koinōnia* (partnership/association) and/or the preservation and renewal of the capacities of its participants to play their part within it.

An important growth point here might be Aristotle's own remark at the end of *Politics* VI.5 (1320a33), 'Destitution is one of the causes of a corrupt democracy', a democracy, that is, in which some citizens see no alternative but to put their own advantage before the common good. In so far as one who is thus destitute has any claim in justice, which might seem to be a moot point, such a claim presupposes not so much the injustice of destitution as such[21] as a positive and public affirmation of the practical ideal of citizenly participation. (An ideal one might think to be worthy of some renewal in the modern world.) At this point, Aristotelian justice$_{[A]}$ needs a hundred and one more such thoughts, notions, and ideas, even as it need multifarious enrichments of justice$_{[A]}$, originating in the exigencies of sustaining at the same time both justice$_{[B]}$ and justice$_{[C]}$. But, noting this, and being primarily concerned to reconnect justice and practical reason,

---

20. The notion of a vital need will surely have essential occurrence in any neo-Aristotelian enumeration of the kind we envisaged in 10.5 of the preoccupations and concerns of those who are to cooperate fruitfully. For the explanation of its systematic absence from Rawls's principles of justice, see Brian Barry, *The Liberal Theory of Justice* (Oxford: Oxford University Press, 1975), pp. 54–5, 114–15.

21. Nor does it presuppose the recognition of any quasi-metaphysical kind of entitlement. Cp. n. 27 below. In this connection and related connections, see Rosalind Hursthouse, 'After Hume's Justice', *Proceedings of the Aristotelian Society* 91 (1990–1): 229–45.

I hasten now to the second part of my comment on Jouvenel's advice to fragment.

A dedicated opponent of the piecemeal approach is likely to protest at the complexity of the conceptual structure of Aristotelian justice and the wide plurality of considerations it will allow to overlap in any context. Such an opponent will protest against the apparent arbitrariness of the process of fragmentation by which Jouvenel delegates to the person making the decision—either to the statesman, or to the magistrate maintaining justice$_{[C]}$, or to the citizen exercising justice$_{[B]}$—the whole duty of satisfying the demands of justice. Here, though, I should counsel Jouvenel to be resolute, stand his ground, and point to a distinction between two distinctions, the distinction between general and specific and the distinction between universal and particular/singular.[22] When a person with justice makes a decision in a place where general principles compete, his determination will normally be highly specific, scarcely general at all. But that does not imply that his judgment is arbitrary—for whether it is arbitrary depends on the quality and content of the ideas or principles in force and the insight with which they are brought to bear. Nor does it imply that the decision is not universally valid, not valid for all contexts which justice and reason find *relevantly similar* to this one. If the decision is a good one, it will have to qualify as valid for absolutely all these contexts. (It is not to be expected, of course, that one who makes a good decision will be in a position to specify with no residue what it requires for a situation to be relevantly similar. *That* is in fact unthinkable.) On a proper understanding of these things, specificity and universality happily consist and cohere.

Finally, a third point: under fragmentation as Jouvenel proposes that, every decision can still arise from a practical and general grasp, on the part of the decider, of the shared or political good and of his or her own part in maintaining, creating, or sustaining that good. Within this sort of fragmentation there can still be a kind of vertical

22. Cp. R. M. Hare, *Freedom and Reason* (Oxford: Oxford University Press, 1963), p. 39. See also p. 352, n. 25, below.

integration down and up and up and down—an incomparably good integration, in fact, if the political good is practically intelligible and conditions are favourable for the instauration, prolongation, and renewal of the idea of the political good. In so far as such vertical integration may demand a certain simplification in the ends that are publicly pursued, it is open to Jouvenel to recommend just that. Here though he will counsel the *polis* and its citizens against *over-reaction*. Let them not fall into sudden despair, under the impact of divers disappointments experienced in the precipitate pursuit of too many ends not well enough considered; let them not, because of that disappointment, abdicate all their powers, there and then, to some supposedly universal market or quasi-market mediating and intervening in all things, whether neutral or freighted with radical import, between citizens and government.[23] Rather than suddenly surrender to the gloomy prescriptions of the liberal marketers, or have Caesar sell off that which is truly Caesar's, let *polis* and citizens, as necessary, simply limit those ends that statesmen and magistrates are to pursue on the public behalf. (First and foremost, let ends qualify through the case for their importance being made by reference to vital needs whose validation as such is morally necessitated by considerations relating to the social tie.)

10.12. So much for my own response to Jouvenel's advice to fragment. But an old-fashioned utilitarian will reject Jouvenel's advice as irrational, as pusillanimous, even as immoral and insensitive to the interests of unnumerable persons who might have benefited from a more ambitious approach. To this Jouvenel must reply that the utilitarian's own trust in centralization is even more irrational than his original distrust of practical reason. Let him pause a little longer

---

23. Jouvenel's former colleagues and associates will be surer than I am of this, but I think he would have warmed to Michael Oakeshott's judgement: 'the main significance of Hayek's *Road to Serfdom* [is] not the cogency of his doctrine, but the fact that it is a doctrine. A plan to resist all planning may be better than its opposite, but it belongs to the same style of politics.' Michael Oakeshott, *Rationalism in Politics* (London: Methuen, 1962), ch. 1, text adjoining n. 28.

before calling into being the enlarged bureaucracy it will require to mount the search for any larger satisfactions than fragmentation can furnish—a larger satisfaction that will soon in any case bring one to the frontier of the humanly unthinkable, and beyond the scope of justice. The next citations convey this point.

If I ask myself the question in what the collective social interests of a society consists, I must envisage in answer the well-being of its members present and future under two aspects, their contentment and their perfection. Not that any real answer is possible; the most I can do is to give myself the illusion of answering by some vasty concept, whose fanatical devotee I shall thenceforward be. Be he philosopher or ruler, whoever claims to be the guardian of the collective social interest is a dangerous man. The highest legitimate aim that men can set themselves is to discover what basic conditions are necessary to the continued existence of a society and favourable to the advancement of the well-being of its members. The most obvious and time-honoured of these conditions is avoidance of destruction by some hostile grouping, of wasting away by the exhaustion of material resources, and of break-up by the dissolution of emotional ties. These are the basic conditions which constitute the least indeterminate part of the collective social interest; consequently they are the part which directs the magistrates most clearly to their duty and presents the smallest target for dissension in political debates. Political dissension, indeed, takes on a sharper edge with every extension of the area of public decision to things which respond more readily to subjective appreciation—things about which there is a natural clash between different preferences and interests, so that any common or commonly accepted decision in regard to them is not possible, but only the destruction of one interest or preference of another. Whereas bitterness is absent from debates if they relate to ends desired by all (and can be made so to appear) as being the necessary condition of and foundation for the various interests which rest and flourish on them. (p. 129)

To suppose that the just authority is one which inaugurates an impeccably just order at all points is the broad way to follies of the most dangerous kind. An authority is just when it gives an example of justice in all the activities proper to itself—and that it finds hard enough. The logical end of the illusions now in vogue is the quite absurd one of a society in which everything would be arranged justly and no-one would have to be just. (pp. 163–4)

These citations make several points, not least a point inimical to Kant's asymmetry claim. But the most immediate reason to give them is to display a quasi-ontological contention Jouvenel is disposed to make against the utilitarian, about the proper subject matter of human justice and the proper ends of the state.

10.13. We reach next for Rawls's response to Jouvenel's counsel of fragmentation. Rawls might say that he was in agreement in the rejection of utilitarianism; that he shared Jouvenel's concern with the proper alignment of the justice of the citizen and the justice of a well-ordered society; that nevertheless he found Jouvenel's own proposals lamentably indefinite. In trying to reconstruct his response, one is reminded of Rawls's remarks in *A Theory of Justice* about intuitionism and the conceptions of justice that he calls mixed, which hold that greater average well-being and a more equal distribution are both desirable ends.

In everyday life we often content ourselves with enumerating common sense precepts and objectives of policy, adding that on particular questions we have to balance them in the light of the general facts of the situation. While this is sound practical advice, it does not express an articulated conception of justice.

One is being told in effect to exercise one's judgment as best one can within the framework of these guidelines. . . . By contrast, the difference principle is a relatively precise conception, since it ranks all combinations of objectives according to how well they promote the prospects of the least favoured. (pp. 317–18)

Here for the record is the difference principle:

Social and economic inequalities are to be arranged so that they are both (a) to the greatest benefit of the least advantaged and (b) attached to offices and positions open to all under conditions of fair equality of opportunity. (p. 83)

If the first citation is a good guide, Rawls would say that Jouvenel and Aristotle have suggested a way of coming to terms with the indefiniteness of the subject matter of the practical, but that theirs is not the best way. In contrast, Rawls's own principle of fair opportunity is designed to ensure that the system of cooperation is one of pure procedural justice. For, *pace* the utilitarian, we badly need to be able to find safe and secure ways to escape the limitless responsibilities utilitarian morality would place upon us, to leave distributive justice 'to take care of itself', but to do so in ways *more principled* than Aristotle or Jouvenel prescribe:

Now the great practical advantage of pure procedural justice is that it is no longer necessary in meeting the demands of justice to keep track of the endless variety of circumstances and the changing relative positions of particular persons. One avoids the problem of defining principles to cope with the enormous complexities which would arise if such details were relevant. It is a mistake to focus attention on the varying relative positions of individuals and to require that every change, considered as a single transaction viewed in isolation, be in itself just. . . . Thus in this kind of procedural justice the correctness of the distribution is founded on the justice of the scheme of cooperation from which it arises and on answering the claims of individuals engaged in it. A distribution cannot be judged in isolation from the system of which it is the outcome or from what individuals have done in good faith in the light of established expectations. If it is asked in the abstract whether one distribution of a given stock of things to definite individuals with known desires and preferences is better than another, then there is simply no answer to this question. (pp. 87–8)

10.14.   At this point, neo-Aristotelian defenders of practical reason must surely make some response to Rawls. Without making any claim to copy the clarity or distinction of Jouvenel's way of writing (the only easy thing to imitate in Jouvenel's style is his addiction to scriptural allusion), I shall put their reply, long though it is, into his mouth, as if he were still alive to make his own comment (the reply will run up to p. 311).

'Professor Rawls and I are at one in wanting there to be a way for justice to take care of itself. Each of us looks in that sense for a procedure. My own procedure is fragmentation or subdivision, a vertically integrated subdivision of questions and problems arising, which enables practical reason to operate in different ways in different places, working from an open multiplicity of principles rooted in a generous but demanding conception of citizenship—a shared conception to be given its realization by virtue of the just$_{[A]}$ acts of citizens who are just$_{[B]}$ (and much else besides) and of statesmen and public servants who act with a whole variety of aims on behalf of a *polis* which is just$_{[C]}$ and much else besides. Justice$_{[A]}$ simply reflects the developing totality of demands to which they have to respond.

'Rawls's way—namely fair equality of opportunity, the difference principle, and all the rest, enforced, one imagines, in the way now familiar enough from America and Britain, by public commissions charged with this or that specific brief—is very different. Nobody can disregard the old watchword *carrière ouverte aux talents,* the need, that is, for every citizen's every talent to be worthily deployed.

(Let no seed fall upon a stony place.) But it seems to me that the way Rawls has to countenance of securing this aim and other aims rests on a deep distrust of practical reason—practical reason as once we knew it, not only from Aristotle, I mean, but also from the everyday procedures of capable persons in public, industrial, and commercial life. All over the world, such distrust has grown apace since *A Theory of Justice* was published—in ways for which one cannot hold to blame any book, least of all Professor Rawls's. Rather, *A Theory of Justice* reflects something that was latent already in the Zeitgeist, which hiding place does not necessarily make this latent thing wise or sensible or immune to criticism.

'This is not the occasion for me to speak of France (where some may claim that our *énarchie* has both maintained and enhanced an older practice of public administration); and after an absence of almost forty years, I no longer know very much of the present reality of the United States. But looking out upon England as she now is, more than fifty years after the prolonged visits I made there at the time of my researches for my book, *Problems of Socialist England*,[24] I think I see what the institutionalization of the mistrust of practical reason has come to signify *in practice*. The thing I see in that country, newly purified of all notions that are professedly socialistic (in the old sense of the term),[25] is a doctrinaire transformation at the level of government of the powerful array of departments of state I once knew into a crazy paving of separate agencies, commissions, and authorities, whose work is defined by simple reference to their satisfaction of certain so-called "targets", targets laid down for them by the residual nuclei of civil servants in residual departments who are still concerned with policy, the briefing of ministers, and the

24. Bertrand de Jouvenel, *Problems of Socialist England,* trans J. F. Huntington (London: Batchworth Press, 1949).

25. 'There is no [longer any] question of ethics here. The end product of society is anyhow taken to be personal consumption: that is, under socialistic colours (!), the extremity of individualism. Nothing quite so trivial has ever been made into a social idea. But it is wrong to accuse our reformers of having invented it: they found it.' Bertrand de Jouvenel, *The Ethics of Redistribution* (Cambridge: Cambridge University Press, 1951), p. 48.

interpretation of the will of Parliament. These are officials very different in training and formation, I might add, from those I once came to know. Nobody could ever have contemplated such an innovation as this (or taken it as flowing from the exigencies of logic!) who understood the singular collocation that one encounters in sound practical reasoning of the specific and the universal, of executive questions and policy questions.

'There is much else to say about this change and how it came about; but here I must narrow the focus to justice, newly evolving conceptions of which surely played as important a part as anything else in the transformations I have just mentioned. Emanating from the agencies I have just spoken of, one sees an army of inspectors and other functionaries whose work is to realize the notions conveyed by a variety of watchwords such as "transparency", "openness", the "public answerability of public institutions", "best procedure", "fair equality of chances". Of course, many or most of these slogans (apart from the all-purpose idea of efficiency, never understood as the incomplete notion that it is until it is specified for a particular purpose or end) are professedly derived, directly or indirectly, from ideas about justice. These inspectors and other functionaries, acting at the same time under the aegis of consumerist dogmas that they repeat from market ideology (a market ideology I recognize but barely recognize as stemming from serious economics), now involve themselves in the day-to-day working of schools, the professions, the public services, the utilities, charitable organizations. ... In response, the organizations that are subject to these inspections and other attentions now find that they themselves have to engage a whole squadron of "managers" of their own, managers who have to be recruited (despite being practically ignorant of the organizations' work and disinclined by their training and formation to see this as a failing) simply in order for the organizations to give themselves the protection they need from the possible criticism of official agencies, who are empowered to apply severe sanctions.

'The ideology that animates the policies that give rise to the procedures I am describing is inseparable from a noble ideal of justice.

But what is the effect of these new developments? A triple loss of confidence between (1) those who do the work of these professions, bodies, or institutions, (2) the new managers of these professions, bodies, or institutions, and (3) the statesmen or politicians who are representative, supposedly, together with their ancillaries and civil servants, of the public. What will be the further outcome of all this? Increasingly, you must expect institutions of diminished moral autonomy, with weakened practical understanding of their own role and devoid of most of the aspirations that are proper to them in any ordinary scheme of things. Already—or so it evidently appears—you have institutions that constantly disappoint the expectations that citizens once had of them.

'It would be a mistake to blame very much of this on bureaucracy as such. Bureaucracy is a long-standing curse of mankind, but perfectly bearable. Bureaucracy as such is not our topic. What is at issue is the culmination of something altogether new. A new form of the passion for justice has combined somehow with various other dissatisfactions that older modes of administration must once have provoked to put into the place of these older modes, a new, arcane, topic-neutral formalism exclusively concerned with the identifying of administrative means to narrowly and would-be explicitly stated ends. The thing society now confronts is a formalism and an associated priesthood of "managers" that precisely celebrates the supposed superfluity of any practical wisdom that draws all its important aims from a shared fund of clear and inexplicit ordinary practical understanding—a new formalism that constantly extends its empire and its prerogatives by taking advantage of every calamity and promising then to insert even more of itself precisely in order to prevent the recurrence of calamity. It gives a new and quite unexpected shape to the dread that I once sought to show haunted Jean-Jacques Rousseau.[26]

26. 'Essai sur la politique de Rousseau', in *Du Contrat Social de J.-J. Rousseau*, ed. Bertrand de Jouvenel (Paris: Le Livre de Poche, 1978), pp. 13–165; *On Sovereignty*, pp. 269–70; 'Rousseau', in M. Cranston, ed., *Western Political Philosophers* (New York: Capricorn Books, 1967).

'For none of this, let me make it clear, is Professor Rawls in any way responsible! Rather I see some of the formulations in his book as a *premonition,* in the English-speaking countries, of something that is larger than him and larger than all of us. Latching onto that book itself, however, I cannot help remarking that, when he envisaged the original position and from thence proposed the difference principle and the rest, together with everything it would take to enforce the difference principle, he took no account of the probability—the inevitability, rather—of the institutional operation of principles such as the innocent-sounding "fair equality of chances" leading in countries smaller and more surveyable than the United States of America to something that would escape all control and demoralize institution after institution. In *Sovereignty,* I say that justice must be the keystone of any social edifice that shall respect the social tie. But I wish now that, there and then, I had given the obvious warning that the keystone cannot pretend to the status and functions of all the other parts of the structure or countermand their requirements. Considerations of justice do not subsume every other consideration. Still less can justice$_{[A]}$ upstage justice$_{[B]}$.

'Another thing that I venture to think about justice in *A Theory of Justice* is that, when the Rawlsian response extends against the neo-Aristotelian conception of justice Rawls's criticism of various other plural conceptions, when it suggests that my own conception "expresses no articulated conception of justice", the Rawlsians are losing track of their own project. Or so I should say if the Rawlsian project is to be understood as an instrument of genuine philosophical discovery. The thing the deliberators must be seen as looking for are good maxims for cooperation and the division of its fruits. It is from that search that justice itself is to be freshly revealed. But it is a search they must conduct in its own terms, namely the prerequisites for *cooperation as such,* if the outcome is to reveal anything about justice. What reason ever was there to suppose that these maxims would come in the format that Rawls expected or partake of the precision that he desiderated? Lack of "articulateness" shows nothing against my view. It only confirms its proper foundation in the practical. As Aristotle would remind us, it is a mistake to look for greater precision than our subject matter (whatever it may be) permits. (Cp. *Nicomachean Ethics* 1094b20 ff.)

'Following that point through, and focusing on the last part of the difference principle, I venture to think that closer attention to his original project would have warned Rawls himself not to transform the notional and temporary obliteration of the particular situations of the deliberators themselves into some principle of cooperation that they would themselves choose in order to remove the "unde-served" or "morally arbitrary" contingencies of natural gifts and for-tunate circumstances. Even from behind the veil of ignorance, the deliberators might easily see the disadvantage of insisting on the "moral arbitrariness" of such blessings—if insisting on it will have the effect of subverting the message of Jesus' parable of the talents, namely one's paramount moral duty to make something (and not just for oneself) of what gifts one has (Matthew 25: 14–30). Contin-gency is not the same as arbitrariness.[27] Nor is distribution as such, equal or unequal, the sole or paramount interest with which justice ought to look out on the world. Prescient deliberators might think it preferable, instead of embarking on a metaphysical crusade against contingency, to embark on the simpler and altogether more positive alternative project of engaging *all* citizens as fully as possible, in as many ways as possible, but each in the way best suited to their own aptitudes and predispositions, with the shared thing in which they all participate, and of removing some of the greater obstacles to this. Let us not confuse the creation of new opportunity (or, even better, the careful maintenance of conditions under which new opportuni-ties are created) with a project for the equalization of opportunity. However careful someone dedicated to the promotion of opportunity

27. Cp. Lucas, *On Justice,* pp. 190–1. Arbitrariness wrongly suggests caprice in the operation of what might otherwise have been well-considered deliberate assignment of natural endowments to particular persons. But, being unthinkable, no such deliberate assignment can be at issue. Similar comment needs to be directed against Rawlsian claims to the effect that 'we do not deserve our place in the distribution of native endowments'. This is a categorial claim about the applicability or non-applicability of the concept of desert, not an ordinary claim about what someone 'doesn't deserve'.

ought to be *not* to promote this at the expense of citizens who have the least opportunity for anything—of course he ought not to do that—the creation (or protection) and the equalisation of opportunity are not at all the same programmes of action. (Indeed equalization is consistent, as so far stated, with the overall *diminution* of opportunity. Let those who are preoccupied with equalization restate the literal purport that they intend.)

10.15. 'This response is already several times longer, I know, than the Rawlsian criticism of my position. But I must not forbear to mention the question of the alignment between the justice of city and the justice of citizen, the matter I was concerned with when I claimed to find an absurdity in the idea of a *polis* being just independently of any citizen's formation in justice or the other citizenly virtues. Since I wrote about that, I find that, in his espousal of his difference principle, Professor Rawls has an apparently comparable concern with such alignment:

The difference principle, however, does seem to correspond to a natural meaning of fraternity: namely, to the idea of not wanting to have greater advantages unless this is to the benefit of others who are less well off. The family, in its ideal conception and often in practice, is one place where the principle of maximizing the sum of advantages is rejected. Members of a family commonly do not wish to gain unless they can do so in ways that further the interests of the rest. Now wanting to act on the difference principle has precisely this consequence. Those better circumstanced are willing to have their greater advantages only under a scheme in which this works out for the benefit of the less fortunate.[28]

The point that I might myself have tried to make about this, if the citation accurately epitomizes Rawls's concern for the said alignment, is how flat and jejune the analogy appears that he is led to construct

---

28. *A Theory of Justice*, p. 105.

between the *polis* and a family and how disturbing are some of the
unintended resonances of this notion of fraternity. But the remarks
I might have made are altogether overtaken by a much more acute
observation by Professor G. A. Cohen.[29] Cohen's argument is as
follows. Suppose those with talents and energy affirm the principle
of difference. Then, if they mean it, they cannot help but commit
themselves to the moral ideal of an equality of primary goods, etc.
For that was the ideal that brought the difference principle into being
in the first place. Thus exceptions to equality will only count as just
where differentiation of reward is indispensable to the good of everyone or else indispensable to the good of the most disadvantaged,
etc. Equality is the presumption. Suppose now that, in accordance
with the difference principle, these people with talent and energy
demand higher rewards than other people. When they do that,
Cohen points out, they will have to think of their own demands for
higher rewards as the demands of an entirely exogenous element in
the situation, and *not* as what they are, namely demands expressing
their own refusal to make proper use of their talents unless they are
differentially rewarded. Such a posture is morally impossible if they
are sincerely committed to the liberal ideal of equality. To suggest
otherwise is an affront to the seriousness that any reasonable person
must attach to the embracing of a political ideal. To hold sincerely
to a political ideal, to mean something by it, is to have been prepared
to think through its implications—at least!—or, if necessary, to *re-
consider it* in the light of those implications.

'I find real force in this argument as directed towards Rawls. It
flows from Cohen's argument that Rawls has a choice. One thing
he can do is to retreat from the claim to which he evidently attaches
importance, namely that in a just society there is a full conscious
accord between the principles that make the society just and the way
in which just citizens live. In the case of retreat, Professor Rawls
must take refuge in a purely procedural justice. The other thing that

29. See G. A. Cohen, 'Where the Action Is: On the Site of Distributive Justice',
Philosophy and Public Affairs 26.1 (1997).

Rawls could do is to advance. He can progress into some better formulation of the principle of difference or a purer philosophy of equality—into an ethos, so to say, of equality.

'That is the choice that Cohen offers. To the reservations that he expresses about Rawls's conception of pure procedural justice, I shall now add just one thing. Rawls has written as follows:

> The main problem of distributive justice is the choice of a social system. The principles of justice apply to the basic structure and regulate how its major institutions are combined into one scheme. Now, as we have seen, the idea of justice as fairness is to use the notion of pure procedural justice to handle the contingencies of particular situations. The social system is to be designed so that the resulting distribution is just however things turn out.[30]

What I would point out is that the last sentence is ambiguous. On the more benign interpretation, it asserts that the social system is expressly designed to *bring it about* that, whatever happens, procedural justice and its principles will give a just outcome. But that is the thing that Aristotle has shown once and for all *cannot* be done. On the other interpretation, Rawls is simply preparing to *stipulate* that something which may not strike anyone as just really is just$_{[A]}$. But stipulation has its price and here, if this be the preferred interpretation, I protest that, in the end, it is not an accident that human beings have always made it a requirement on human justice that one should in principle be able to *see* as just that which really is just. It is in this vicinity too that we find the original impulse that brings into the law considerations of equity.

10.16. 'In effect, then, Cohen and I agree in the importance we attach to justice$_{[B]}$, in rejecting pure procedural justice as Rawls offers it, and in denying any claim that Rawls might make to have aligned

30. *A Theory of Justice*, pp. 274–5.

justices [A], [B], and [C]. This is a remarkable degree of agreement. The question that remains, though, is whether Cohen himself has succeeded in aligning the justice$_{[B]}$ of a citizen with the justice$_{[C]}$ of a *polis*. According to him, the best way to remove the moral incoherence that he finds in the thoughts of persons seeking to live justly$_{[B]}$ by the difference principle lies in some purer, more single-minded adherence among the just$_{[B]}$ to equality in the sense of the word that is made prominent by the difference principle. No doubt that will remove the incoherence Cohen was concerned with. But I fear that it may introduce another.

'How well does the purer ideal and ethos of equality consort with the ordinary day-to-day thought about justice$_{[A]}$ by which just$_{[B]}$ citizens appraise the moral quality of everyday acts, their own and other people's, and fulfil the myriad day-to-day obligations that sustain the justice$_{[C]}$ of the *polis?* These ordinary thoughts—thoughts we have no idea how to dispense with—only rarely make any reference to equality in the sense of the word that occurs in Rawls's difference principle. (Indeed, in the absence of any prescribed standard by which all should live, equality is not even, in the parlance of the logicians, an effective notion. It is scarcely, then, unless transformed in a way I shall shortly propose, a notion of the kind that it would need to be for us to live by it.) Not only do such ordinary ideas lack any explicit reference to equality. They often prescribe acts that seem to run counter to it. Even where there is no outright conflict, our certainty that what we are doing is just usually has nothing at all to do with any certainty we might feel that the outcome of our doing the act will be to promote equality. (See the reply I give to D.W. at 10.7 *ad fin.*) If the purport of Professor Cohen's "ethos of equality" relates to the same notion of equality that animates the difference principle, then it will need to be explained how well it will cohere even with everyday morality. The truth is, though, that that which is morally attractive in Cohen's idea of an egalitarian ethos relates almost entirely to thoughts that find proper expression in Rawls's construction of the case for Rawls's relatively uncontroversial *first principle* of justice "each person to enjoy an equal right to the most extensive system of liberties compatible with a like system of liberty for all". That which is compelling in Cohen's case for an egalitarian ethos does not go beyond its endorsement of the idea which Rawls's first principle endorses of the equal standing *as citizens* of all the citizens of a *polis*.'

10.17. So much for an imaginary Aristotelian response made by Jouvenel to Rawls. The persisting importance of Cohen's objection to Rawls lies not so much in the case that it builds for equality's or egalitarianism's requiring a less permissive difference principle as in the more general constraint that the objection suggests. This is a constraint upon any philosophy of justice that shall answer to the requirements that Cohen and Jouvenel (as we reconstruct him) impose, each in his own way, on the realizations of justice$_{[A]}$, justice$_{[B]}$, and justice$_{[C]}$. The ordinary ideals to which the acts of the *polis* or its statesmen and magistrates are answerable and the ordinary ideals to which the acts of the citizen are answerable are not exactly the same, but they need to cohere. If justice$_{[B]}$ and justice$_{[C]}$ are to stand in the constituting and synergetic relations that Cohen and Jouvenel contemplate, if they are to fulfil their respective functions, then justice$_{[A]}$ must spring from public and private ideals and conceptions of justice$_{[A]}$ that agents can comprehend, make their own, be anxious to see realized, invest with value, uphold along with the other things they care about, and so on—all within a conception of the shared thing that they hold in common and that commands their adherence and their loyalty. The way forward still seems to be to side with Cohen against Rawls but then with neo-Aristotle against Cohen (who is surely open to some of the criticisms urged in 7.19 ff.).

10.18. At this point, and close to the end, let us give to Jouvenel one last word:

'Almost everyone insists nowadays that the proper end or aim of justice is equality. How then can I have been so doubtful of egalitarianism as a philosophy of justice? A soft answer turneth away wrath (Proverbs 15:1). To those who have introduced equality into justice in the ways that I have criticized as divorcing the justice of the *polis* from the justice of human being themselves, let me say that the idea itself of equality is indeed sacred. But, in the first instance, equality is to be sought in the relation of one person to another in the totality of particular rights, duties, and shared expectations and conceptions that is demanded by the security of our cooperation and the friendship we sustain among strangers. This totality, the residue of prolonged experimentation in fruitful cooperation and the precipitate of a myriad moral responses to the ordinary experience of it, could never be deduced from a pure or newly milled conception of equality or proportionality. But these words, "equal" and "equality", are a fit celebration of the status of a thinking and acting free citizen of a *polis* of thinking and active free persons, a *polis* which, by virtue of its laws, its constitution, and the dispositions of its citizens, by virtue of the sum of their relations to one another and the social tie that is thereby secured, prolongs its however unspectacular happiness and protects it from some of the worst evils that threaten it from within and without.'

10.19.   Properly to conclude, let us abandon neo-Aristotle and go back to the real Aristotle. Aristotle says in *Eudemian Ethics* 1241b13–15:

A constitution is a kind of justice. For a constitution is a *koinōnia,* a partnership for sharing. And it is by its justice that every shared thing (*koinon*) maintains itself.

Here, and in similar claims made by Aristotle (compare *Politics* 1253a37–8), a constitution is not a blueprint, a prescription, a mere diagram. Still less is it a Bauplan for the creation of just persons. Rather, the constitution of a *polis* is the manner in which the *polis* lives already. See *Politics* 1253b37–9:

The constitution of a polis is in a sense the life of the *polis.*

Moreover, not any or every would-be constitution can be lived. It is one thing to say, truly enough, that the law secures obedience 'by power of habit' (1269a20). It is another thing to commit oneself to the claim that the human capacity to form habits and form associations has power to issue in benign dispositions even if the framework that contains it does not sustain and encourage impulses to promote the political good.

There are all sorts of problems, conceptual, historical, practical, and other, in understanding the genesis of a just *polis*. To Jouvenel, as to Aristotle, the thing that must seem most doubtful of all in the second supplement to Kant's 'Perpetual Peace' is his *claim of asymmetry*, his claim that it is not for morality to bring into being a good constitution, but that it is for a good constitution to bring about a good level of moral culture among human beings. (Unless of course the criteria for a 'good constitution' comprise its power to engage with human motivations and dispositions! But that simply subverts the denial that what is at issue is a question of back and forth.)

10.20. The dialogue staged here between Rawls, Jouvenel, Cohen, and Aristotle will make no converts amongst Rawlsians. So far as they are concerned, these questions lie well beyond the ordinary reach of the kind of philosophical contestation attempted here. Maybe the most one could hope to have shown is that the justice of Rawlsianism and the justice of neo-Aristotelianism are so different, are involved with such different philosophical work, that they are incommensurable. Incommensurable or not, however, they compete for the same space of concepts in one and the same arena of activity. It remains to be seen—let us watch with interest and see—whether, at each future twist and turn of history and at each stage in the perdition of practical knowledge and ordinary trust, the world will be able to dispense entirely, or dispense even to the degree to which it at present seeks to dispense, with every distinctively neo-Aristotelian contention concerning justice.[31] Rawlsians may continue to claim that conceptions such as Rawls's give the more perfect expression to human ideals of democracy and legitimacy. Surely, though, these ideals cannot displace absolutely every other consideration. Cannot enough be enough? At a moment so unpropitious for pre-liberal conceptions, it cannot be unfair to leave the very last word with Aristotle:

Many things that are held to be democratic destroy democracies, and many things held to be oligarchical destroy oligarchies. . . . It is possible for an oligarchy or a democracy to be satisfactory even though they have diverged from the [theoretical] ideal. If one strains either of them further, first one will make the polity/ constitution worse, and finally one will make it not a polity/ constitution at all. (*Politics* 1309b21–2)[32]

31. Here at least might be found a kind of test which could transcend some of the dialogical difficulties Alasdayre MacIntyre enumerates in *Whose Justice? Which Rationality?* (London: Duckworth, 1988). See pp. 342–51, especially p. 345.

32. I want to make special acknowledgement of the advice or help and the encouragement I have received in rewriting this lecture from Véronique Munoz-Dardé, Stephen Mulhall, and Daniel Mahoney.

III

Metaethics

Introductory note

1. At 1.1, we framed the questions (A) and (B). These having
been answered as best we can answer them, first for the moral realm
and then in outline for the moral-cum-political realm, question (C)
now looms into view. With (C) there enters the question of the status
of ethical utterances and the whole business of metaethics, or
thinking about ethical thinking. That business is easier to understand
if we go back to the time when the word 'metaethics' entered into
philosophy. It needs to be said, though, that metaethics is the least
suitable of all the subjects treated in this book for an introductory
work. I have set out the most accessible part of this subject in Lecture 11. The reader may prefer to go straight to that.

2. In part V of *The Logical Syntax of Language*, Rudolf Carnap
wrote:

> Once philosophy is purified of all unscientific elements [meta-
> physical sentences, for instance, or moral sentences, all sense-
> lessly purporting to refer to transcendental entities], only the
> logic of science remains. . . . [The] logic of science takes the
> place of the inextricable tangle of problems known as philos-
> ophy. . . . All philosophical problems which have any meaning
> belong to syntax. . . . The logic of science is the syntax of the
> language of science.[1]

1. Rudolf Carnap, *The Logical Syntax of Language,* trans. A. Smeaton (London:
Kegan Paul, Trench, Trubner & Co., 1937), originally published as *Logische Syntax der
Sprache* (Vienna: Springer, 1934).

Lectures 7 and 8 will have prepared the reader for the way in which these and other declarations from members of the Vienna circle either aroused moral philosophers to sheer disbelief (prompting them to attack verificationist criteria of meaningfulness or to expose the inability of the positivists to avoid trespassing outside the limits of thought and speech they had themselves set up); or else gained acceptance for the positivist contention that ethical utterances say nothing but simply express and/or stimulate feeling (A. J. Ayer, C. L. Stevenson); or else incited philosophical moralists to sympathetic reconstrual of the positivist contention (see Lecture 7, and R. M. Hare's account of the rational purport of certain commands and prescriptions).

The typical response of a present-day moral philosopher to a claim such as Carnap's would probably owe something to the first or the third of these reactions. To be fully worthy of the name of response, it could not of course ignore the issues of the meaning and meaningfulness of ethical utterances. But, as we shall see in Lectures 11 and 12, there is plenty to say about that. Meanwhile, in introducing those lectures, my concern is to record and comment upon the way in which Carnap's proposal combined with positivist doctrines of cognitive significance to bring into being the idea that whatever was worthwhile in anything that had passed up to then for moral philosophy ought really to be revamped as metaethics and presented as something morally neutral. Complete neutrality, I shall soon say (see section 6 below), is a false requirement for moral philosophy—as false as the requirement would be of moral zealotry. First, though, a little more about the general purport of part V of Carnap's book.

Carnap was well aware that, contrary to his conception of philosophy as the syntax of the logic of science, philosophy has a strong semblance of concerning itself closely with all sorts of non-syntactical subjects—with properties, relations, numbers, and objects of reference themselves, as well with truths, facts, sense, meanings, aboutness, etc. Carnap's reaction to this appearance was to invoke a threefold distinction: between (1) *syntactical sentences,* where philosophy seemed to him to be engaged as *The Logical Syntax of Lan-*

guage said it should be; (2) *object sentences,* which were ordinary non-philosophical sentences about the objects studied by some reputable and unproblematic first-order discipline—such sentences belonging to the language of that discipline; and (3) *pseudo-object sentences,* among which were philosophical sentences. These last have the appearance of object sentences, for they present themselves, Carnap says, *in the material mode.* Many of these sentences will indeed be nonsensical, he thought. In certain favourable cases, however, things may be better than they appear. As transposed *into the formal mode,* the philosophical sentence 'Redness is a quality', for instance, can be reconstrued as ' "Red" is an adjective'. Similarly, 'Five is a number' may be beneficially transposed (Carnap suggests) into 'Five is a number-word'. And 'Yesterday's lecture was about Babylon' need not be understood as (metaphysically) *about* the town of Babylon, being better interpreted as follows: 'The word "Babylon" occurred in yesterday's lecture.'

None of these translations will strike us as satisfactory (or even as necessitated by Carnap's more hospitable understanding in the earlier parts of the book of what syntax is). Still less can they be mandatory. Indeed, in the next phase of his thought, Carnap seems to have abandoned them. But it was at this point—it was within months of the translation of *The Logical Syntax of Language* into English— that the idea seems to have arisen that some analogous treatment might be *especially* suitable for the philosophical understanding (never mind how cognitively meaningless they were) of the utterances of first-order ethics. In the study of such utterances' true role and their semblance of meaningfulness, a new science of 'meta-ethics'—the word was already gaining some currency by the year 1938—would enable the serious philosopher to study ethics without any risk either of falling into nonsense or of incurring questionable commitments that might otherwise arise from using an ethical term *in propria persona* (from his or her own mouth, so to speak). So far as the ethical subject matter was concerned, it seemed not to matter that Carnap himself had already seen some of the difficulties of the general position he had been defending in *Logical Syntax of*

Language about the nature of philosophy or had joined in the public defence of Tarski's semantic and entirely objectual treatment of truth.

If the charm of Carnap's translations was already fading by the mid-1930s and the syntactic view of the rest of philosophy was on its way out, the formal mode still had a long future in front of it in philosophical ethics. Once the idea of 'metaethics' had secured its peculiar hold, A. J. Ayer and many others—for reasons they took to be internal to the subject of morality itself—continued to expect that metaethics would be for the moral philosopher what rubber gloves are for the doctor or orderly. Thus Ayer: 'all moral theories are neutral as regards actual conduct. To speak technically they belong to the field of metaethics, not ethics proper'.[2] Hare differed from Ayer with respect to the *outcome* of metaethics. Hare and Ayer agreed, however, with respect to the complete neutrality of the starting point. In *Language, Truth and Logic*,[3] even before he had adopted the expression 'metaethics' (the earliest occurrence of the word I know of in his writings dates from 1949), Ayer had already maintained that the only kind of ethical sentence which a philosopher can put forward declaratively and in the role of philosopher was a definition or a comment upon a definition.

3. Today, long after the demise of verificationism, few if any present day philosophers take the rubber glove view of metaethics. But few have said what their positive view is. That which follows is a proposal. It is at variance with the tradition that Ayer represented, but it is based upon the writings that moved Carnap himself beyond *Logical Syntax of Language* conceptions into a concern with a more fully objectual semantics. In the present, my proposal will stand or fall with its power to make sense now of the better things moral philosophy can do when it addresses questions such as (C) or when en route to such questions.

2. A. J. Ayer, 'On the Analysis of Moral Judgements', *Philosophical Essays* (London: Macmillan, 1954), p. 246.
3. A. J. Ayer, *Language, Truth, and Logic* (London: Gollancz, 1936).

4. Let us begin with words of Alfred Tarski that Carnap would have found familiar:

We must always distinguish clearly between the language *about* which we speak and the language *in* which we speak, as well as between the science which is the object of our investigation and the science in which the investigation is carried out. The names of the expressions of the first language [called the *object language*], and of the relations between them, belong to the second language, called the *metalanguage* (which may contain the first as a part [or else contain translations of expressions of the object language]). The description of these expressions, the definition of . . . the concept of consequence [for instance], of provable sentence, possibly of true sentence . . . [and] the determination of the properties of these concepts is the task of the second theory which we shall call the *metatheory*. (1931/6)[4]

the language on the basis of which the semantics of the given [*object language*] is to be developed . . . we shall call the *metalanguage*. The most important point in . . . construction [of this metalanguage] is the problem of equipping [it] with a sufficiently rich vocabulary. But the solution of this problem is prescribed by the particular nature of the semantical concepts. In fact semantical concepts express certain relations between objects (and states of affairs) referred to in the [object] language discussed and expressions of the [object] language referring to these objects. (1936)[5]

From these citations and the works whence they come, the general picture that emerges is this. We begin with a discipline relating to some subject matter consisting of things that are in the world (phys-

---

4. Alfred Tarski, *Logic, Semantics, Metamathematics*, ed. and trans. J. H. Woodger (Oxford: Oxford University Press, 1956), p. 176.
   5. Ibid. p. 403.

ical bodies or animals or places . . .) or are as if in the world (numbers, sets . . . and values). That discipline, science, or theory is stated in the *object language*. So soon as we speak of this object language itself, however, and find ourselves talking about its terms, predicates, etc.—talking of these *and* of the objects that the terms of the object language refer to or that satisfy or fail to satisfy the predicates—we are extending the object language into the *metalanguage*. The object language (or some translation of it) must then be a part of the metalanguage. Finally, in finding something to say about the object language itself in its relation to the science, theory, or outlook that it expresses and the things it is concerned with, we build a *metatheory*, which treats of consequence relations and consistency relations between object language sentences, and treats of truth, reference, satisfaction, definability . . . or whatever else.

The subject matter of morality is a very special case among subject matters, and the analogy sustaining the idea of metaethics rests on a parallel between metatheory and metaethics that is far from perfect. As we have already seen many times, first-order ethics is neither a science nor a theory. The language of first-order ethics is not formalized. It only gives partial expression to first-order ethics itself. But, once the idea of metaethics is floated, none of this needs to stand in the way of an aspiration to the effect that we should mark the distinction between ethical object language and ethical metalanguage; that the best of that which now passes under the name of metaethics, sieved free of philosophical terms that are ill defined or question-begging, should graduate to the new condition of a metatheory for ethics; that the said metatheory should see itself as concerned, beyond all engagement in first-order ethical thinking, with issues *about* that sort of thinking, with its notions of consistency and implication, its aspirations to truth, and the whole variety of forms of argument or persuasion for which it makes houseroom. On the terms I am proposing, one could even say that, however intermittently, we have long since been deep into metaethical or second order inquiry—albeit informally, discursively, and in a mostly participative-cum-descriptive rather than a spectatorial way.

5. In accordance with this proposal, Lectures 11 and 12 will have a straightforward claim to belong to metaethics. I give due warning that they will combine to suggest that there is in fact no need to devise notions of semantic meaning that are peculiar to ethical vocabulary. But the analogy we have seen give life to the idea of metaethics did not depend on the possibility or desirability of a separate semantics or speech act theory for the language of ethics.

What then is new about question (C)? Only that it requires us to try to pass a verdict upon the epistemological or metaphysical pretensions of ethical discourse—something there has been no previous call to do. In Lectures 11 and 12, our response to the questions of objectivity and objective truth will be to emphasize first, in a manner foreign to the usual paradigm of the metaethical, not only the practical subordinacy of such metaethical issues to the real nature of first-order ethical thought, but also their *logical and theoretical subordinacy* to it. In the provinces of metaphysics or epistemology or philosophy of language conducted as autonomous branches of philosophy, there is no power to determine *in advance* the limits of cognitive significance, of objectivity, or of candidature for plain truth. The conclusion I draw from this is that no metaethical term of art or metaethical contention ought to be arrived at *wholly in advance* of the study of first-order ethical thinking as it actually is—unless the plan is simply (how dispiriting that would be!) to *stipulate* the answer to questions such as (C).

6. One last word more about the rubber glove conception. In the Tarskian picture, the metalanguage and metatheory associated with a given subject matter or theory normally need all of the expressive power of the object language together with all the conceptual resources of the theory, discipline, or outlook to which the object language gives expression—and then they need more. In so far as we apply this finding to the case of ethics and metaethics, the conclusion into which we are led is that (notwithstanding the expectations aroused by the distinction between the 'material mode' and the 'formal mode') ascent to the metalanguage leaves intact all the

resources and all the commitments of the object language. It cannot free the ethical metatheorist from the semantic entanglements of the ethical object language. A theorist who has some specific need to escape these things will contrive better to do so by going back to the level of the object language and explicitly refusing to use the expression that carries a cargo he finds suspect, or by saying from the outset that he finds it suspect (either morally or otherwise). This at least appears to be a true insight into the ethical. There is no other way to point the finger of suspicion at some expression in the object language of ethics than to start out on the process we began to describe in the closing pages of Lecture 1 (from 1.12 onwards).

11

Objectivity in ethics

Two difficulties, two responses

A more heartening fact about the cultures of man
  Is their appalling stubbornness. The sea
Is always calm ten fathoms down. The gigantic
  anthropological circus riotously
Holds open all its booths.

William Empson, 'Sonnet'

11.1. In *Ethics: Inventing Right and Wrong*,[1] John Mackie subsumed the difficulties he claimed to see in the idea of ethical objectivity under two heads. First there was the metaphysical peculiarity of such things as values or obligations,[2] this peculiarity importing the need to postulate a faculty of moral intuition for the detection of obligations and the value properties G. E. Moore called nonnatural properties. Secondly there was the 'variability of some important starting points of moral thinking and their apparent dependence on actual ways of life' (p. 49)—'the well known variation in moral codes from one society to another and from one period to another, and also the difference in moral beliefs between different

---

1. Harmondsworth: Penguin, 1977.

2. 'If there were objective values then they would be entities or qualities or relations of a very strange sort, utterly different from anything else in the universe. Correspondingly, if we were aware of them, it would have to be by some special faculty of moral perception or intuition, utterly different from an ordinary way of knowing everything else. These points were recognized by Moore when he spoke of non-natural qualities, and by the intuitionists in their talk about moral intuition' (p. 38).

groups and classes within a complex community' (p. 36). These difficulties are sharply stated and still on the record. Under the names Mackie gave them of *queerness* and *relativity*, they are still at work in philosophy.[3]

11.2.   For the response to queerness, let us look first where Mackie himself looked when he sought to compensate us for that which his chapter 1 seemed to sweep away. In the place of the outlook of moral objectivism, Mackie proposed a form of moral constructivism. In the tradition instituted by Protagoras, the fifth century B.C. sophist, this was to be built up from the idea that morality was a device, 'a system of particular sort of constraints on conduct—ones whose central task is to protect the interests of persons other than the agent and which present themselves to an agent as checks on his natural inclinations or spontaneous tendencies to act' (p. 106). Morality was to be 'a device for counteracting limited sympathies' and alleviating, in ways prefigured by G. J. Warnock,[4] the inveterate tendency for things to go very badly. It was to be addressed to the standing causes of that tendency.

When Mackie drew closer to the actual business of implementing the construction and looking for ways to offset the narrowness of men's sympathies, rationality, intelligence, and information, he set out with telling and interesting examples various 'prisoner's dilemma' situations. He brought to the constructional task all sorts of insights of Darwin,[5] Hobbes, and Hume. He was never tempted, though, to

---

3. Compare, from the other side of the argument, Hilary Putnam in *The Collapse of the Fact/Value Dichotomy* (Cambridge, Mass.: Harvard University Press, 2003): 'The positions that are still defended by the proponents of a fact/value dichotomy are variants of non-cognitivism and of relativism. But non-cognitivism founders, as we have seen, once we appreciate what I have been calling the entanglement of fact and value; while the relativism derived from contemporary scientism threatens to toss much more than ethical judgments into the bag of truths that are valid only from some local perspective or other' (p. 42). Putnam says that into this bag will go almost everything that ordinary people know how to say.

4. G. J. Warnock, *The Object of Morality* (London: Methuen, 1971).

5. For the case of Darwin, compare Mackie's p. 113 and Darwin's *The Descent of*

try to contrive the whole core of first-order morality from games-theoretical or evolutionary ideas. Remarking on the inadequacy of prudence, self-interest, and long-term self-interest to sustain the construction that he had in mind, he said:

> there can be no doubt that many real-life situations contain, as at least part of their causally relevant structure, patterns of relationship of which various simple 'games' are an illuminating description. . . . Such simplified analyses . . . show . . . how the combined outcome of several intentional actions, even of well-informed and rational agents, may be something no one of the agents has intended or would intend. But from our point of view the game theory approach merely reinforces the lessons that we have extracted from the arguments of Protagoras, Hobbes, Hume, and Warnock. The main moral [we have already extracted from them] is the practical value of the notion of obligation, of an invisible and indeed fictitious tie or bond, whether this takes the form of a general requirement to keep whatever agreements one makes or of various specific duties like those of military honour or of loyalty to comrades or to an organization. . . .
> . . . The real weakness of the Hobbesian solution lies not in anything that the games theory models show but in what, just by being models, they leave out. . . . The Hobbesian solution is . . . like a house of cards . . . and it is inflexible in the same way. A structure is more likely to be able to bend in response to changing forces without collapsing if it is held together by ties of which some are less conditional than those of prudence. (pp. 119–20)

I shall quarrel shortly with the claim of fictitiousness, but the wisdom that is manifest in everything else that is here prefigures the vigilance

---

Man (1871), p. 166, a position whose reputability is refurbished by Mackie himself in 'The Law of the Jungle', *Philosophy* 53 (1978). See 2.13.

and unerring insight that distinguish Mackie's efforts elsewhere in the book to supply what he calls 'the content of the device' which he has announced that he will take morality to be. Not only (as Mackie says) is self-interest a needlessly narrow resource from which to draw palliatives for prisoner's dilemma predicaments and their variants or for state-of-nature situations. It gradually becomes evident, even though Mackie never quite says so, that there is no real possibility of specifying in advance *the one objective* that the morality device is to encompass. It is true that, at one point (p. 193), Mackie mentions the 'well-being of active intelligent participants in a partly competitive life'; but the occasion for this formulation is Mackie's remarking on its unsatisfactoriness as an overall objective. Nor is he preparing at this point to identify, either inaccurately (by his standard) or else too hopelessly vaguely for most constructive purposes, an even larger or more inclusive objective—'the flourishing of human life', for instance, or 'general human well-being'—in relation to which he can propose to us an ethic of consequentialism. Indeed, when it comes to it, Mackie rejects consequentialism.

By what method then does the construction proceed? Mackie's real method is this. As he moves from topic to topic and question to question, he draws constantly upon the reservoir of implicit knowledge that we all have, but make explicit only piecemeal and in given contexts, of what matters in this or that sphere of activity. At need, Mackie draws freely upon this reservoir. From hence, of course, and from his power to interpret the point of what he finds, his rare judgment and good sense.[6]

Mackie might find this a disappointing description. But I should reply that he ought not to complain. For this is the *right* method. The fact that he needs to follow it only mirrors the oft-repeated failure of moral philosophy, well documented by Mackie himself, to settle peacefully for any utilitarian aim or deontological aim or other

---

6. See, for instance, Mackie's temperate and sensible treatment, which stands out among others offered by authors of an empiricist outlook, of the Principle of Double Effect (pp. 160–8).

specific aim as 'the (overall) aim of morality'. In truth, the inner or enactable aim of morality, the real aim of morality, is inseparable from the everyday meaning of everyday life and its everyday extensions and elaborations. It is something practically apparent but apparent only within the business of life itself. There is everything to be said for starting, as Warnock and Mackie do, with some foundational purpose or purposes (countering the narrowness of human sympathies, say). But there is no question of advancing from these to the specification of an overall end that would be required for purposes of reconceiving morality as a means to that end. It begins to appear that the idea that morality is a *device* (or a means to an end) is either, as literally understood, false—or else, as charitably understood, uncomfortably close to vacuous.[7]

11.3. If something you think you hoped for is lost by your concurring in this last contention, well, something else can be gained by reflection upon this reservoir which Mackie draws upon of practical or implicit knowledge. The thing we gain is a vivid reminder of the possibility of inward ends or purposes or concerns which, in the business of their life at a given place and time, participants in a first-order ethic will steadfastly adhere to as if by second nature, distinguishing readily, however essentially contestably, between these concerns and other concerns that *can* be abandoned and may have to be. Is it not here, in the sphere of the unforsakeable, that we find the true source of the deontological ideas and categorical requirements that Mackie insists upon our retaining in first-order morality? If there is this to be gained, then how can we acquiesce in Mackie's redescribing a categorical requirement as an appeal to an 'invisible and fictitious tie or bond' of obligation or as depending for its force on mysterious 'intrinsically prescriptive entities' which he says that 'ought' and 'must' purport to invoke? What need is there for these mysteries?[8]

7. I expect that something analogous has already been said about analogous proposals to conceive of law as an economic device.
8. Here I make response to a point Mackie notes at p. 27.

This remark leads on to yet another thought Mackie never meant us to have. Is Mackie looking in the right place for truth and objectivity? Aren't truth and objectivity best looked for in the difference between good and bad first-order thinking within the subject matter that Mackie's book reintroduces to us—and that it vindicates for us by displaying it to us as, piece by piece, *not pointless* but more or less indispensable to us? This is a subject matter we need no longer see as littered with the nuts and bolts of the constructivist, but as provided with the purport and density proper to a mode of thinking that is fully fledged and engaged with all sorts of other life-purposes by reference to which it is constantly proved and tested.

First-order morality is very unlike elementary arithmetic. But that does not forbid a comparison under one chosen aspect. Consider here the efforts of a philosopher of arithmetic who seeks to reconcile us to the wondrous ontology of natural numbers by showing how naturally and seemingly inevitably it is cantilevered from the first of the indefinitely many needs that arithmetic is to subserve, namely that of counting the ordinary objects of human experience. Just as we can see the achieved satisfaction of all these needs as sustaining, well enough, the ontology of natural numbers and the corresponding ideology (conceptual apparatus) of their properties, can we not see the inward or lived accumulated aims of ethical thinking as sustaining the proper ontology and ideology of first-order ethics? If so, why should not the distinction that ordinary agents make between good and bad thinking about what to say about such and such an act (or such and such a character, or such and such a situation) instantiate the *general* distinction between true and false? If ethical thinking about such things is in good shape, cannot ethical properties and value properties be as distinctive as you like, provided that it serves an ethical aim for them to be thus or so? On the view I am trying to make visible, an assertion invoking ethical properties will not aspire to a different kind of status from a factual assertion; and there need not be any *dichotomy* between getting it right in matters of ethics, however distinctive that is, and getting it right in matters of fact.[9]

11.4. Here it seems necessary to explain a little more carefully what there is to mean by such claims as this, as well as to indicate what it would take to justify them. What shall we mean?

By 'ethics' we can mean something we know how to explain copiously by examples, examples that are dead centre. 'Matter of fact' will be harder, however. It is instructive to remember in this connection the logical positivists' repeated efforts and repeated failures to say what a factual predicate was.[10] Almost anything we think we can simply assume here will beg the question against some reputable opinion. But let us go by another way.

Look at some of our strongest cases of simple plain truth among judgments, any true judgments that you like. This is my suggestion. Then study what in such cases is to be expected of the property of truth. In this way, excogitate the Fregean marks of the concept *true*.[11] Then, with these in mind, look carefully at real-life ethical reasoning or persuasion at its best and most convincing. Discover what judgments it can even endorse as prompted to us by there being (for one who grasps fully the sense and reference of the sentence expressing the judgment) nothing else to think but that so and so. (Not nothing else *for us* or *here* or *now* to think. That is too weak.) Then ask yourself how narrowly to conceive the general idea of there being nothing else to think. Surely it does not need to be confined to the realm of the necessary or confined to that which we reach by deduction. Before you decide about that, listen to Charles Sanders

---

9. For another account of the non-dichotomy, namely Hilary Putnam's to be found in *The Collapse of the Fact/Value Dichotomy*, see Lecture 12, n. 20.

10. The reasons for their failure are vividly illustrated by the remarkable short history of these endeavours which Putnam provides at *The Collapse of the Fact/Value Dichotomy*, p. 21.

11. For marks of truth and a continuation of the themes that ensue upon them in moral philosophy, see 12.2, 12.3. See also my *Needs, Values, Truth* (amended 3rd ed., Oxford: Oxford University Press, 2002), pp. 115, 147, 152.

Peirce on the subject of thinking and the idea, as he advances it, that thinking is not to be conceived to 'form a chain which is no stronger than its weakest link', but as 'a cable whose fibers may be ever so slender provided they are sufficiently numerous and intimately connected'.[12] Finally, when you have made up your mind about all that, spell out your remaining reason for supposing that ethical judgments could never enjoy the properties corresponding to the marks of plain truth. If this reason has to do with their remoteness from perception, well, ask yourself whether, from scratch, you could hope to establish any special status for perception itself without recourse to modes of thinking that only the Peircean conception will certify as genuine argument.

On this kind of approach, there will be no instant answer to the question whether ethical findings are or are not matters of fact. There will be no instant answer, but, *in so far as* first-order ethical thinking seems to muster powers of persuasion and criticism that are rooted in a genuine subject matter, and *in so far as* the cognitivist thinks he can answer Mackie's argument from relativity, how should he characterize the non-dichotomy of fact and value? Like this, I suggest: the concept *factual judgment* or *judgment with a truth-value* and the concept *ethical judgement* will be different concepts—such a distinction is there to be made, just as the concept *mouse* and the concept *mammal* are different concepts (for 'concept', see 12.2, n. 2)—but this distinctness does not preclude a judgment's being both a factual and an ethical judgment. Compare the way in which the distinct concepts *mouse* and *mammal* will each collect any particular mouse you please, Timmy Willy or Johnny Townmouse or whichever, within their extensions. Ethical judgments could be a subset

12. C. S. Peirce, *Collected Papers,* ed. C. Hartshorne, P. Weiss, and A. W. Burks (Cambridge, Mass.: Harvard University Press, 1931–58), vol. I, p. 265. In citing Peirce here, I am not preparing to endorse an anti-realist or pragmatic conception of truth. Just the reverse. In an essay in the *Cambridge Companion to C. S. Peirce,* ed. Cheryl Misak (Cambridge: Cambridge University Press, 2005), I argue that the best reconstruction of Peirce will make him an operationalist or pragmaticist not about truth but about sense or significance.

of factual judgments even if they were an utterly special and essentially contestable subset. In this way, we can have a clear *difference* between the ethical-as-such and the factual-as-such without any dichotomy between their proper provinces. The hope of making good some claim of this sort is the characteristic hope of ethical objectivism or moral cognitivism.

11.5. Do these explications, dispositions, and proposals complete the response to the argument from queerness? Not quite. We have deprecated Mackie's mockery of certain curious things he claims to find, and which we might refuse to find, within the ontology or ideology of the working portion of our own first-order ethical system. But we have not yet engaged with Mackie's charge that objectivism needs to postulate a curious faculty of intuition by which human beings can detect the presence of valuational and other non-natural properties.

The first point that needs to be made here is that a non-natural property is something less strange than Mackie seems to suppose. A non-natural property is simply a property that does not conform to Moore's first characterization of 'nature' and 'natural'.[13] I paraphrase and adapt that characterization as follows. A predicate stands for a natural property if it is indispensable to the exposition or development of some natural science (or to some similarly strictly empirical-cum-explanatory mode of investigation). A non-natural property is simply one that is *not* like that. It is a myth and the opposite of the truth that our grasp of properties that are natural in this sense is better than our grasp of the non-natural.

Is there not something queer, though, about the epistemology of the non-natural properties that are value properties? Here I shall refer to Hilary Putnam's recent book, *The Collapse of the Fact/Value Dichotomy:*

---

13. G. E. Moore, *Principia Ethica* (Cambridge: Cambridge University Press, 1903), p. 41.

How could there be 'value facts'? After all, we have no sense organ for detecting them . . . Consider the parallel question: 'How could we come to tell that people are *elated?* After all, we have no sense organ for detecting elation.' . . . [Answer:] Once I have acquired the concept of elation, I can see that someone is elated. . . . Perception is not innocent; it is an exercise of our concepts. (pp. 102–3)

This is to say that, once you have the concept of elation, you know what to look for. In looking for that, you can use any kind of perception or any mode of investigation that suits the case. Similarly, then, consider the ethical predicate 'considerate'. That which marks out or delimits or descries or discriminates the property of considerateness in acts or attitudes or human characters is an essentially ethical interest, in pursuit of which we can deploy any kind of perception or any mode of investigation or any associated concept that suits the case.[14] The presence of *such* properties, that is of value properties, is ascertained by all the multifarious means that are called for by the exercise of our grasp of this or that ethical concept. Such properties are to be conceived *in the light of what it takes to exercise that grasp*—not vice versa. A particular ethical property, we might

---

14. Confronted with the argument from queerness and the mockery of 'intuition', Aristotle could have given a similar gloss on his own use in ethical contexts of the word *aisthesis*. This, moreover, is a point it ought also to be safe to credit the Aristotelian philosopher W. D. Ross with understanding. Short-sightedly but excusably, Ross never realized that he needed to explain to his future critics what Aristotle meant by *aisthesis* in the two or three parallel passages of Aristotle that he was apt to quote to the effect that the 'decision lies in perception'. (Compare *Nicomachean Ethics* 1109b23, 1126b4, 1143b6.)

Ross, the arch-intuitionist supposedly (but let's stick to the historical figure W. D. Ross), scarcely ever uses the word 'intuition' at all unless to record the findings of what Aristotle called *aisthesis*. It is unimaginable that he would have been prepared to say that intuition was a dedicated faculty for hunting down, as if by smell or taste, the non-natural properties. Why then is Ross called an intuitionist? Well, in the end, he called himself one; see his *Foundations of Ethics* (Oxford: Oxford University Press, 1939). He must have thought that, subject to careful explanation, this was harmless. History has proved him wrong. If he wanted to be understood, he should not have moved beyond the position of *The Right and the Good*.

say, is to be identified or singled out as the property which the reasonable exercise of the grasp of such and such a concept, as regulated by criticism, hunts down. Only at his peril can Mackie's moral sceptic deny that there is such a quarry to hunt down or deny that there is such a property; just as it is at his own peril that a metaphysical naturalist will deny, if we are looking for a prime between 5 and 13, that there are primes. The objectivity of the reasonable exercise of the grasp of an ethical concept is not established by reference to the product of some *independent* understanding of the property. (Why should it need to be?) It is established by those who exercise it and engage fairly with fair first-order criticism.

Something tells me this is the moment to close down on the argument from queerness. Yet something else prevents. For I hear Protagoras and Mackie protesting in these terms: you have denied that a first-order ethic is a device, but not that it is a human invention. If man is the measure, then how can man himself treat ethical judgments as objectively true or false? How can man treat an ethical assertion as recording how things are out there independently of him or her who makes the assertion? I reply: does 'man is the measure' mean that it is a matter of stipulation what to say about (say) this or that action by NN? That is implausible and it does not follow from morality's being an invention. (Nor does it follow from morality's being an invention that just any invented ethos will count as a morality—or that one is just as good as another.) Or does 'man is the measure' mean that to discover or decide about the moral quality of this or that act or character must regard, either directly or indirectly, the nature of man or the expectations or aspirations of man? Does it mean that the act or character has to be measured on some *human* scale of values, the scale of values that human beings themselves have arrived at? That is more plausible, but it does not imply that, when we subject things to that scale, it is going to be up to us, who are human beings, which concept, whether *admirable* (say) or *execrable,* the action in question falls under. For someone to jump to that conclusion is analogous to a confusion of sense and reference, the confusion of the significance of a sentence—which, if you insist, you can call stipulation or invention—and its truth-value, which cannot be stipulated.

'All right,' someone may say. 'I will guard against that confusion. But do you want to allow sense to just any old supposed subject matter that someone may propose, however apparently vacuous or nonsensical?' Answer: no, I don't. The candidate subject matter must have a point, however inward and imperfectly articulate this may be, and it must engage in a proper multiplicity of ways with things that we can find out about or pursue or care about in the rest of life. But the subject matter of ethics does manifestly do all these things—as Mackie himself took pains to show. That is not all. If we think about this matter from the inside then we shall discover within us a wealth of further knowledge, however inexplicit, about the inner aim that animates the whole business, and regulates it critically. Morality is not just one among numerous possible ways of thinking about how we are impinged upon from without. It is our response to things which, in the light of certain distinctive unforsakeable concerns, matter distinctively. Our sense of how they matter and why they matter is something we come to understand progressively more exactly, moreover, as we join with others in the business of applying or refusing to apply one or another ethical predicate to that which we confront or look out upon in the ordinary business of work, survival, or participation in shared enterprises. Here is how, in the course of our exploration and colonization of the world, we arrive at our sense of what notions emerge from the crucible of shared experience as indispensable to us. Here is how we gain a more and more exact understanding of what considerateness, or callousness, or kindness, or brutality, or proportionality . . . amount to, and what they count for, in an act chosen or contemplated, in an action done, or in its outcome.[15]

15. The particular cognitivist outlook that shapes so many of the formulations of this lecture will remain incomplete so long as we postpone the effort to reconstruct a natural history of the grasping of ethical concepts and the elaboration and handing down of the language in which they are expressed. In the interim, see 2.9 and 2.11 and 10.4–6; also Sabina Lovibond, 'Ethical Upbringing: From Connivance to Cognition', in Sabina Lov-

11.6. The second difficulty Mackie brought against objectivity in ethics was the relativity of morals. Someone might say this: your answer to the objection from queerness will pass muster if first-order ethical thinking has the kind of soundness the objectivist postulates; but in reality human beings at large *fail to converge* in their findings about the presence or absence in given objects or situations of ethical properties. If ethical questions were somehow on all fours with questions of fact, then those who understand an ethical question ought under favourable conditions to start to agree on an answer to it—or else be eager to discover what obstructs the way to agreement. Where is this agreement or this eagerness?

For determined objectivists, there has been a temptation to try to flatten this objection once and for all, as often as not by ignoring the link Mackie saw between the difficulty that he called relativity and the difficulty he called queerness. Crediting Mackie and others who raise this question with a genuine curiosity about the nature of ethical thinking itself, I shall proceed much more circuitously, starting from a famous essay by Montaigne entitled 'On the Cannibals'. The essay's claim to our attention, let me say, does not depend on its counting as an early work of empirical ethnography. Its claim depends on the resource and canny enterprise that the author demonstrates in the practicality of the confrontation with cultural difference. It gives the lie to the automatic assumption that the ethical cannot be a subject matter where critical agreement will accumulate.

11.7. In La France Antartique or (as we should say) Brazil, a 'seemingly boundless territory', there live (discovered, as Montaigne

---

ibond and S. G. Williams, eds., *Identity, Truth and Value* (Oxford: Blackwell, 1996, 2000); David Wiggins, *Needs, Values, Truth,* ch. 5. For a place where an altogether fuller account might begin, see Vygotsky's account of thought, speech, and meaning as this is set out in David Bakhurst in *Consciousness and Revolution* (Cambridge: Cambridge University Press, 1991), ch. 3. For a supplement to Hume, well emphasizing among other things the part that language plays in 'affix[ing] signs to all sorts of objects and qualities and excit[ing] trains of thought which would never arise from a mere impression of the senses, and if they did arise could not be followed out', see Charles Darwin, *The Descent of Man,* part II, ch. 21.

intimates, not very long before the moment of writing) a people with customs very different from our own. Despite the gap between them and the French or the Spanish or the Portuguese . . . , there are things we can learn from them. Montaigne says that such peoples as these will appear barbarous. But they are

> barbarous only in that they have been hardly fashioned by the mind of man, still remaining close neighbours to their original state of nature. . . . Their purity is such that I am sometimes seized with irritation at their not having been discovered earlier. . . . It irritates me that neither Lycurgus [the Spartan lawgiver] nor Plato had any knowledge of them. . . . I would tell Plato that those people have no trade of any kind, no acquaintance with writing, no knowledge of numbers, no terms for governor or political superior, no practice of subordination or of riches or poverty, no contracts, no inheritances, no divided estates, no occupation but leisure, no concern for kinship—no clothing, no agriculture, no metals, no use of wine or corn. Among them you hear no words for treachery, lying, cheating, avarice, envy, back-biting or forgiveness. . . .
>
> They dwell along the sea-shore, shut in to landwards by great lofty mountains, on a stretch of land some hundred leagues in width. They have fish and flesh in abundance which bear no resemblance to ours; these they eat simply cooked. . . . They get up at sunrise and have their meal for the day as soon as they do so; they have no other meal but that one. . . . They spend the whole day dancing; the younger men go off hunting with bow and arrow. . . . In the morning, before their meal, one of their elders walks from one end of the building to the other, addressing the whole barnful of them. . . . He preaches two things only: bravery before their enemies and love for their wives. . . . They believe in the immortality of the soul: souls which deserve well of the gods dwell in the sky where the sun rises; souls which are accursed dwell where it sets.[16]

16. Michel de Montaigne, *The Complete Essays,* trans. and ed. M. A. Screech (London: Allen Lane, 1991), p. 231 ff.

So far, so good. However utterly different the lives may be that these people lead, however many of our virtues or vices they fail to cultivate, the virtues that they do practise are instantly recognizable to us. Such people might even seem to us to represent a golden age. They might. But now we learn a little more about the battles in which they are constantly schooled to be resolute. Montaigne continues:

> These peoples have their wars against others further inland beyond their mountains. They go forth naked, with no other arms but their bows and their wooden swords sharpened to a point like the blades of our pig-stickers. Their steadfastness in battle is astonishing and always ends in killing and bloodshed. They do not even know the meaning of fear or flight. For a long period they treat captives well and provide them with all the comforts which they can devise. Afterwards the master of each captive summons a great assembly of his acquaintances. He ties a rope to one of the arms of his prisoner and holds him by it, standing a few feet away for fear of being caught in the blows, and allows his dearest friend to hold the prisoner the same way by the other arm. Then, before the whole assembly, they both hack at him with their swords and kill him. This done, they roast him and make a common meal of him, sending chunks of his flesh to absent friends.

The brave warriors already have plenty of wholesome food to eat. Why then, we may wonder, do they eat their enemies?

> This is not, as some think, done for food—as the Scythians used to do in antiquity—but to symbolize ultimate revenge. As a proof of this [mark the following]: [when some of our natives] noted that the Portuguese, who were allied to their enemies, practised a different kind of execution of [those they took] prisoner— which was to bury them up to the waist, to shoot showers of arrows at their exposed parts and then to hang them—, they thought that these men from the Other World [that is Europe],

who had scattered knowledge of many a vice throughout their neighbourhood . . . , were greater masters than they were of every kind of revenge . . . , [and] they began to abandon their ancient method and adopted that one.

This regrettable change in the customs of primitive people is the occasion for Montaigne to make one simple and entirely deliberate comparison between what he knows of sixteenth-century Brazil before the arrival of the Portuguese and sixteenth-century France:

[I am not dismayed] that we should note the horrible barbarity in a practice such as theirs [the Brazilians]; what [does dismay me] is that while judging correctly of their wrong-doings, we should be so blind to our own. I think there is more barbarity . . . in lacerating by rack and torture a body still able to feel things, in roasting him little by little and having him bruised and bitten by pigs and dogs (as we have . . . seen in recent memory (*de fraîche mémoire*) . . . among our fellow citizens and neighbours—and, what is worse, in the name of duty and religion)—than in roasting him and eating him after his death. . . . We can indeed call those folk barbarians by the rules of reason, but not in comparison with ourselves, who surpass them in every kind of barbarism. Their warfare is entirely noble and magnanimous. It has as much justification and beauty as that human malady allows. Among them it has no other foundation than a zealous concern for courage. . . . They are still in that blessed state of desiring nothing beyond what is ordained by their natural necessities: for them anything further is merely superfluous. The generic term which they use for men of the same age is 'brother'; younger men they call 'sons'. As for the old men, they are the 'fathers' of everyone else. . . . They require no other ransom from their prisoners-of-war than that they should admit and acknowledge their defeat. Yet . . . you cannot find one who does not prefer to be killed and eaten than merely to ask to be spared.

Finally, contemplating the imminent future of these people and his European countrymen's constantly creeping corruption of them, Montaigne relates that

> Three such natives, unaware of what price in peace and happiness they would have to pay to buy a knowledge of our corruptions, and unaware that such commerce would lead to their downfall—which I suspect to be already far advanced—, pitifully allowing themselves to be cheated by their desire for novelty and leaving the gentleness of their regions to come and see ours, were at Rouen at the same time as King Charles IX. The King had a long interview with them: they were shown our manners, our ceremonial and the layout of a fair city. Then someone asked them what they thought of all this and wanted to know what they had been most amazed by. They made three points; I am very annoyed with myself for forgetting the third, but I still remember two of them. In the first place they said (probably referring to the Swiss Guard) that they found it very odd that all those full-grown bearded men, strong and bearing arms in the King's entourage, should consent to obey a boy rather than choosing one of themselves as a Commander; secondly—since they have an idiom in their language which calls all men 'halves' of one another—[they said] that they had noticed that there were among us men fully bloated with all sorts of comforts while their halves were begging at their doors, emaciated with poverty and hunger: they found it odd that those destitute halves should put up with such injustice and did not take the others by the throat or set fire to their houses.

These people are cannibals, Montaigne has told us. They have not perceived what a malady warfare really is. They have not found their way beyond vendetta towards any law- or custom-based resolution of blood-feuds (we can confidently surmise). So their preoccupation with virtue is much taken up with military forms of courage. But the chief thought Montaigne prompts us to have about them is that their charity *(agape)*, their asceticism, and their unconcern for the merely material far excels that of any European. In so far as these primitive peoples strive for anything beyond the perfecting of their personal merit, they effortlessly surpass any European in the innocence of their amusements, their dignity, and their capacity to live in contentment. When Montaigne questioned one of them who was a commander among them ('our sailors calling him a king') and asked him

> what advantage he got from his high rank, he told me that it was to lead his troops into battle; asked how many men followed him, he pointed to an open space to signify as many as it would hold—about four or five thousand men; questioned whether his authority lapsed when the war was over, he replied that he retained the privilege of having paths cut for him through the thickets in their forests, so that he could easily walk through them when he visited villages under his sway.
>
> Not at all bad, that.—Ah! But they wear no breeches.

11.8. Montaigne was a thinker deeply influenced by Pyrrhonism and doubt, especially doubt of philosophical systems. Yet, despite the restraint and gentle indirection for which Montaigne is so justly celebrated—his fully considered thoughts about unperverted nature are not deducible from the opening passage, for instance—this particular essay appears to carry a cargo of moral commentary that is disarmingly positive and direct. Even if Montaigne's account of the cannibals were less carefully researched than Montaigne makes as if to suggest—even if it came to be proved that he has taken no more trouble to assure himself of its accuracy than he has to assure himself of the historical actuality of the stories he makes use of from (say) Plutarch—that need not diminish the simplicity of his ethical purpose. If there are specifically philosophical problems to be found here, maybe the chief among them is not his but ours—for us to ensure that our own supposedly rigorous methods of describing and classifying ethical positions and metaethical positions should not close off a space that ought to be held open for the sort of response to moral diversity that Montaigne exhibits for us. His aim is to recruit anyone, anywhere, who will listen.

Or so I assert. Yet someone might say this: yes, Montaigne seeks to recruit anyone, anywhere, who will listen. But that is a very weak claim. For Montaigne is clearly a relativist. It is in that capacity that he calls for tolerance towards the cannibalism of these people. His appeal is for us to judge the cannibalism of these Brazilians *by their standard.* The one great objection that is ready and waiting for him to urge against the Christians of sixteenth-century Europe—if only he would deploy it—is that constantly, in all sorts of ways, these Christians act against their own professed standard. But then (the critic will say), with everything so arranged, Montaigne spoils the whole thing. For he seems to judge Christians *and* cannibals from a standard that is neither sixteenth-century Brazilian nor simply sixteenth-century Christian. He wants to look at things from the point of view of *both*—or else of neither. This is more humane (the critic says) than it is justifiable or consistent with his own suggestion that we should not try to look beyond the laws of our own country.[17]

17. Here the relativist interlocutor surely makes reference to the ninth/tenth paragraph of 'On the Cannibals', where English translations have given the impression that Montaigne asserts that we have no other criterion of truth or right reason than the example and form of the opinions and customs of our own country. The French text of the relevant sentences reads as follows: 'Or je trouve, pour revenir à mon propos, qu'il n'y a rien de barbare et de sauvage en cette nation, à ce qu'on m'en a rapporté, sinon que chacun appelle barbarie ce qui n'est pas de son usage; comme de vrai, il semble que nous n'avons autre mire de la vérité et de la raison que l'exemple et idée des opinions et usances du pays où nous sommes. Là est toujours la parfaite religion, la parfaite police, parfait et accompli usage de toutes choses.' The following seems to be a fairly literal translation: 'I find that there is nothing barbarous or savage in this people judging by what I have been told—except that [except in so far as] everyone will call barbarous that which is at variance with his own customs or habits. For indeed it seems that we have no other target for truth-seeking and reasoning than the example or stereotype of [represented by] the beliefs and customs of the country to which we belong. It is there, in that country, that we have the perfect religion, the perfect constitution, the best way of doing anything!'. The last sentence is clearly ironical. It surely looks forward to the last paragraph of the whole essay, as well as backward to the first. These first and last paragraphs dramatize Montaigne's insistence on our liability to mistakes and misapprehensions in findings of barbarity. If so much is correct, then we can surely take seriously

The critic is imaginary. But if there is such a critic, I say his stricture is multiply mistaken. Montaigne does not condone cannibalism or vengeance at all. He does not praise perpetual warfare as the ideally admirable mode of being for the Brazilians. He does not even say that these goings on are all very well when judged by the relevant local standard. Out of his own mouth, he says explicitly that war is a malady and cannibalism an evil. He also insists, however, and this of course is the chief thing, that cannibalism is *less* bad than sixteenth century European modes of behaviour towards convicted criminals or convicted heretics. It is one thing to roast someone after they're dead, another to roast them alive, and so on. The criticisms Montaigne conveys of his countrymen are criticisms not of inconsistency between their acts and their own professed beliefs but of inhumanity, inhumanity that Christians should be ashamed of. The stance in which he is sustained by the comparison of Brazilian and Christian morals is a stance not so much of relativism as of outright *engagement,* engagement presumably in the cause of the creation of a world in which human beings may dwell in a security and peace unwonted in Montaigne's own lifetime.

11.9. To say this much is not to position Montaigne with respect to Mackie, whose engagement, in its own way, is not less than Montaigne's. The contrast is with other positions that take their cue from the phenomenon to which Mackie gives the name of relativity.

One such position inserts into the content of a moral judgment an implicit reference to a moral code. Thus (the position says) the act of eating one's enemies satisfies the predicate 'right-for-sixteenth-century-Brazil'; and this same act also satisfies the predicate 'wrong-

---

and give due weight to the 'il semble que'. We can also allow more weight to what *precedes* the 'sinon que' ('except in so far as') than to what follows it. After 'sinon que', Montaigne is only reporting that he has the same difficulty as everyone else in fighting free of parochial misconceptions.

I am indebted here to my colleague Dr Wesley Williams—not only for his help with these particular sentences but also for his generous encouragement and friendly reassurance in the matter of understanding Montaigne.

for-sixteenth-century-France'. Speaking in the twenty-first century, we must say that cannibalism is wrong-by-our-system and cannibalism was not wrong-by-the-Brazilian-system. Such relativity might suggest that it is pointless to sit in judgment on the verdicts of another system or to insist on one's own. But, whoever else may think in this way, Montaigne does not. 'On the Cannibals' begins in strongly conciliatory fashion with the life of these people, then provokes us to a strongly adverse judgment upon the native Brazilians, then conciliates us afresh and equally strongly in their favour. The essay treats disagreement and our condemnation of cannibalism first *as a fact,* but then as a challenge to Montaigne's best powers of persuasion. It is by his deployment of those powers that Montaigne's readers are to be brought round to see the native Brazilians as much better than they (his readers) are—something his readers did not expect.[18] There is no trace here of the idea that moral judgment appeals to a standard that is purely local to time, place, or culture or is answerable only to some local say-so. The claim that he and his readers surpass the Brazilians in every kind of barbarism appeals to something Montaigne aspires to make it compulsory for everyone to think; and they are to think this with reference to all of a range of acts that the sixteenth-century French do and that the Brazilians do, each set of acts being understood *for what these acts are, in their context.*

Here is a second attempt at relativism. It has sometimes been maintained that, as predicated of moral judgments, the properties of truth and falsehood are really relative to a system of moral assessment, so that the sentences 'Eating people is wrong' and 'Harming one's enemies is wrong' could be true relative to Christian morality of sixteenth-century France (however little heed may have been paid there to the second precept) and false relative to sixteenth-century native Brazilian morality. This relativism shifts its attentions from the

18. 'Nous les pouvons donc bien appeler barbares, eu égard aux règles de la raison, mais non pas eu égard a nous, qui les surpassons en toute sorte de barbarie.' ('We can indeed call these folk barbarians by the rules of reason, but not in comparison with ourselves, who surpass them in every kind of barbarianism').

content of the judgment (that was the first variety) to the verdict on
that content. But careful reflection will find nothing at all for the
words 'relative to Brazilian morality' to mean in the combination
'false relative to Brazilian morality', except 'false *according to* Brazilian morality'. And then, in that construal, all that is being said is
that, *according to Brazilian morality,* eating one's enemies is right
whereas, *according to* (some) *Christian morality,* it is wrong. This
simply records an apparent difference of opinion. It leaves us where
we were, in the manner of a bare anthropological record or a trav-
eller's narrative. Or else—if it is taken to silence all further discussion—it leaves us worse off. It could have no relevance to Montaigne's efforts.[19]

There is a simpler and third thing to mean by relativism—one
now sees—less technical, less charged with philosophical theory.
This is that morality essentially consists of moralities in the plural,
and that moralities in the plural are different and always at loggerheads with one another. This purports to be a statement of fact.
The statement is turned into philosophy when someone adds something—namely that there is no vantage point from which to arbitrate
between different moralities; or else that for each person the only

---

19. Of course, if the verdict 'true according to Brazilian morality', as predicated of
'Eating one's enemies is right', be taken *not* to silence discussion, then it is more hospitable to Montaigne's reflections than the previous version was. At least it leaves 'right'
and 'wrong' with the ordinary use that we attribute to them. It points in the wrong
direction, however, as one may see by asking how crucial it is to Montaigne whether
his reports of Brazilian beliefs and practices have the accuracy we demand of a careful
historical report. Surely it is not crucial *in itself.* For the real purpose of the essay is to
enlarge the range of moral possibilities we can take account of when we are engaged
with questions of how human beings are to live. The reason why Montaigne says he
sets store by artless testimony is that he knows that we know that moral possibilities
count for little in the absence of their possible exposure to actual usage and real human
feelings. One might say without paradox or play that the raison d'être for the narration
is the commentary, a commentary that treats the scenes depicted as representing one
moral possibility which then reveals further moral possibilities that ought to interest us.
In providing that commentary, Montaigne discloses his own thoughts (or himself, as he
often says). But chief among the purposes here of disclosing these thoughts is to unlock
faction, to conciliate, to instruct, to persuade, to make us look harder at what we usually
do or feel before we respond in our own habitual way.

proper vantage point is that which is locally laid down. Here we come closer, in a sense, to engaging with Montaigne—except of course that he might want to qualify the finding of fact: 'always at loggerheads'. Montaigne would also reject the philosophical addendum. For in his essay he seems to suggest a method for *finding* a more than merely local vantage point from which to understand a particular difference that seems to have come into question. Diversity of customs may or may not amount to disagreement—we must not confuse these things—and the better practice may or may not be the familiar one. The first things to be attended to, though, are the local meanings of the acts that are in question, the reasons these meanings sustain for doing such acts and the other beliefs that come into play. Unless we pay heed to these things, we shall not see the good in that which is strange or the bad in that which is familiar.

Let us call such an outlook as this contextualism (not relativism). Philosophically speaking, it might be seen as a bequest from Aristotle.[20] In Aristotle and those who have followed him, this outlook coheres well enough with the general thought that, despite the manifest differences in the ways in which different peoples (and different people) are introduced to morality and participate in it, there is a common core of morality, which finds its expression in a whole variety of different acts in a variety of different contexts.[21] Mon-

20. Here is a provisional statement of contextualism: No act or practice can be assessed as right or wrong, good or bad, etc. without the full specification of circumstances and context (context embracing, in some versions, the identity of agents). An act or a practice is a response in some situation to something somehow discriminable in that situation or a framework that contains that situation.

Properly understood, contextualism may be expected to have both ethical and metaethical consequences. But, strictly speaking, its life starts elsewhere, in the shape of a logico-grammatical reminder: properly to situate an act or a practice or an instance of a practice is the necessary preliminary to passing judgment on *that act, that practice*, or *that instance*. Unless we do this, we shall scarcely know what we are passing judgment upon.

21. Downwind from Aristotle's famous discussion of natural justice (contrast customary or legal justice) in *Nicomachean Ethics* V.7, there are countless further expressions of the thought. For a modern exposition of it, see Aurel Kolnai, 'Moral Consensus', *Proceedings of the Aristotelian Society* 70 (1969-70), to which I am indebted in my account of the third kind of relativism. For an expression a hundred years on from

taigne's essay illustrates very well what such a core might comprise, the notions or ideas that Europeans and cannibals had in common, for instance. It also mentions ideas the cannibals did not recognize and ideas the cannibals had that Europeans were not fully prepared for. Here, though, it prepares us for the thought that his countrymen would benefit by taking seriously the native Brazilian idea of human beings as halves of one another; just as, the other way round, the Brazilians stand in need of the European idea of reparation/blood-price and an understanding of the self-renewing evil of vendetta.

The Aristotelian thought is indispensable, then, in so far as we are concerned with shareable notions or ideas and the duty both to husband and to increase our store of them. It is less clear, though, whether, on the level of *judgments* that may be critically agreed, the idea of a common core is the way forward for the objectivist eager to learn something from Montaigne. On the level of agreement in moral judgments themselves, maybe it is better to bracket the question of identifying verdicts that *already* command universal agreement. A better question is what verdicts can or *could,* on the basis of reasonable persuasion, command agreement. The philosophical point of paying heed to Montaigne's essay is surely not for the moral

---

Montaigne, see bk I, ch. 2 of Leibniz's *New Essays:* 'since morality is more important than arithmetic, God has given to man instincts which lead, straight away and without reasoning, to part of what reason commands. . . . These instincts do not irresistibly impel us to act: our passions lead us to resist them, our prejudices obscure them, and contrary customs distort them. Usually, though, we accede to these instincts of conscience, and even follow them whenever stronger feelings do not overcome them. The largest and soundest part of the human race bears witness to them. The Orientals, the Greeks and the Romans, the Bible and the Koran agree in that. . . . One would have to be as brutalized as the American savages to approve of their customs, which are full of a cruelty surpassing even that of the beasts. However, these same savages have a good sense of what justice is in other situations; and although there may be no wicked custom which is not permitted somewhere and in some circumstances, nonetheless most of them are condemned most of the time and by the great majority of mankind. This did not come about for no reason; and since it has not come about through unaided reasoning it must in part be related to natural instincts. Custom, tradition and discipline play their part, but natural feeling is what causes custom to veer mainly in the right direction as regards our duties.' G. W. Leibniz, *New Essays on Human Understanding,* trans. P. Remnant and J. Bennett (Cambridge: Cambridge University Press, 1981), pp. 92-3.

philosophers to be appointed to the high office of keepers or interpreters of the human code of morality, as if it were a body of ratified
law. Rather, the point is for us to study the interpretive power of
contextualism as Montaigne practises it, and to perceive the reach
of criticism across difference and the reach of agreement over difference. What we then get from the essay is not only a sense of the
power of moral notions or ideas in moral dialogue, but a new intimation also of the *actual variety* of modes of ethical persuasion. It
is the second of these things (attention to which is a precondition I
believe of any sensible prolongation at all of philosophical metaethics) which might prompt us to hope for the possibility that *sometimes* one who undergoes discursive moral persuasion on some particular matter or question, and who fully understands what is being
said and the context for which it is being said, might be left with
nothing else to think but one thing—*even if* such persuasion is 'a
cable whose fibers may be ever so slender provided that they are
sufficiently numerous and intimately connected'. (See above, 11.4)

11.10. This is all very well, the anti-cognitivist will say, but what
if there are well-formed questions that cannot be answered in this
dialectically satisfying way? I answer that objectivism in ethics, or
moral cognitivism (as one might say), comes without *a priori* assurance that it *must* be right, or prevail over the whole range of ethical
questions. Nevertheless, with disagreements of the kind that the objector has in mind, it will be sensible to try to discover what other
disagreements (e.g. historical or theological disagreements) subsist
in the area, whether parties in disagreement really mean the same
by their words, and what previously unknown or neglected ideas,
indispensable nevertheless to human purposes, might be usefully
proposed to those who appear to be in genuine dispute.

What is the final destination of this way of seeing these issues? Is
the *telos* aspired for a compendious morality equipped with an answer to every well-formed question that might in practice be asked,
or a global ethic with pretensions to match, and to run in tandem
with, the pretensions of some total political/economic global order?

Nothing could be more absurd or give rise more readily in practice to yet new forms of ignorance and endless new and proportionately unjustified subversions by stronger countries of the political or economic fabric of those that are weaker. Setting aside reservations concerning the prospect of the west's exporting the most suspect features of what is called democracy (exporting it without any mention of the warnings of Tocqueville or Mill or of the danger that the less serious interests of the majority can swamp the truly vital interests of a minority), I say that, so far as ethics is concerned, the suggestion rests on rank confusion.

For, first, a morality does not consist of a set of moral propositions, even a very large one. Moral judgments are indeed partial expressions of the findings or demands of some particular mode of being and its associated sensibility. But there is simply no question of collecting up a whole mass of moral judgments arrived at by some combination of Montaigne's methods and philosophical good will in order for these judgments to represent or construct or create an ethic, a morality, or a whole manner of life for citizens of the new world-order. For (1) judgments are only half of the story (the later half) and (2) moral judgments themselves, even when spelled out, cannot even be understood as they are intended except against the background of a lived understanding that will never be fully articulated. In the absence of such a background, you have no hope of being understood exactly as you intend to be understood even if you say something as simple as 'It is wrong to say what is not true/ what you don't know is true/what you know is not true . . . '.[22] In the absence of such a background, which it would be an endless process, that is impossible, to spell out fully explicitly, you could not even keep in balance, as is second nature to us, the conflicting claims of a pair of fully compacted proverbs such as 'He who hesitates is lost' and 'Look before you leap'.[23] In so far as globalism

22. This is to say that injunctions of these kinds cannot be replaced by an exact instruction or precept. On this point, I should like to refer to the remarkable and importantly sensible essay on lying and truth-telling in Leszek Kolakowski's book, *Freedom, Fame, Lying and Betrayal: Essays on Everyday Life* (London: Penguin, 1999).

23. I owe the example and the expression 'compacted' to Christopher Ricks. See his

will dilute or seek to dispense with the moral counterpart of that sort of understanding and put nothing of comparable power or strength in its place (and how could it do so?), it can as well destroy morality as enhance it.²⁴

Essays in Appreciation (Oxford: Oxford University Press, 1996), p. 323. Consider again 'The truth will set you free' and 'Human kind cannot bear very much reality'.

24. Lest this remain obscure, let me illustrate the point by reference to the United Nation's so-called Millennial Development Goals announced in July 2002. They are: (1) to eradicate extreme poverty and hunger; (2) to achieve universal primary education; (3) to promote gender equality and empower women; (4) to reduce child mortality; (5) to improve maternal health; (6) to combat HIV/AIDS, malaria, and other diseases; (7) to ensure environmental sustainability; (8) to develop a global partnership for development. Well, who can be against any of these things? The question is not of course whether one is for them or against them, but the danger that such approved formulations and the priorities that they encapsulate should upstage local perceptions and interpretations of what is locally needed or intended.

Imagine goal (2)'s being interpreted in the boardroom of an international company or the external aid department of a foreign government, six thousand miles from the intended beneficiaries of assistance in the furtherance of such goals. Prescind from all local understanding and then, from within that vacuum, try to consider whether it is a good idea to persuade some national government or charity to fund a scheme to take word-processors to the Berbers or the Bedouin and cause them to adapt their method of education accordingly? Stop, you say! Nobody is going to suggest *that!!* All right, I reply, for the moment, I expect that you are right. So let us consider goal (8) instead, together with the UN resolution on which it rests: 'we are committed to making the right [*sic*] to development a reality for everyone and to freeing the entire human race from want. We resolve therefore to create an environment—at the national and global levels alike—which is conducive to development and to the elimination of poverty' (sects. 11-12, General Assembly resolution, 55th session 55/2, New York, 6–8 September 2000). Suppose, then, that the question revolves around a vast dam scheme of great interest to international contractors and projected for the Narmada River (say) by an Indian state government or two or three such—a dam scheme projected (in some sense) democratically but in defiance of the interest of indigenous peoples who are outnumbered by middle-class city-dwellers (reminding one again of the warnings of Mill and Tocqueville). Suppose that the construction work for the water scheme will benefit enterprises that export goods and services from some country that is a candidate to help fund the aid scheme. Suppose these enterprises pay their taxes to this country, and benefit its balance of payments. How will it be decided whether this constitutes a beneficial step towards goal (8)? On what basis will it be decided? Into a vacuum that sort of scheme will rush. Into a partial vacuum, it will also rush.

Proposals of such kinds—relating to schemes which this is not the place, and I am not the person, to try to pass judgment upon—could be multiplied beyond all present necessity. In a footnote concerned with the indispensability of implicit knowledge, the present necessity is only to illustrate the effect of setting out international goals within a context of understanding that is, *from the nature of the case,* insufficiently rich or

There is a second confusion for us to guard against here, a confusion between *generality* (as understood in contrast with *specificity*) and *universality* (a judgment's holding over *all* of the so specified or stated range of cases or instances)—the confusion so usefully exposed (for purposes of his own) by R. M. Hare.[25] I think that those who dream of a world ethic do not think of it as given in terms that are endlessly specific or that can only be mobilized or made articulate by drawing upon an existing way of being. They are apt to think of it as offering us *prima facie* answers to all questions that are likely to be proposed to it, answers given in terms that are at once usefully general and helpfully prescriptive. If that is the dream, however, let me point out that it is only with the help of contextualism that we have any evident hope of formulating moral judgments that will hold universally and for absolutely all cases (that is, for all cases that fall under descriptions that enter into the question that is under consideration). And contextualism only comes to the rescue of universalism by making full use of the conceptual resources of specificity. Montaigne's readers are convicted of being more barbarous than the Brazilians by a would-be universal or would-be incontrovertible standard that is brought to bear upon the specifics of what they do and the specifics of what the Brazilians do, each set of customs being understood for exactly what it is, in its context. In so far as universality is achieved in cases of this sort, it is almost entirely at the expense of generality.

Does *that* at least help Mackie's argument from relativity? Not at all. It suggests that, once we understand better what sort of thing a first-order ethic is, we can hope to see distinct ethical systems as neither at loggerheads nor aiming at unity, but as simply aspiring in

robust to withstand commercial or political exploitation and abuse and insufficiently informed by the local realities of a myriad very diverse supposed beneficiaries.

25. See his *Freedom and Reason* (Oxford: Oxford University Press, 1963), p. 39. As I should see it, this is a distinction between something that concerns the content of the sentence used to make a judgment and something that concerns the success or unsuccess of that judgment with respect to all pertinent cases. In so far as content is analogous to sense and valuation is analogous to reference, the confusion is analogous to a sense–reference confusion.

their distinctness and the specificity of their *verdicts* to universality. They aspire to be correct (as contextually interpreted) while holding themselves answerable to any case anywhere. On these terms, we become open to the further reflection that, by their nature, ethical systems have *within them* powers of regeneration, reparation, and renewal that will always invite the efforts of moralists, satirists, and other analogizers who strive to make their participants follow their ethical commitments through. The objectivist's faith is this: that, when or if participants do try to follow through, when they recant what they must recant in order to persevere in this process, disagreement and conflict can diminish. Compare the ratchet mechanism that now sustains the once extremely uncommon opinion that there is something wrong with slavery. And now we are back where we were in the response to the queerness objection (see 11.2, 11.4, and 11.5). We are back in the metaethical business (entirely foreign to Montaigne) of plotting the philosophical significance of all the ways in which morality gives the appearance of a real subject matter fully answerable in its own way to the true.

11.11.   A word more, before we end, about this earnest character, the moral objectivist. In the poem from which our epigraph is taken, William Empson begins by describing the totalitarian efforts of 'thinkers' and 'hopers' to counter totalitarianism and their pious hopes that, once 'the loony hooters' (Hitler and Mussolini, perhaps) have been squared, things can be 'reconverted to be kind and clean'. Then come the lines of the epigraph. Then, lest cheerfulness break in, the poem switches course to intimate that collectivism itself may have its origin in the same depths as does the rest of the gigantic circus. So after the cheerfulness, poetic resignation.

The objectivist, by contrast, is not resigned. An objectivist who is any good at objectivism can acquiesce as happily as Montaigne (critically, that is) in the gigantic anthropological circus. He will gain some of the same comfort as Empson from the calmness of the sea ten fathoms down. Maybe, with Humean optimism and a literal-mindedness sadly at variance with the spirit of Empson's poem, he will conceive of these depths as holding within them not only the obstinacy of the human will, despite everything, to find the way to survive, not only the innate tendencies that are expressed in self-love, benevolence, imagination, and reason, but also the capacity to look for notions or ideas of (say) solidarity, reciprocity, need, desert, responsibility, virtue. . . . But what does the objectivist say comes of this mass of stubborn potentiality? Well, on the level of the actual, everything depends (he will say) on what ideas (and what acceptations of what ideas) do actually take hold—and it depends on human dispositions, *hexeis* as Aristotle would say, *Bildung*, or ethical formation (as Sabina Lovibond says in her book of this name).[26] The objectivist is not a prophet. He reflects gloomily perhaps that bad ideas (or bad acceptations) tend to drive out good. More cheerfully, he reflects that a new and practical preoccupation with the idea of formation could counteract that vexatious tendency. It is up to us, though, to cultivate that preoccupation, up to us to hold on to what we do have, and up to us to subvert that which subverts it. But no predictions! (Contrast the cheerful belief, just perceptible in Hume's essay 'Of the Standard of Taste', that, in the end, the better judgment will prevail over the worse.)[27]

11.12. I have digressed. About relativity, I have claimed that we do not need to see distinct ethical systems (even ethical systems that share in many ideas) as aiming at unity, but as aspiring to universality (in Hare's sense). Maybe relativists are really disappointed unifiers or globalists. But globalism, in so far as this is a creed or a crusade rather than a description of certain tendencies that pose certain new and serious problems (not least problems of bad ideas driving out good), is a misunderstanding of true internationalism. True internationalism has no need to confuse an aspiration to universality in its judgments with the aspiration to propound a mass of general

26. Sabina Lovibond, *Ethical Formation* (Cambridge, Mass.: Harvard University Press, 2002).

27. In David Hume, *Essays Moral, Political, and Literary,* ed. E. F. Miller, rev. ed. (Indianapolis: Liberty Classics, 1987).

judgments[28] or to attempt general prescriptions about millennial goals for the world (which will be interpreted over and over again to reflect the preoccupations of states that are powerful, but unpractised in self-examination, and are caught between the benevolent impulses of their citizens and the insatiable demands of an economy that they dare not contemplate trying to set in a different direction). True internationalism would do better to start out from the place where Montaigne and similar thinkers have left off, with the exploration, the accumulation, and the critical deployment of ideas or notions that human societies find they really can share—and with the more specific humanitarian missions that local knowledge, tempered by justice, will second or that human constitution itself (at least as it appears to a *médecin sans frontières*) will confidently endorse. With declarations against torture, genocide, imprisonment without charge, slavery, forced labour, etc., we are in the home territory of the international spirit at its finest and least controversial, the universally valid proscription of specific evil. It is a tragic mistake

28. A witness to this is the one great philosopher who stands out from his times as an internationalist, a diplomat, and a theorist of international law and justice—as well as a logician. I mean Leibniz, who held that 'justice is that which is useful to a community . . . a community not of a few, not of a particular nation, but of all those who are part of the City of God, so to speak'. (See Leibniz, *Political Writings*, trans. and ed. Patrick Riley (Cambridge: Cambridge University Press, 1988), p. 39.) For Leibniz, the closest then visible approximation to such a City and the best prospect for peace in Christendom was the Holy Roman Empire. But in accord with his understanding of that prospect, he himself refused to renounce Lutheranism. He upheld the plurality and distinctness of the German Electorates, principalities, duchies, etc., and upheld the right of princes who were not electors to send *legati* not *deputati,* ambassadors not mere agents, to congresses, conferences etc. (See 'Caesarinus Fürstenerius', in *Political Writings*, ed. Riley., p. 111 ff.) Leibniz equally upheld the virtue of patriotism. When they learn all this, people are apt to smile or to repeat Russell's slanderous account of Leibniz's moral character (see his *History of Western Philosophy* (New York: Simon & Schuster, 1945), bk III, ch. 31) adding perhaps that Leibniz was sadly mistaken in supposing that the emperor would in the future be mindful of his Christian duty to protect from injustice all the divers peoples within the extent of his *imperium*. But failure is one thing, lack of principle is another. Think twice, think three times, before you accuse Leibniz, a tireless peacemaker and friend of mankind, of insincerity or time-serving. Having ourselves distinguished for ourselves between generality and universality, let us credit our predecessors with some inkling of the same distinction.

to suppose that these can be a paradigm for the positive and general prescriptions of 'global ethics'.

It is time to conclude. As I have characterized it, moral objectivism is not so much a cut-and-dried doctrine as an outlook, an outlook of qualified second-order optimism relating not to the future but to the conceptual and critical resources and the power of first-order ethical thought. The importance of Mackie's arguments from queerness and relativity, properly construed, is that they combine, when each is explained in the light of the other, to represent a serious challenge to that qualified optimism—a challenge that demands from objectivists and anti-objectivists alike a close attention to the actual resources available to first-order ethical thought as well as a new interest in the business of moral persuasion.

12

Miscellanea metaethica

Objective and non-objective; subjective and non-subjective; convictions that make a difference, guide action, etc.

A country may be overrun by an armed host, but it is only conquered by the establishment of fortresses. Words are the fortresses of thought.

William Hamilton

[It] was the Edinburgh logician Sir William Hamilton who said that a good new term is like a fortress to dominate a country won from the forces of darkness. But those forces never sleep and will strive . . . to recover lost territory.

P. T. Geach

12.1. Lecture 11 was dedicated to setting out the essentials of moral objectivism, a position to which even its critics seem to allow the right to acceptance pending the appearance of persuasive refutation. Morality itself, Mackie thought, precisely depended for the

Lecture 12 completes Lecture 11. Like Lecture 11, it draws on a presentation made at a Boston Colloquium held in honour of Hilary Putnam in October 2003 and on a paper (published in Brad Hooker, ed., *Truth in Ethics* [Oxford: Blackwell, 1996], not all of it reproduced or recapitulated here) for a *Ratio* conference which was held in the University of Reading in 1995. A reader who sets out on this lecture without having any previous acquaintance with philosophy of language may wish to omit (or skip read) all of 12.3 except the first and the last six paragraphs. Or else Lecture 11 is a perfectly good stopping place.

purposes of its ordinary work on our preserving and respecting—
even if only at the level of necessary illusion—most of its whole
apparent substance. The outstanding question, to which he returned
a negative answer, was how much of that substance morality could
have at a non-illusory level.

Lecture 11, in seeking to counter the difficulties that Mackie urged
against the positive, optimistic, or objectivist answer to that outstanding question, denied that Mackie had sustained his arguments
either from queerness or from relativity. By way of conclusion, I
shall fill out the grounds for that denial and pursue certain closely
related matters, before leaving the question (C) to its own devices.

12.2. *Objective versus non-objective.* If a subject matter, a province
of thought, or a field of inquiry or activity admits of a distinction
between correct and incorrect ways of going about things, if it distinguishes correct and incorrect lines of thinking or doing, then the
possibility will exist there for commentary, for adjudication, and for
praise and blame directed at the particular thoughts (or acts) had
(or done) by particular agents at particular times. Along these lines,
one will expect to find claims to this sort of effect: that, in this or
that field of practical or theoretical endeavour, *this* is the right way
to go about such and such; that *that* is a bad way; that one has, in
trying to ϕ, to aim to ψ. (Compare Lecture 9, n. 13.)

Such claims, where a propositional content rests upon something
inherently practical, are familiar enough within the realm of craft or
skill and the practical arts. In that realm, moreover, the truth or
falsity of practitioners' assertions seems to be a relatively straightforward matter. But can this finding not be adjusted—if with care, then
without very much distortion—to the moral realm?[1] It is true that,

---

1. Any adaptation in the opposite direction, of the practical to the speculative, with
the speculative conceived in the intellectualist way that is familiar within philosophy, will
lead no doubt to a grave misrepresentation of the practical. This will be a misrepresentation similar to those that we were protesting against in Lecture 10 and elsewhere. By
contrast, the thing I am proposing here is to learn what we can from contemplating a
reverse adaptation, if only for that portion of the intellectual or speculative that lies within

for the case of morality, such a finding would rest on conceiving it as keyed to purposes analogous to the purposes that are internal to the practical arts. On such a conception, morality will have to be keyed to the unforsakeable human purposes (not necessarily open to finite enumeration) already touched upon in 11.3. It has to be keyed constitutively to the internal purposes (an open-ended set, see 9.22) which support our whole understanding of the moral 'must', 'ought', 'right', 'wrong', 'forbidden', and condition the sense of our vocabulary of evaluation. Nobody denies that, by their nature, such unforsakeable purposes are essentially contestable. If that is found difficult—if the idea that this is a difficulty amounts to more than a simple muddle between two different kinds of '-able' (a *moral* and a simply *logical* modal, so to speak)—then the problem can be confronted head-on, at the right moment. The more immediate task, though, is to characterize the objective, as it applies or fails to apply to this or that or the other class of judgments.

The suggestion I defend is this. A subject matter is objective if and only if enough of the questions that are posed within it admit of answers that are substantially true—simply and plainly true, that is.

What then is plain truth? On the view I take, truth is indefinable, something we grasp by being drawn into a set of practices that culminate in speaking, understanding, and thinking. The concept of truth is immanent in the norms of success and unsuccess that govern these activities. But still we may ask: what is truth like? Even if truth is indefinable, that ought not to exclude there being sorts of things we can say about it.

So what kind of property is truth? In other places, I have tried to construct a basis on which one might begin to determine certain *marks* of the concept of truth.[2] Such marks (I say) are to be excog-

---

a realm such as the ethical. At this point, we are continuing in a line of argument upon which we first set out in 9.5.

2. I use the word 'marks' and the word 'concept' in Frege's sense. (See his essay 'Concept and Object' in *Translations from the Philosophical Writings of Gottlob Frege*, ed. Peter Geach and Max Black (Oxford: Blackwell, 1952, 1960), p. 42 (later editions

itated from the ideas we have of what flows from the difference
between getting something right and not getting it right in the business of speaking, understanding, or thinking. It is there one must
look if one wants to know what truth is like. I think that an enumeration of marks of truth might begin as follows:

(1) if x (a proposition, or thought, or belief, or thing said, a pu-
    tative instantiation of the concept *true*) is true, then x passes
    muster in the dimension of assessment in which x demands,
    by virtue of being the sort of thing it is, to be assessed, and
    this will be the primary dimension for its assessment;
(2) if x is true, then, if conditions are fully hospitable to inquiry,
    those who understand x will tend to converge upon x, and
    the best explanation of this convergence will be inconsistent
    with the denial of x;
(3) if x is true, then x has content and x says something about
    something;
(4) if x is true, then x is true by virtue of something;
(5) if x is true and y is true, then the conjunction of x and y is
    true—indeed (lo and behold!) every truth must be consistent
    with every other truth; . . .[3]

---

are not recommended). A concept is what a predicate stands for. Take the predicate
'rabbit'. To ascertain the marks of the concept *rabbit,* collect up all the predicates that
can replace the letter 'F' in the sentence 'Everything that is a rabbit is F'. The marks
of the concept *rabbit* are the concepts that these predicates stand for. For the marks of
true, see my *Needs, Values, Truth* (Oxford: Oxford University Press, 2002), pp. 115, 147–
52. For the idea of *elucidation* by specifying marks, see in the same work pp. 182, 188–9,
314 n.2. For an improved account of what is involved in the business of interpretation,
on which the whole business of finding the marks of *true* depends, see now my 'Meaning
and Truth Conditions', in J. Hale and C. Wright, eds., *A Companion to the Philosophy
of Language* (Oxford: Blackwell, 1997).

   3. Note that (4) is akin to a schema. It is not intended to suggest quantification over
entities (distinct from ordinary things and their properties or relations) that 'make' sentences or statements true. Its meaning is best suggested by an example. To say that a
truth such as 'Snow is white' is true by virtue of something or answers to something is
only to say that this sentence can't, given its meaning, be true unless snow *is* white. In
this explanation we rely on the possibility of showing or suggesting something more

In their collectivity, marks such as these represent a partial elucidation of the notion of truth. There is of course no question of collecting up all the materials provided by (1) (2) (3) (4) (5) . . . and transforming the result into a philosophical analysis (informative necessary and sufficient conditions) of genuine truth. The impossibility of doing that is evidently no obstacle to our ascertaining some of the more important marks a judgment may be expected to possess if the standard of correctness it satisfies within its subject matter is indeed a standard for genuine truth.

12.3. *Can ethical judgments aspire to a correctness equivalent to ordinary truth?* For purposes of the ethical subject matter the most interesting among general requirements such as (1)–(5), and the most threatening, will appear to be mark (2). We claimed in Lecture 11 (see there 11.6) that it must have been a thought of some such requirement as (2) that made it so natural for Mackie to follow up his anti-objectivist argument from queerness with his argument from relativity.

Let *x* be a putative truth, mooted as such at some place and time.

---

general by means of a particular example. If we were setting out to 'define' truth by such means, that would be useless or worse. For purposes of explaining what we mean by '*x* is true by virtue of something' it is neither illicit nor useless.

On so-called redundancy and deflationary views of truth, this substantialist approach will appear entirely misguided. But such views originate in a serious mistake, one which I try to expose as such in 'An Indefinibilist cum Normative View of Truth and the Marks of Truth', in Richard Schantz, ed., *What Is Truth?* (New York: De Gruyter, 2002). See especially pp. 321–4.

Not all anti-substantialist views of truth rest on the fallacy that I seek to expose in that place. But among those that do not rest on it, as among 'minimalist' views, there is less principle than it may appear. Crispin Wright, for instance, in the first essay in Hooker, ed., *Truth in Ethics*, claims that there cannot be *more* to the property of truth than resides in the platitudes he begins to enumerate (platitudes not altogether unlike the propositions from which I have sought to derive some of the marks of truth). The first trouble I have with this claim is that, understandably enough, Wright does not *complete* the list of platitudes. The second trouble is that the platitudes themselves might well unfold into something whose collective import was very demanding indeed, not to say substantial. See the critique I offer in the appendix (not recapitulated here) of my own contribution in the same volume.

Suppose various thinkers pay attention to the subject matter where x belongs and they disregard that which is extraneous to x's actual content. Suppose they fully understand the sentence or sentences ' . . . ' in which x is expressed, and they grasp that which is at issue with the question whether or not . . . Suppose each of these thinkers is primarily concerned not to end up in agreement with the majority of other thinkers but to respond to *that* very question. Then, if conditions are not adverse for reflection or inquiry, and x belongs to a subject matter where there can be genuine truth, how can there help but be a tendency for thinkers to arrive at similar conclusions?

Here surely we find a conceptual connection between truth and convergence—a presumptive connection, unidirectional and no licence at all to argue from simple agreement back to truth, but a conceptually grounded presumptive connection nonetheless and all of piece with the natural idea that in convergence of the kind we have described we may see *a response* which thinkers concur in making to that which really is so. Unluckily though, at least in this formulation, (2) gives trouble. I note for instance that, in cases where conditions hospitable to inquiry are very hard to envisage and principled convergence of the kind we have described is more or less excluded, (2) will be far too easy to satisfy. Wherever the satisfaction of (2)'s antecedent ('conditions fully hospitable', etc.) is in effect *ruled out,* the conditional will be verified by the impossibility of the antecedent. That, however, is a hindrance to setting the strict standard by which anti-objectivists such as Mackie and his allies or putative moral cognitivists and objectivists want the subject matter of ethics to be tested.

In the cause of supplementing or reinforcing (2), consider now the mark of truth we numbered (3): if x is true then x has a content and says something about something. In itself such a claim is entirely platitudinous. That may yet be an advantage, however, if (as I believe) the spelling out of (3) can reveal the general basis (so far unspecified) on which we may inquire what truth itself is like and look for ways to subject moral cognitivism to a sterner test.

Suppose x has a content and there are words in which to express this content. If so, then there will be a subject matter within which things can be singled out and properties ascribed to things in accordance with a norm that associates the application of each and every predicate with an interest or point that animates a common understanding of the property it stands for. (Compare 11.5.) These will be the terms on which a sentence *s* that expresses *x* will have its meaning. If *s* has meaning then *s* must be open to semantic interpretation. But how else can that hold, one might ask,[4] but by virtue of there being some condition that those who know the language that *s* belongs will accept as the condition under which it is true? Or, putting that matter as Ludwig Wittgenstein does at *Tractatus Logico-Philosophicus*, 4.022:

A Satz [any sentence in significant use, that is] shows how things stand if it is true. And it says that they do so stand.

What can we learn from all this about truth itself? Relatively little if we confine ourselves to the knowledge of the concept of truth that speakers of the language possess who are at home in the subject matter where *s* belongs and understand what *s* says. For their grasp will be practical. They will recognize entirely without reflection what it requires for *s* to be true. Suppose however that, in the interest of

4. One might ask this. But, if one does, then critics may say that, by this move, *the whole question is begged* that Lectures 11 and 12 have aimed to treat as an open question still to be determined. 'This question cannot be treated as open if you begin by assuming that the interpretability of an ethical sentence amounts simply to its having a condition of *truth*.'

It is important to counter this objection. I point out first that the argument in progress is entirely general and turns upon the link between the sense of a sentence and the interpretability of utterances of the sentence. From this argument certain marks of truth will emerge. But at no point in the course of my attempt to show that ethical judgments that deserve acceptance really can have these very marks shall I *assume* that we know already that ethical judgments are true or false. Of course, if the moral cognitivist position I defend fails, that will leave me with a problem about how moral utterance is to be interpreted. But the fact that this would be a problem or usher in theories of ethical discourse I currently reject is *not* the argument for my denial that it is excluded in principle that ethical judgments as such should possess marks of truth such as those we have generated.

theory (for that is what metaethics forces us into), we try to reconstruct or recapitulate in theoretical terms that which speakers recognize simply practically. Then we shall assign particular references
to the terms in the ethical object language, assign particular properties to the predicates and particular relations to its relation words
. . . and state the rules of combination by which these devices can
be combined in sentences by which things can be said. What is it
then—what shall we say at the level of theory that it turns on—for
such a semantic reconstruction of ours to be correct or faithful to
the norms of the language it is concerned with? The only good
answer I know is this: applying our reconstruction, confronting the
whole conduct of speakers and taking their utterances as expressive
(for the most part) of what they think, do we or do we not end up
attributing to these people beliefs (and other propositional states)
that are intelligible in the light of *some reality or other,* something
or other that is available to subject and interpreter alike, which we
take to impinge upon them? And can we—this is the second part
of the same test—can we make sense of what these speakers do or
strive for or seem to care about if, subsuming all their efforts under
some (however provisional and revisable) canon of human practical
reasonableness, we seek to understand their efforts and conations in
the light of the beliefs and other propositional attitudes that their
utterances prompt us to ascribe to them on the basis of the said
reconstruction?[5] A sentence *s* has content just if there is a way of
interpreting *s* that meets both these requirements.

How to connect this answer with the notion of truth? Suppose
that, as regards meaning and interpretation in general, so much is
correct. Suppose that neither of the two conditions just given is
really replaceable. (For how could either be replaced without jeop-
ardizing the very possibility of a shareable public content?) Suppose
that, as regards utterances which cannot be interpreted as direct
responses to something impinging equally upon the receptivities of
subjects and of interpreters, we resolve to interpret these as *canti-*

---

5. For this criterion, see John McDowell, 'Truth Conditions, Bivalence and Verificationism', in Gareth Evans and John McDowell, eds., *Truth and Meaning* (Oxford:
Blackwell, 1976).

levered from that which can satisfy more straightforwardly the first of the two conditions upon public intelligibility. Suppose finally that *Tractatus* 4.022 sustains the thought that there is a key equivalence to be had between a sentence *s*'s having a meaning by virtue of which it can be used to say that *p* and the interpretability of *s* ensuring that *s* is true if and only if *p*. (The force of this schema is to commit one who asserts it to each and every claim that results from replacing the letter *p* by a declarative English sentence.) Then we arrive at a cardinal question: *if the said equivalence is to hold, and interpretability involves that which we have said it involves, then what must truth be like?* Here surely, is the thread of Ariadne that leads us back to the marks of truth.

Two-thirds of our task is complete. So now, in the light of the Wittgensteinian equivalence let us return to the task of replacing (2). Having in mind the first part of the double test of interpretive fidelity, I suggest this:

(2') If *x* is true and *x* lies within the part of a given subject matter that impinges more directly upon a conscious subject, then, if *x* says that *p*, there will be circumstances under which a thinker can come to believe that *p* precisely because *p*.

What is meant here by 'the subject believes that p precisely because *p*' or (more clearly) 'because *p*, the subject believes that *p*'? A general answer will be wanted. My suggestion is that someone believes that *p* precisely because *p*—an important but special case of believing that *p*—just if there is a good explanation of their coming to believe that *p* which leaves *the explainer himself* no room to deny that *p*. The picture we need is one of something or other which is 'there anyway' for those who can attend to it, something that impinges on the awareness of the explainer/interpreter and which he can see as impinging no less forcefully upon subjects whose thoughts he is to characterize and interpret. It is to this that subjects are responding correctly when their judgments are true. Here is one part of the whole story alluded to at 11.5, n. 15.

The mark of truth (2') and our gloss upon it, given as they are in terms of believing that p precisely because p, can only be understood with the generality we need if we are ready to understand the verb *impinge* first by reference to the case of sense perception and then metaphorically or analogically. We need to understand *impinge* as admitting (in the same way as *because* and the idea itself of explanation do) a whole variety of realizations. If we proceed by examples, however, I think they will discover to us that we can do this.

The first example may as well be perceptual: 'Look, the cat is on the mat. So, given John's perceptual capacities and his presence near the cat, no wonder he believes the cat is on the mat. There is nothing else for him to think about the cat and the mat.' This explanation, which leaves no room to deny that the cat is on the mat, answers the question, 'Why does John believe the cat is on the mat?'

Next, and in the second place, consider the analogous but utterly different question, 'Why does Peter believe $7 + 5 = 12$?' and an explanation that runs on the following pattern: 'Look, $7 + 5 = 12$; no calculating rule that makes it possible to use numbers to count things leaves room for any other answer. [Explainer proves this.] So no wonder Peter, who understands the calculating rule which leaves no room for any other answer, believes that $7 + 5 = 12$.'

Let us call such explanations for the existence of a belief *vindicatory explanations* of the belief. On their basis we see the belief as coming into being precisely because there is no real alternative. By the same token, ethical objectivism will be committed (simply by virtue of its commitment to the possibility of truth in ethics) to saying that an ethical subject matter, no less than perceptual and arithmetical subject matters, will admit vindicatory explanations of (at least some) moral beliefs. An example might run as follows: 'Look, slavery is wrong, it's wrong because . . . [here are given many, many considerations, fully spelled out, appealing to what someone already knows and understands if they know what slavery is and what "wrong" means, all these considerations working together to leave no alternative, for one who is so informed, but to think that slavery is wrong]; so no wonder twentieth-century Europeans, who would accept that . . . and whose beliefs are so many of them down-wind of such considerations as . . . , believe that slavery is wrong. They believe that it is wrong for just the kind of reasons why there is nothing else to think but that it *is* wrong.'

Ethical objectivism, so characterized, represents a strongly but not crudely cognitivist conception of the subject matter of morals. It is not necessarily an inferentialist conception. In so far as it is a Humean conception, involving the seamless collusion of passion with thought and thought with passion, each repeatedly focusing and sharpening the other, it is not inferentialist. (See 2.2 ff.) But it did not need to be inferentialist to be cognitivist. It ought to be obvious, though (see Lecture 11), that it is far from obvious whether ethical objectivism is correct, or to what extent it is. For in advance, we cannot know for sure whether or how often we *can* assemble perceptions or put together considerations ' . . . ' that will combine to leave nothing else to think.[6] But *that* seems to be the thing that is at issue when we ask whether the property which passes for the truth of ethical judgments has the marks (2') and (4). Condition (2') is not a trivial requirement.

12.4. *Vindicatory expanations continued.* Much hangs for objectivism as so defined on the idea of a vindicatory explanation. In commentary on proposals similar to those advanced in the foregoing section, and in reaction to my claim that there can be vindicatory explanations for beliefs such as the belief that slavery is wrong, Bernard Williams was apt to insist that it is not enough for an objectivist to show how, if one describes the institution of slavery as 'slavery' and one brings to the task all the ideas and sentiments marshalled by names like 'injustice', 'inhumanity', 'exploitation', then there will be nothing else to think but that slavery is wrong.[7] The reason why it is not enough is that to reach the conclusion in *that* way leaves

---

6. The point is enlarged upon in my 'Moral Cognitivism, Moral Relativism, and Motivating Moral Belief', *Proceedings of the Aristotelian Society* 91 (1990–1).

7. See, for example, his essay in Brad Hooker, ed., *Truth in Ethics*.

open the possibility that there is another way to categorize institutions such as (those we call) slavery and thus another way to evaluate them.

Suppose that, at the turn of the eighteenth century, Clarkson or Wilberforce or some person devoted to the abolitionist cause asserts that slavery is wrong and insupportable. And suppose that someone else, looking for an explanation of this conviction of theirs, claims that the best way to explain their conviction is to see it as *the only reasonable response* to what confronted them. Suppose he then undertakes to explain in the vindicatory way why it is that Clarkson or Wilberforce has come to believe that slavery is insupportable. The things that the explainer has to show—*given* that Clarkson and Wilberforce, to whom the question of right or wrong posed itself, attended to the institution that we call 'slavery'—are then (a) why they grasped or categorized that institution as slavery and (b) why, categorizing it so, they saw it as brutal, inhuman, exploitative, unjust, and wrong. The issue (a) between Williams and me is whether, once the moral question (of right and wrong, etc.) *has come into focus*, there is any way to avoid categorizing slavery as slavery.

So much might have been agreed, I think, between Williams and myself—as might the importance of the non-inferentialist framework in which to situate the formation of moral beliefs. The thing I would now ask is this. How much does it count against the possibility of a would-be vindicatory explanation of Wilberforce's and Clarkson's convictions that *someone else,* with a different outlook from theirs, might have categorized the practice we call slavery as a commercial practice (indeed many British and Americans did so categorize it, and even some West Africans did) and might then have described it as 'wasteful but profitable'? I readily agree that nothing prevents someone with an outlook at variance with Wilberforce's or Clarkson's from seeing the practice we call slavery as a commercial practice pure and simple. But, *once the question arises* of right and wrong, injustice, etc., someone's seeing the practice as a commercial practice will scarcely exempt that person from seeing it *also* as exploitation. Williams might have asked how an objectivist could show that just anyone who is willing to take up the moral point of view will have to subsume the institution of slavery under the concepts it is subsumed under in Wilberforce's and Clarkson's denunciations of its injustice and insupportability. But my answer to this challenge is to say that anyone with a rival or alternative view will need to show the moral and practical workability of a scheme of moral ideas which, in the face of the phenomena such as the slave trade and all its historical effects, dispenses with ideas like 'slavery', 'using human being as means, not ends', etc. In pitting this alternative scheme of moral ideas against Clarkson's and Wilberforce's scheme, we are bound to discover that the workability of moral ideas cannot be judged idea by idea but only by comparing whole systems that make use of an idea with whole systems that dispense with it. Such comparisons will sometimes be complex and difficult, no doubt—equally difficult for defenders of moral positions and for critics who criticize in good faith. But that hardly shows that such comparisons cannot be conclusive. It does not disprove the objectivist claim that to dispense with the concept of slavery in the actual circumstances of the slave trade as it actually was would be to dispense with altogether too much that makes up the idea of morality itself. I agree with Williams that the strength of moral *deixis,* argument and persuasion is not the kind of thing that can be shown by *a priori* considerations about truth. But *a priori* considerations about the connections between truth, objectivity, cumulative conclusiveness, and vindicatory explanation do have the merit of suggesting what we shall need to look for—and what according to objectivism we shall sometimes find—among the products of persuasion. As always, we need to ascertain whether there really is any other way to think about the matter. (A moral question, not a barely logical one—just as, in the first of the three vindicating explanations given at 12.3, the question was perceptual, not barely logical.)[8]

8. Edmund Fawcett tells me that Thomas Clarkson placed before the Privy Council in 1788 a diagram of the slave ship *Brookes,* showing slaves tightly packed and chained in row upon row. Many councillors for whom the diagram conjured up the reality of a slave ship found that, try as they might, they could not escape the passions of horror

So much for the defence of the conception of 'objective' offered in 12.2 and 12.3. It is harmonious enough, I believe, with the rough and ready ordinary acceptation of the word, in so far as there is one.

What then shall we call the opposite of 'objective', understood in that way? Let us say 'non-objective', leaving open the possibility that the term 'subjective', which is so often used for this purpose, should have a content of its own. If 'subjective' does have a content of its own, then it remains to be discovered what the relation is between the non-objective and the subjective. If anything of any interest is to come of this bit of metaethics, we must begin at the beginning and ask what the subjective is. But here, remember, at the moment of introducing technical terms into philosophy, we cannot rely on our given natural language to secure significations. We must exert ourselves to fix them ourselves, securely and correctly.

12.5. *Subjective versus non-subjective.* My suggestion is this. A subject matter is subjective if it pertains to/arises from the states, responses, etc. of *conscious subjects* and if questions about this subject matter are answerable to a standard that is founded in these states, responses (etc.) of subjects (compare Lectures 2 and 3); or else (where no such standard is in the offing at all) the subject matter is subjective if questions about it are answerable *only* to these states, responses, etc.

Because this is a wide and inclusive definition of 'subjective', ethical subjectivism can take various forms and receive highly various expressions:

Protagoras [restricted]: man is the measure of all [valuational] things.

---

and revulsion attendant upon the very thought of such a spectacle. Once given the ordinary ethical interest that they were there to deploy, or so he suggests, these councillors could see through the diagram into a moral reality that thus impinged upon them. See 11.5, third paragraph. (Having seen *this*, could they then have dispensed with the categorization 'slavery'?) Cp. also Lecture 9, on ideas of recognition and solidarity. To recognize as other human beings the animate beings thus chained up is what focuses the *receptivity* to that reality.

[A possible] *David Hume: x* is good if and only if *x* is such as to arouse approbation.

[The real] *David Hume:* 'There is just so much vice or virtue in any character as every one places in it, and 'tis impossible in this particular we can ever be mistaken.'[9] (This might appear to be a mere agreement view. But Hume is headed towards something more subtle than this. Witness the essay 'Of the Standard of Taste'.)[10]

Refined Humean subjectivism: x is good if and only if *x* is such as to *deserve* (N.B.) or *merit* approbation.[11]

Thomas Hobbes: 'But whatsoever is the object of any mans Appetite or Desire; that is it, which he for his part calleth *Good:* And the object of his Hate, and Aversion *Evill;* And of his Contempt, *Vile* and *Inconsiderable.* For these words of Good, Evill, and Contemptible, are ever used with relation to the person that useth them: There being nothing simply and absolutely so; nor any common Rule of Good and Evill, to be taken from the nature of the objects themselves; but from the Person of the man (where there is no Common-wealth;) or, (in a Common-wealth,) from the Person that representeth it; or from Arbitrator or Judge, whom men disagreeing shall by consent set up, and make his sentence the Rule thereof.'[12]

[*All subjectivists*]: ultimately statements of value are answerable only to such standards as are set by human feelings and human responses, these feelings and responses not necessarily being isolated from the contributions of reason or imagination.[13]

---

9. *Treatise of Human Nature*, III.ii.8, Selby-Bigge, p. 547.

10. *Essays Moral, Political, and Literary*, ed. E. F. Miller, rev. ed. (Indianapolis: Liberty Classics, 1987).

11. Cf. A. J. Ayer, *Freedom and Morality* (Oxford: Clarendon Press, 1984), p. 30; and J. McDowell, 'Values and Secondary Qualities', in T. Honderich, ed., *Morality and Objectivity: A Tribute to J. L. Mackie* (London: Routledge, 1985), pp. 117–20.

12. *Leviathan*, (1651), bk 1, ch. 6 (reprinted in Everyman's Library, London: Dent, 1914, 1963, p. 24).

13. Contrary to what might be supposed, this does *not* restrict value to that which engages with human interests or promotes human advantage. It is up to the sentiments what they will engage with, or up to the sentiments together with the reasons that they give themselves for the stance they take up.

Vulgar Subjectivism: (a) '*x* is good', as said by me, means no more than 'I like it' or (at best) (b) 'we like it'.

Some of these positions are more familiar than others. The objections to Vulgar Subjectivism are familiar. Variant (a) makes disagreement impossible. (See G. E. Moore, who seems unaware of subjectivisms that are not exposed to this objection.)[14] Variant (b) misrepresents the content of disagreement.[15]

Against Refined Subjectivism, some may object that it depends on not analysing away the moral terms 'deserve/merit'. It is crucially important here whether the subjectivist does or does not take himself to need to engage in this analysing away. It is doubtful, though, whether Hume, for instance, believing as he does that taste and morals are 'altogether new creations', ought to believe that, in order for its existence or nature to be explained, moral language has to be *explained or analysed away*. (Here compare also the approach of J. L. Mackie.)

If Hume is a subjectivist according to these proposals, then in what should he have said that the subjectiveness of moral thought and language consisted? Perhaps in this: value terms have their sense by being annexed to properties in objects of our attention that call for certain shareable responses—the responses to these objects that the objects *make appropriate*.[16] The fact that these responses are appropriate is owed to a scale of values whose recognition is of course downwind of the fabric and constitution of *conscious human subjects*.

14. G. E. Moore, *Ethics*, chs. 3 and 4 (Oxford: Oxford University Press, 1912).

15. *Emotivism*, not treated here, seeks at this point to save vulgar subjectivism from the Moorean objection by importing something called *emotive meaning*—one of philosophy's more problematical, not to say gratuitous, inventions. See my *Needs, Values, Truth*, p. 186.

16. Cf. McDowell, 'Values and Secondary Qualities'; my 'Truth, Invention and the Meaning of Life', *Proceedings of the British Academy* 62 (1976), reprinted in my *Needs, Values, Truth* (Oxford: Blackwell, 1987): and 'A Sensible Subjectivism', in *Needs, Values, Truth*.

12.6. *Historical note.* Under 'objective', the *Oxford English Dictionary* tells us this: that the scholastic philosophy made the distinction between what belong to things *subjectivē* (Latin adverb) or as they are 'in themselves' (on the one hand) and (on the other hand) what belongs to them *objectivē* (Latin adverb), or as they are presented to consciousness. (Here the subject is the item which some thought or perception is concerned with. It is the subject in a grammatical sense.) In later times, the custom of considering the perceiving or thinking consciousness as pre-eminently 'the subject' brought about the different use of these words which now prevails in philosophy (and which prevails in our proposals). According to this way of thinking, what is considered as belonging to the perceiving or thinking self is called 'subjective' and what is considered as independent of the perceiving or thinking self is called in contrast 'objective'. So 'objective' and 'subjective', as it were, changed places!

It is important to notice that, in the last sentence of our report of the *Oxford English Dictionary,* the word 'objective' is used as an opposite of 'subjective'. That runs contrary to the recommendations at the end of 12.4 above. Attending immediately to this emergency, let us emend the dictionary's account by thinking of 'objective' as connoting *positively* that which relates to things in themselves. Compare the scholastic account of 'subjective' taken scholastically. (Forget then the stipulation of independence, whatever that may be, of the perceiving self. Make no ruling about it.) But the *general* explanation of *objective* is better as given in 12.2 and 12.3 above.

12.7. *Following through.* Clearly the 'objective/non-objective' contrast and the 'non-subjective/subjective' contrast are two different contrasts. So when people seem to contrast 'objective' and 'subjective', first ascertain whether they are scholastics. *Then,* provided they're not scholastics, go on and ascertain whether they have begun with the subjective and defined the objective by forming its complement; or whether they have begun with the objective and called its complement (everything that is other than objective as the objective will have been defined) the 'subjective'. Ask how they defined the one they began with. If they haven't done either of the things just mentioned, then inquire whether they have done the best thing (which is what we have done here) and defined 'objective' and 'subjective' separately. If so, what accounts do they give of each? Always bear in mind, though, the awful possibility that they may not know what they're doing or have no idea what has been done on their behalf.

It would be a long business, though not impossible, to stop here in order to chronicle in terms of the possibilities we have reviewed the various uses that various philosophers have made of 'objective' and 'subjective' and the preconceptions that they have attached (with or without justification) to the subjective, notably that of non-objectivity. Let us only pause long enough to treat the case of Hume.

Hume has impressive arguments for the claim that moral judgments are subjective in the better sense that we explicated in 12.5. In the *Treatise* he supposes that they are also not objective. Contrast, however, the mere agreement view at p. 547 (in Selby-Bigge) with the more-than-mere-agreement view expressed later, at p. 620. In Hume's later writings, which are replete with optimism about the resources of moral argument and the prospects of principled agreement, anti-objectivism is gradually and progressively qualified and relaxed. He never, however, avows anything tantamount to proper objectivism.

It is hard sometimes not to expound Hume's theory in as as-if narrative style: 'Human beings came into the world, they devised a scale of values, and *thenceforth* ingratitude (for instance) was in itself hateful and despicable.' But matters do not need to be expounded in this way and it is better if they are not. (Cp. 11.5 on 'man is the measure'.) The human scale of values is timeless or (if you prefer) it reaches backwards and forwards *to all times*. The fact that *its recognition* has the history it has need not deter Hume from thinking ingratitude as hateful or despicable in itself.[17] He thinks it is des-

---

17. It is true that, in paragraph eighteen of 'The Sceptic', from the same phase of his thinking as the *Treatise*, Hume says that 'objects have absolutely no worth or value

picable and hateful in itself. But he does not affirm objectivism or anything tantamount to it.

If you are satisfied so far, then pause, consolidate, and consider, in returning to our two distinctions, the following situation. Somebody says this to you: Never mind the terminological fuss that your author is now engaged in. You don't need to. It's *obvious* how to distinguish the objective and the subjective. A paradigmatic instance of the objective would be the question of the outdoor temperature at Kew Gardens on 20 May 1993 at noon GMT. A representative instance of the subjective would be the question of the fairness or otherwise of the scales operative on that day for the remuneration of the grades of gardener employed there on that day. Surely there is a manifest and conceptually overwhelming difference between these kinds of question.

The right reply to this is not to suggest that questions of the second sort might shade off into question of the first sort (or vice versa). Until the first thing is clearer, namely the point of the contrast being illustrated, that is feeble and worse. (Shade off along what dimension of similarity?) The right reply is to ask what it is that the first illustration, the temperature, is meant to be paradigmatic or

---

in themselves'. (See *Essays,* ed. Miller.) But, on pain of contradiction, the word 'absolutely' must be taken here in its full and original sense, that is in its contrast with 'relative', a word Hume does sometimes use. (Compare paragraph eight, the first sentence, where modern punctuation would delete the semicolon.) Hume's view is that objects have value in themselves but that such a claim is to be construed as relative to our standard, not to an absolute standard. It is noteworthy that in the footnote to paragraph seventeen, where he mentions the 'famous doctrine supposed to be fully proved in modern times "that tastes and colours, and other sensible qualities, lie not in the bodies, but merely in the senses" ', he then says 'the case is the same with beauty and deformity, virtue and vice. *This doctrine however takes off no more from the reality of the latter qualities than from the former*' (my italics). At this juncture it is well to remember also that Hume himself did not accept the 'famous doctrine'. See *Treatise,* I.iv.4: 'After the exclusion of colours, sound, heat and cold from the rank of external existences, there remains nothing which can afford us a just and consistent idea of body' (Selby-Bigge, p. 229).

It would be silly to assert that Hume ever settled down to the position I am urging upon the reader. In so far as Hume cannot do so, that may be because, in relevant respects, his position has some of the same difficulties as Mackie's.

representative of and then to put the same question about the second illustration, the pay scales and their fairness. There are too many different ways of reading the proposed contrast. Until we know which way is intended, examples cannot clarify the distinction that purports to be introduced here. It is not even clear whether the objector's distinction of objective and subjective is intended to sort things into two mutually exclusive kinds. (If that be intended, then more needs to be said about whether there are degrees of objectivity; and more needs to be said about why the second example cannot aspire to any degree of objectivity.) Or is the distinction intended one that sorts items into two *presumptively* non-overlapping kinds? (In which case more needs to be said to *argue* for the non-overlap of their extensions.) Or else, is the objective/subjective distinction a distinction like that between being a mammal and being a mouse, where the things distinguished are indeed distinct but being a mouse is simply a special case of being a mammal? See 11.4. (No doubt there are other possibilities, too.)

Similar tricks will be tried upon you concerning *fact* and *value*, or *is* and *ought* (or, in the philosophy of mind, with regard to the mental and the physical). As technical terms, such labels can be introduced in pairs that are definitionally exclusive, but in that case we should first announce the fact/non-fact distinction and the *is/* non-*is* distinction, leaving the status of value and the status of *ought* to be argued on their merits. (Are valuational questions not factual questions? Why not? Are *ought* questions not a species of *is* questions?) Or all four terms can be introduced as distinct items, each being positively characterized. Then, as we have seen, the question of their interrelation will remain open until it is argued further. Such still, after 2,500 years, is the chaos in some parts of moral (and mental) philosophy. Philosophers can confuse you in this matter without even intending to take advantage of you. If words are to be the fortresses of thought—indeed, if thought is to have any fortresses at all—then we must be careful to choose words that are maintained either by determinate usage or else by careful, correct definition.

The possibility has now loomed of a given moral question's being both subjective *and* objective. It is this that seems to create the prospect of vindicating the consensus that slavery is wrong or unjust and doing so by means of by considerations (which need not be expected to work simply or only inferentially upon subjects' convictions) that both appeal to standards that are founded in sentiment and yet leave nothing else to think but that slavery is wrong. (See 12.2 above. See also 11.4 and 11.9.) It is this that helps to create the prospect of conclusive arguments being made by the gradual accumulation of the right sorts of consideration.

12.8. *Further remarks.* In so far as it represents a high optimism about the latent resources of first-order ethical consciousness, such a position really does deserve to be called objectivist. Riding on the hope of reaching moral truths and moral knowledge, it must count as a form of moral cognitivism. Once upon a time, indeed well within living memory (in the mid-twentieth century), cognitive aspirations of this sort would have been accused of 'naturalism'. Once the charge was clarified, the verdict might well be: 'The cognitivist is guilty as charged.' Everything would depend on what was meant. But there is much to be said for reserving the term 'naturalism' either for something much more general, namely the broadly anti-metaphysical approach of writers like Hume to the phenomenon of human morality—or else for something much more specific and of which we are innocent, namely the kind of analysis of moral concepts that G. E. Moore singled out for his first and most central attack upon naturalism.[18]

In the form in which I have advocated the position—see 11.5—the kind of objectivism defended here will be classified by its opponents as 'descriptivist'. It attracts this label, which seems clearer than 'naturalistic', because it sees ethical terms as making a specific and distinctive contribution to the truth-conditions of sentences that express

18. See the account of nature and natural suggested by the remarks on p. 41 of *Principia Ethica* (Cambridge: Cambridge University Press, 1903), already discussed in the second paragraph of 11.5. See also Casimir Lewy, 'G. E. Moore and the Naturalistic Fallacy', *Proceedings of the British Academy* 52 (1966): 251.

moral judgments, and it sees the commendatory or approbatory force of such terms (where that force is present and in operation) not as an *extra input* to their full meaning but as *resulting from that which they already mean*. If 'considerate' means what it means and it assembles its extension in the special way described in 11.5, then no wonder calling someone 'considerate' will tend to be heard as praise or as approbation of that person.[19] And no wonder that failure awaits all attempts to hit off in non-moral terms the exact specification that ethical concerns and preoccupations have worked up into the finished ethical sense of 'considerate'. There is indeed a distinction between the factual or truth-evaluable as such and the ethical as such, but there is no dichotomy that needs to be conceived as calling into being a specifically non-factual form of meaning. See 11.5 and 11.6.[20]

19. Putting the matter in terms of the now standard terminology of the theory of speech acts devised by J. L. Austin, one might say: no wonder the *locutionary* (or descriptive) force of 'considerate' makes possible *illocutionary* acts of approving or praising or commending. And no wonder then that the right person's praising someone in the right context will probably have the effect—the *perlocutionary effect*—of causing them to be preferred for a certain position.

The key to this classification of speech acts (in the sense of 'act' everywhere in use in this book) may be derived from the following example. A farmer who utters to ramblers (hikers) the significant words 'There is a bull in that field' does a *locutionary act*. By doing that act, he *says that* there is a bull in the field. By doing that act of saying, he does the *illocutionary act* of warning the ramblers. By doing that act of warning, he produces the *perlocutionary effect* of diverting the ramblers to another route.

20. Given the account which 11.5 has rendered of the sense of 'considerate', and given its concinnity with things I have quoted from Hilary Putnam, it seems important to contrast the cognitivist account that I have been offering here of ethical vocabulary, and to contrast my rejection of the fact–value dichotomy, with the account of these matters offered in Putnam's *The Collapse of the Fact/Value Dichotomy* (Cambridge, Mass.: Harvard University Press, 2002).

In that book, as in other works with similar intent, the case against the dichotomy of fact and value begins with a distinction (which is treated as more than the ordinary distinction I should see of more specific from less specific or of evaluative from practical) between *thick* predicates (such as 'cruel') and *thin* predicates (such as 'wrong'). In these works the thick/thin distinction is almost always made, however, in the terms furnished by anti-cognitivism. On the view I take, this does the entanglement thesis no good. Indeed, it subverts its whole cognitivist motivation.

Putnam writes: ' "Cruel" simply ignores the supposed fact/value dichotomy and cheerfully allows itself to be used sometimes for a normative purpose and sometimes as a descriptive term" (p. 35). How fully emancipated (I ask) is this way of characterizing and upholding entanglement from R. M. Hare's use of 'descriptive' and 'purely descriptive'? For Hare, a term like 'cruel' is to be unpacked into a 'descriptive complex' generative of truth-conditions (but how on the prescriptivist picture is this complex to be characterized?) and one other component, namely a prescription (not a command but something analogous to a command) which has come to be attached to the descriptive complex, simply signifying that any act answering to *that* description is one you ought not to do. The trouble is that, working by this Harean conception, Putnam's opponent, namely the *disentanglement theorist himself*, will be very happy to say that ' "cruel" cheerfully allows itself to be used sometimes for a normative purpose and sometimes as a descriptive term.' That is what he could have predicted. (In some uses of 'considerate', the prescription will be present, in others not.) Again, he could claim to have predicted that 'the terms used in history, sociology . . . ' (see Putnam, p. 63) would be 'ethically coloured'. For when you colour something, it will already have *its own describable outline.* In that case the 'description' will have been complete before the colour arrives. ('Coloured', I conclude, is the wrong metaphor for use by an entanglement theorist.)

These are the sort of reasons why I doubt Putnam ought to use 'describe' in the way he does in the passage that we began from (at p. 35) in the course of stating his entanglement thesis—or in the way he does two pages earlier (p. 33), where he *seems,* in something like Hare's fashion, to equate describing *as such* with describing the simply sensible or physical. It is a real mistake to think of describing as in principle somehow more limited than evaluating. Not only is it a tactical mistake for an opponent of Hare. It is entirely unclear why we should *not* 'describe' an act as inhumanly cruel, or the perpetrator of the act as a scoundrel and a knave. (In any case, who can seriously believe that there is any chance of giving the 'ethically uncommitted' or 'pure' description that 'scoundrel' and 'knave' piggy-back upon?)

What then ought the entanglement theorist to say about describing and what should he say about the properties which, in describing something, we attribute to it? The theorist should say, as we have, that that which marks out or delimits or descries or discriminates the property of cruelty (say) in acts or attitudes or human characters is an *essentially ethical* interest. If that is correct, though, then an entanglement theorist must absolutely not make the disentanglers a present of the possibility of some limited notions of describing. Rather, *describing* x must now stand in the same sort of general relation to *true of* x and *actual property of* x (any old actual property of x) as the general relation in which *saying/stating* stands to *true* and to *fact.*

Entirely in line with that, another thing which the proponent of the entanglement should say is this: 'The fact–value dichotomy is at bottom not a distinction but a thesis, namely, the thesis that ethics is not about matters of fact.' Happily, though, *this* formulation—entirely characteristic of entanglement—is not mine but Putnam's. See p. 19 of his book. It's from *this* sentence that I believe we should move outwards and onwards.

According to the thesis of entanglement so clarified, we probably need to say one thing more: if we describe an act as 'cruel' while disclaiming all intent to judge the act, then we must be deliberately prescinding from the outlook and interest that first attached 'cruel' to certain acts/attitudes/characters. That is one way and the *only* way in which

The idea that, in all its varieties, the ethical (or the aesthetic) should generate an ordinary sense, reference, and extension for items of moral (or aesthetic) vocabulary provokes deep disquiet among philosophers of a would-be modern temperament. The only condition on which it seems they could even contemplate such an idea is for the cognitivist to be prepared to recite after them the magical words, 'Even so, the ethical *supervenes on* the non-ethical.' Given the near total confusion about what in ethics this is meant to mean,[21] it might seem to be safe for the cognitivist to comply with this stipulation. Nevertheless, it would be *wiser* for him, rather than affirm or deny the apotropaical formula, to ask what perplexity or difficulty the spell is meant to hold off or preserve anybody from.

Even at this late hour, some will urge it against the position espoused in these pages that Mackie ought really to have located the queerness of moral values in their *causal inertia;* that Mackie ought to have said that the moral quality of an act or a character doesn't feature in the causal explanation of any event, situation, or state of affairs that exists, happens, or comes to pass. To this I reply with a question: are we really meant to believe that the courage of a soldier or the charity (benevolence, kindness, considerateness . . .) of a Samaritan will not figure in any explanation of anything that exists or comes to pass?

Among anti-cognitivists, others will ask how a mere belief about a matter of fact (or a belief about a mere matter of fact) can be an action-guiding or a culture-affecting force. But a moral conviction, expressive as it is of a state of being whose genealogy in a person recapitulates a historically given sensibility's origination in self-love, benevolence, reason, and imagination, is not a *mere* belief. Nor is it

---

we can describe an act as cruel *and* in effect disclaim the intent to pass judgment on it. We can do this, of course, but the *meaning* of the word 'cruel' itself is not affected by this prescinding. The dislocation that results is not at the level of locution, meaning, or truth-conditions. It is at the level of illocution.

21. See my *Needs, Values, Truth,* p. 197, n. 18; see also Sabina Lovibond, 'Reply to McNaughton and Rawling', *Proceedings of the Aristotelian Society* 104 (2003–4): 185–201.

a belief about just any old state of affairs. It will relate to a state of affairs of one of the kinds that *that* kind of sensibility with that origination discerns. How could a conviction relating to *such* a state of affairs help but have its effect upon action? Look back where the conviction comes from.

Concluding overview

In Part I we rest the positive case for morality—see questions (A) and (B) of 1.1 (cp. 1.12)—upon a challenge to find any better or more durable expression of the dispositions of benevolence and self-love that a human being will discover within himself or herself.

In Part II, we explore one distinctively political expression of the morality that arises from these dispositions.

In Part III—see question (C) of 1.1—we try to show that first-order ethical thinking really can be more or less what it represents itself as being; that that which is peculiar to moral judgments does not relate to their orientation towards truth (they do not differ in this respect from other judgments) but relates to the multiplicity and contestability of so much of that to which their ordinary sense (signification) makes them answerable. Moral judgments' orientation towards truth is in no way diminished by the fact that their sense is an artefact arising from the same processes of invention and discovery which have furnished a first-order ethic suitable to defend the unforsakeable concerns of its participants/inventors/discoverers. Not just any imaginary ethic or imaginary would-be standard of morals will befriend or sustain in that special way these unforsakeable concerns. On this rests the objectivity, such as it is, and the universality (contrast generality) that Montaigne has shown us the way to attribute to the ethical.

Over and over again, but only obliquely and in passing, we have touched upon the ancient question (which in 1.1 we labelled (D)) of the relation that moral virtue bears to happiness, to contentment . . . or to whatever we shall nominate 'our being's end and aim.'[1]

---

1. The phrase is Pope's: 'O Happiness! Our being's end and aim! / Good, pleasure,

It is a significant as well as an obvious truth that no passable (or truly ethical) first-order human ethic can be humanly unliveable— that a first-order ethic of any merit must even extend and elaborate, constitutively as well as by its instrumentality, the conditions of human felicity. From this it simply does not follow, however (as we saw in Lecture 6), that we can condense the whole of morality into the principle 'Actions are right in proportion as they promote happiness, wrong as they tend to produce the reverse of happiness' (whether with or without the gloss, 'By happiness is intended pleasure and the absence of pain; by unhappiness pain and the privation of pleasure'). Any such summation attempts too direct and unidirectional a connection between virtue and happiness. (Compare 11.2). So simple a connection cannot be what one is thinking of if one feels drawn to concur in Hume's cheerful opinion, 'the happiest disposition of the mind is the virtuous'.

It was in Lecture 9, at 9.18 following, that we came closest to supporting Hume's declaration. It would be foolish though to claim too much for that which was argued there. The inscrutability of happiness itself, the confusion or superficiality of so many of our ideas about it, the fact that this confusion and superficiality so easily becomes evident to us, the open texture and inherent contestability of the concept of the reasonable . . . all this does indeed discourage the thought that the 'choice between virtue and vice' or that between concern and indifference can be a prudential choice between different means to some clear end, or a choice entirely unconstrained by claims upon us that are *already* ethically committal. So much is not perhaps controversial. Neither this point, however—nor yet the related point that such a choice can scarcely be an existential choice (a choice, for instance, as Aristotle almost seems to say at *Nicomachean Ethics* 1095a23, between entirely disjoint lives of virtue, of public esteem, and of pleasure or prosperity)—will carry us all the way to the place where the doctrinaire moralist would like us to settle down, namely, the patent falsehood that our notions of un-

---

ease, content! Whate'er thy name: / That something still which prompts th'eternal sigh, / For which we bear to live, or dare to die.' *Essay on Man* (1734), Epistle IV, lines 1–4.

happiness, deprivation, and misery are too unclear, too silly, or too superficial for criminality to appear to a truly rational person as a reasonable means of escape from these evils.[2]

There is no such easy victory to be gained on this ground. The thing we might do better to claim is that, once we prepare to take our moral notions as they are and on their merits, once we undo the theorist's readiness in matters of moral notions to go constantly against the grain, once we forget our predetermined expectations for the configuration of the conceptual landscape, moral philosophy may yet reveal to us the real rhyme and reason of some of our untheorized ethical ideas, responses, and conceptions, the pattern in which they lie. . . . By these means, moral philosophy may yet reveal (as Glaucon and Adeimantus demanded) that which is loveable about at least some of these ideas, responses, and conceptions, and show forth to each of us what is admirable and enviable even in some of the moral dispositions to which we have ourself the least chance of attaining.

2. Are there really no situations where survival itself can seem to a reasonable person to require that self-love claw back something—or almost everything—from benevolence and the other sentiments and dispositions into which benevolence leads? The real question here is surely what should count as the *measured* response to such situations.

A note on five texts

Aristotle's *Nicomachean Ethics,* translated by W. D. Ross, is available in the World's Classics series published by Oxford University Press (1954, 1959, 1961). Subsequent editions and impressions from 1980 incorporate some alterations. Among the beauties of Ross's translation is the strangeness (for us and for the Greeks themselves) that it so well conveys of the original and of the challenge that this strangeness presents to associative and reflective imagination. For present purposes, there is only one other translation I know well enough to recommend, an excellent supplement and counterweight for Ross, constantly to be collated with Ross, namely Roger Crisp's in the Cambridge Texts in the History of Philosophy series (Cambridge: Cambridge University Press, 2000). The reader will find an invaluable companion to Aristotle in *Essays on Aristotle's Ethics,* ed. Amélie O. Rorty (Berkeley: University of California Press, 1980).

Among translations of Kant, I recommend that of Lewis White Beck, *Foundations of the Metaphysics of Morals* (Indianapolis: Bobbs-Merrill, 1959), a translation to be constantly compared with and backed up by that of H. J. Paton, *The Moral Law: Groundwork of the Metaphysics of Morals* (London: Hutchinson, 1948, 1951), which is published simply as *Groundwork of the Metaphysics of Morals* in the United States (New York: Harper & Row, 1964).

Hume's *Treatise of Human Nature* and *Enquiries Concerning Human Understanding and Concerning the Principles of Morals* were edited by L. A. Selby-Bigge (Oxford: Oxford University Press), most lately published as revised by P. H. Nidditch in 1975 (*Treatise*) and 1978 (*Enquiries*). In so far as it is necessary to use page references to Hume, as well as references to parts and sections, these are to the revised Selby-Bigge editions. In order to show (not without risk of being proved wrong) how I construe Hume, I frequently modernize Hume's punctuation.

Hume's *Essays Moral, Political, and Literary* are currently available in an edition by F. C. Miller (Indianapolis: Liberty Classics, 1987).

Index

compiled by Keith Allen